CW00924297

# Great Deaths

Grieving, Religion, and Nationhood in
Victorian and Edwardian Britain

# Great Deaths

Grieving, Religion, and Nationhood in
Victorian and Edwardian Britain

by
John Wolffe

*A British Academy
Postdoctoral Fellowship Monograph*

*Published for* THE BRITISH ACADEMY
*by* OXFORD UNIVERSITY PRESS

*Oxford University Press, Great Clarendon Street, Oxford* OX2 6DP

*Oxford New York*
*Athens Auckland Bangkok Bogota Bombay*
*Buenos Aires Calcutta Cape Town Dar es Salaam*
*Delhi Florence Hong Kong Istanbul Karachi*
*Kuala Lumpur Madras Madrid Melbourne*
*Mexico City Nairobi Paris Singapore*
*Taipei Tokyo Toronto Warsaw*

*and associated companies in*
*Berlin Ibadan*

*Published in the United States by*
*Oxford University Press Inc., New York*

*British Library Cataloguing in Publication Data*
*Data available*

*ISBN 0-19-726238-4*

*Phototypeset by Intype London Ltd*
*Printed in Great Britain*
*on acid-free paper by*
*Creative Print and Design Wales*
*Ebbw Vale*

# Contents

# List of Plates

*(between p. 214 and p. 215)*

# Preface and Acknowledgements

Like many research and writing projects, this one had its origin in a combination of personal experience and serendipitous discovery. Some of my own earliest recollections of public events relate to prominent deaths. In November 1963, aged four, I was conscious of stunned reactions from my parents to unexpected news on the radio. John F. Kennedy had just been assassinated in Dallas. I have more extended memories of the death and funeral of Sir Winston Churchill in January 1965, although I have no recollection of, for example, the 1964 general election. Over two decades later, having completed my earlier monograph on mid-nineteenth-century anti-Catholicism, I was looking for a new research project that would develop my overall interest in religious influences in modern Britain. Browsing in the British Library catalogue, I noticed with interest the enormous quantity of publications, particularly sermons, arising from the Duke of Wellington's death and funeral. What, I wondered, do they reveal about the cultural, political, and religious climate of 1852? From that initial idea and question, this book has developed.

From the outset my interest has been not merely in responses to death itself, but in what such events tell us about other central historical problems, above all national consciousness and the influence of religion. The premise that underlies this book is that the history of death, like the history of religion with which it is intertwined, has a significance that goes far beyond the particular sub-specialisms directly associated with its study. Indeed, whereas the extent of religious influence and experience is open to legitimate debate, the comprehensive impact of death is beyond question. Just as the management of its extensive consequences in personal life is by no means solely a matter for doctors, lawyers, and undertakers, its historical study raises questions that extend far beyond thanatology. At a time when research for this book was already well advanced, the extensive public response to the tragic death of Diana, Princess of Wales in 1997 provided striking confirmation of the wide-ranging implications of the theme.

A monograph is defined by the *Oxford English Dictionary* as a 'separate treatise on a single object or class of objects'. This book fits the definition insofar as it is focused on a particular category of events, the deaths of selected prominent individuals in the United Kingdom between the 1840s and 1910. It does, however, challenge the widespread implicit assumption that monographs are firmly located within a specific narrow field of study. If monographs are to have a continuing viable and useful role in the evolution of historical understanding, they need to build the bridges inherent in their subject matter, and to be accessible to scholars in a variety of specialisms, as well as to map out particular islands of study. It is in the terms of this aspiration that I hope this book will be judged. The potential scope of the relevant sources is virtually inexhaustible, and very different, more narrowly focused, books could be written concentrating exclusively on, say, press reactions, religious observance, or the detailed technical organization of funerals and mourning. My own approach has been to pursue a variety of sources and aspects of public reaction in some depth, but without any pretension to exhaustive coverage. If by so doing I succeed in demonstrating the wider importance of the subject and provide a stimulus to others to engage in further detailed research I shall be well content.

I am indebted above all to the British Academy, which provided essential support at all stages of this project. They appointed me to a Postdoctoral Fellowship in 1988, which I held for two years before taking up my present post at the Open University in 1990. They subsequently part-funded a period of sabbatical leave in 1995, and have contributed to research expenses. I am delighted that they have shown further commitment to the book by selecting it for publication in their postdoctoral fellowship monographs competition. My warm thanks go to former colleagues in the Department of History at the University of York, which provided a most congenial environment during the early stages of the research. I also greatly value the support, both practical and more intangible, received over the last decade in the Faculty of Arts at the Open University, which contributed substantially to the direct and hidden costs of research, and where many valuable trains of thought and enquiry have been stimulated.

I am pleased to acknowledge the gracious permission of Her Majesty Queen Elizabeth II to make use of manuscript material and to reproduce a photograph from the Royal Archives at Windsor Castle. I gratefully acknowledge similar permission from the other following private owners of manuscript material: His Grace the Duke of Norfolk, Viscount Esher, Mr C. A. Gladstone, the College of Arms, the National Trust (Disraeli Papers), the Dean and Chapter of St George's Chapel, the Dean and Chapter of St Paul's Cathedral, and the Dean and Chapter of Westminster Abbey. I apologise to anyone whose copyright I have inadvertently infringed. I am further indebted to the Dean and Chapter of Westminster, and to the British Library for permission to reproduce visual material. I would also like to express my warm appreciation of the vital assistance received from numerous archivists and librarians in both private and public institutions.

An earlier version of part of Chapter Three first appeared as 'Responding to National Grief: Memorial Sermons on the Famous in Britain 1800–1914', *Mortality*, 1 (1996), 283–96, and an earlier version of passages in Chapter Eight first appeared as 'The End of Victorian Values: Women, Religion and the Death of Queen Victoria', in W. J. Sheils and Diana Woods, (eds.), *Studies in Church History 29: Women in the Church* (Oxford, 1990), 481–503. I acknowledge with gratitude permission to reuse this material from, respectively, Carfax Publishing Limited (website http://www.tanf.co.uk/journals), and the Ecclesiastical History Society.

Many other friends and colleagues have contributed substantially to this book. I am grateful in particular to Hugh McLeod and David Bebbington, who have read the whole typescript on behalf of the British Academy, made many useful comments, and saved me from various errors. I have also benefited much from the comments of participants at conferences and seminars where I have read papers that served as early drafts of chapters, and those who have discussed the work with me in more informal contexts. I would like in particular to thank Edward Bailey, Sheila de Bellaigue, Tim Benton, Jay Brown, Arthur Burns, Tony Coulson, Mark Hutchinson, Peter Jupp, Aila Lauha, Mark Noll, Gerald Parsons, Dick Pierard, Edward Royle, Mark Smith, Peter Van Rooden, Tony Walter, and my mother, Mary Wolffe. Wendy Clarke and Miriam Selwyn have provided invaluable secretarial support. Janet English and James Rivington have constituted a most congenial and efficient link with the Publications Department of the British Academy. Last but not least, I want warmly to thank personal friends and relatives for their practical support. Many have been generous both with hospitality on research visits and with encouragement and interest in the project.

J. R. W.

# List of Abbreviations

| | |
|---|---|
| AddMS | Additional Manuscript |
| BL | British Library |
| BodL | Bodleian Library |
| CA | College of Arms Archives |
| CBCM | Cardiff Borough Council Minutes |
| CCL | Cardiff Central Library |
| DavP | Davidson Papers, Lambeth Palace Library |
| DerP | Derby Papers, Liverpool Record Office |
| DisP | Disraeli (Hughenden) Papers, Bodleian Library |
| EM | Earl Marshal's Papers, Arundel Castle |
| ETCM | Edinburgh Town Council Minutes, Edinburgh District Archives |
| GAS | Glamorgan Archives Service |
| GG | Glynne-Gladstone MSS, St Deiniol's Library, Hawarden |
| *ILN* | *Illustrated London News* |
| LC | Lord Chamberlain's Office |
| LCA | Leeds City Archives |
| LPL | Lambeth Palace Library |
| MCCD | Minutes of the Municipal Council of the City of Dublin, Dublin City Hall |
| MEC | Minute Book of the Exeter Chamber/Council, Devon Record Office |
| NCL | New College Library, Edinburgh |
| NLS | National Library of Scotland |
| PRO | Public Record Office |
| QVJ | Queen Victoria's Journal |
| RA | Royal Archives |
| RGS | Royal Geographical Society |
| TCD | Trinity College, Dublin |
| WA | Westminster Abbey Muniments |

# I

# 'The paths of glory lead but to the grave': Approaching the Deaths of the Famous

> The boast of heraldry, the pomp of pow'r
> And all that beauty, all that wealth e'er gave
> Awaits alike th'inevitable hour:
> The paths of glory lead but to the grave.[1]

Thomas Gray's familiar lines, first published in 1751, introduce a paradox that lies at the heart of this book. Gray, reflecting primarily on the 'unhonour'd dead', recalled the ultimate inescapable fate of all humanity. Similar thoughts ran through the mind of a clergyman called to the deathbed of an octogenarian a century and a half later, as he wrote to his wife of the 'dear old lady' who was 'simply worn out'. This particular clergyman, however, was Randall Davidson, Bishop of Winchester and soon to be Archbishop of Canterbury. The 'dear old lady', who had given her name to a whole age, was Queen Victoria. Thus, although Davidson felt the personal dimension of what was happening, he also saw it as 'a solemn moment in English History, or the history of the world'. Such had been the length of the reign that the death of the sovereign lacked 'any precedent within people's memory or knowledge' and the constitutional implications were stirring some unease. 'It does', he went on, 'give one suggestive thoughts about *national* life and its meaning.'[2] It is with such 'suggestive thoughts' and their cultural, religious, and political implications, that this book is to be concerned.

In a personal sense the endpoint of life was indeed the same for Victoria as for the most obscure of her subjects. Much of the public

---

[1] H. W. Starr and J. R. Hendrickson (eds.), *The Complete Poems of Thomas Gray* (Oxford, 1966), 38 ('Elegy Written in a Country Churchyard', lines 33–6).
[2] Lambeth Palace Library [LPL], Davidson Papers [DavP] 19, no. 101B, Davidson to Mrs Davidson, 21 Jan. 1901.

fascination with this and other comparable events hinged on precisely this point: the deaths of the famous were a disconcerting reminder of one's own mortality and that of one's own family and friends. Nevertheless the aftermath of such prominent deaths differed greatly from that following the deaths of ordinary people. On the day after Queen Victoria's death on 22 January 1901 a remarkable scene was witnessed in St Paul's Cathedral on an otherwise ordinary winter weekday afternoon. Without any invitation, the building was 'filled from end to end', with more than 5000 people 'all in deep mourning, and all as still and reverent as any congregation could be.'[3] Such a manifestation of public feeling suggested that Davidson's sense of the gravity and spiritual significance of the event was shared by very many of his compatriots. During the next few weeks obituary columns, public meetings, and church services, culminating in the funeral itself, testified to the depth of national and world-wide emotion focused on this single human being.[4] In the events following Victoria's death 'the pomp of pow'r' was still very much in evidence.

The theme of this book is public responses to the deaths of prominent individuals in the United Kingdom between the 1840s and the First World War. The underlying criterion for inclusion of a personage has been a sufficient degree of status and familiarity for his or her death to impinge on the consciousness of the whole nation, rather than merely on a circle, however extended, of personal affinity, acquaintance and reputation. In this initial chapter the context of the book will first be established and its main themes introduced. Subsequently, a brief survey of responses to prominent deaths in Britain between the seventeenth century and the early nineteenth will provide historical background for the detailed examination of the Victorian and Edwardian periods in the chapters that follow.

## Death, Religion and Nationhood

The very universality of death serves to check generalization: in any given historical period the permutations of its incidence in relation to age group, social class, circumstances, personality, cultural and religious beliefs are almost infinite. Thus the field is particularly exposed to swings and inconsistencies of interpretation between narrowly focused studies on the one hand and attempts at synthesis on the other. In 1965 Geoffrey Gorer gave a seminal impetus to the sociological study of contemporary death in England, but his historical perspective was limited. John Morley's account of Victorian attitudes to death, published in 1971, began to open up the

[3] DavP 506, fos. 12–13, William Sinclair to Davidson.
[4] For further detail, see below Chapter 8.

knowledge of the particular period covered in this book. The work of the architectural historian, James Stevens Curl, was also valuable on its own terms, but did little to establish the wider context in which cemetery and memorial design needs to be seen. Philippe Ariès's massive study of western attitudes to death since the early Middle Ages, published in English in 1981, was both courageous and premature. Ariès suggested that the rise of individualism in the later Middle Ages undermined the calm acceptance of a 'tame' death current in earlier centuries. At a later date, he argued, Romanticism promoted the 'beautiful death' of the nineteenth century, and served as a focus for emotional and spiritual expression.[5]

Such wide brushstrokes are rightly being subjected to close scrutiny, although the process still has a long way to go. In 1989 Ralph Houlbrooke likened the field 'to a vast continent whose coasts are disputed by rival bands of colonists while much larger inland tracts remain unexplored.' After a further decade of research, an increasing number of conferences and publications, and the commencement of an interdisciplinary journal, *Mortality*, in 1996, one might take satisfaction in the indications that, to develop Houlbrooke's analogy, the limits of exploration have been pushed back from the Atlantic seaboard to the Appalachians. In particular Pat Jalland has provided a detailed account of attitudes to death in upper and middle class Victorian families, while two recent works of synthesis, one from an anthropological and religious studies perspective, the other from an historical viewpoint, have provided valuable points of reference for future scholarship.[6]

The social sciences provide some helpful insights for historical analysis. A death, except of a person already entirely isolated from the social fabric, is necessarily disruptive of the pattern of life of the survivors. Only during the twentieth century did marginalization of individuals before death, through hospitalization, institutionalization or merely living alone, become

[5] G. Gorer, *Death, Grief and Mourning in Contemporary Britain* (1965); J. Morley, *Death, Heaven and the Victorians* (1971); J. S. Curl, *The Victorian Celebration of Death* (Newton Abbot, 1972); J. S. Curl, *A Celebration of Death* (1980); P. Ariès, *The Hour of Our Death* (1981), 1–28, 409–74 and *passim*. For helpful summaries and critiques of the views of Ariès and others, together with extensive bibliographical information, see J. Whaley (ed.), *Mirrors of Mortality: Studies in the Social History of Death* (1981), 1–14 and D. L. D'Avray, *Death and the Prince: Memorial Preaching before 1350* (Oxford, 1994), 177–84, 285–6.

[6] R. Houlbrooke (ed.), *Death, Ritual and Bereavement* (1989), 8; P. Jalland, *Death in the Victorian Family* (Oxford, 1996); D. J. Davies, *Death, Ritual and Belief* (1997); P. C. Jupp and C. Gittings (eds.), *Death in England: An Illustrated History* (Manchester, 1999). Further dimensions are indicated by studies of other countries, notably T. A. Kselman, *Death and the Afterlife in Modern France* (Princeton, NJ, 1993) and G. Laderman, *The Sacred Remains: American Attitudes to Death 1793–1883* (New Haven, 1996).

commonplace.[7] Anthropological investigation of non-western societies has provided a framework for understanding the way in which in the past more closely-knit communities in Europe would have reacted to the death of one of their members. In Arnold Van Gennep's work the rituals associated with death were set in the wider framework of other 'rites of passage' that accompany changes in the status of an individual. All such rites, Van Gennep argued, involve the three stages of separation, transition (or liminality), and reincorporation. These three stages can be equated respectively with the deathbed, the period before the funeral, and the funeral itself and its aftermath (which may continue for many years). Throughout the process two strands of change are operating. On the one hand there is the situation of the dead person, whose earthly remains are moved from the place of death into a coffin and subsequently into the grave, and whose soul is perceived as moving to another sphere of existence. On the other hand there is the adjustment made to the social fabric of the survivors, who first experience loss, then live through its direct consequences in the liminal phase associated with mourning and the funeral, and finally reorganize their lives to operate without the dead person.[8]

The particular theme of this book extends analysis of these processes from the sphere of personal grief to wider national life. Whereas on the death of a private individual, the process of grieving and readjustment merely involved family, friends and certain specific social institutions, the potential scope of this book extends to numerous aspects of religion, politics, society and culture. Such events thus offer a fruitful vantage-point from which insights into values and beliefs can be gained. This approach draws theoretical support from Douglas Davies's argument, built on insights derived from the pioneering early twentieth-century French sociologists Émile Durkheim and Robert Hertz, that the body can be viewed as a microcosm of society. Davies also argues, following Maurice Bloch, that the emotions and rituals following the death of an individual can be a spur to change and renewal among the survivors.[9] This analysis can be applied to the understanding of private bereavement, but operates with particular force when the body in question is that of an individual familiar to millions. The death of such a body is thus a challenge to society itself, but one that can be overcome by the assertion of a trans-

---

[7] M. Mulkay, 'Social death in Britain' in D. Clark (ed.), *The Sociology of Death: Theory, Culture, Practice* (Oxford, 1993), 31–49.

[8] A. Van Gennep, translated M. B. Vizedom and G. L. Caffee, *The Rites of Passage* (1960), 10–11, 146–65; R. Huntington and P. Metcalf, *Celebrations of Death: The Anthropology of Mortuary Ritual* (Cambridge, 1979), 8–13 and *passim*.

[9] Davies, *Death, Ritual and Belief,* 9–19.

cending reality. That transcendence may well carry dimensions of supernatural belief, but also is a prompt to the intensified expression of the
shared values and convictions of the group as a whole. Conversely, where
such shared values are lacking or illusory, the death of a prominent person
may expose that deficiency and serve to break whatever fragile and superficial consensus existed.

Here there is a direct link with the investigation of national identity and
nationalism in nineteenth-century Britain. This subject has been relatively
neglected by scholars, probably because of the absence of the kind of
readily identifiable ideologies, political movements and formative events,
such as the 1848 revolutions, that can be investigated on the continent.[10]
There is moreover an intimidating complexity in an investigation that
immediately has to come to terms with the multinational diversity of the
United Kingdom. From this political and cultural reality arises the need
both to appreciate the ambiguities between Englishness and Britishness and
to trace the maintenance and development of an awareness of separate
identity in Ireland, Scotland, and Wales, not to mention powerful regional
and local consciousness.[11]

As a political entity 'The United Kingdom of Great Britain and Ireland'
was defined by the institution of the monarchy. The person and image of
the reigning sovereign was a central expression of its cultural cohesion.
Moreover, with Victoria's elevation to be Empress of India in 1876, the
powerful symbolism of the Crown as a pivot of imperial unity was
reinforced. Such ties were never more clearly exposed than when the death
of the sovereign subjected them to a temporary hiatus. Nor were monarchs
the only source of such cohesion. When the Duke of Wellington died in
1852, Alfred Tennyson's profoundly patriotic poetic response reflected his
awareness of the role of such larger than life individuals in defining and
sustaining an awareness of nationhood:

> A people's voice! we are a people yet.
> Though all men else their nobler dreams forget,
> Confused by brainless mobs and lawless Powers;
> Thank Him who isled us here, and roughly set
> His Briton in blown seas and storming showers,
> We have a voice, with which to pay the debt

---

[10] For reflection on this neglect see G. Newman, *The Rise of English Nationalism: A Cultural
History 1740–1830* (1987), pp. xvii–xxiii.
[11] These complexities are being explored in a growing body of recent work, notably L.
Colley, *Britons: Forging the Nation 1707–1837* (1992); K. Robbins, *Nineteenth-Century Britain:
Integration and Diversity* (Oxford, 1988), and J. Wolffe, *God and Greater Britain: Religion and
National Life in Britain and Ireland 1843–1945* (1994).

Of boundless love and reverence and regret
To those great men who fought, and kept it ours.[12]

Veneration for Wellington could indeed overcome much of the social and national division otherwise apparent among those who mourned him. Similarly, when William Ewart Gladstone, with his Scottish blood, English birth, Welsh residence and Irish political sympathies, died in 1898, the ties of common identity within the United Kingdom were powerfully apparent. In the meantime the memory of men such as David Livingstone, dying in Africa in 1873, and Charles Gordon, killed at Khartoum in 1885, served to give the empire a sense of purpose and legitimacy derived from the sacrifice of such perceived martyrs. Further dimensions of national consciousness were reinforced by Disraeli's apotheosis after 1881, while figures such as Thomas Chalmers, Daniel O'Connell and Charles Stewart Parnell provided a stimulus to awareness of distinctive identity in Scotland and Ireland.

The deaths of the famous drew people to church in unusually high numbers and also stirred prolific religious and quasi-religious discourse. While such events were, by definition, exceptional, when taken in conjunction with each other they provide evidence of changes and continuities in official and popular religiosity during the course of the period. Normally, theological and literary reflection on issues relating to death, judgement and the afterlife was a step removed from the everyday experience of church congregations, except of course for dying and bereaved individuals. On occasions of national mourning, however, these issues were brought suddenly to the forefront of the collective consciousness. Important insights can therefore be gained into changing patterns of belief and religious teaching.[13] Meanwhile, the nature of religious practice can be explored, in relation to matters such as liturgy, the use of hymns and music, and attitudes of different denominations. Above all there were the dimensions of participation and observance as experienced by ordinary people. Many attended services in church buildings, but there was a wider spectrum of involvement through gatherings outside churches, watching processions, or participation in ritual and symbolic observance such as the wearing of

---

[12] C. Ricks, *The Poems of Tennyson*, 3 vols. (2nd edn., Harlow, 1987), ii. 487 ('Ode on the Death of the Duke of Wellington', lines 151–8). Tennyson originally wrote 'His Saxon in blown seas . . .', but changed it to Briton in 1864, a suggestive illustration of the complexities of national identity alluded to above (E. F. Shannon and C. Ricks, 'A Further History of Tennyson's *Ode on the Death of the Duke of Wellington*', *Studies in Bibliography*, 32 (1979), 145).

[13] For background information on these themes see G. Rowell, *Hell and the Victorians: A Study of the Nineteenth-Century Theological Controversies Concerning Eternal Punishment and the Future Life* (Oxford, 1974) and M. Wheeler, *Death and the Future Life in Victorian Literature and Theology* (Cambridge, 1990).

mourning or the closing of shops. A premise underlying the analysis of this book is that clear-cut distinctions between 'religious' and 'secular' individuals and actions, problematic at any time, are especially inappropriate in relation to events such as those here under consideration. The consideration of such material thus provides an important enhancement both to knowledge of the place of the institutional churches in society and culture, and to studies of folk religion.[14]

The concept of civil religion as developed with particular reference to the United States by Robert N. Bellah, is potentially relevant and useful here.[15] It has been defined as 'the widespread acceptance by a people of perceived religio-political traits regarding their nation's history and destiny. It relates their society to the realm of ultimate meaning, enables them to look at their political community in a special sense, and provides the vision which ties the nation together as an integrated whole.'[16] Any straightforward application of the American model to Britain would though be problematic. In consistency with the separation of church and state, the language of civil religion in the United States sets a clear distance between itself and the doctrinal teaching of the Christian churches.[17] In Britain on the other hand the assumption and the aspiration that the nation was not merely generally religious but explicitly Christian, was still fundamental, and was expressed through the constitutional links of church and state and their ritual and ceremonial concomitants. This context gave full legitimacy to specifically Christian visions of the nation, including Evangelical reformism, residual High Toryism, and the Broad Church and liberal Anglican traditions deriving from Thomas Arnold and Samuel Taylor Coleridge. The Free Churches might campaign for disestablishment, but in doing so their aspiration was for the ending of narrow religious privilege rather than the de-Christianiz-ation of national life. Moreover, even as the Victorian period saw a relaxing of many of the historic legal consequences of Anglican and Presbyterian establishment, there was a notable recovery in the role of the monarchy both as a national emblem and as a Christian symbol. Thus in Britain civil religion was not something distinct from Christianity, but rather a complex hybrid of Christian and national inspirations and practices. Such a phenom-enon defies tight theoretical categorization, but it is a fruitful field for empirical historical investigation.

To serve the purposes of the analysis a case-study approach has been

[14] For my own synthesis and evaluation of existing scholarship on these topics see Wolffe, *God and Greater Britain*, 48–97.
[15] R. N. Bellah, 'Civil Religion in America', in R. G. Jones and R. E. Richey (eds.), *American Civil Religion* (1974), 21–44 (originally published in *Daedalus*, Winter 1967).
[16] R. V. Pierard and R. D. Linder, *Civil Religion and the Presidency* (1988), 22–3.
[17] Bellah, 'Civil Religion', 26–30.

adopted. Any attempt to achieve within a manageable compass an account of the responses to the deaths of all public figures in the period would inevitably be doomed to failure. Accordingly detailed consideration has been concentrated on nine cases, the Duke of Wellington (1852), Prince Albert (1861), David Livingstone (1874), Disraeli (1881), General Gordon (1885), Prince Albert Victor, Duke of Clarence (1892), Gladstone (1898), Queen Victoria (1901) and King Edward VII (1910). Other instances, notably Thomas Chalmers (1847), Daniel O'Connell (1847), Palmerston (1865), Prince Leopold, Duke of Albany (1884), and Charles Stewart Parnell (1891) will receive some attention, to the extent that they serve to illuminate particular themes in the book. The selection of the nine cases for close examination largely reflects their exceptional prominence. It includes the two monarchs who died during the period (Victoria and Edward VII), a quasi-monarchical figure (Albert), three of the handful of non-royal figures to receive publicly-funded funerals (Wellington, Livingstone and Gladstone),[18] and the most charismatic statesman of the age (Disraeli). The Duke of Clarence was in 1892 second in line to the throne after his father the Prince of Wales, and his tragically early death stirred a massive outpouring of public sentiment. The case well illustrates the phenomenon that reaction to a death was fuelled as much by symbolic associations as by a consciousness of objective loss. The case of General Gordon was *sui generis*, prompting an outpouring of sentiment that, together with responses to Livingstone's death a decade earlier, was especially influential in inspiring the religious and patriotic mythologies of Empire.

The survey of pre-Victorian developments in the remainder of this chapter, will establish the context for Chapter Two, which offers an analysis of responses to the Duke of Wellington's death in 1852, of the setting and planning of his funeral, and of the impact of that 'great solemnity'.[19] Chapters Three and Four then pursue particular themes through the period as a whole. In Chapter Three dimensions of the organized religious response to prominent deaths are examined, with reference in particular to funeral sermons, the development of the funeral services themselves, and parallel memorial services held throughout the country. Chapter Four then develops the local dimension of the analysis, based on an examination of five cities, beginning with two contrasting English provincial centres, Exeter and Leeds, and then turning to Cardiff, Edinburgh and Dublin, as points of focus respectively for Welsh, Scottish and Irish reactions. In each case the organized religious aspects of the aftermath of prominent deaths are set in the wider context of local response and civic development. An opportunity is

---

[18] For an indication of how rare this distinction was, see Appendix.
[19] Ricks, *Tennyson*, ii. 490, line 244.

also taken briefly to introduce further case studies centred on funerals that took place in or near the cities under examination.

The four subsequent chapters then revert to the central national perspective and address the remaining eight case studies, grouped in pairs in order to give focus to particular strands in the overall analysis. Thus Chapters Five, Six, and Seven are all concerned with the period between the 1860s and the 1890s, and are directed to the Empire (Livingstone and Gordon), politics (Disraeli and Gladstone), and royalty (Albert and Clarence) respectively. Chapter Eight then carries the discussion into the early twentieth century through Victoria and Edward VII. Here too threads are brought together from the preceding chapters insofar as in the responses to the deaths of these two monarchs one can observe the culmination of a wide range of developments apparent during the course of Victoria's reign. In all these four chapters, as in Chapter Two, attention is centred particularly on the available evidence for the general public mood in the aftermath of the death, on the range of religious and quasi-religious comment, and on the context, content, and significance of the funerals. Merely procedural and technical matters relating to the organization of funerals are not considered in detail, although the Appendix provides an overview of the various agencies involved and of significant shifts in chains of command and responsibility. Discussion is concentrated on the initial period between the death and the end of the funeral ceremonies, and, although allusions are made to subsequent commemoration and memorialization, no attempt is made to cover these later phases in a systematic manner. Nor should treatment of immediate responses be regarded as comprehensive: several of these cases would be worthy of a book in their own right,[20] and issues treated as relatively peripheral in much of the present study, notably the international dimensions of such events, would merit much more detailed analysis.

Finally in Chapter Nine, the most prominent cases occurring between 1910 and the end of the twentieth century will be briefly surveyed, and in the light of that longer perspective conclusions will be drawn. Further engagement with theoretical perspectives is largely postponed until this point.[21] Earlier discussion would run the risk of setting an unrealistic agenda for study of a complex historical reality on the basis of sometimes fragmentary sources. In concluding this book, however, it will be appropriate

---

[20] One already has been so treated, albeit in a narrative rather than analytical fashion. See J. M. Packard, *Farewell in Splendor: The Passing of Queen Victoria and Her Age* (1995).

[21] For a recent valuable survey of literature see J. Woodward, *The Theatre of Death: The Ritual Management of Royal Funerals in Renaissance England, 1570–1625* (Woodbridge, Suffolk, 1997), 1–14.

to build on the detailed empirical evidence of the preceding chapters in exploring wider patterns of historical, religious and cultural development.

## From the Stuarts to the Victorians

In a short perspective the dominant reaction to prominent deaths often appeared to be a resort to conservatism and tradition in the face of disruptive and painful events. When considered over a longer span of time, however, responses appear much more mutable. Broadly speaking, a survey from the sixteenth century to the late nineteenth produces an impression of a wheel slowly turning full circle. The period began with a phase of widespread mourning and elaborate funerals, and continued through one of much more limited reactions, and ended with an era when death was again a spur to extensive 'celebration'. Within this general trend significant fluctuations can be discerned, partly arising from the popularity or otherwise of particular individuals, partly from other attendant circumstances. In the earlier part of the period attention naturally centres on funeral rites themselves as the best documented aspect of reaction. Responses to the deaths of sovereigns provide the most obvious thread for tracing such developments.

The funerals of the Tudor monarchs were on a grand scale. Henry VIII's death in 1547 was followed by extended religious and secular ceremonial that appeared to reflect genuine depth of popular feeling.[22] When Elizabeth I died in 1603 the indications are that the public felt a similar mixture of genuine grief combined with a momentous sense that an era had ended, resembling that apparent on Queen Victoria's death three centuries later. Her funeral in Westminster Abbey was an elaborate occasion preceded by a long procession in front of large crowds.[23] In terms of cost, however, it was to be dwarfed by the obsequies of her successor James I in 1625 and of his consort, Anne of Denmark, in 1619. Even when some allowance is made for inflation, the expenditure of £50,000 on James's funeral as opposed to £11,305[24] on Elizabeth's revealed more about the pretensions of the early Stuart monarchy than its popularity: James and his son Charles I evidently took the view that funerals were an opportunity for impressive display. This period indeed saw a high-point of what Jennifer Woodward has dubbed the 'theatre of death', in which, despite iconophobia stirred by

---

[22] P. S. Fritz, 'From "Public" to "Private": the Royal Funerals in England, 1500–1830', in Whaley, *Mirrors of Mortality*, 62–3; C. Gittings, *Death, Burial and the Individual in Early Modern England* (1984), 216–20.

[23] O. Bland, *The Royal Way of Death* (1986), 26–34.

[24] Gittings, *Death, Burial and the Individual*, 226–7.

the Reformation, elaborate royal mortuary ritual was used as an important channel for the focusing and stimulating of loyalty to the living monarch.[25]

The Civil War, however, was followed by a significant reduction in the scale of royal funerals. Charles I, following his execution in 1649, was buried with minimal ceremony costing only a few hundred pounds. Parliament was anxious to prevent the funeral from becoming a spectacle and insisted that the king be interred at Windsor rather than Westminster Abbey, thus showing its awareness of the political significance of funeral rites.[26] When Charles II died in 1685 there was a reversion to precedents derived from the funeral of James I. Nevertheless, there were changes: public grief in 1685 was perhaps more genuine and widespread than it had been in 1625, but the funeral itself was 'private', taking place at night, establishing a pattern that was to be followed until after the death of William IV in 1837.[27] The untimely death of Mary II in 1694, at the age of thirty-one from smallpox, appears to have stirred deep popular emotion, and brought a stronger, but temporary, reversion to earlier precedents. Her distraught husband William III, supported by the council, spared no expense on the impressive lying-in-state and funeral ceremonial, which cost even more than that provided for James I. Preachers edified their congregations with sermons on the mysterious workings of providence and Henry Purcell's anthems for the service provided a lasting contribution to English music. As John Evelyn put it, there was 'Never so universal a mourning'.[28]

During the eighteenth century, however, the deaths of monarchs did not give rise to strong feeling or expensive display. The funerals of William

[25] Woodward, *Theatre of Death, passim.*

[26] Bland, *Royal Way of Death*, 35–56; Gittings, *Death, Burial and the Individual*, 226–7. From the late thirteenth century to the eighteenth all sovereigns were buried at Westminster with the exception of Edward II (Gloucester), Henry IV (Canterbury), Henry VI (Chertsey, moved to Windsor), Edward IV (Windsor), Richard III (Leicester), Henry VIII (Windsor), Charles I, James II (St Germain-en-Laye) and George I (Hanover). It is significant that of these nine exceptions, five had been deposed or killed. The burial of two of the others, Edward IV and Henry VIII, at Windsor reflected a passing vogue for the recently-built St George's Chapel, while the choice of Hanover for George I confirmed his weak identification with Britain. However George II was the last sovereign to be buried at Westminster: all his successors were interred either at Windsor or at nearby Frogmore. Cf. M. Bond, 'The Burial Places of English Monarchs', *Report of the Society of the Friends of St George's and the Descendants of the Knights of the Garter*, 1969–70, pp. 30–40.

[27] Bland, *Royal Way of Death*, 72–4; Fritz, ' "Public" to "Private" ', 69–71. The term 'private' was relative rather than absolute, denoting in particular that the role of the heralds in the proceedings was much reduced (Ibid., 79). For further information see Appendix below.

[28] Bland, *Royal Way of Death*, 78–81; Fritz, ' "Public" to "Private" ', 65–8; W. Sherlock, *A Sermon Preached at the Temple Church December 30 1694 upon the Sad Occasion of the Death of our Gracious Queen* (1694).

III (1702) and Anne (1714) confirmed the pattern of private nocturnal interments,[29] while comments on these national bereavements suggested calm acceptance and even recognition of positive advantage from the change of sovereign. Thus a preacher on William III's death considered the providential black and white chequering of human lives and, while recognizing the qualities of the late monarch, he ended with a eulogy of praise on the new Queen.[30] Twelve years later, Anne's shade might well have had cause to ponder not only the fragility of life but also the transience of popular enthusiasm, when it was suggested that the timing of her death meant a providential deliverance from High Church influence and the designs of Pope and Pretender.[31] Anne, of course, had her devotees, but attitudes to her death reflected ecclesiastical and political party, more than national consensus. A loyal versifier complained of a 'Vile degenerate race':

> With Pride, they Vaunt it o'er Great ANNA's Hearse,
> Lampoon her Reign, and high Exult in Verse.
> Their Canker'd Breasts, with utmost Hatred burn,
> And dare Rejoyce, when all the World does Mourn.[32]

The suddenness of George I's death in 1727 inspired reflection on the uncertainties of the world, but grief was qualified by praise for the perceived virtues of the new monarch and gratitude for the peaceful maintenance of the Protestant succession.[33] In the Hanoverian period there was no taboo against speaking ill of the dead. When Queen Caroline, George II's consort, died in 1737, the following lampoon was offered as her epitaph:

> Here lies unpitied by Church and State
> The Subject of their Flattery and Hate . . .
> Fawning and Haughty, when familiar, rude,
> And never civil seem'd but to delude:
> Inquisitive in trifling mean affairs,
> Heedless of publick good, or orphan's tears.
> To her own offspring mercy she deny'd,
> And unforgiving, unforgiven, dy'd.

---

[29] Bland, *Royal Way of Death*, 84–8; ' "Public" to "Private" ', 71–2.

[30] N. Brady, *A Sermon upon Occasion of the Death of our Late Sovereign King William; and Her Present Majesty's Happy Accession to the Crown* (1702).

[31] B. Stinton, *A Discourse of Divine Providence: Occasion'd by the Demise of Her Late Majesty Queen Anne, and the Happy Accession of our Present Sovereign King George* (1714).

[32] *Britannia's Tears: A Satyrical Dirge by Way of Lamentation on the Deplorable Death of Her Late Gracious Majesty Queen Anne . . . and as a Chastisement to all Her Merry Mourners* (Dublin, 1714), 12–13. Dissenters, gratified that Anne's demise prevented Royal Assent being given to the Schism Act, were prominent among the Whig 'merry mourners'.

[33] I. Watts, *The Religious Improvement of Publick Events* (1727).

Other reactions to the Queen's death took a more positive view of her character, but it was evident that there was no consensus of adulation.[34] Likewise, the predominant reactions to the premature death of Frederick, Prince of Wales, in 1751, were either muted or cynical.[35] George II's own demise in 1760 does not appear to have stirred much sincere mourning and, although his funeral procession was, according to Horace Walpole, 'a noble sight', the subsequent burial service was a disorderly and poorly-attended affair.[36]

A contrasting development from the mid-seventeenth century onwards was for a very small and select number of prominent non-royal personages to receive grand public funerals. The precedent was set following the death of Oliver Cromwell in 1658, when an effigy, with regal trimmings, was conveyed in a splendid procession from Somerset House to Westminster. This case was exceptional and reflected the struggles of the vulnerable Protectorate régime to maintain its legitimacy after Cromwell's death. Charles II's government, though, came close to emulating it when General Monk, Duke of Albemarle, who had played a central role in the Restoration, died in 1670. The King at once resolved to pay all the expenses of the funeral himself and plans by Garter King of Arms on the basis of several (unspecified) precedents were agreed by the council. An effigy of the Duke in full armour lay in state at Somerset House as Cromwell's had done.[37] A woodcut of the subsequent procession to Westminster Abbey shows a carefully arranged display of heraldry and gradations of rank culminating with an elaborate horse-drawn funeral car.[38] Such events remained rare, however, and the only comparable eighteenth-century examples were the funerals of the Duke of Marlborough (1722)—the costs of which were met by the family

---

[34] *Verses on the Death of Her Late Most Excellent Majesty Queen Caroline* (1738).

[35] Bland, *Royal Way of Death*, 97–8.

[36] Gittings, *Death, Burial and the Individual*, 228–9; Colley, *Britons*, 229–30.

[37] The body itself was kept in a separate private room and privately interred in the Abbey on the evening before the funeral. As with Cromwell's funeral (Bland, *Royal Way of Death*, 57), the public ceremonial was thus entirely detached from the deceased's mortal remains. The use of effigies was discontinued in the course of the eighteenth century (Fritz, ' "Public" to "Private", 77n) but a transitional phase was apparent at Marlborough's funeral in 1722 when the coffin was conveyed openly, with 'a compleat Suit of Armour, Steel gilt, lying on the Coffin, Vizor clos'd' (*The Order of the Procession at the Funeral of His Grace John Duke of Marlborough* (1722), 5). The heralds initially proposed the use of an effigy for the Earl of Chatham's funeral in 1778, but the suggestion was not implemented (PRO, LC 2/35).

[38] F. Sandford, *The Order and Ceremonies used for, and at the Solemn Interment of the . . . Duke of Albemarle* (1670).

rather than the Crown—and of William Pitt (the Elder), Earl of Chatham, in 1778.[39]

The decline in the observance of prominent deaths in the eighteenth century should not be overstated: grand aristocratic funerals continued to occur, and substantial crowds were still drawn to the spectacles afforded by royal obsequies and the preparation for them.[40] Nevertheless there was a relative contrast with the periods before and after, which calls for some explanation. It was in part attributable to organizational factors. In the seventeenth century the College of Arms and the Earl Marshal had taken the central role. Their key concern was to ensure an appropriate and precisely regulated degree of heraldic display, based on precedents dating back to the Tudor period. Such ceremonial had originally had an important social and political function in providing a public display of hierarchy and order. By the eighteenth century, however, the culture had become less receptive to such visual didacticism and, with a growing consciousness of privacy, the Hanoverian dynasty, like the nobility as a whole, became increasingly restive at close heraldic regimentation and the heavy fees charged by the College of Arms. There was a shift of organizational initiative from the Earl Marshal to the Lord Chamberlain, who was more directly answerable both to the sovereign and to the government. This change was confirmed by the holding of funerals in the evening and the change during George III's reign of the royal burying place from Westminster to Windsor. A manuscript ceremonial for the funeral of Princess Amelia in 1810 pointedly noted that it was to be 'conducted entirely by the Lord Chamberlain's office without the Heralds by His Majesty's express commands'. On the other hand, especially on the death of the sovereign, the heralds could not normally be excluded altogether and the arrangements made reflected the sometimes uneasy compromises between the Lord Chamberlain's Office and the College of Arms.[41]

Wider factors were also relevant. In the decades after 1688, relative political stability together with the declining practical importance of the monarchy meant that the death of the sovereign no longer seemed to be a moment of potential crisis that needed to be smoothed by ritual expressions of continuity.[42] The deaths of non-royal political leaders were more likely to take place in retirement and hence did not usually have obvious practical consequences. At the same time the growing individualism that, Clare

[39] Gittings, *Death, Burial and the Individual*, 232; W. Coxe, *Memoirs of the Duke of Marlborough*, 3 vols. (1896), iii. 423–5.
[40] Gittings, *Death, Burial and the Individual*, 207–8; P. Fritz, 'The Trade in Death: The Royal Funerals in England, 1685–1830', *Eighteenth-Century Studies*, 15 (1981–2), 294–6.
[41] PRO, LC 2/41; Fritz, ' "Public" to "Private" ', 75–9.
[42] Gittings, *Death, Burial and the Individual*, 228.

Gittings argues, brought an intensified sense of irreplaceable loss and personal sorrow to bereavement in private life,[43] worked against strong identification with relatively remote public griefs. It also became harder for an idealized vision of monarchy to transcend the obvious human limitations of the men and women who actually wore the crown. Moreover as the Reformation and the subsequent era of baroque display gave way to the Enlightenment, the predominant religious climate of the age also weighed against elaborate ritual or spiritually-charged funeral sermons.[44]

By the early nineteenth century, however, renewed political and national insecurity following 1789, currents of religious revival, and the beginnings of a more 'Romantic' attitude to death all stimulated change. Lord Nelson's victory and death at Trafalgar in 1805 gave rise to an unprecedented breadth and depth of public response. Unlike earlier military heroes, such as Albemarle and Marlborough, he had died not in retirement when his achievements were fading into memory, but at the moment of his greatest triumph. Thus grief for Nelson was coupled with gratitude for his defeat of the French and Spanish fleets and with patriotic assertion at a time of ongoing national crisis. One of many versifiers contributed additional verses to 'Rule Britannia':

> Rest, rest in peace, bright Honour's son.
> Thy sires above will smile on thee;
> Glorious thy race on earth was run,
> Who dar'd to die, to keep us free
> Then mourn Britannia, Britannia's sons, so brave,
> Your laurels strew o'er NELSON's grave.[45]

The clergy and ministers who preached memorial sermons echoed such sentiments in Christianized form. Thus, for example, a Bath minister dwelt on the 'invigorating influence' of patriotism and considered Nelson's death to be a 'model of true heroism'. He had now received 'a beautiful crown': the admiration of the nation coupled with the hope that his soul lived in Christ.[46]

The funeral at the beginning of January 1806 was a spectacular pageant. It began with a lying-in-state at Greenwich, which was besieged by large

---

[43] Ibid., 14.
[44] For detailed analysis of the relationship between religious change and the history of death in the early modern era see R. Houlbrooke, *Death, Religion and the Family in England, 1480–1750* (Oxford, 1998).
[45] *Neil's Pocket Melodist, or, Vocal Repository*, no. xxii.
[46] J. Gardiner, *A Tribute to the Memory of Lord Nelson* (Bath, 1805).

crowds,[47] and the body was then conveyed in a barge procession to White-hall. On the following day the grand progress continued to St Paul's, attended by a numerous array of naval and military officers and of nobility. The Prince of Wales attended, breaking the tradition that royalty did not attend funerals of subjects, however distinguished.[48] The coffin was carried on an elaborate funeral car designed to resemble a ship. The proceedings concluded with Evensong and the burial service, and the interment of the body in the crypt beneath the dome of the cathedral.[49] Accounts of the ceremonial dwelt explicitly on the messages it was intended to convey:

> No expence has been spared, no form omitted in any respect, to make this procession awfully grand; showing to our enemies, and the world at large, the veneration in which we held him in remembrance, and rousing the spirit of the living heroes of the present day, by displaying the estimation paid to the deceased who have signalised themselves in their country's cause, and died fighting for her welfare.[50]

Another observer noted that the magnificence of the spectacle was at least equal to that at the interment of past sovereigns and observed that it had drawn 'thousands' to the metropolis from substantial distances.[51]

Nelson's funeral initiated a period of more extensive public acknow-ledgement of the deaths of the great, a trend that was confirmed a few weeks later when the Younger Pitt was given a public funeral at Westminster Abbey amidst heraldry and pageantry, and in the presence of three royal dukes.[52] Nevertheless the affair was not uncontentious: the resolution to grant a public funeral had been a matter for lengthy debate in the Commons,

---

[47] A. Y. Mann, *The Last Moments and Principal Events Relative to the Ever to be Lamented Death of Lord Viscount Nelson* (1806), 30–3.

[48] *The Order to be Observed in the Publick Funeral Procession of the Late Vice-Admiral Horatio Viscount Nelson* (1806). Despite his evident devotion to Albemarle, Charles II did not attend his funeral; at Marlborough's funeral George I and the Prince of Wales showed their sympathy by sending their coaches, but did not attend in person (*Funeral of Duke of Marlborough*); at the Earl of Chatham's funeral royal non-participation was supposed to be politically-motivated and attracted adverse comment (Mann, *Death of Lord Nelson*, 24–6). The tradition that the sovereign in person did not attend the funeral of a subject was maintained for another century, and was only decisively breached by George V's participation in the interment of the Unknown Warrior in 1920.

[49] *Services and Anthems to be Used upon Thursday the 9th Day of January 1806, being the Day Appointed for the Public Funeral of the Late Lord Viscount Nelson* (1806).

[50] Mann, *Death of Lord Nelson*, 27.

[51] *An Official and Circumstantial Detail of the Grand National Obsequies at the Public Funeral of Britain's Darling Hero, the Immortal Nelson* (1806?), 4.

[52] *Order to be Observed in the Publick Funeral Procession of the Late Right Honourable William Pitt* (1806).

and eighty-nine votes were cast against it.[53] On the day 'the crowd was by no means great'.[54] By contrast, the funeral of Pitt's great rival Charles James Fox, also at Westminster Abbey later in the same year, was not formally a public one, but the streets were 'immensely crowded'.[55] Unlike Nelson, statesmen could not in death wholly transcend the controversies and affinities of their lives. The prospects for royalty were rather better, however: from 1817 onwards a significant cluster of royal deaths in the space of a few years—Princess Charlotte (1817), Queen Charlotte (1818), the Duke of Kent (1820), George III (1820)—attracted widespread popular interest. Even here, however, there were limits to consensus, as was to become dramatically apparent in the aftermath of Queen Caroline's death in 1821.

The formative event was the death of Princess Charlotte in childbirth on 6 November 1817 at the age of twenty-one. The sudden demise of George III's only legitimate grandchild at a time of political insecurity stirred worries about the succession of a kind that had been absent since the early eighteenth century. Moreover it was a genuine and profound tragedy of a kind that was of common occurrence in private life in those days of high maternal mortality. During the reign of George III the monarchy had gained in popularity through cultivating an image of ordinary and accessible family life.[56] Hence the untimely death of his granddaughter could be regarded, in Harriet Martineau's words, as 'a calamity that demanded the intense sorrow of domestic misfortune.'[57] Thomas Chalmers saw the event as stirring the recognition that the royal family were 'partakers of one common humanity with ourselves' and believed that there was not 'a peasant in the land, who is not touched to the very heart'.[58] There was an outpouring of literary, religious, musical and artistic tributes.[59] On the day of the Princess's funeral at Windsor, churches all over Britain were filled with people who found in the forms of Christianity an apparent source of comfort, meaning and communal coherence in the face of the

---

[53] *The Times*, 28 Jan. 1806.

[54] *The Times*, 24 Feb. 1806.

[55] *The Times*, 11 Oct. 1806.

[56] Colley, *Britons*, 232–5.

[57] Quoted S. C. Behrendt, *Royal Mourning and Regency Culture: Elegies and Memorials of Princess Charlotte* (Basingstoke, 1997), 1.

[58] T. Chalmers, *A Sermon Delivered in the Tron Church, Glasgow, on Wednesday Nov. 19 1817, the Day of the Funeral of HRH the Princess Charlotte of Wales* (Glasgow, 1817), 17–18.

[59] Behrendt (*Royal Mourning*) provides detailed and insightful analysis of this material. See also E. Schor, *Bearing the Dead: the British Culture of Mourning from the Enlightenment to Victoria* (Princeton, NJ, 1994), 196–229.

pathos of the event and the constitutional insecurity it generated.[60] Also apparent in the response to Princess Charlotte's death were strong links between collective grief and national consciousness. Chalmers asserted that 'It is in this way, that through the avenue of a nation's tenderness, we can estimate the strength and steadfastness of a nation's loyalty. . . . Oh! is it possible that these can be other than honest tears, or that tears of pity can, on such an emergency as the present, be other than tears of patriotism.'[61] Whereas the response to Nelson's death had demonstrated the appeal of the Romantic British hero, that to Princess Charlotte's showed that awareness of the tragedies of the royal family could stimulate other powerful currents of nationality. The very consciousness of individual human frailty that appears to have lessened the impact of royal deaths in the eighteenth century was, with enhanced sympathetic identification with the sufferings of others,[62] to become a key factor in their widespread emotional resonance in the changing cultural context of late Georgian and Victorian Britain.

While the deaths of Queen Charlotte and of George III were hardly unexpected in the course of nature, and for the King was recognized as a merciful release from the indignity and suffering of his last years, the inevitable when it came still stirred widespread grief.[63] On the day of his funeral, the churches were densely crowded and even the aisles 'filled with well-dressed persons'. This description betrays the social limits of church-going, which operated even on this occasion. It is unclear, however, whether the poor stayed away by choice or because there was no room for them: in the streets the 'lower ranks' were observed wearing mourning, and all the shops were closed.[64] Memorial sermons for both the King and the Queen confirmed the linkages between idealized family life, religion, and patriotism that had been so conspicuous in November 1817.[65]

---

[60] 'Scoto-Britannicus' (Thomas McCrie), *Free Thoughts on the Late Religious Celebration of the Funeral of HRH The Princess Charlotte of Wales* (Edinburgh, 1817). For discussion of McCrie's own trenchant critique of the majority response see Schor, *Bearing the Dead*, 212–18. See also below, 117.

[61] Chalmers, *Princess Charlotte*, 18–20.

[62] Schor, *Bearing the Dead*, 11, 34–40. Schor attributes this trend to the formative influence of Adam Smith's *Theory of Moral Sentiments*.

[63] As *The Times* put it, 'Although the time to weep for a virtuous man is not properly when he ceases to exist, as when that existence ceases to be a source of comfort to himself or of usefulness to others, yet will our late Monarch's actual death be deeply, though perhaps not rationally, mourned.' (31 Jan. 1820).

[64] Robert Southy (pseud.), *Authentic Memoirs of our late Venerable and Beloved Monarch, George the Third* (1820), 420; *The Times*, 17 Feb. 1820. Cf. L. Colley, 'The Apotheosis of George III: Loyalty, Royalty and the British Nation 1760–1820', *Past and Present*, 102 (1984), 94–129.

[65] For examples see W. B. Collyer, *The Royal Preacher* (1818); T. T. Biddulph, *National Affliction Improved* (Bristol, 1820).

A further indication of personal identification with deceased royalty was a strong interest in the process of dying itself. Princess Charlotte's last agony was narrated in detail in commemorative pamphlets, one of which defended its prurience in the following manner:

> We know the delicacy of the subject; we know that the weaknesses of nature (feminine nature) are not fit to be exposed to the eye, and that no rude hand should approach the veil that conceals them; but we feel that the present is a case of public and national interest, which if it does not justify, will excuse a liberty that would be, under other circumstances a reprehensible breach of decorum.[66]

Accounts of 'last moments' of other royalty were widely circulated. In 1820 there were complaints that those around George III had been remiss in not issuing sufficient bulletins to meet the 'natural and laudable anxiety of the public'.[67] After the Duke of York died in 1827 there were complaints that his doctors had provided insufficient information during his illness. The omission was subsequently redressed with the publication in the *Annual Register* of a detailed memorandum by the Duke's secretary, Sir Herbert Taylor, on the closing days of his life.[68] On George IV's death in 1830 the somewhat gruesome details of the post-mortem were published in the newspapers.[69]

On the other hand, if royal deaths were seen as a very public affair, royal funerals were treated as private or semi–private occasions. Money was a good measure of scale: expenditure authorized by the Lord Chamberlain's department on George III's funeral in 1820 was just under £26,000, less than half that for Mary II's in 1694.[70] The change of burial place to Windsor diminished further the potential for direct public participation. As funerals were held in the evening, an overnight stay was necessary for those who came from London, and the accommodation available in the small town was very limited. Moreover the ceremonial was almost entirely contained within the walls of the castle itself. George III, George IV, and William IV all died in the castle, lay in state in the state apartments, and were buried

---

[66] *The Virtuous Life and Lamented Death of HRH The Princess Charlotte, including Every Interesting Particular Relative to Her Accouchement and Death!* (1817?), 24.

[67] *Authentic Memoirs of George III*, 406; *Radicals and True Patriots Compared; or Living Evidences from New York of Paine's Character and Last Hours Contrasted with those of the Patriotic Duke of Kent and the late great and good King George III* (1820).

[68] J. Sykes, *An Account of the Death and Funeral Procession of HRH Frederick Duke of York* (Newcastle-upon-Tyne, 1827), 6; *Annual Register*, 1827, 442–60. There is a facsimile of Taylor's original memorandum in the British Library [BL], Additional Manuscript [AddMS] 47142, fos. 41–66.

[69] *The Times*, 2 July 1830.

[70] Fritz, ' "Public" to "Private" ', 78.

in the royal vault underneath St George's Chapel without their remains ever leaving the precincts. On the death of the sovereign, there was an opportunity for the public to view the lying-in-state, but difficulties of access meant that even many of those who had succeeded in travelling to Windsor were unable to gain admittance.[71] Other royal bodies, such as those of Princess Charlotte and her infant, were brought 'privately' to the castle before ceremonies commenced. Despite strong public interest, Princess Charlotte's body only lay in state for a few hours, in an 'exceedingly small' room with only one door to which no one was admitted without a pass ticket.[72] Subsequently, although spectators were allowed into the courtyards of the castle, their admission had to be regulated by tickets, and the number who could witness the full-scale processions was much smaller than would have been the case had they walked through the streets (see Plate 1). Moreover, much of the nave of St George's Chapel was cleared of seating to allow room for the procession and only a very select few could be admitted to the service. The total seating capacity for the funeral of Princess Amelia was only 423 and it seems unlikely that it would have been greater on subsequent occasions.[73] Processions themselves allowed for a carefully-regulated ordering of aristocracy, rank and precedence, but for no participation by the common people, unless one counted the soldiers who lined the route bearing flambeaux and the Eton boys admitted to standing room in the chapel.[74]

There were, however, noteworthy exceptions to this pattern. The Duke of Kent, fourth son of George III and father of the future Queen Victoria, died at Sidmouth in Devon in January 1820. There accordingly had to be a long journey across southern England to bring the body back to Windsor. The cortège was accompanied out of Sidmouth by a carriage procession of local dignitaries, in front of 'an immense concourse of spectators from the surrounding country'. Its subsequent progress was marked by tolling bells and closed shops in the various towns through which it passed, giving an altogether more public dimension to the proceedings than occurred in the case of the Duke's relatives who had died in locations closer to Windsor.[75]

On the other hand the aftermath of the death of the King's estranged

---

[71] BL, AddMS 47142, fo. 30; *The Times*, 16 Feb. 1820; *Authentic Memoirs of George III*, 418–9; J. Sykes, *An Account of the Last Moments and Death of His Majesty King George the Fourth* (Newcastle-upon-Tyne, 1830), 23–5.

[72] BL, AddMS 47142, fo. 12; *Life and Lamented Death of Princess Charlotte*, 43.

[73] Ibid., 51; *The Times*, 17 Feb. 1820; PRO, LC 2/41. PRO, WORKS 21/5/8/4 is a plan of the fittings in St. George's for the funeral of William IV in 1837 which is consistent with the arrangements described for earlier royal funerals.

[74] *Ceremonial for the Interment of His Late Most Sacred Majesty King George the Fourth* (1830).

[75] *The Times*, 14 Feb. 1820.

wife Queen Caroline at Hammersmith on 7 August 1821 indicated that public mourning, even for royalty, could be subversive as well as affirming of consensus. Caroline's death was the last act in the drama that had begun with her return to England on her husband's accession in 1820 to claim her rights as Queen. It had continued with her 'trial' before the House of Lords for her alleged marital infidelities and her exclusion from the Coronation. In the course of these indignities she became a focus for popular sentiment and Whig and radical protest. In the opinion of *The Times* 'She died as she had lived, a Christian heroine, and a martyr.'[76] Accordingly, from the government's point of view, it was desirable that the funeral should be conducted as briskly and inconspicuously as possible in order that it should not become a focus for further unrest.

Initially, circumstances seemed promising. The Queen herself had decided not to risk a final posthumous confrontation with her husband by demanding burial at Windsor, and had instead left directions in her will that her remains should be sent off for interment in Brunswick three days after her death.[77] This however proved easier said than done. A scheme to move the body down the river from Hammersmith and straight out to sea was abandoned when the complications and dangers were vigorously represented by the Admiralty.[78] Accordingly there was no alternative to moving the body to Harwich by road, a journey that went through London and would take at least two days. In the meantime the King was on his post-Coronation visit to Ireland, and with a spitefulness that pursued his wife beyond the grave, was embarrassingly reluctant to order court mourning and resentful of any consequent disruption to his schedule.[79] The Prime Minister, Lord Liverpool, was acutely conscious of the political risks inherent in the affair. The late Queen's attendants and supporters were anxious to prevent shabby treatment of their mistress's remains and well aware of the popular sympathy which they could command. Liverpool wrote to Lord Londonderry (Castlereagh) that 'As long as the Queen lived, it might not unreasonably be apprehended that any concession wd. be followed by some fresh Demand. Now, all her demands are at an end, and the only consideration should be, how we can close the business most

---

[76] *The Times*, 6 Aug. 1821. For analysis of the Queen Caroline affair see T. W. Laqueur, 'The Queen Caroline Affair: Politics as Art in the Reign of George IV', *Journal of Modern History*, 54 (1982), 417–66; L. Davidoff and C. Hall, *Family Fortunes: Men and Women of the English Middle Class 1780–1850* (1987), 150–5; Colley, *Britons*, 265–8.

[77] BL, AddMS 38563, fo. 413 Copy of codicil to Queen Caroline's will, 5 Aug. 1821.

[78] BL, AddMS 38289 (Liverpool Papers), fos. 351–2, Melville to Sidmouth, 12 Aug. 1821.

[79] Ibid., fos. 320–1, Liverpool to Londonderry?, 10 Aug. 1821; fos. 322–3, Liverpool to the King, 10 Aug. 1821.

quietly and without offence.'[80] Lady Hood, wife of the Queen's Chamberlain, particularly resented the fact that the Queen, who had never been accorded the dignity of a military escort during her lifetime, should now be 'guarded' on her last journey, in order to check protest. She foresaw 'mischief' and 'bloodshed' as likely to arise from such provocation of the people.[81]

The procession left Hammersmith on Tuesday 14 August. When it reached London it encountered military detachments stationed in Hyde Park to prevent it proceeding directly east through the City. Shots were fired, several people were reported killed, and the procession was diverted along Edgware Road and what is now Marylebone Road. The government's intention had been that it should skirt the City to the north, but a barricade erected by the crowd succeeded in turning it down Tottenham Court Road, along the Strand and through the heart of the City of London.[82] The war of nerves between the government and the populace continued as the procession journeyed on through Essex. At Chelmsford, which was not reached until 4 a.m. on the next day, the body was laid in the church while the attendants rested. Despite the hour, the building was crowded 'with persons, most of them in deep mourning, taking a melancholy interest in the fate and sufferings of departed Royalty.'[83] Here, at quarter to five in the morning, the Queen's executor, Stephen Lushington, who had already disclaimed responsibility for the arrangements because of government interference, took up his pen to vent his fury to the premier. 'My Lord', he wrote, 'these proceedings require no comment from me; if they do not by bare recital satisfy your Lordship of their gross indecency no observations of mine can avail.'[84] Liverpool reluctantly agreed that the cortège would be permitted to stop for a second night on the road. The halt was made at Colchester where large crowds gathered and the undertaker vainly attempted to keep people out of the church. While his back was turned a plate was fixed to the coffin bearing the words 'Caroline of Brunswick, the injured Queen of England', wording stipulated in the Queen's will, but unacceptable to the government. Following remonstrations with members of the local corporation, the church was cleared and the obnoxious plate removed.[85] On the third day the increasingly ramshackle procession eventually reached Harwich, where the body was taken on board ship with minimal ceremonial. 'Such', in the eyes of an anonymous pamphleteer, 'was the beggarly manner

---

[80] Ibid., fos. 342–3, 12 Aug. 1821.

[81] Ibid., fos. 328–30, Lady Hood to Liverpool, 12 Aug. 1821.

[82] *The Times*, 15 Aug. 1821; *An Authentic and Impartial Account of the Funeral Procession of Her Late Most Gracious Majesty Queen Caroline* (1821?), 6, 15–16.

[83] Ibid., 20.

[84] BL, AddMS 38289, fos. 370, 376–7, Lushington to Liverpool, 14, 15 Aug. 1821.

[85] PRO, LC 2/52, report from undertaker (Bailey).

in which those who wield the power of Great Britain thought fit to dismiss from their shores the body of their Queen. But the line of conduct which they in their folly thought fit to pursue, only serves to render the affection with which the people regard her memory more striking by the contrast.'[86]

The preaching of funeral sermons provided a final focus for such affection and for the expression of the sentiments that the Queen had stirred in life. One Dissenting minister recalled that many had asked 'with a sort of eager and tumultuous earnestness' whether he would preach on the occasion. He did so, but tried to calm emotions by religious reflection and upholding the virtues of social harmony. Nevertheless, he somewhat pointedly prayed that 'the royal and noble should henceforth set a fine pattern of domestic purity and peace to the humbler orders'.[87] Other preachers were altogether less circumspect, praising the late Queen, repudiating the charges against her, and extolling the virtues of radical patriotism, defined by one minister as 'an admiring and ardent love of the people'.[88]

At one level Queen Caroline's funeral was an exceptional event with qualities of tragic farce that were not to be repeated on any subsequent occasion. In other respects, however, it demonstrated the potential for such occurrences to become a focus for popular sentiment. Given more favourable circumstances, both government and monarchy could harness such feelings to their advantage. This potential was not fully realized until much later, but the arrangements for the Duke of York's funeral in 1827 suggests that the lesson was not entirely lost on George IV. The Duke, the second son of George III, had been heir to the throne. As commander-in-chief of the army and a staunch opponent of Catholic Emancipation he had been an important figurehead for political conservatism.[89] There was thus a considerable incentive to mitigate the consequences of his demise, by turning his funeral into an impressive display of loyalty to the Crown. Such would seem to have been the King's intention when he took personal charge of the arrangements and ordered that they 'should be public and

---

[86] *Authentic and Impartial Account*, 23. The charge that the government's treatment of the Queen's remains was 'beggarly' is only partially borne out by the records of the Lord Chamberlain's department which show expenditure of £8,930, admittedly only a third of the cost of George III's obsequies, but still significantly more than the £6,283 spent on the Duke of Kent's funeral (PRO, LC 2/49, LC 2/52).

[87] J. Clayton, *A Discourse on the Death of Her Late Majesty the Queen* (1821), 7–8, 21.

[88] C. Berry, *A Sermon on the Death of Caroline, Queen of England* (1821); W. J. Fox, *A Funeral Sermon for Caroline Queen of England* (1821), 26.

[89] J. T. Allen, *A Sermon Preached in the Parochial Chapel of Clitheroe . . . on occasion of the . . . Death of HRH Prince Frederick Duke of York and Albany* (Clitheroe, 1827), 5–7, 10. Cf. R. Bradley, *Britain in Sorrow for the Loss of a Prince and a Great Man* (Manchester, 1827).

magnificent'.[90] Unlike most of his relatives, the Duke died in London, and this chance facilitated the decision to hold a lying-in-state on 18 and 19 January 1827 at St James's Palace, which was much more accessible to the populace than Windsor Castle. Attendance during the two days was estimated at between forty and fifty thousand, and a dangerous press of the crowds around the entrances suggested considerable public interest. On the following day the Duke's remains were taken to Windsor in a daylight procession that drew large crowds, and involved over 2,500 troops. On arrival after nightfall, before the funeral at St George's, the cortège passed through the streets of the town, with the route lined by Life Guards and infantry.[91] As so often with George IV's schemes, reality did not measure up to conception. The management of the lying-in-state was chaotic. The crowds who had been led to expect more extensive military display were audibly disappointed by the procession, while those at Windsor could not even see it because of inadequate lighting. Members of the congregation at St George's went to sleep on the floor while waiting for the service to start, and the protracted and badly managed ceremonies in the chapel in the January cold resulted in the illness of several distinguished participants. The King was furious.[92] Nevertheless in the opinion of *The Times* the public response had demonstrated that the people had a genuine regard for the late Duke. The ceremonial was echoed by displays of loyalty in the provinces: for example, in Newcastle-upon-Tyne members of the local Orange Lodge and Friendly Societies processed through the streets to a church service.[93] Despite the farcical aspects of the proceedings a significant precedent for a more public form of royal funeral had been set.

Whereas the reigns of George II and George III between them spanned ninety-three years, the subsequent reigns of George IV and William IV amounted to a mere seventeen years. This obvious chronological fact is worth emphasizing, because it substantiates the impression that between the 1810s and the 1830s royal deaths, and even the death of the sovereign, lost the aura of novelty that was apparent between 1817 and 1820, and was to recur in 1901. The diarist Charles Greville was struck on George IV's death in 1830 by the 'small apparent sensation' that it generated. This impression was even stronger on the death of William IV in 1837 when,

[90] L. Strachey and R. Fulford (eds.), *The Greville Memoirs 1814–1860*, 8 vols. (1938), i. 167 (12 Feb. 1827).

[91] Sykes, *Duke of York*, 14, 18.

[92] *The Times*, 22 Jan. 1827; *Greville Memoirs*, i. 168. As late as 16 January the Home Secretary, Peel, had not been informed of the regulations for the lying-in-state and had accordingly been unable to make arrangements to police them (PRO, LC 2/54, fo. 26, Peel to the Duke of Montrose).

[93] Sykes, *Duke of York*, 23.

he noted, 'the Crown has been transferred to the head of the new Queen with a tranquillity that is curious and edifying'.[94] An American visitor, in Edinburgh at the time of William IV's death, noted that 'The reign of the late monarch was closed, and that of the youthful Queen commenced, without any extraordinary demonstrations of feeling on the part of the people of Scotland.'[95]

In the case of George IV at least, familiarity quite literally bred contempt. His misdeeds were censured in obituary comment; the event of his death could be used as a basis for flippant advertising of patent medicine; the day of his funeral, despite the outward trappings of grief, had a holiday atmosphere.[96] *The Times*, in a subsequently notorious leader, declared:

> The truth is . . . that there never was an individual less lamented by his fellow-creatures than this deceased King. What eye has wept for him? What heart has heaved one throb of unmercenary sorrow? Was there at any time a gorgeous pageant on the stage more completely forgotten than he has been, even from the day on which the heralds proclaimed his successor? . . . If George IV ever had a friend—a devoted friend in any rank of life, we protest that the name of him or her has not yet reached us.[97]

On the other hand, the forms of mourning had their own institutional and cultural momentum. Clergy preaching funeral sermons tried to cultivate some charity towards the late monarch and to turn the thoughts of their congregations to spiritual matters; the event gave rise to displays of civic loyalty and solidarity; within the limits of Windsor, the funeral was an impressive spectacle.[98] Nevertheless, even on the death of William IV, who appears to have stirred rather greater genuine affection than his brother, it was still hard to escape the impression of sham and superficiality in official and popular reactions. On visiting the lying-in-state, Greville found it like a scene in a theatre, somehow detached from reality, and he complained of the 'wretched mockery' of the funeral with 'all this pomp and pasteboard crowns, and Heralds scampering about'. Even though the procession was imposing, the service was 'intolerably long and tedious'. Greville reflected that, were he himself a king, he would wish to abandon such outward trappings in favour of greater sincerity of mourning.[99]

Indeed, it seems that some surviving members of the royal family

[94] *Greville Memoirs*, iii. 376 (25 June 1837).

[95] George Barrell Cheever in *New York Observer*, 23 Dec. 1837.

[96] *Greville Memoirs*, ii. 1, 4 (16, 18 July 1830); *The Last Moments of our Late Beloved Sovereign George IV* (1830?); *The Times*, 16 July 1830.

[97] *The Times*, 16 July 1830.

[98] A. C. L. D'Arblay, *The Vanity of All Earthly Greatness* (1830); W. B. James, *National Blessings a Ground for National Gratitude and Obedience* (1830); Sykes, *George the Fourth*, 23–6.

[99] *Greville Memoirs*, iii. 382 (9 July 1837).

reached a similar conclusion. When the Duke of Sussex died in 1843 he broke with tradition by choosing burial at Kensal Green Cemetery rather than at Windsor. Although his funeral was 'with all Honors suitable to the Remains of a Prince of the Blood Royal', the setting naturally limited the scale of the ceremonial.[100] The choice of Kensal Green was seen as affirming solidarity between the late Duke and those less privileged than himself.[101] The preference for privacy and modesty was at its most apparent in the case of Queen Adelaide, William IV's widow, who died in 1849 having left instructions that she should 'have as private and quiet a funeral as possible. I particularly desire <u>not to be laid out in State</u>, and the funeral to take place by <u>Daylight</u>, no procession.'[102] Her funeral took place at Windsor, but Queen Victoria was, accordingly, 'pleased to sanction a departure from the usual Ceremony observed in the Funerals of the Kings and Queens of the Realm'.[103]

Despite the perception that such ceremonies had a 'usual' form, the Victorian era in reality inherited a confusing range of precedents. It would have been scarcely politic to note in 1849 that the most recent instance of the death of a queen consort had been that of the unhappy Caroline in 1821. Even without that particular case, it was apparent that the ambiguities between 'public' and 'private' ceremonials were very considerable. Funerals at Windsor were too exclusive to focus on the royal family the kind of national pageant that had centred on Nelson in 1806, but still too much regulated by tradition and a perceived need for pomp and ceremony for them to appear a sincere reflection of private grief. The ambiguities were reflected in continuing uncertainty about the exact roles of the various agencies involved in the organization of funerals.

At the same time, despite the uncertain management of ceremonial, a wider view of reactions to prominent deaths in the early nineteenth century suggests that they did indeed have a significant formative role in the development of national consciousness. Nelson's funeral was the centrepiece of extensive popular feeling, and reactions to the deaths of Princess Charlotte and George III were widespread and sincere. The aftermaths of the deaths of Queen Caroline and of the Duke of York indicated the political potentialities of such occurrences in the expression of competing concep-

---

[100] PRO, LC 2/45, fo. 196.

[101] Mrs. J. H. Gregory, *Lines on the Interment of HRH the Late Lamented Duke of Sussex in Kensall Green Cemetery* (1843?). Bland (*Royal Way of Death*, 152) speculates that the Duke's choice of Kensal Green was actually motivated by his wish to be buried with his wife who would not have been eligible for Windsor. The relative magnificence and prominence of his tomb shows the limits of his democratic sympathies.

[102] BL, AddMS 46358, fo. 105 (facsimile).

[103] PRO, LC 2/70/12, p. 1.

tions of patriotic identity. Even the repetitions of conventional forms on other occasions were not without their importance in confirming a seemingly uncontested continuity of the constitutional fabric in unsettled times. At the beginning of Queen Victoria's reign, as at its end, reactions to death played a significant part in shaping the world of the living.

# 2

# 'The last great Englishman is low': Burying the Duke of Wellington

Bury the Great Duke
With an empire's lamentation,
Let us bury the Great Duke
To the noise of the mourning of a mighty nation . . .[1]

On Tuesday 14 September 1852 the Duke of Wellington died suddenly at Walmer Castle in Kent. Although he had some of the inevitable frailties of old age, he had remained active and in essentially good health. Accordingly his death, from a series of epileptic fits, took the nation by surprise.[2] Once the initial shock had passed, however, there was a predominant sense of timeliness and appropriateness in the Duke's end. He would be missed, but his decease had been long anticipated—*The Times* had its obituary already at proof stage[3]—and the apparently painless, quick and dignified end of a man of eighty-three could hardly be grounds for particular regret. The news reached Doncaster on the morning of the St Leger, but, Charles Greville recalled, 'most people were too much occupied with their own concerns to bestow much thought or lamentation on this great national loss'.[4] At Hereford the Three Choirs Festival was in full swing. The 'Dead March' was played before the evening oratorio on 16 September and seen as reflecting a unanimous sentiment in the audience. On the following day, however, the programme continued and the mood appeared anything but sombre.[5]

Nevertheless Wellington's unparalleled eminence induced a profound

---

[1] Ricks, *Tennyson*, ii. 481 (lines 1–4).

[2] For the circumstances of Wellington's death see E. Longford, *Wellington Pillar of State* (1972), 398–400.

[3] J. K. Laughton (ed.), *Memoirs of the Life and Correspondence of Henry Reeve*, 2 vols. (1898), i. 263.

[4] *Greville Memoirs*, vi. 360 (18 Sept.). Greville acknowledged that Doncaster on St Leger day might not be representative of the mood of the nation, but it is not clear what evidence he had for sentiment elsewhere.

[5] *The Times*, 17, 18 Sept. 1852.

sense that his passing was an 'event', an historic moment needing to be marked in a correspondingly weighty manner.[6] Within a few days, the absorbing question for the public had become not the import of the death itself, but, as the *Illustrated London News* put it, 'when, where, and with what state and ceremonial the great Duke of Wellington should be buried?'[7] Those involved in the planning of Wellington's funeral cannot have been unaware of the grand pageant held in France in December 1840 to mark the return of Napoleon's remains from St Helena for interment at Les Invalides, and a sense of parallelism between Wellington and his great adversary was very much apparent.[8] The funeral did not take place until 18 November, when it constituted one of the grandest and most expensive state occasions of the nineteenth century, exceeding in magnificence the obsequies of all recent sovereigns. It seems that it left a much stronger impression on those who witnessed it than did the news of the death itself. Gladstone noted in a single sentence the fact that he was 'astounded' when the Duke died, but devoted an uncharacteristically lengthy entry to his account of the funeral.[9] Of a sample of thirty-four published sermons on the Duke's death, only eleven were preached in the second half of September, two during October, and the remaining twenty-one on the day of the funeral or on the Sunday immediately succeeding it.[10]

The form of Wellington's splendid apotheosis was in no way predetermined and was shaped by the specific contingent assumptions and decisions of those who planned and organized it. The events of September to November 1852 are well documented and worthy of examination in some detail, illustrative as they are of the aspirations and meaning accorded to the funeral itself, and providing as they do a yardstick against which later such events can be assessed. Subsequently a wider range of reactions to the Duke's death and its aftermath will be examined. The analysis of the response to this particular seminal event will serve both as chronological focus and point of reference at the earlier end of the period under detailed

---

[6] *ILN*, 18 Sept. 1852, pp. 214, 225–6. Gathorne Hardy's sense of occasion and timeliness was characteristic of many: A. E. Gathorne-Hardy (ed.), *Gathorne Hardy First Earl of Cranbrook: A Memoir*, 2 vols. (1910), i. 85.

[7] *ILN*, 25 Sept. 1852, p. 241.

[8] Gilbert Martineau, *Le Retour des Cendres* (Paris, 1990).

[9] M. R. D. Foot and H. C. G. Matthew (eds.), *The Gladstone Diaries*, 14 vols. (Oxford, 1968–94), iv. 455, 469 (18 Sept., 18 Nov. 1852). Other memoirs that support this conclusion include those of the eighth duke of Argyll, Sir Robert Morier and Lord Redesdale (Bertram Freeman-Mitford). The exceptions were likely to be people who knew Wellington personally: for example see R. Edgecumbe, *The Diary of Lady Frances Shelley 1818–1873*, 2 vols. (1913), ii. 308–9.

[10] The sample was a random selection from the collections in the Bodleian Library, the British Library and Manchester Central Library.

consideration, and will also serve to introduce themes that will be more fully developed in the chapters that follow.

Six hundred miles away from Walmer, Queen Victoria and Prince Albert were at Balmoral, where the Prime Minister, the fourteenth Earl of Derby, was currently a visitor. Following an indecisive general election earlier in the year, Derby was the leader of a minority Conservative administration. When the news reached Victoria and Albert they were away from Balmoral for an overnight trip to a distant part of the estate.[11] Initially, they 'entirely disbelieved' it, the Duke's death having been erroneously reported on various previous occasions. When confirmation was received, the Queen wrote to Derby, that the news 'grieved and distressed her—as it must everyone of her Countrymen most deeply. England has lost the greatest man she ever had . . . the Crown the most loyal devoted and faithful servant it ever had, and the Queen personally a friend and adviser who cannot be replaced. It is impossible at first to believe that "the Duke" is dead. This loss the Queen fears will be very severely felt.'[12] Victoria, unlike the great majority of her subjects, experienced a sense of genuine personal bereavement in the loss of a man who had become something of a father figure. Even in her immediate reactions, however, these emotions combined with her perception of the national significance of what had happened. From the outset, fully supported by Albert, she was determined that the funeral should correspond to her sense of the Duke's worth. Meanwhile, Derby wrote to the Duke's son, Lord Charles Wellesley, leaving him in no doubt of his view that the nation would wish to pay 'every tribute of veneration to the greatest man of this age'.[13]

On Friday 17 September Victoria and Albert returned to Balmoral and discussed with Derby what was to be done. Their most urgent concern was the succession to the Duke's numerous offices, especially that of commander-in-chief, where it was important to avoid a prolonged interregnum.[14] That very day Derby wrote to Lord Hardinge to offer him the command of the army, informing him at the same time of the Queen's wish that it should go into mourning as if for a member of the royal family.[15] The

[11] Royal Archives, Windsor Castle [RA], VIC/E 2/1, Phipps to Prince Albert, 15 Sept. 1852.

[12] RA, Queen Victoria's Journal [QVJ]: 16 Sept 1852; Liverpool Record Office, Derby Papers (14th Earl) [DerP] 101/2, The Queen to Derby, 16 Sept. 1852; A. C. Benson and Viscount Esher (eds.), *The Letters of Queen Victoria 1837–1861*, 3 vols. (1907), ii. 478, The Queen to the King of the Belgians, 17 Sept. 1852.

[13] DerP 181/1, 16 Sept. 1852. Wellington's eldest son and heir was at Baden Baden at the time of his father's death, and did not arrive back at Walmer until 17 September, another reason why initial decision making was slow (*The Times*, 18 Sept. 1852).

[14] *Letters of Queen Victoria*, ii. 476–7, Memorandum by Prince Albert, 17 Sept 1852.

[15] RA, VIC/E 2/7.

funeral was also discussed, and it was agreed that it should be a public one. Accordingly Derby wrote again to Lord Charles Wellesley, strengthening the position he had taken on the previous day, by conveying the anxiety of the Queen and the Prince that any arrangements made by the family 'may not be such as to prevent Her Majesty from marking in the most public manner her regard for his memory and her sense of the national loss'.[16]

Something of a hiatus ensued over the weekend while the constitutional and ecclesiastical position was considered. There were two interrelated difficulties. First, Parliament had not sat since the general election and there was doubt whether the Crown could formally order a public funeral and all the consequent expenditure without a resolution of both houses. Derby therefore decided that the funeral should not take place until after Parliament met in November.[17] He would have been reluctant to summon it early because of the vulnerability of his government's position in the Commons. The government was aware that Lord Nelson's funeral in 1806 had been ordered during the recess on the responsibility of ministers,[18] but this precedent was disregarded. Colonel Phipps, Albert's private secretary, wrote:

> The public tribute of veneration to the greatest man of the age would have a double weight if called for by the unanimous Voice of the nation speaking through their representatives and their aristocracy, instead of being ordered by the personal Will of the Sovereign, and as there is not a man in England who would not wish to take a part in this last sad mark of Veneration, it is very desirable that the ceremony should take place when the greatest number of people are assembled in London, and have therefore an opportunity of assisting at it.[19]

The consequent decision that the funeral would be delayed until mid-November raised a second difficulty. The family confirmed that the Duke had left no instructions for his funeral and were happy to hand over arrangements to the government, but they were anxious that there should be proper ecclesiastical sanction for leaving the body unburied for so long. Accordingly the late Duke's clerical nephew, the Revd Gerald Wellesley, was deputed to negotiate with the government.[20]

---

[16] DerP 181/1.

[17] *Letters of Queen Victoria*, ii. 477.

[18] RA, VIC/E 2/18, Walpole to the Queen, 20 Sept. 1852.

[19] RA, VIC/E 2/21, Phipps to Gerald Wellesley, 22 Sept. 1852.

[20] RA, VIC/E 2/26, Marquess of Douro (i.e. 2nd Duke of Wellington, who declined to use the title immediately in deference to his father's memory) to Derby, probably 18 Sept. 1852; QVJ: 20 Sept. 1852.

In the meantime the Home Secretary, Spencer Walpole, who was the senior responsible member of the government in London, was close to panic. Assorted unfounded rumours regarding the funeral plans were circulating in the newspapers, and on Sunday 19 September he twice scribbled letters to Derby urging that a decision be made immediately.[21] On the following day Gerald Wellesley called on Walpole to explain that the family were uneasy about a proposal, favoured by the Queen, to have two funerals, an initial private one, followed by the public interment in due course.[22] Meanwhile Derby, in consultation with the Queen, decided to announce that a public funeral 'with all the solemnity due to the greatness of the occasion' would indeed take place in November.[23] Phipps wrote to Gerald Wellesley urging him to use his good offices to persuade the family to accept this outcome.[24] Despite continuing private reservations, they agreed, and the body was accordingly left at Walmer Castle until 10 November, without any funeral rites taking place, but with a guard of honour posted.[25]

Derby also announced that the Duke would be laid to rest in St Paul's Cathedral, 'there to rest by the side of Nelson—the greatest military by the side of the greatest naval chief who ever reflected lustre upon the annals of England'.[26] This choice, crucial in retrospect in confirming the position of St Paul's as the pre-eminent shrine for the nation's naval and military heroes, was not a wholly obvious one in prospect. Leaving aside the possibility that the Duke might, like many aristocrats, have been buried on his country estate, at Stratfield Saye near Reading,[27] Westminster Abbey provided a metropolitan alternative. It was one advocated by Walpole, on the grounds both that the Duke had been a statesman as well as a soldier, and that, whereas at St Paul's the place of honour directly under the dome was already occupied by Nelson's sarcophagus, at Westminster there was a vacant vault in the corresponding central location under the great tower.[28] John Delane, the editor of *The Times*, also initially assumed that the burial would be at Westminster.[29] Derby, however, stood by his 'strong opinion' that St Paul's was the right place.[30] The decision was influenced, one might infer, by awareness that emphasis on military rather than political memories of

[21] DerP 153/1.
[22] RA VIC/E 2/18, Walpole to the Queen, 20 Sept. 1852; QVJ: 21 Sept. 1852.
[23] *The Times*, 23 Sept. 1852. Derby's original letterbook copy is in DerP 181/1.
[24] RA, VIC/E 2/21, 22 Sept. 1852.
[25] DerP 153/1, Walpole to the Queen, 23 Sept. 1852 (copy); Longford, *Wellington*, 402. The body was embalmed (Longford, *Wellington*, 400), and presumably the coffin was sealed.
[26] *The Times*, 23 Sept. 1852.
[27] *The Times*, 17 Sept. 1852.
[28] DerP 153/1, Walpole to Derby, 19 Sept. 1852 ('Sunday 1/2 past 9 p.m.').
[29] A. I. Dasent, *John Thadeus Delane Editor of 'The Times'*, 2 vols. (1908), i. 140.
[30] DerP 181/1, Derby to Walpole, 21 Sept., 2 Oct. 1852.

the Duke were likely to be a basis for a much stronger national consensus at the funeral.

The delay in holding the funeral was entirely attributable to the wish to associate it with the meeting of Parliament, and did not arise from any perception that the time would be necessary in order to make essential preparations. Derby now let nearly a week go by before taking any further action. Only on 28 September did he write to the Earl Marshal (the thirteenth Duke of Norfolk) asking him to have plans drawn up, specifying the desirability of including the greatest possible number of people in the ceremonial and suggesting that every regiment in the army should be represented.[31] Norfolk delegated the task to Sir Charles Young, Garter King of Arms, and on 6 October submitted the results of his work to Derby, who forwarded them to Prince Albert. Albert made a number of changes— such as cutting out the sons of peers—with a view to making the length of the procession more manageable. He also heightened its military character by implementing the suggestion originally made in Derby's letter of 28 September, which Young had apparently hitherto disregarded.[32] This process of decision-making illustrates an important general point about the planning of such ceremonials. The College of Arms, with the Earl Marshal at its head, based its schemes entirely on precedent, and the government of the day could do little to change them. Only the sovereign, or in this case Albert as her acknowledged personal representative, had the recognized authority to vary precedent. There was accordingly an inherent bias towards conservatism in arrangements except when the sovereign was actively involved.

Meanwhile the Lord Chamberlain's Office found that its own records were very imperfect and accordingly carried out detailed research on previous public funerals back to 1670 so as to establish the relevant precedents and glean other useful information. The resulting reports[33] suggested that past events had a level of clarity and consistency that had been lacking in reality, but they provided an important basis for planning. The sheer magnitude and complexity of the tasks that the various agencies had to complete in little more than six weeks was beginning to dawn upon them.

Only on 4 October did the Dean of St Paul's, Henry Hart Milman, receive the government's formal notification that the funeral was to take place in his cathedral. He was understandably irritated and concerned at the manner in which time was being wasted and warned that immediate action was necessary if the cathedral was to be fitted up in time for the

---

[31] DerP 181/1.

[32] DerP 42/1, Norfolk to Derby, 6 Oct. 1852; Prince Albert to Derby, 11 Oct. 1852; draft ceremonial with annotations in Albert's hand.

[33] PRO, LC 2/75, partially reproduced in the Appendix, below.

service.[34] Spencer Walpole, however, had little sense of urgency about the funeral arrangements and busied himself rather with visiting the cathedral to inspect the site of the Duke's tomb. He proposed moving Nelson's sarcophagus off centre in order to make room for Wellington's alongside it, thereby literally implementing Derby's public statement on 20 September that the two heroes would be placed side by side.[35] Milman countered with the proposal, which was eventually adopted, that Nelson should stay where he was and that Wellington be placed nearby along the central axis of the crypt.[36]

The arrangements for the lying-in-state provided further matter for procrastination and for debate over symbolism and practicalities. Derby initially suggested Whitehall Chapel.[37] Walpole agreed that it was appropriately located close to the Horse Guards, but he was concerned that the exit staircase was small and narrow. He suggested Chelsea Hospital as an alternative, by analogy with Greenwich Hospital, which had been used for Nelson.[38] Norfolk, when consulted, shared Walpole's concern over access, but pointed out that the decision was actually one for the Lord Chamberlain, the Marquess of Exeter.[39] Exeter's officials had certainly been considering the matter, but their efforts only muddied the waters further with two additional suggestions, Apsley House (the Duke's London residence) and Westminster Hall, without making any clear recommendation in favour of any of them.[40] The impasse had to be resolved by the Queen and the Prince who on 11 October gave their verdict in favour of Chelsea Hospital.[41]

A full month had now passed since the Duke's death and the slow rate of progress was beginning to attract public comment. On 2 October the *Illustrated London News* queried whether it was really necessary to allow two months to make the arrangements, and suggested that, if it was not, Parliament might be summoned earlier to provide the necessary constitutional sanction.[42] On 14 October *The Times* complained that 'absolutely nothing has been done, except to fill up the vacant offices, and post sentries at Walmer'. The newspaper reported a by now widespread suspicion that Derby was attempting to make 'a party gain of a public loss' by spinning

---

[34] DerP 181/1, Derby to Walpole, 2 Oct. 1852; St. Paul's [Cathedral Library, Chapter Minutes,] Memoranda [Concerning the Duke of Wellington's Funeral]; DerP 42/1, Milman to Derby, 4 Oct. 1852; 153/1, Walpole to Derby, 5 Oct. 1852.

[35] DerP 153/1, Walpole to Derby, 4 Oct. 1852.

[36] DerP 42/1, Milman to Derby, 4 Oct. 1852.

[37] DerP 177/2, Derby to Walpole, 28 Sept. 1852.

[38] DerP 153/1, Walpole to Derby, 30 Sept. 1852.

[39] DerP 42/1, Norfolk to Derby, 6 Oct. 1852.

[40] PRO, LC 2/75.

[41] DerP 42/1, Prince Albert to Derby, 11 Oct. 1852.

[42] *ILN*, 2 Oct. 1852, p. 273.

out the Duke's obsequies for as long as possible in order to secure a suspension of normal political hostilities and extend his own precarious tenure of power. However, on the very same day, Victoria and Albert returned to Windsor from Scotland and on Saturday 16 October a two-hour summit meeting attended by Albert, Derby, Hardinge and Milman at last gave a much-needed impetus to exertion.[43] Even though, according to Milman, it only actually settled 'certain preliminary arrangements',[44] thereafter the pace of activity quickened. On Monday 18 October workmen finally moved into the cathedral; the Office of Works was instructed to begin preparations for the lying-in-state (although the governors of Chelsea Hospital did not agree to its use until 21 October), and designs were commissioned for the funeral car and for the fittings at Chelsea.[45] The latter were evidently produced expeditiously, as they were approved by the Queen on 22 October.[46] The designs for the funeral car took longer, and its subsequent construction was perforce a very rushed job, a factor that contributed to the deficiencies of the eventual result.[47]

The essential policy decisions had now been taken, but during the frenetic weeks that ensued many problems continued to exercise officials. The route of the procession was not finalized until quite a late stage. Hardinge had proposed that it should start from the Horse Guards, again in conscious parallelism to Nelson's funeral, which had started from the Admiralty, and this was the arrangement eventually adopted. At an intermediate stage, however, in late October, Apsley House was very actively under consideration.[48] The final route started from the Horse Guards, but then took a long loop past Buckingham Palace, along Constitution Hill, past Apsley House, along Piccadilly, St James's Street and Pall Mall to rejoin at Charing Cross what would have been the direct line from Horse Guards to St Paul's. The extension suggests responsiveness to concerns that the route should be long enough to accommodate the enormous crowds expected.[49]

A further serious concern was public safety and good order. Recollections of Chartist demonstrations were still fresh in the memory and although the purpose was very different, the prospect of multitudes assembling

---

[43] RA, QVJ: 14, 16 Oct. 1852; St Paul's Memoranda.

[44] Ibid.

[45] Ibid; PRO, LC 2/40, fo. 139.

[46] PRO, LC 2/40, fo. 142.

[47] *The Times*, 2, 4, 17 Nov. 1852.

[48] CA [121], Wellington's Funeral [Correspondence], fo. 24 (first sequence), Young to Walpole, 22 Oct. 1852.

[49] For examples of these concerns see PRO, HO 45/4096/6, John Masterman, MP, docketed by Walpole 'his representations shall have every attention' and CA, Wellington's Funeral, fo. 15 (second sequence), F. Hutchinson Synge to the Earl Marshal, 1 Nov. 1852.

on the streets of the capital still occasioned some unease. Indeed difficulties started even before the body left Walmer. Walpole initially rejected a request from the inhabitants of Deal that they should be allowed to visit the remains, from fear that visitors from outside the neighbourhood would take advantage of the arrangement. Subsequently, however, 9,000 people were allowed to file past the coffin on 9 and 10 November.[50] The body was transferred to London on the evening of 10 November, with a minimum of ceremonial, using the quiet station at Deal and without formal partici- pation from the local authorities.[51] The coffin was scheduled to arrive in London at 11.30 p.m., and was unloaded at the goods station at Bricklayers Arms rather than the passenger terminal at London Bridge. Nevertheless, despite these precautions, significant crowds gathered to watch the cortège, both in Kent in the evening and in London in the small hours of the morning.[52]

By contrast the difficulties of maintaining order at the lying-in-state were seriously underestimated, even though the earlier research by the Lord Chamberlain's Office had noted that there had been problems at both Nelson's and the Duke of York's funerals.[53] On the first day of public opening, Saturday 13 November, the police failed to control the flow of visitors, a crush ensued and several people were killed (see Plate 2). The commissioner of the Metropolitan Police, Sir Richard Mayne, openly admitted that, unduly influenced by the limited public interest at the funerals of William IV in 1837 and the Duke of Sussex in 1843, he had seriously underestimated the likely size of the crowd. Only 225 officers had been deployed at the beginning of the day, but numerous reinforcements were brought in after trouble had developed.[54] Thereafter the police presence was substantially increased, from a total of 879 men on 13 November to 1,379 on Monday 15, 1,792 on the Tuesday and 1,877 on the Wednesday, and further serious accidents were prevented.[55]

The major preoccupation, of course, was the funeral itself on 18 November. The erection of stands and viewing platforms along the pro- cessional route was monitored and controlled in evident awareness of the

[50] PRO, HO 45/4096/15; Longford, *Wellington*, 401.

[51] PRO, HO 45/4096/26–8, 31.

[52] PRO, HO 45/4096/27; *The Times*, 11 Nov. 1852; *ILN*, 13 Nov. 1852, p. 395. According to *The Times* the body actually arrived in London at 12.30 a.m. Longford (*Wellington*, 401) says it was 3 a.m., but her authority for this is unclear.

[53] PRO, LC 2/75.

[54] *ILN*, 20 Nov. 1852, p. 430.

[55] PRO, MEPO 5/26/159. The *ILN* quoted slightly different figures and indicated that some of these men were held in reserve.

potentiality for a disastrous collapse.[56] On 13 November Mayne issued his orders for crowd and traffic control on the day. These, in contrast with his initial arrangements for the lying-in-state, constituted a careful and well-considered plan, including the erection of barriers to control access to the processional route. Notice was served that 'the Police will take immediate steps to remove persons whenever it becomes necessary for the general safety'.[57] Military detachments were placed in reserve for the eventuality of serious trouble. There was, however, confusion about the numbers of soldiers required, especially within the City of London: on 16 November Hardinge still felt he was being given inadequate information.[58] *The Times*, its concerns understandably heightened by the accident at the lying-in-state, was seriously worried about the potentiality for a catastrophic breakdown in crowd control and public order.[59] In the event, however, the 5,058 police[60] deployed on the day proved adequate to maintain good order without any need for support from the army, a testimony both to the effectiveness of Mayne's planning and to the primarily consensual and docile mood of the crowd.

The allocation of places in the procession and tickets for the cathedral was at times an extremely delicate matter, given the sensitive issues of precedence and privilege that inevitably arose. The resolution of these matters was ultimately the responsibility of the Earl Marshal, apart from the minority of tickets retained by the Dean and Chapter of St Paul's to meet their own requirements and those of the City of London. There was substantial initial friction over the allocations between the government and the cathedral, which was jealous of its own rights.[61] Milman signed all the 10,000 or so tickets personally in order 'to shew that the right of entrance into the Church was in the Dean and Chapter'.[62] The Earl Marshal was submerged with requests for tickets. Individuals, such as a William Pollard Urquhart, who claimed to be a cousin of the Duke's long-deceased wife, presumed upon the most tenuous connections.[63] The numerous public and voluntary bodies who pressed their claims could be more troublesome. Sir

[56] CA, Wellington's Funeral, fo. 50–2 (first sequence); PRO, HO 45/4096/19, 39; WORKS 37/5/4, 6; *The Times*, 5 Nov. 1852.

[57] Metropolitan Police Office, *Funeral of the late Field Marshal Arthur Duke of Wellington* (BL Tab.597.a.1(1)).

[58] PRO, HO 45/4096/32, 34, 35, 38, 40, 43, 48.

[59] *The Times*, 18 Nov. 1852.

[60] PRO, MEPO 5/26–159.

[61] PRO, WORKS 21/37/2/28–32; CA 121, fo. 25 (first sequence), Young to Milman, 22 Oct. 1852.

[62] St Paul's Memoranda.

[63] CA, Wellington's Funeral, fo. 5 (second sequence), Urquhart to Norfolk, 1 Nov. 1852; fo. 6 Norfolk to Urquhart, 3 Nov. 1852.

Richard Brown, leader of the baronets, cited royal patents of James I giving his Order a place at public solemnities. He noted that they had walked in procession at the funeral of the Duke of Albemarle in 1670.[64] Norfolk replied that he had no command from the Queen to include them, at which Brown appealed directly to the sovereign, accusing her of departing from precedent and violating historic covenants between the Crown and his Order.[65] His protests appear to have been ignored, and Young noted that these claims had been made on previous occasions and not accepted.[66] There was concern that the Lord Mayor of London might press his claim to take precedence within the City even over Prince Albert, but this matter was amicably settled.[67] A simmering dispute between the corporations of Dublin and Edinburgh as to which of them should be regarded as the second city of the United Kingdom was brought to a head by the funeral arrangements and proved more awkward to resolve. Officials attempted a compromise, allocating benches in St Paul's to the two cities jointly, but unfortunately the Scottish councillors arrived to find their Irish counterparts already in possession of the more prestigious front seats. An altercation ensued, and 'the difference was eventually arranged for the time by the Lord Provost of Edinburgh and the Lord Mayor of Dublin agreeing to sit together in the middle of the front Bench with their Councillors beside them to the left and right respectively'.[68]

Whereas many eager to attend had to be excluded, the possibility that others might be absent stirred different anxieties. Victoria and Albert were particularly concerned that the attendance at the funeral should symbolize the solidarity of the European powers that had fought against Napoleon, in the face of the rise of Louis Napoleon in France. The Queen wrote on 22 October: 'The dear old Duke's funeral to which Austria, Prussia, Russia and Portugal are sending representatives to attend, will be a salutary reminder of former days and may serve as a wholesome sedative.'[69] Subsequently there was confusion and disappointment. The Austrians declined to be represented because of a perceived British insult to one of their generals, a decision that alarmed and infuriated Victoria.[70] She urged her uncle, King Leopold of the Belgians, to ensure that his sons, who were

[64] Ibid., fos. 34–5 (first sequence), Brown to Norfolk, 30 Oct. 1852.
[65] Ibid., fo. 36 (first sequence), Norfolk to Brown, 6 Nov. 1852; fo. 38, Brown to the Queen, 8 Nov. 1852.
[66] Ibid., unfolioed, Young to T. W. Talbot (Derby's private secretary), 15 Nov. 1852.
[67] DerP 42/1, Norfolk to Derby, 6 Oct. 1852.
[68] Edinburgh District Council Archives, Town Council Minutes, [ETCM] 259, pp. 121–2, 28 Dec. 1852.
[69] RA, QVJ.
[70] RA, QVJ: 10 Nov 1852.

already in England, took part in the funeral, pointedly reminding him that Waterloo is in Belgium.[71] In the event the Belgians and numerous other nationalities were represented. Even the French were willing to be magnanimous.[72] The Foreign Secretary, Lord Malmesbury, was adamant that the Duke's foreign titles as well as his British ones must be read over the grave.[73]

Meanwhile at St Paul's, Milman and the organist, John Goss, were worrying about the liturgical and musical arrangements. On 21 October the Dean wrote that 'the more I calculate the mass of woollen and of obese humanity, which will crowd the Cathedral, the more I am concerned that we must have a great force and volume of sound'. He then thought he would need seventy men.[74] By the second week of November the choir had swelled to 120, eighty men and forty boys, but Goss still thought this insufficient, and asked for 200.[75] The eventual arrangement was to supplement the 120 singers in the choir by a further forty in the organ gallery with the instrumentalists.[76] Even the choice of music raised tensions between tradition and vested interests on the one hand, and a wish to give some place to contemporary work on the other. The emphasis was on continuity with the past. An offer by the leading church musician of the day, Samuel Sebastian Wesley, to provide a new setting of the sentence 'Man that is born of a woman' to replace the standard setting by William Croft (1677–1727) was rejected. Handel and Purcell predominated, but the inclusion of anthems by Mendelssohn and Goss himself constituted a significant gesture to more recent music.[77]

The involvement of so many different agencies and bodies in the funeral preparations was an obvious source of confusion, especially as co-operation was limited by awareness of privilege and self-interest. The Earl Marshal and the heralds were not beholden to the government of the day, least of all to one as fragile and inexperienced as Derby's was, and saw their responsibility as being directly to the sovereign and beyond her to the archaic traditions of their offices. St Paul's Cathedral was a proud corporate body, liable in the aftermath of recent controversial church reforms to be especially sensitive to any violation of its rights and privileges. The Lord

[71] RA, VIC/Y 97/41, 44, The Queen to King Leopold, 26 Oct., 9 Nov. 1852.
[72] Earl of Malmesbury, *Memoirs of an Ex-Minister*, 2 vols. (1884), i. 365.
[73] CA, Wellington's Funeral, fo. 14 (first sequence), Malmesbury to Addington (under-secretary at Foreign Office), 10 Nov. 1852.
[74] PRO, WORKS 21/37/3/1.
[75] PRO, WORKS 21/37/3/10.
[76] St Paul's Memoranda. PRO, WORKS 21/37/3/12 records payment of a slightly smaller number, but this was presumably an incomplete return.
[77] RA, PP/VIC/1852/A93, Wesley to Milman, 23 Oct. 1852. The Queen (RA, QVJ: 18 Nov. 1852) stated that Albert chose all the music, but it is not clear whether this included the music in the service as well as the marches played by the military bands in the procession.

Chamberlain's Office and the Office of Works were both responsible to the Crown, but they had their own concerns over demarcation of function and diverse perceptions of appropriate procedure. The police and the military were heavily dependent on civilian assessments of the need for their services, most of all within the limits of the City of London where responsibility for public order rested with the Lord Mayor. Some key individuals, notably Mayne (his initial misjudgement over the lying-in-state apart) and Milman, showed themselves to be extremely competent within their own spheres of responsibility, but there was a lack of overall co-ordination. Prince Albert was much more than a figurehead, but was hardly in a position to provide leadership of an executive kind. Lord Derby had other preoccupations and the relative lack of references to the funeral in his correspondence after early October indicates that thereafter he abdicated direct responsibility. A more energetic and ambitious Lord Chamberlain might have made considerably more of that role, but Lord Exeter appeared content to react to events rather than to shape them. Given the weaknesses in organization it was remarkable that the funeral took shape as successfully as it did, an indication of strong underlying consensus about Wellington and the way in which he should be commemorated.[78]

A full description of the ceremonial on November 18—of the procession that took nearly two hours to pass, of the mechanical problems associated with the funeral car, of the privileged thousands who waited for many hours in the crammed cathedral, of the acknowledged splendid pathos of the service itself—would take up many pages.[79] Such an account, moreover, would be a distraction from our present purpose, which is to consider the impact that the event had upon those who participated in it or observed it. Any one individual was of course normally limited to one viewpoint, whether a position on the processional route or a seat in the cathedral, although Gladstone, with characteristic energy and precision, managed to watch the procession at an early stage on its route and then to travel by river with fellow MPs to attend the service at St Paul's.[80] For those not present in central London at all, reactions were likely to be shaped by a sense of general awareness of the national mood or by specific parallel occasions in which they themselves participated.

The perceptions of the Queen and Prince Albert, as the ultimate architects of the pageant, provide a noteworthy starting point. They were both genuinely and profoundly moved. As Victoria watched the procession she found it difficult to restrain her tears. She found the funereal music of the military bands, especially the Handel 'Dead March', especially harrowing.

---

[78] Cf. *The Times*, 16 Nov. 1852.
[79] For a modern account see Morley, *Death, Heaven and the Victorians*, 80–90.
[80] *Gladstone Diaries*, iv. 469.

She considered the funeral car 'very gorgeous' and felt it 'made an indescribable impression upon me'. Albert reported to her the moving service in the cathedral. He had been particularly touched by the sight of so many elderly generals paying tribute to their former supreme commander and by Goss's anthem 'And the King said' which had made everyone weep.[81] As immediate emotions settled, the royal couple also reflected on the international symbolic significance of the occasion. Victoria wrote to Frederick William IV of Prussia to thank him for sending distinguished representatives to the funeral and to express the hope that the co-operation of the powers of Europe manifest at Waterloo would be resurrected should there be a new threat to peace from France.[82] Albert followed this up with a more informal letter to the King's brother, the future Kaiser William I, recalling that no eye was dry as Wellington sank to his place of rest. With the Duke, the symbol of the 'old glorious time' had been carried to its grave just at the time when the symbol of an earlier danger was being re-established in France. Germany, Albert hoped, would remain united in the face of this challenge. The tone of emotive nostalgia coming from the pen of a man of only thirty-three born several years after Waterloo is striking, the more so when it was addressed to the eventual reluctant figurehead of the German Empire.[83] The Duke's funeral helped to lengthen the already long shadow of recollection of Waterloo to influence international relations in the later decades of the century.

Analysis of wider reactions to the Duke's apotheosis is inevitably heavily dependent on the accounts of the articulate, generally élite, minority who wrote diaries and memoirs. Nevertheless some suggestive impressions emerge. The lying-in-state generated mixed reactions. Gathorne Hardy described it as a 'gorgeous spectacle in admirable taste' and Ronald Gower, then aged seven, one of many children taken to see it, recalled thirty years later its 'profound solemnity'.[84] The Queen noted that her daughters were 'quite overcome' and her sons 'much impressed'.[85] Even Greville, who had been so scathing about William IV's lying-in-state fifteen years before, thought that it was well done.[86] Nevertheless, he, like other more sophisticated observers, also found it 'theatrical' rather than really moving. Robert Morier dwelt at some length on the defects: the hall was too small for the purpose, and the catafalque being placed against the end wall had 'too

---

[81] RA, QVJ: 18 Nov. 1852.

[82] RA, VIC/I 28/115, 30 Nov. 1852.

[83] RA, VIC/I 28/116, 1 Dec. 1852. I am indebted to Professor Frank Eyck for assistance with the translation of this letter, and for discussing its significance with me.

[84] *Gathorne Hardy A Memoir*, i. 85; R. Gower, *My Reminiscences*, 2 vols. (1883), i. 117–8.

[85] RA, QVJ: 11 Nov. 1852.

[86] *Greville Memoirs*, vi. 369–70 (16 Nov.).

much the look of a "buffet" '. He too used the word 'theatrical', feeling that all the surrounding splendour distracted attention from the coffin itself, and that the spectacle 'said . . . nothing of Death'.[87] Lord Shaftesbury judged that 'It was fine, very fine, but hardly impressive; signs of mortality, but none of resurrection; much of a great man in his generation, but nothing of a great spirit in another; not a trace of religion, not a shadow of eternity.'[88] Although the hospital chapel opposite the hall had been left open, there are indications that others found the absence of religious allusions troubling.[89] A further difficulty arose from the layout of the room and the pressure of the crowds, which meant that visitors were moved on too rapidly fully to take in and reflect on the scene. Even the Queen, who presumably was allowed much more time to stand and stare than most of her subjects, commented that she 'could hardly say we saw all that was there'.[90] Tacit awareness of the difficulties inherent in staging a successful lying-in-state are indicated by the absence of any attempt to hold a comparable ceremony until the death of Gladstone in 1898, on which occasion the much larger setting of Westminster Hall was to be used along with simpler furnishings.[91]

Reactions to the funeral itself were similarly mixed. The military part of the procession gave rise to strong emotions, stirred by the solemn music, the reversed arms and the mournful demeanour of the troops, who were likely to feel the Duke's loss as acutely as any section of the population. Observers were also deeply touched by the sight of the dead man's riderless horse being led along behind his bier.[92] Other parts of the procession were, however, less enthusiastically received. Despite Albert's efforts to limit the number of civilian carriages, the irresistible demands for representation by bodies associated with the Duke and for the participation of great civic and state officers generated a lengthy procession. It appeared ill-assorted and too much shaped by archaic heraldry and considerations of precedence and status. It seemed redolent more of the pretensions of those taking part than of genuine mourning for the Duke, even if it did have an important symbolic function in representing Wellington's widespread civil as well as military associations. The funeral car was particularly controversial. Although the *Illustrated London News* described it as 'magnificent' and the

[87] Mrs R. Wemyss, *Memoirs and Letters of the Rt Hon Sir Robert Morier*, 2 vols. (1911), i. 118–9.
[88] E. Hodder, *The Life and Work of the Seventh Earl of Shaftesbury*, 3 vols. (1887), ii. 388 (quoting Shaftesbury's diary for 18 Nov. 1852).
[89] *The Times*, 12 Nov. 1852; *Leeds Intelligencer*, 20 Nov. 1852, quoting W. F. Hook's sermon referring to 'minute critics . . . carping at the ceremonial'.
[90] *The Times*, 12 Nov. 1852; Wemyss, *Morier*, i. 119; RA, QVJ: 11 Nov. 1852.
[91] See below, Chapter 6.
[92] *Gladstone Diaries*, iv. 469; Wemyss, *Morier*, i. 120; Lord Redesdale, *Memories*, 2 vols. (1916), i. 87.

object of 'universal admiration', private observers were much less enthusi-astic.[93] The reactions of Miss Napier, daughter of General Sir Charles James Napier, are worth quoting at some length because they illustrate well some of the expectations and emotions focused on the Duke's funeral. They unwittingly indicate how it was located in a transitional phase between the traditionalist legacy of heraldic funerals, and a dawning expectation that such occasions should fully encapsulate and express the perceived national mood of the moment:

> Every thought had been concentrated on the one idea of presently beholding the coffin of the dead, the central object of all this mighty emotion, of all this wide respect. There should at least have been nothing incongruous in the bier on which it was borne to the grave. No trappings could add any magnificence to the tribute of the nation's heart. He should at least have been borne along on this last journey with the grandeur of simplicity. Instead of which, Behold! a lumbering pile creaking heavily on its 6 low wheels! A confused heap of banners and ill-wreathed laurels tossed disorderly about; a tasteless mound of bronze and gilding and black and silver mingled without reason; surmounted by a tawdry flapping canopy ill-sustained by four weak sloping rods. It was an insult alike to the great assemblage and to the dead. At the sight of it mortifications manifold struggled within one. Our national character for some propriety of taste was compromised when it might have been vindicated. There was blemish at the very central point of attraction; and worse than all the memory of the well-known simple tastes of the dead were outraged by such clumsy barbarism. Oh! that they had laid him on a gun carriage and covered the coffin with his cloak, instead![94]

Miss Napier's advocacy of the 'grandeur of simplicity' was a noteworthy anticipation of the attitudes that were to shape the funerals of Gladstone, Victoria and Edward VII.

Similar ambivalence was apparent among those privileged to attend the service inside St Paul's. They had been spared the distracting sight of the ponderous progress of the funeral car, but they had endured a chilly and frustrating wait while its mechanical deficiencies held up the unloading of the coffin. Moreover in the rush the workmen had had to leave their tasks unfinished and hence the intended effect of the fittings, especially the exclusion of all natural light, was somewhat marred. Here too, as in the procession, the marriage of pageantry and mourning was a somewhat

---

[93] *ILN,* 20 Nov. 1852, p. 431; Wemyss, *Morier,* i. 120–1; *Greville Memoirs,* vi. 370 (21 Nov.); Bodleian Library, Oxford [BodL] MS.Eng.misc.b.96, fos. 338–9 (MS account by Miss E. A. Napier).

[94] Ibid.

uneasy one. On the other hand Albert's feelings about the stirring dignity of the group of old soldiers around the coffin were widely shared, and the music appears effectively to have inspired powerful reflections among the congregation. For most, the supreme moment came when the platform bearing the Duke's coffin was lowered very slowly into the crypt.[95] The young Ronald Gower was watching from the gallery and felt that the scene had left a mark on his memory 'that will endure as long as I can recall aught of earthly sights or sounds'.[96] The Duke of Argyll similarly found the scene 'indelibly impressed on my memory as one never to be forgotten'.[97]

Implicit even in negative reactions to aspects of the funeral was the presumption that this was a great national occasion in which the mood could transcend minor irritations, even if these jarred on the mind as inappropriate and disappointing. The question remains, however, as to how far that élite perception was borne out by the attitudes of the crowd on the streets of London, estimated at up to one and a half million,[98] and by the remainder of the population unable to watch the ceremonial in person. Solidly verifiable answers are elusive, but well-founded inferences can be drawn.

It should first be noted that the sheer size of the crowd made it the largest public gathering of the period. Even if the more extravagant estimates are scaled down to one million, it would mean that the equivalent of nearly half the population of the metropolis and almost 5 per cent of the people of Great Britain were physically present at the Duke's funeral.[99] It was the first state occasion in history when cheap trains were available to bring numerous people into London from considerable distances, many of whom braved the dank late autumn weather by spending much of the night before the funeral on the streets.[100] Several observers noted a mood of growing excitement on the streets on 17 November as the crowds began to gather.[101] Correspondingly widespread interest was apparent in the more than a quarter of a million people who had visited the lying-in-state, and the 100,000 who were to visit St Paul's in the week after the ceremony to view the cathedral before the funeral fittings were taken down. In both cases it seems very likely that the period of opening was insufficient to

[95] Gladstone Diaries, iv. 469; H. H. Milman, Annals of St. Paul's Cathedral (1869), 492–4; Gathorne-Hardy A Memoir, i. 85; Duke of Argyll, Autobiography and Memoirs, 2 vols. (1906), i. 367.
[96] Gower, Reminiscences, i. 118.
[97] Argyll, Autobiography, i. 367.
[98] The Times, 19 Nov. 1852.
[99] The population of Great Britain at the 1851 census was 20.82 million and that of London 2.48 million (B. R. Mitchell, Abstract of British Historical Statistics (Cambridge, 1962), 6, 21).
[100] The Wellington News (1852), 1; ILN, 27 Nov. 1852, p. 467; Morley, Death, Heaven and the Victorians, 85–6.
[101] Gathorne Hardy A Memoir, i. 85; Gladstone Diaries, iv. 469; The Times, 18 Nov. 1852.

meet demand and that many who might have wished to attend were disappointed.[102]

Second, it was apparent that the crowd cut across social class and age. Those with the requisite financial means had ample opportunity to hire a room or at least a seat overlooking the route. It was estimated that 200,000 such places were available.[103] Nevertheless the streets were still very crowded, an indication that those of lower social and financial status indeed turned out in large numbers.[104] At the lying-in-state, despite the dangers from the throng, many parents brought small children along, wishing that they should experience a perceived historic moment for themselves.[105] The majority of the parents—like the Queen and Prince Albert—would themselves have been born during the thirty-seven years that had elapsed since Waterloo.

Third, the crowd was remarkably well behaved. Apart from the crush at the lying-in-state on 13 November, which was attributable to inadequate policing rather than to any disorderly spirit, and a minor disturbance in the Strand when some attempted to follow the procession,[106] the whole sequence of events passed off without any recorded public order problems. Such an outcome could not have been achieved by a mere five thousand policemen had the mood not been fundamentally consensual. Observers were struck and moved by the silence of the crowds, especially as the procession passed, and by the almost universal wearing of sombre dress and signs of mourning.[107]

Finally, a similar state of mind was apparent outside the capital. In provincial towns and cities local mayors and corporations called on shops and businesses to close for the day, instructions which appear to have been generally if not universally observed.[108] Civic processions to cathedrals and principal churches were watched by large crowds, as, for example, in Leeds where 'The silence and decorum of a sabbath day was strictly observed in all the principal thoroughfares . . . But the most satisfactory feature of the

---

[102] *The Times* reported the following attendances at the lying-in-state: 12 Nov. ('private view'), 10,800; 13 Nov., 46,834; 15 Nov. (open until 9 p.m.), 79,699; 16 Nov., 58,448; 17 Nov. 65,073, a total of 260,854. 104,828 people visited St Paul's in the week after the funeral, and officials proposed unsuccessfully that the period of opening be extended for another week in order to allow more to attend (PRO, WORKS 21/37/3/68–78).

[103] *The Times*, 17 Nov. 1852.

[104] *The Times*, 19 Nov. 1852; *The Wellington News*, 1–2. Redesdale (*Memories*, i. 88) recalled the refusal of a 'poor old woman' to sell him a wreath fallen from the funeral car, a further illustration of lower class fascination with the occasion.

[105] *The Times*, 16 Nov. 1852.

[106] Morley, *Death, Heaven and the Victorians*, 86.

[107] BodL, MS.Eng.misc.b.96, fos. 334–5; Redesdale, *Memories*, i. 87–8.

[108] *The Times*, 19, 20 Nov. 1852.

day's solemnities was the orderly and becoming demeanour of the humbler classes in the spending of the holiday, and particularly during that portion of it which was devoted to religious services.'[109] In Bristol the young Marianne Farningham, although herself a Nonconformist, squeezed into the packed cathedral for the memorial service and recalled that the playing of the 'Dead March' . . . affected me greatly'.[110] In Exeter the cathedral was similarly thronged by 'thousands . . . fervently and earnestly taking part in the solemn devotions'.[111] A further indication of widespread provincial fascination with the Duke's funeral was the 'extreme and unprecedented' sales of copies of the *Illustrated London News*, amounting to a total of nearly two million for the numbers of 20 and 27 November.[112]

Dissentient voices were rare. The Chartist *Star of Freedom* portrayed Wellington as a superannuated relic of past despotism, and viewed the discussion of his funeral with thinly veiled contempt. It judged the ceremonies to be a waste of public money.[113] A similar line was taken by Samuel Carter, an MP and former Chartist, who described the funeral as a 'national folly' and 'man paying idolatrous worship to the clay of his fellow worm.'[114] Patrick Brewster, another erstwhile Chartist sympathiser and Minister at Paisley Abbey, also thought that veneration for the Duke was misplaced. War was an ugly and undesirable business, and the Duke's services as soldier and statesman had in any case been rendered to the ruling classes rather than the mass of the people. Wellington had no place among 'those noblest of heroes and patriots and philanthropists who have devoted their lives to the glorious cause of human emancipation and human progress', and was accordingly deficient in the qualities of a really great man. Brewster considered the funeral to be 'a gorgeous pageant to impose upon the ignorant and unreflecting'.[115] An unusual critical note from within the establishment was struck by an Oxford-educated chaplain to the Queen, Arthur Philip Perceval, who took particular exception to the 'revolting' delay in the Duke's interment. Perceval considered that in any case a public funeral was not justified. Granted the Duke's distinction as a soldier, his failures and lack of integrity as a politician since 1815 made such recognition inappropriate. Perceval objected particularly to the Duke's alleged tendency to treat

---

[109] *Leeds Intelligencer*, 20 Nov. 1852.

[110] M. Farningham, *A Working Woman's Life: An Autobiography* (n.d.), 64.

[111] *Exeter Flying Post*, 25 Nov. 1852.

[112] *ILN*, 4 Dec. 1852.

[113] *Star of Freedom*, 18 Sept. 1852, pp. 81, 85; 25 Sept. 1852, p. 98; 20 Nov. 1852, p. 253.

[114] *Hansard* third series, 123, cols. 213–4.

[115] P. Brewster, *Wellington 'Weighed in the Balance' or War a Crime, Self-Defence a Duty* (Paisley, 1853). For another similar view see C. Harpur, 'Wellington' in G. Dutton (ed.), *The Heritage of Australian Poetry* (South Yarra, 1976), 31–2.

'religious principle' as a matter of 'secondary and comparatively trifling value'.[116]

Such public questioning of the legitimacy of the whole proceeding appears, however, to have been limited to a few eccentrics, whether of the right or the left, even if there were others who, like Gathorne Hardy, privately wondered whether 'it be right to make all this parade for the dead'.[117] A more widespread attitude was not objection to the funeral, but rather a tendency to treat it as a mere spectacle, divorced from any real sentiment of mourning for the Duke. The *Illustrated London News* reporter who visited the lying-in-state on 13 November noted that during all the hours he had spent in the throng he had not heard Wellington named by those around him.[118] Numerous entrepreneurs, from the owners of houses overlooking the processional route to the vendors of cheap memorabilia, were very ready indeed to use the occasion as an opportunity for financial gain, and in some cases for swindling and extortion.[119] The *Star of Freedom* found ample evidence to support its own cynicism regarding the public mood: 'We saw crowds of decent-looking people, hungry, tired and dirty, coming from "the sight", and indulging in jokes and laughter, and we noticed a considerable number of drunken men and women with any quantity of short pipes. But we did not see—we really did not—and we grieve to make the announcement—one solitary tear.'[120]

Nevertheless such evidence needs to be weighed against the widespread testimony to the prevalence of mourning dress and the respectful, hushed, demeanour of the crowd as the procession passed. The 'jokes and laughter' and the drinking may be interpreted as a natural psychological reaction against an earlier more sombre and serious mood, not to mention the unpleasant physical conditions experienced by those standing on cold, muddy, rain-soaked streets for many hours. Granted that it was hard to grieve deeply for a man of eighty-three who had already been dead for two months, the fact remained that the crowds turned out in their hundreds of thousands, waited patiently, and bought souvenirs; while the better off parted with substantial amounts of good money to hire rooms and seats from which to view the procession. The sense of occasion was evidently a powerful one, even when it is recognized that many would have been stirred not so much by any real sentiment of mourning or veneration for the Duke himself, as by a wish to observe a grand spectacle and to participate in an

---

[116] A. P. Perceval, *Thoughts on the Delayed Interment of the Remains of the Late Duke of Wellington* (1852).

[117] *Gathorne-Hardy A Memoir*, i. 85.

[118] *ILN*, 20 Nov. 1852, p. 430.

[119] *ILN*, 27 Nov. 1852, p. 486; *The Autobiography of George Harris* (1888), 186–7.

[120] 20 Nov. 1852, p. 225.

historic community and national event.[121] Miss Napier's observations ring true:

> to some I suppose it was but a pageant marching by, but to many, how much more! Yet the very speakers whose own words had ... betokened that what had been passing before their eyes had stirred nothing of deeper significance within, were prompt to criticize the crowd, and pronounce sweeping judgement on 'the people' who had borne themselves so well; deciding that they were there but to make holiday and stare. I do not believe it. Doubtless, as we did ourselves, they felt for a portion of the time the distraction of the surrounding circumstances; but if one nature be common to us all, and all poetic faith be not in vain; if reverence for greatness gone have any power upon the soul, who shall dare to affirm that any heart there was not for some short time at least stirred by emotion deeper than usual, and uplifted to higher thoughts. If so, if but for a few short moments, who shall say it was in vain.[122]

*The Times* judged that Wellington's funeral was indeed a focus for 'the strong currents of feeling and of thought which go to form the spirit of a nation'.[123] Thomas Cooper, himself a former Chartist, felt that by the time of his death the Duke had outlived the Radical antagonism he had stirred in the 1820s and 1830s and was now felt to be a very personification of England. His own childhood had been passed 'amid the noise about Wellington's battles' and as he watched the funeral procession pass out of sight along Piccadilly he 'thought that a great connecting link of our national life was broken'.[124] The consensus was not universal, but it was certainly dominant.

Moreover there was no lack of writers and speakers ready to articulate 'higher thoughts'. It was true that the occasion lacked any one authoritative interpreter and that politicians, more sensitive than others to the risk of bathos, generally confined themselves to warm though relatively matter-of-fact tributes to the Duke. A notable and revealing exception was that of Disraeli, then Chancellor of the Exchequer, who, speaking in the Commons on 15 November, attempted a more flowery interpretation of the public mood:

> In an age of utility, the most busy and the most common-sense people in the world find no vent for their woe, and no representative for their sorrow, but the solemnity of a pageant; and we—who are assembled here for

[121] Cf. *ILN*, 20 Nov., p. 434.
[122] BodL, MS.Eng.misc.b.96, fos. 340–1.
[123] 19 Nov. 1852.
[124] *The Life of Thomas Cooper Written by Himself* (1872), 353. I am much indebted to Dr Timothy Larsen for this reference.

purposes so different—to investigate the sources of the wealth of nations, to bury ourselves in statistical research, to encounter each other in fiscal controversy—we offer to the world the most sublime and touching spectacle that human circumstances can well produce—the spectacle of a Senate mourning a Hero.[125]

Unfortunately for Disraeli, the high-flying sentiments of his speech were subsequently brought painfully down to earth when he was found to have plagiarized a substantial passage from an eulogy by Thiers on the Marshal de Saint-Cyr.[126]

Even though they thus lacked a worthy lead from statesmen, the journalists, poets, and preachers needed little encouragement in seeking to find a deeper meaning in the Duke's death and apotheosis. Leader columns throbbed with purple passages, and innumerable poets, good, bad, and indifferent, attempted tributes.[127] Clergy reflected on the event in their sermons, whether preached at memorial services held on the day of the funeral, or at normal Sunday services. Their utterances were of some importance in shaping and reflecting the public mood, because church services were for many a key mechanism for expressing a sense of communal involvement in the distant ceremonial.[128] Sermons were also much the most common genre in free-standing published comment on the Duke's death: of 111 items in the British Library catalogue published in 1852 and containing the words 'Duke' and 'Wellington' in their titles, 62 were sermons. Consideration of this material accordingly provides an instructive basis for analysis of the interface between religion and national consciousness expressed in the aftermath of the Duke's death. Four themes merit particular comment: the sense of the passage of time; the Duke as an exemplar of Englishness; his funeral as a 'national solemnity'; and awareness of the providential hand of God in British history.

Tennyson's famous line in his Ode, 'The last great Englishman is low', which has provided the title for this chapter, was a poetic rather than objective statement. Its implicitly negative view of the present and future was questioned at the time, but the poet qualified it with the following line, 'Mourn, for to us he seems the last'. In so doing he seems to have captured the mood of the moment in which the Duke's death was seen as marking the end of an era.[129] For example, Prince Albert perceived it as symbolizing

[125] *Hansard* third series, 123, cols. 153–4.

[126] R. Blake, *Disraeli* (1966), 335. Blake has no doubt that the plagiarism was inadvertent.

[127] *ILN*, 11 Dec. 1852, pp. 526–7.

[128] For systematic discussion of the relationship of organized Christianity to national mourning, see below Chapter 3.

[129] Ricks, *Tennyson*, ii. 482 (lines 18–19); E. F. Shannon, 'The History of a Poem: Tennyson's *Ode on the Death of the Duke of Wellington*', *Studies in Bibliography*, 13 (1960), 162.

the passing of 'the old glorious time', mourned the decline of 'the Spartan virtues' and bemoaned the current rule of 'Calico and Cant'.[130] Another poet characterized his contemporaries as 'children of evening', but went on to see the Duke's funeral as a point of new beginnings as well as of conclusions:

> 'Tis a whole glorious Aeon that ye trust
> To the grey Past with him who lieth low!
> This day with chant and funeral march we go
> From out the Old. Beneath our hero's bust,
> We stand upon the threshold of the New![131]

Tennyson similarly located Wellington in a longer perspective of history, from 'our England's Alfred' to the imagined future reader 'far on in summers that we shall not see'.[132]

Clergy too dwelt on the implications of the passage of time, and on the Duke as representative of his nation and age. In this context their discourse was shaped by the scriptural parallels suggested by their texts, such as the deaths of Jacob and Joseph in the closing chapters of Genesis, David's lament over Abner in 2 Samuel 3:38, 'Do you not know that a prince and a great man has fallen this day in Israel?' and David's own epitaph in 1 Chronicles 29:28, 'Then he died in a good old age, full of days, riches and honour'. Old Testament parallels of this kind were noticeably more popular than New Testament ones, a preference which enabled remembrance of Wellington to feed on the rich culture of memory in ancient Israel, and gave scope to preachers who wished to make explicit the perceived parallel between biblical Israel and modern Britain. For example, a Lincolnshire clergyman expounded the Abner parallel at some length and then went on to assert that 'it was given to this great man (Wellington) to be the *Judge* of our Israel, in peace as in war, for a term of patriarchal duration'.[133] *The Times* too was similarly sufficiently struck by the applicability of 2 Samuel 3:38 to quote it in its leader on the morning of the funeral, while the *Illustrated London News* noted and welcomed the richness of implicit scriptural allusions in Tennyson's Ode.[134]

Preachers also presented the Duke's passing as illustrative of the inevitability of death for all and the consequent ultimate evanescence of human

---

[130] RA, VIC/Y 149/53 Prince Albert to Stockmar, 6 Oct. 1852; VIC/I 28/116, Prince Albert to the Prince of Prussia, 1 Dec. 1852.

[131] S. Evans, *Sonnets on the Death of the Duke of Wellington* (Cambridge, 1852), 8, 14.

[132] Ricks, *Tennyson*, ii. 489, 490 (lines 188, 234).

[133] R. Reade, *The Conqueror's Rest* (1852), 8.

[134] *The Times*, 18 Nov. 1852; *ILN*, 27 Nov. 1852, p. 483 (the echo of Isaiah 63 in the 'Nelson' passage, lines 8off. was particularly noted).

achievements. For example, William Brownlow, Rector of Wilmslow, recognized the death as marking an epoch in the history of the country, but, taking as his text Ecclesiastes 12:5, spent much more time speaking on the need for preparedness for the eternity that succeeded physical death.[135] As Francis Close, Vicar of Cheltenham, pointed out, great as the Duke was, he had died like other men, and he called on the living to lay the recognition of this fact to heart.[136] The incumbent of Walmer, who had preached in the Duke's presence a mere two days before his decease, was understandably particularly struck by the suddenness of the event, and urged his hearers to ensure that they were spiritually prepared for unexpected death.[137]

The irony that the 'last great Englishman' had in fact been born in Dublin does not appear to have attracted notice outside Ireland,[138] and the Duke was widely portrayed as, in the words of *The Times*, 'the very type and model of an Englishman'.[139] There was, however, a notable lack of precision in expanding on what this meant in practice. For the Marquess of Bath, speaking in the House of Lords, it implied 'devotion to the sovereign, and attachment to the constitution',[140] but such conservative political virtues were hardly consensual. For Tennyson, as for others, the Duke's outstanding quality was his straightforward sense of duty, reflecting lack of self-seeking and a fidelity to 'right' and to 'truth' imbued with 'saving common-sense'.[141] One of the few attempts at more specific elaboration of Wellington's contributions to national character was, in a further revealing irony, made by a Scotsman, the popular Presbyterian preacher John Cumming. In a crowded lecture at Exeter Hall, attended by members of the late Duke's family, he enumerated qualities such as his sound judgement, simplicity of aims, his reliance on righteous means, his abnegation of self, and his equanimity in the face of adverse circumstances.[142] Cumming also hinted in a memorial sermon that the associations stirred by the Duke made him not merely a representative, but even the normative, model of national achievement. He stated that Wellington 'occupied a larger space in our history, in our successes, in all that constitute that beloved thing we call *country*, than any other man for many a day'.[143] Such an identification ultimately transcended definition.

[135] W. Brownlow, *A Sermon Occasioned by the Death of . . . the Duke of Wellington* (Manchester, 1852), 6–12, 15, 19.
[136] F. Close, *National Obsequies Sanctioned by Holy Writ* (1852), 17–19.
[137] W. B. Holland, *A Sermon Preached in the Parish Church of Walmer on September 19th 1852* (1852).
[138] *Freeman's Journal*, 18 Nov. 1852.
[139] 15 Sept. 1852.
[140] *Hansard* third series, 123, col. 34.
[141] Ricks, *Tennyson*, ii. 482, 489 (lines 32, 186–9, 202).
[142] J. Cumming, *Wellington: A Lecture* (1853), 18–32; *ILN*, 4 Dec. 1853, pp. 522–3.
[143] J. Cumming, *The Lord Taketh Away* (1852), 17–18.

Christian eulogists of the Duke found themselves confronted with the problem of assessing his spiritual state and prospects in a context where adverse judgements might well appear unpatriotic. Some nevertheless gave offence by speaking of him as a lost soul, while others acknowledged themselves unsure of the Duke's eternal fate; more dodged the issue by pleading lack of information on the matter or by expressing charitable hopes for his salvation.[144] Some, however, were confident that Wellington was a true Christian believer, and accordingly found it easy to undergird patriotism with religion. Such was Cumming's approach, citing witnesses who had seen the Duke at prayer, noting his warm support for the Church of England, and his reverence for the Bible. Accordingly, he believed that the great soldier would be found amongst 'the noble armies of the sky'. Cumming urged that Wellington be memorialized by bringing the gospel and the Bible to the whole population and hence proving 'to brave hearts that still beat in the midst of us, that we are a country worth defending'. He thus appropriated the Duke's name to give patriotic fervour to his own Evangelical concerns.[145] Meanwhile Charles Boutell, curate of Litcham, Norfolk, argued that Wellington's apparently secular qualities, notably his famous sense of duty, were in fact rooted in a genuine and constant Christian faith. Boutell hoped that Wellington's example and death would give 'fresh life to the slumbering spirit of national heroism', an aspiration that accordingly carried religious as well as patriotic undertones.[146] For Thomas Hugo, preaching at St Botolph's, Bishopgate, the Duke's most salient and worthy characteristic was his loyalty to the Church of England, and his example inspired a seamless web of religious and patriotic devotion to 'the monarch he served, the Church which he venerated, and the land that he loved'.[147]

A sense that the funeral was, in the words of the Bishop of London, Charles James Blomfield, 'a great national religious solemnity'[148] can also be found in non-ecclesiastical interpretations of the event. The *Illustrated London News* highlighted the centrality of church buildings in the ceremonial, both St Paul's itself, 'our sublime Protestant Cathedral', and the parish churches throughout the land from whose towers bells were simultaneously tolled at 3 p.m. on the day of the funeral.[149] Tennyson wrote:

---

[144] F. H. Maude, *The Mighty Man of Valour* (Ipswich, 1852), 12ff.; T. Archer, *'The Duke' A Sketch* (1852), 30; J. H. Bowhay, *A Pulpit Tribute to the Memory of His Grace The Duke of Wellington* (1852), 13.

[145] Cumming, *Wellington*, 51–86.

[146] C. Boutell, *The Hero and His Example* (1852).

[147] T. Hugo, *The Voice of the Dead* (1852), 19, 23.

[148] C. J. Blomfield, *The Mourning of Israel* (1852), 12–13.

[149] *ILN*, 30 Oct. 1852, p. 353; 27 Nov. 1852, p. 462.

> More than is of man's degree
> Must be with us, watching here
> At this, our great solemnity.[150]

In Leeds, despite the predominant Nonconformist and Liberal ethos of the town, the parish church was crowded with a 'vast congregation' on the day of the funeral. Two thirds of the town council were present. The Vicar, the prominent High Churchman Walter Farquhar Hook, took his inspiration from the biblical parallel of Hezekiah. Wellington, he said, exhibited 'an ideal of the English character' and the lavish tribute being paid to him was an entirely appropriate expression of patriotic devotion. Jesus's lament over Jerusalem gave Christian legitimacy to such patriotism, although loyalty to one's own country could not justify the violation of due justice to other nations. Such enlightened patriotism was being encouraged by the honours being paid to Wellington. 'Let us', Hook urged, 'glory in the fact that we are Englishmen, and remember that as Englishmen we are to set an example to the world'. A 'true English heart' would welcome all aspects of the current ceremonial, whether national or religious in character. After such rousing patriotic exhortation, Hook finally turned his discourse in a more exclusively Christian direction, by asserting that the 'hero', and the 'father of his country' was also a believer in Jesus, and urging his hearers to emulate him and lay hold of the promise of resurrection. His efforts in articulating a patriotic consensus had clearly struck a strong chord with his hearers, because the members of the corporation present offered to pay for the publication of the sermon.[151]

There were further whole-hearted clerical endorsements for the perceived mood of the occasion. Francis Close argued from biblical precedents that it was entirely right to pay lavish honour to such a great 'Benefactor of his country' in a funeral that was 'truly a British spectacle'.[152] Others warmly welcomed the pageant as a stirring demonstration of the consensus of 'an entire nation', 'a free, a brave and a sober-minded people'.[153] Nevertheless, many preachers felt the need to balance such celebratory observation with more sobering reflection on the transience of earthly honours. The point was made particularly starkly by Christopher Wordsworth in his sermon in Westminster Abbey on the Sunday after the funeral. 'The funerals of the dead', he observed, 'are the best preachers to the living, and *public* funerals are *national sermons*.' He emphasized the frailty of all human achievements and the certainty of resurrection and judgement.

---

[150] Ricks, *Tennyson*, ii. 490 (lines 242–4).

[151] *Leeds Intelligencer*, 20 Nov. 1852.

[152] Close, *National Obsequies*, 7–11, 13, 15.

[153] C. J. Heathcote, *A Sermon Preached on the Sunday After the Funeral of the Duke of Wellington* (Hackney, 1852), 4; William N. St Leger, *The World Passeth Away* (1852), 15.

Substantial extracts were printed by the *Illustrated London News* and thereby received a very wide circulation.[154]

Finally, preachers made explicit the sense of providentialism in the Duke's career that was implicit in Tennyson's repeated exhortation to 'render thanks to the Giver'.[155] Here too one can discern a graduation from straight-forward theological endorsement of the secular national mood, through the assertion that divine Providence acted through Wellington as the supreme protector of England,[156] to more distinctively Christian emphases. Some expressed these through perceiving a wider moral and spiritual purpose that went beyond national aggrandizement: for example, the annihilation of Napoleon's tyranny, or the downfall of papal power in Europe.[157] Several clergy saw the Duke's military achievements both in India and in Europe as establishing the providential preconditions for subsequent British procla-mation of the gospel to other lands, thus fulfilling an essential divine purpose.[158] Others, again, dwelt on the more transcendent and mysterious workings of the deity. To Edward Miller, the Duke was the 'battle-axe of God', holding a role in the divine purposes analogous to that of Cyrus in the Old Testament, and preparing the way for the Second Advent.[159] Another approach was to emphasize the workings of providence not so much in the Duke's life as in his death, arguing that through the removal of a human pillar of the state, the nation was being called to a renewed awareness of its dependence on God and its ultimate accountability to the Almighty.[160]

The Duke's death and its aftermath thus admitted of manifold interpre-tations. Underlying them all, however, was a consciousness of a weighty event that touched deep springs of national and religious feeling. No one other than a sovereign had ever been buried with comparable magnificence, nor was to be again until Sir Winston Churchill died in 1965. The creation of a ceremonial that, with all its limitations, was genuinely designed to attract mass participation and ownership, marked a significant shift away from the hidebound traditions of the heralds and of the royal household, which had shaped earlier nineteenth-century royal funerals. Such a spec-tacular expression of public mourning undoubtedly assumed a dynamic of

---

[154] *ILN*, 27 Nov. 1852, p. 479.

[155] Ricks, *Tennyson*, ii. 483 (lines 44, 47).

[156] As an example, see G. Croly, *A Sermon on the Death of the Duke of Wellington* (1852).

[157] Holland, *Sermon in the Parish Church of Walmer*, 10; J. A. Hatchard, *Romanism Overthrown by Wellington* (1852).

[158] H. Howarth, *On Human Greatness* (1852); F. E. Gretton, *Barzillai: The Very Aged, the Very Great Man* (1852), 10–15; J. E. Dakeyne, *Virtutis Fortuna Comes* (Wolverhampton, 1852), 11.

[159] E. Miller, *The Battle-Axe of God* (Chichester, 1852).

[160] Cumming, *The Lord Taketh Away*, 4–8, 14–15; J. Bedford, *Britain's Loss and Lesson* (Stockport, 1852), 22–4.

its own that was disproportionate to the extent of sincere grief for the Duke. It was thus both a high point in the extravagant mourning customs of early Victorian Britain, and a trigger of reaction against them.[161] Meanwhile, the focus on St Paul's both as the centre of ceremonial and the place of interment also greatly reinforced the image of the cathedral as a potent physical symbol of nationhood that powerfully encapsulated the linkage of the Church of England to the state and military glory.

One recurrent theme in contemporary attempts to explore the meaning of the Duke's funeral was, as *The Times* put it, that it was 'rather ... an act of self-respect, than one of honour to his cold remains'.[162] Wellington's apotheosis formed part of a sequence of events at mid-century, notably the 'Papal Aggression' of 1850, the Great Exhibition of 1851, and the outbreak of the Crimean War in 1854, which both illustrated and reshaped the dimensions of British national consciousness.[163] A specifically Protestant sense of national identity was still strong, and it had its echoes in interpretations of the Duke's career and funeral. At the same time, Protestantism could no longer provide the dimensions of overarching consensus that it had offered in the eighteenth century. Behind the numerous impulses that contributed to make up the 'solemnity' of 18 November 1852, one therefore detects a searching for alternative articulations of nationhood, still linked to religion, but also drawing on secular aspects of the national past as a springboard for facing the future with a clearer sense of identity. In a very real sense therefore, Wellington's funeral was not so much an end, as the beginning of a process of partial reinvention of the nation through its response to death, the working out of which across a longer timespan will be explored in the chapters that follow.

---

[161] Cf. Jalland, *Death in the Victorian Family*, 196–7.
[162] 18 Nov. 1852.
[163] For my further analysis of this context see Wolffe, *God and Greater Britain*, 111–122.

# 3

# 'O God our help in ages past':
# The Churches and National
# Mourning

From the Orkneys in the far north, to sea-girt Cornwall in the south, from the hills and dales of Cumberland to the flat shores of the Medway and the Thames, in proud minster churches like our Gloucester, in quiet village churches like our houses of prayer on the Cotswolds—on that grey, sombre Wednesday—was one mighty solemn funeral service.[1]

In such terms the Dean of Gloucester articulated his perception of the nation's observance of the funeral of the Duke of Clarence, Queen Victoria's grandson, on 20 January 1892. This evocation of national solidarity focused upon Anglican religious observance implied a forgetfulness of the diversity of late Victorian religion and irreligion, but it still contained much more than a grain of truth. An essential characteristic of the decades covered by this book, which corresponded approximately to the period between the invention of the electric telegraph and the advent of broadcast radio, was that it was possible for people to know with some speed and precision about events taking place at a distance without being able to listen to them or watch them. In the television age the urge to feel a sense of participation in a funeral taking place in London or Windsor can be satisfied in people's homes; in the nineteenth and early twentieth centuries alternative mechanisms had to be sought. Throughout the country, the churches played a central role in meeting this need, drawing larger than normal congregations on Sundays and even weekdays following a death and often holding well-attended special services on the day of the funeral. It is true that motives could be mixed, as Thomas Chalmers had observed at the time of Princess Charlotte's funeral in 1817. He complained of

men, whose taste for preaching is very much confined to these great and

[1] H. D. M. Spence, *England's Demonstration of Sympathy and Loyalty* (1892, privately printed RA/VIC/Z 98/23).

national occasions—who, habitually absent from church on the Sabbath, are yet observed, and that most prominently, to come together in eager and clustering attendance, on some interesting case of pathos or politics—who in this way obtrude upon the general notice, their loyalty to an early sovereign, while, in reference to their lord and master, Jesus Christ, they scandalize all that is Christian in the general feeling.[2]

Nevertheless, for whatever reasons, they did come to church, and the evidence of numerous newspaper reports indicates that they continued to do so throughout the nineteenth and early twentieth centuries. The nature and content of the preaching and the services offered to them, which form the main subject matter of this chapter, were therefore matters of much more than narrowly ecclesiastical interest.

The analysis in this chapter will commence with a survey of the attitudes contained in funeral and memorial sermons, which were the centrepiece of church services on such occasions. Through the adoption of a long perspective, from the death of Nelson in 1805 to that of Edward VII in 1910, points of reference will be suggested for changes and continuities in religious attitudes to death. Later in the period, the spoken word, although still important, appears to have receded a little in prominence, in services designed to express a greater sense of communal solidarity and participation, notably through the singing of hymns. The content of such events, both the actual funeral services and parallel local commemorations, were also a significant reflection of changes in the religious world displayed at a crucial interface with the wider society and culture.

## Funeral Sermons

Memorial sermons and orations have attracted some attention from scholars of earlier periods, both as a significant literary genre and as a neglected source of evidence regarding political and other beliefs. The great majority of speakers, of course, sought to conform to convention rather than to challenge it, but when viewed over extended periods the changing perceptions of what constituted that convention can be very revealing.[3] In nineteenth-century Britain full-flown secular funeral orations were rare, but funeral sermons delivered in church were very widespread, their popularity

---

[2] Chalmers, *Princess Charlotte*, 6.
[3] J. M. McManamon, *Funeral Oratory and the Cultural Ideals of Italian Humanism* (Chapel Hill, 1989); D. L. D'Avray, 'The comparative study of memorial preaching', *Transactions of the Royal Historical Society* fifth series, 40 (1990), 25–42; D'Avray, *Death and the Prince*.

reviving after relative decline in the eighteenth century.[4] Strictly speaking they were memorial rather than funeral sermons in that they were not normally delivered at the funeral itself, but at a separate special service or at a scheduled service on a Sunday close to the date of the death or funeral. The intention of preachers was to link tribute to the deceased to the drawing of spiritual lessons for the living. Often the subjects were relatively obscure individuals, to whom tribute was paid in their own church or locality, and such occasions drew substantial congregations of friends and acquaintances.[5] Sometimes indeed the very ordinariness of the subject was dwelt on by preachers as a means to encourage emulation of their qualities by the survivors.[6] Dramatic deaths in the experience of particular congregations could be turned towards exhortation by their pastors, as in the eloquent title of a published sermon by a Hampshire clergyman: *The Duty of Watchfulness Enjoined on the Church Collectively, and on Individuals Particularly, Lest the Lord Coming Suddenly either in Person or in Providence, Should Find us Sleeping, Being the Substance of a Sermon Occasioned by the Most Awful Sudden Death of the Late Mr Thomas Paul of Gosport, who Fell in his Pew and Instantly Expired, in the Midst of the Congregation, during Divine Service, at Gosport Church, on Sunday Morning, November 20th, 1836.*[7]

The deaths of prominent people gave, however, a particular stimulus to widespread preaching of this kind. As the Leicester Dissenting minister Robert Hall explained in a sermon on Princess Charlotte, acknowledged as a classic of the genre, such events were worthy of especial note both because they touched the whole kingdom, and because the very elevated station of the deceased in life pointed up the ultimate vanity of all human aspiration when laid low by death.[8] Their popularity had lessened somewhat in the eighteenth century: the printed British Library catalogue lists twenty-three sermons on Mary II (1694), but only fourteen on William III (1702), eleven on Anne (1714), ten on George I (1727) and eighteen on George II (1760). In the early nineteenth century, however the numbers shot up: there were eighty-one sermons on Princess Charlotte (1817), seventy-five on George III (1820), sixty-five on the Duke of Wellington (1852), and seventy

---

[4] A. A. Fry, *A Dissertation Upon Funeral Orations* (1839), 14–17; Houlbrooke, *Death, Religion and the Family*, 323–6.

[5] On Census Sunday in 1851 a Primitive Methodist Chapel Steward in Hull noted that an evening congregation of 880, as opposed to an average of 580 was due to 'a Funeral Sermon being preached'. (PRO, HO 129/520/28).

[6] F. Baker, *An Address Delivered to the Children of the Sunday School, Bank Street, Bolton, on the Death of a Sunday Scholar* (Bolton, 1826); T. Thornton, *Religion in Humble Life: A Sermon on the Death of Betty Adamson, A Weaver* (1863).

[7] R. Bingham (1836).

[8] R. Hall, *A Sermon Occasioned by the Death of Her Late Royal Highness the Princess Charlotte of Wales* (Leicester, 1818), 12–20.

on the Prince Consort (1861). These four personages stand out a long way ahead of any others in terms of the numbers of published sermons, the next most numerous for the period 1800 to 1914 in the British Library listing being Queen Victoria (1901) with sixteen and the Duke of York (1827) with thirteen. Nevertheless, it is possible to find at least a handful of sermons for almost any person of note. It seems reasonable to suppose that published sermons and others summarized in the newspapers were representative in sentiment and outlook, albeit probably superior in literary quality, to the countless unrecorded sermons. The specific motives for publication are usually obscure, but would generally seem to reflect a readiness of the clergy to respond to a genuine public demand for such literature while also taking the opportunity to enhance the profile of their own names and views. There was an upsurge in publication of funeral sermons in the late Georgian period, after a relative paucity of examples from the eighteenth century, but by the end of the nineteenth century the genre appears to have been again in decline. The fact that noticeably fewer sermons were published on Queen Victoria than on her husband or her grandfather suggests that the memorial sermon was becoming rather less central in the response to national bereavement than it had been at an earlier date. The four individuals who gave rise to the most numerous published sermons suggest the two main contexts in which death stirred the deepest response. These were either untimely and tragic deaths like those of Charlotte and Albert, or conversely the ending of lives such as those of George III and the Duke of Wellington that had seemed to define a whole era. Princess Charlotte's death in 1817 was a particularly important defining moment in the development of funeral sermons, the combination of tragic personal circumstance and national insecurity generating an intensity of public interest and religious reflection unprecedented as least since the similarly untimely death of Queen Mary II in 1694. Wellington was the only non-royal figure to generate published sermons on the scale of sovereigns and other prominent members of the royal family.

For much of the nineteenth century the pattern of most memorial sermons was to begin with sustained exposition of an appropriate biblical text, with the connection with the current bereavement at first kept implicit. The preacher would then explicitly refer to the death that had occurred and turn to a panegyric on the deceased, drawing out moral and spiritual lessons. Sermons usually concluded with a direct exhortation to the hearers to be mindful of their own mortality, spiritual state, and eternal prospects. During the last third of the century the tendency was for sermons to become much shorter: the printed text of many earlier examples would have taken anything up to two hours to deliver, whereas by 1900 the norm was half an hour or less. The structure also became softer and more fluid, with biblical exposition becoming more compressed or even incidental, the panegyric less didactic in emphasis, and preachers offering spiritual comfort to their hearers rather than direct challenges to repentance. Obviously the picture was variegated by theological and ecclesiastical diversity but the general trend is clear enough.

The panegyric element in the sermons of course related primarily not to death itself but rather to the qualities in the life of the deceased that were considered worthy of admiration and emulation. It is noteworthy that even if preachers generally sought to present their subjects in the most favourable possible light, there was up to the middle of the nineteenth century at least, no taboo against the inclusion of some more critical and negative comment. It is true that few were as forthright as a preacher on the death of Queen Caroline in 1821: 'The private virtues, and individual qualities of monarchs, and their connections, are not the cause of this mark of respect being paid them. Were it so, I fear few sermons would ever be preached upon such occasions.'[9] Nevertheless a preacher on George IV openly acknowledged that the late monarch was not faultless and was indeed subject to 'those vices and errors which particularly attach themselves to rank and greatness'.[10] Adulation could still be qualified in relation to Wellington in 1852. It was suggested by some that his military career, even if not morally reprehensible, still made him something less than a moral ideal. There was also criticism of his record as politician on two fronts. In the eyes of the arch-Tory George Croly, Wellington had, by conceding Catholic Emancipation in 1829, perpetrated a 'national calamity', whereas the Dissenter Henry Barnett recalled that he had opposed the 'righteous claims' of the people at the time of the Reform Bill of 1832.[11] In the last quarter of the century, however, preachers tended carefully to avoid controversial ground. For example, the author of a sermon on the death of Disraeli acknowledged that his subject had had his faults, but disclaimed any knowledge of them. On the day of Gladstone's funeral H. Montagu Butler noted in passing that assessments of the deceased as a statesman differed, but affirmed that all would agree regarding his moral grandeur.[12] The closest thing to criticism of Queen Victoria apparent in a sermon was a brief mention of the charge that she had mourned too long for Albert. Even this, however, was immediately turned on its head with the suggestion that even though she might have withdrawn from the pomp of royalty she

[9] Berry, *Sermon on the Death of Caroline, Queen of England*, 7ff.

[10] James, *National Blessings*, 28.

[11] H. N. Barnett, *The Victor Vanquished* (1852), 15,18; Croly, *Wellington*, 43–4.

[12] J. A. Atkinson, *Lessons From the Life of the Earl of Beaconsfield, KG* (Manchester, 1881), 5; H. M. Butler, *An Address Delivered in Great St Mary's Church, Cambridge . . . at the Hour of the Interment . . . of the Right Hon William Ewart Gladstone* (Cambridge, 1898), 10.

still honoured her essential obligations.[13] The retreat from even well-founded and moderate criticism of the deceased in memorial sermons was consistent with the weakening of theological convictions concerning imminent divine judgement. Belief in the universality of God's love began to make human judgement seem distasteful or even impious.

Preachers did not usually give particular attention to the process of dying itself, but viewed the subject's life as a whole. The evidence from sermons would therefore imply a revision of the perception of nineteenth-century expectations shaped by Philippe Ariès's concept of the 'beautiful death'.[14] There was always a gulf between the ideal of the good death in religious literature, and the unpredictable and messier practice,[15] and the clergy were well aware of this human reality. They recognized that modes of dying were inevitably diverse and, even in the earlier part of the period, they did not usually put forward any particular normative or ideal model. Certainly the prolonged deathbed amidst loving relatives and quiet religious reflection had its appeal. William IV was judged to have had his latter days brightened by the preparation of his soul for death and the sympathy of his devoted wife; Gladstone's dignity and courage in his prolonged and painful terminal illness was seen as 'the old warrior ... vanquishing death by submitting to it'.[16] However spiritual expectations were not generally stereotyped: although a minority of clergy searched anxiously for evidence that the dying had made explicit professions of faith,[17] most seemed content rather to assess the spiritual state of the deceased by reference to their manner of life rather than death. Even the cleric who directly asked in the title of his sermon *The Patriot Palmerston: Was He Saved?* dwelt not so much on the late Prime Minister's deathbed but on the more general character of his later years, his elevation of Evangelicals in the church and his contacts with devout Christians. Such evidence led the preacher to answer his own question affirmatively, albeit tentatively.[18] Attention to the deathbed was a more regular feature of sermons on individuals of acknowledged Christian conviction, but even then the treatment could sometimes be cursory. Thus a sermon on William Wilberforce dealt briefly with his last hours, and then quickly reverted to reflection on his public life.[19]

The sudden death of a young person, such as that of Princess Charlotte

---

[13] J. Harrison, *A Queen Indeed* (1901), 13.

[14] Ariès, *Hour of Our Death*, 409–74.

[15] Jalland, *Death in the Victorian Family*, 17–38.

[16] T. F. Dibdin, *The Patriot King* (1837), 14–17; C. Garnett, *Mr Gladstone: Scholar, Statesman, Saint* (Manchester, 1898), 3.

[17] For example A. Fletcher, *A Sermon on the Death of Her Late Majesty Queen Caroline* (1821), 20.

[18] R. W. Dibdin, *The Patriot Palmerston: Was He Saved?* (1865).

[19] A. C. L. D'Arblay, *The Path of the Just* (1833), 33–4.

or the Duke of Clarence, was viewed as an awesome tragedy, explicable only in terms of some inscrutable divine purpose.[20] Older people were urged to be spiritually prepared for such an eventuality, but for those in middle life or old age whose past conduct suggested an underlying readiness to meet their maker, a swift, relatively painless, end was to be welcomed. Nelson fell mortally wounded as a 'model of true heroism' and then survived just long enough for 'the Christian [to] supersede the hero'.[21] Wellington's sudden death was considered an appropriate end to his life, especially as he had demonstrated his spiritual preparedness by regular attendance at divine worship.[22] After Thomas Chalmers was found dead in bed in 1847, having retired apparently in good health the previous night, an American preacher presented his abrupt demise as a form of 'translation' granted to one of great spiritual attainments.[23]

The teaching on death contained in the sermons was shaped by a noticeable preference for Old Testament texts, which prompted preachers to dwell primarily on the lessons to be drawn from the life of the deceased and to exhort preparedness for death, rather than to speculate on the nature of eternity. Even some favoured New Testament texts, such as Revelation 3:19, 'Those whom I love, I reprove and chasten; so be zealous and repent', were used as a basis for general spiritual reflection and exhortation rather than for discussion of the nature of the afterlife.[24] Sermons on passages such as the raising of Lazarus, or 1 Corinthians 15, which contain the most full-blooded New Testament teaching on the bodily resurrection, were unusual. This reticence may well have arisen in part from the unspoken uncertainties of clergy regarding the real spiritual state of the deceased, but they may also suggest a lack of theological confidence in tackling such themes. Many sermons tended to dwell simply on the unchangeableness and dependability of God in eternity in contrast to the transience of earthly life. Until the last third of the century congregations were routinely warned of the inescapability of divine judgment, but there was little explicit discussion of the joys of heaven on the one hand or the pains of hell on the other.

There was, however, a substantial minority of preachers who specifically addressed the nature of the afterlife, and in doing so showed a considerable variety of emphases. Four categories can be identified. First, the grave was

---

[20] Hall, *Princess Charlotte*, 60–1; Anon., *Christus Consolator* (1892), 9–19.

[21] Gardiner, *Lord Nelson*, 19; Anon., *A Sermon Preached on the Sunday After the Funeral of the Rt Hon Lord Viscount Nelson* (1806), 12.

[22] J. Baines, *Honourable Sepulture the Christian's Due* (1852), 11.

[23] W. B. Sprague, *A Discourse Commemorative of the Rev. Thomas Chalmers* (Edinburgh, 1847), 14–15.

[24] C. S. Hawtrey, *A Funeral Sermon on the Death of . . . the Princess Charlotte Augusta* (1817).

viewed as a place of rest and sleep, although not necessarily of extinction. Preachers were prepared to use Old Testament texts such as Job 3:17 'There the wicked cease from troubling, and there the weary are at rest', and Ecclesiastes 9:10 'there is no work or thought or knowledge or wisdom in Sheol, to which you are going', which expressed an essentially ancient Judaic rather than Christian concept of the condition of the dead.[25] Sometimes however this prospect was softened with the promise of eventual resurrection.[26] Second, the dead were pictured as being already in a state of conscious glory and bliss, a state visualized by the Revd Benjamin Mardon in relation to William IV:

> Let us ... indulge the hope that for the good which he has effected, he has freely exchanged an earthly for a heavenly crown, and though not occupying one of the highest stations in the heavenly kingdom (reserved perhaps for the brightest talents, when united with the purest and noblest acquisitions of virtue) has heard pronounced to him the plaudit of approbation, 'Well done, good and faithful servant'.[27]

A refinement of this view, apparent at a later date, was the perception that the dead were provided by God with new avenues for activity and personal growth.[28] Third, there was emphasis on the resurrection of the dead, sometimes linked to apocalyptic expectation. Jesus was the mighty conqueror over the terrors of death and those who trusted in him could be confident of restoration to life at his Second Coming. The exact state of the dead in the interim was, as in the New Testament, left as something of a mystery.[29] Finally, there was the assertion that the dead watched over the living, who would eventually be reunited with them. Unlike the first three views this one does not appear to have been current among preachers until the end of the period. It gradually gained acceptance partly as a result of Anglo-Catholic doctrinal emphasis on the communion of saints; partly

[25] J. Evans, *A Sermon Preached at the Independent Chapel, Malmesbury ... Occasioned by the Death of ... Queen Caroline* (1821); J. Bentley, *A Sermon Preached on ... Occasion of the Death of Lord Beaconsfield* (1881). Cf. Rowell, *Hell and the Victorians* (Oxford, 1974), 19–20. Julie Rugg ('From Reason to Regulation: 1760–1850' in Jupp and Gittings, *Death in England*, 213–14) notes that belief in heavenly reunion found extensive expression in art and literature earlier in the century.

[26] Brownlow, *Wellington*.

[27] B. Mardon, *The Evanescence of Human Glory* (1837), 17–18,

[28] R. R. Rodgers, *Queen Victoria* (Birmingham, 1901), 10–17. Geoffrey Rowell (*Hell and the Victorians*, 15) follows Paul Tillich in relating this view to contemporary notions of progress, and characterizes it as 'an immortality of self-realization, rather than an immortality of salvation'.

[29] D. Wilson, *Death the Last Enemy of Man* (1827), 17, 22–4; W. M. Falloon, *A Prince and A Great Man Fallen* (Liverpool, 1861), 12–18; W. Conway, *The Victory Over Death* (1865), 6–16.

because the clergy were evidently responsive to Victorian popular idealiz-
ation of family life and willing to endorse implicitly the idea that the
hereafter would see a recovery of a perfected domesticity.[30] James Fleming
made a particularly eloquent statement of this view in a sermon in the
private chapel at Windsor Castle following the death of the Duke of
Clarence. Preaching on Hebrews 12:1, Fleming argued that the 'cloud
of witnesses' were not saints, but pardoned sinners, our loved ones gone
before. We may be far nearer to them than we think; we are in communion
with them 'in the perfected love of God' and we shall meet again 'as man
meets man', all clothed in white.[31]

The existence of such a diversity of views on the afterlife is consistent
with the work of Geoffrey Rowell and Michael Wheeler on the literary and
theological controversies relating to matters of heaven, hell and judgement
during the Victorian era.[32] As Rowell points out, such differences of
emphasis were inherent in the Christian tradition from the very beginning,
influenced as it was by Hellenistic ideas of the immortality of the soul,
alongside the apocalyptic hope in the resurrection of the body.[33] During
the Victorian period the growing influence of both liberal and Catholic
ideas brought further variety and controversy. Nevertheless the sermon
evidence is significant because it shows that such uncertainties and diver-
gences were not limited to scholars and highbrow literary circles, but were
also reflected in the teaching given by the clergy to ordinary congregations.
Moreover, although the variety of ideas increased as the nineteenth century
went on, even in pre-Victorian years there had been substantial differences
in belief. Views of the experience of the dead, as of the dying, were by no
means stereotyped and uniform. It is particularly noteworthy that the mid-
Victorian theological reaction against the doctrine of eternal punishment
was anticipated by the widespread reluctance even of earlier nineteenth-
century preachers to engage explicitly with this issue.

Although preachers were quick to draw out personal implications for
their hearers from the deaths of the famous, there was an awareness that
such public deaths contrasted with the domestic deaths of ordinary people.
While domestic death stirred the powerful feelings of a few, public death
awakened the more diffuse sympathy of the many.[34] The sermons suggest,

[30] J. A. Atkinson, *In Memoriam Victoria and Albert* (1901), 6; Anon., *The Long Home* (1910),
11–12; B. Pollock, *Fellowship with the Departed* (1911), 10–12; cf. Rowell, *Hell and the Victorians*,
9–10.

[31] J. Fleming, 'The Cloud of Witnesses' (unpublished sermon preached in the private chapel
at Windsor Castle on 28 Feb. 1892, RA, VIC/Z98/36).

[32] Rowell, *Hell and the Victorians*; Wheeler, *Death and the Future Life*.

[33] Rowell, *Hell and the Victorians*, 18–23.

[34] J. W. Cunningham, *A Sermon Preached . . . On the Death . . . of George the Third* (1820), 4.

however, that, just as a family unit facing the loss of one of its members had to redefine and reassert its identity through the rituals of grieving, clergy preaching on the deaths of people who had been central to national life saw themselves as responding to the associated collective insecurities of the nation. Accordingly they sought to give their hearers a renewed patriotic sense of meaning and direction. There were four broad mechanisms by which memorial preaching served to foster and consolidate national consciousness: celebration, accountability, sympathy and inclusiveness.

Celebration may seem a provocative word when used in relation to death, but it still encapsulates much of the sermon comment on the deaths in old age of those who had been seen to characterize a whole era, above all George III, the Duke of Wellington, and Queen Victoria. Preachers had an opportunity to project through the image of the deceased those qualities that they themselves perceived as most fundamental to national life. George III was viewed as 'the perfect Englishman', a role model for his people, above all in his attachment to the joys of home. His influence had defined and lifted the moral and spiritual tone of the nation.[35] The Duke of Wellington was portrayed as the pre-eminent hero, the supreme protector of the nation, and God's agent in overcoming bondage and idolatry from India to Spain, and raising England to new heights of national eminence. His passing ended an epoch and gave rise to inevitable feelings of nostalgia, but it was to be hoped that the contemplation of his death would give 'fresh life to the slumbering spirit of national heroism'.[36] Queen Victoria was felt to have been the mother of her people, who had greatly raised the prestige of the monarchy and upheld the place of religion in national life. Her beneficent reign had been 'the most glorious ... in human history'.[37] Its ending marked the passage of time and the ringing of the 'knell of the departed century'.[38]

In other cases celebration was more muted and patchy, but instances can still be noted. Despite Nelson's death, Trafalgar was hailed as a great national deliverance; the much-maligned Duke of York had still been a bulwark of Protestant England and an inspiration to others to appreciate their exalted national privileges.[39] Despite their personal moral failings, George IV and William IV had still presided over years of great national

---

[35] Ibid., 7–18; S. Crowther, *A Sermon Occasioned by the Lamented Death of His Majesty King George the Third* (1820).

[36] Boutell, *The Hero and His Example*, 13–15; Brownlow, *Wellington*, 15; Croly, *Wellington*, 6; Gretton, *Barzillai*.

[37] A. M. MacLean, *Queen Victoria and Her Time* (Edinburgh, 1901), 11; C. W. Sandford, *The Queen and Mother of Her People* (Oxford, 1901).

[38] M. Hyamson, *In Memoriam Queen Victoria 1837–1901* (1901).

[39] R. Cecil, *The Pageant is Over* (1852, preached 1806); Bradley, *Britain in Sorrow*.

achievement and peaceful constitutional reform.[40] Even though the Prince Consort's life had been tragically cut short, he had brought about a 'moral revolution', making royalty a pattern for the family lives of the nation and setting an example of diligence and piety.[41]

On the other hand the unpredictability of death and its frequent untimeliness was perceived as a powerful sign of the nation's accountability to God, and of the overruling and sometimes deeply mysterious hand of divine providence in human affairs. Nelson's death, despite its mitigating circumstances, was still viewed by some as an indication of God's anger with the nation, of abuse of privileges and of over-reliance on the arm of flesh.[42] Preaching on the assassination of the Prime Minister, Spencer Perceval, in 1812, William Van Mildert pointed out that the deaths of the righteous were not a divine judgement on the deceased, but that they might well be a chastisement for those who survived.[43] Assertions that the nation was being judged for inadequate repentance and lack of gratitude for divine mercies were especially widespread at the time of the death of Princess Charlotte in 1817, even if there was a degree of circumspection in identifying the specific failings that had outraged the deity.[44] The death of the Duke of Kent in 1820 inspired further examination of the mysteries of providence and judgement, as did the tragic death of William Huskisson in a railway accident in 1830.[45]

By the time of the death of the Prince Consort, however, such a viewpoint, although still widely held, was beginning to be rather less of a matter of consensus. John Cumming, who in other respects held to very conservative theological positions, attacked the view that national sins were being punished, even if he still saw events as overruled by the providential hand of God.[46] Over the remainder of the century allusions to divine purpose and judgement became much more hesitant. In 1887 the sudden death of the Earl of Iddesleigh was viewed as a solemn lesson and a call to national brotherhood, and that of Duke of Clarence in 1892 led to generalized speculation about the possible links between national sin and national sorrow. In neither case, however, was the event explicitly attributed

---

[40] James, *National Blessings*, 15–24; C. Stovel, *National Bereavement Improved* (1837), 9.

[41] C. J. Vaughan, *The Mourning of the Land, and the Mourning of the Families* (Cambridge, 1861).

[42] J. Styles, *A Tribute to the Memory of Nelson* (Newport (IOW), 1806), 119–21.

[43] W. Van Mildert, *A Sermon Preached . . . on the Occasion of the Assassination of the Rt Hon Spencer Perceval* (1812), 5.

[44] T. F. Bowerbank, *A Sermon Preached in the Parish Church of Chiswick, Middlesex* (Chiswick, 1817); Hall, *Princess Charlotte*, 56.

[45] T. Gilbart, *Britain's Song* (Dublin, 1820); S. Saunders, *A Sermon Occasioned by the Death of the Rt Hon William Huskisson* (Liverpool, 1830).

[46] J. W. Brooks, *The Rod of the Almighty* (Nottingham? 1861); J. Cumming, *From Life to Life* (1861), 18–19.

to divine agency.[47] For example, the most the Dean of York was willing to say was that the death (which occurred in January) was God's Epiphany that 'man is born to trouble'. It reflected mysteries beyond human power to unravel, but the day would eventually come when 'thoughtful minds will look back upon the present time, and acknowledge that our dear young Prince has not lived, nor died, in vain'.[48]

As the perception of death as divine judgement receded, there was a renewed emphasis on the moral power of grief to inspire national solidarity and sympathy. This thread was picked up, sometimes with explicit allusion to memories of Princess Charlotte, when Prince Albert died in 1861. In the opinion of one Wesleyan minister 'since that period [1817] the national emotion has never been so deeply stirred, and the tribute of a nation's grief has never been so warmly and touchingly expressed as at this present moment'. The bereaved Queen could be assured of 'the spontaneous tribute of a nation's sympathies and a nation's tears'.[49] It was a grief felt by every individual, and one that was both national and Christian, a 'becoming witness to the unity . . . of our people.'[50] On the Duke of Clarence's death in 1892 such perceptions were reiterated and expanded in their geographical range: 'Wherever the English tongue is spoken there will be Human Sympathy—true and deep and honest Human Sympathy. Addresses, newspaper reports, telegrams, private letters, whatsoever else, will be no mere expressions of etiquette; but the outcome of a broad and generous love that *knows* because it has *suffered*.'[51] The preacher thus hinted at the growing tendency in this period for people to identify their personal bereavements with those of the royal family. Such sympathy with the throne, in the eyes of another preacher, was an invaluable safeguard of political stability and an inspiration to national prayer and repentance.[52] Edward VII's death in 1910 was judged to have made the 'whole world kin'. The Archbishop of Canterbury, Randall Davidson, was stirred to preach in Westminster Abbey a sermon that linked older perceptions of providence to the more recent emphasis on human sympathy. England's story, he suggested, was interwoven with signs of divine guidance, which were especially apparent in the solidarity of purpose evident at times of national grief and celebration.[53]

---

[47] J. Fleming, *The Death of a Patriot* (1887); A. R. MacEwan, *The Distress of Nations* (Glasgow, 1892).

[48] A. P. Purey-Cust, *God's Ordering, Our Sufficiency* (York, 1892), 9–10, 15.

[49] J. Jeffreys, *Princes and Great Men* (1862), 5–8.

[50] Falloon, *Prince and a Great Man*, 4–5; W. B. Flower, *An Extract from a Sermon on the death of HRH the Late Prince Consort* (1862), 4–5.

[51] Anon., *'He that Comforteth' A Plain Sermon on the Death of HRH the Duke of Clarence* (1892), 8.

[52] *Christus Consolator*, 13, 18–19.

[53] H. M. Butler, *For Kings and All that Are in High Places* (1910), 6; R. T. Davidson, *From Strength to Strength* (1910).

Finally, memorial sermons provided an opportunity for affirming the inclusiveness of the nation, especially in relation to groups that might be perceived as marginal or disadvantaged. In general, sermons did not betray much awareness of geographical or denominational origin: preachers, even in Scotland and Ireland, were concerned rather to participate in a uniform national observance. Some Dissenters, however, especially in the early part of the period, could not resist the temptation to point up their own worth and loyalty. Thus George III was held to have 'entertained the most heart-felt respect for all conscientious Nonconformists', while William IV's death provided an occasion for an exposition 'of the cardinal principles upon which the Protestant Dissenters of this country have shown their patriotism and loyalty to the House of Brunswick'.[54] Jews were even more fulsome than Dissenters in their responses to royal deaths: in 1830 one rabbi responded to the King's death with an extended comparison between the late monarch and King David and, with an unusual theological confidence, advanced proofs that George IV was even then enjoying glory.[55] On the death of the Duke of Clarence, the Chief Rabbi noted with satisfaction that the deceased had attended a Passover service and had showed considerable interest.[56]

On the other hand Roman Catholics were relatively much slower to preach memorial sermons, and no independently published examples have been found. In 1861 *The Times* reported that in only a few Roman Catholic sermons in London on the day before Albert's funeral was 'even a passing allusion' made to the loss.[57] It was not until the death of Queen Victoria in 1901 that Catholic sermons were widespread, although even then many priests appear to have limited themselves to reading pastoral letters from their bishops. Father Bernard Vaughan, preaching at the Spanish Place Church, London, paid eloquent tribute to the late Queen and affirmed the 'unswerving loyalty' of Catholics to the throne.[58] A common theme of sermons reported in the *Tablet* was an emphasis on the extent to which toleration of Catholicism had advanced during the Queen's reign.[59] In similar vein, after Edward VII's death, Cardinal Bourne, in a sermon at Westminster Cathedral, praised the late King's courtesy and consideration towards his Catholic subjects.[60]

---

[54] J. Morison, *Patriotic Regrets for the Loss of a Good King* (1820), 20; J. E. Good, *Britannia's Tears at the Decease of Her Sovereign* (Gosport, 1837), advertisement.

[55] S. Meyer, *A Funeral Sermon on the Death of His Late Majesty George IV* (1830).

[56] H. N. Adler, *The Nation's Lament* (1892), 9–10.

[57] *The Times*, 23 Dec. 1861. Cardinal Wiseman did, however, issue a pastoral letter expressing Catholic sympathy with the Queen.

[58] *The Times*, 26 Jan., 4 Feb. 1901.

[59] *Tablet*, 2 Feb. 1901, pp. 189–93.

[60] *The Times*, 9 May 1910.

The Church of England, for its part, was, by the end of the nineteenth century, showing itself increasingly magnanimous towards those who had dissented from it. Thus in 1889 in a memorial sermon on the militant Nonconformist John Bright, the Dean of Manchester emphasized the principles he held in common with the deceased and expressed the hope that the union of hearts apparent at the funeral would be turned to practical account. He concluded by quoting and applying to Bright, with minor adjustments, Tennyson's lines on that 'last great Englishman', the Duke of Wellington.[61]

By the end of the century funeral sermons were less authoritative than they had been in shaping the public mood. Nevertheless the *Scotsman* acknowledged that even in 1901 they still had a worthwhile role to play: 'Other public voices may in our day have come into competition with the pulpit and deprived it of the singular prominence and power it once possessed, but there is evident ground for the sober judgement that, if its influence is relatively less than it was, its ability and eloquence was never greater nor more general throughout the churches.'[62] Certainly, the extensive and detailed reporting of funeral sermons on Victoria and Edward VII in the national and local press shows that, even in the first decade of the twentieth century, they remained an important channel for the shaping of national sentiment following a prominent death. As throughout the nineteenth century, their success was founded on the capacity of preachers to articulate wider public emotions and to set them in a spiritual perspective that rang true for their congregations.

## Churchmen and the Development of Major Funerals

During the first half of the nineteenth century the sermon served as the primary channel for religious acknowledgement of a prominent death. From the 1860s onwards, however, clergy showed an increasing interest in using the content and symbolism of funerals and memorial services as a whole to affirm a sense of wide participation. In doing so they sought to direct the thoughts of participants to an awareness of spiritual dimensions, while also serving the institutional cause of the churches in general, and the Church of England in particular, by asserting and confirming their central role in national mourning. Such endeavours reflected and reinforced a trend apparent at the same period in the funerals of private individuals, where increased attention was being given to the church service.[63] Memorial

---

[61] J. Oakley, *The Mid-Lent Gospel* (Manchester, 1889), Preface, pp. 22–4.

[62] *Scotsman*, 31 Jan. 1901.

[63] J. Litten, *The English Way of Death: The Common Funeral Since 1450* (1991), 171.

services throughout the country had their focal point in the actual funeral services in London or Windsor. Accordingly consideration of trends in the nature and liturgical content of these central events sets an essential point of reference for discussion in the next section of commemorations elsewhere.

In the first half of the century, the clergy had showed little will or capacity to shape major funerals, contenting themselves with the walk-on roles scripted for them by precedent and heraldic regulation. Indeed for royal funerals at St George's Windsor, the Dean had to submit to the indignity of handing over the keys of the chapel to a representative of the officer of state responsible for the whole ceremonial, the Earl Marshal for the funerals of sovereigns, the Lord Chamberlain for those of other members of the royal family.[64] The Chapter was left with no control over arrangements other than narrowly liturgical ones. On occasions they even had to lobby officials to obtain a limited number of tickets for their own use.[65] Following the funeral of Princess Sophia Matilda in 1844 the Dean of Windsor complained to the Lord Chamberlain of 'the evils arising from the present mode of conducting these mournful ceremonials'. He was particularly concerned about the damage done to the fabric of the chapel by the extensive temporary fittings and the bad effects on the organ of the dust and dirt generated by the associated building works. Furthermore, divine service had had to be suspended for eighteen days.[66] At Queen Adelaide's funeral in 1849 a memorandum noted that only Windsor clergy with an official role were to be admitted to the chapel.[67]

The two great London churches were better placed than St George's to develop a role less subordinated to royal and government officials. At St Paul's in 1852 Dean Milman's active involvement in the arrangements for the Duke of Wellington's funeral began to establish a new direction. Within the cathedral he and his organist, John Goss, were able to plan and implement a service that was generally perceived by the privileged minority who were present as an inspiring and uplifting climax to the Duke's obsequies.[68] Lord John Manners expressed his 'very great and unexpected delight at the conception and execution of the whole religious service: than which I can conceive nothing more effective or sublime'.[69] The Bishop

---

[64] For examples see CA [86], Minute of Proceedings Funeral of William IV, copy letter of Dean of Windsor 27 June 1837; PRO WORKS 21/5/13/25, warrant from Lord Chamberlain to Dean of Windsor. This practice apparently originated in the reign of George IV, owing to a breakdown in relations between the King and the Chapter of St George's (St George's Chapel Archives, III.o.1, Henry L. Cust to Earl de la Warr, 3 Jan. 1845).

[65] CA [84], Funeral of William IV, fo. 24, Henry Cust to Sir William Woods, 6 July 1837.

[66] PRO, LC 2/44, Dean of Windsor (Hobart) to Lord Chamberlain, 23 Jan. 1845.

[67] CA [108], Funeral of Queen Adelaide.

[68] St Paul's Memoranda.

[69] Ibid., Manners to Milman, 23 Nov. 1852.

of London also congratulated Milman 'on the perfect success of your arrangements for the solemn ceremony . . . every part of them was admirable, the music most correct and efficient, everybody was greatly struck with the procession of the clergy'.[70]

In 1863 the appointment of Arthur Penrhyn Stanley as Dean of Westminster placed at the head of the Abbey Chapter a man with an even stronger sense of history and of the national role of his institution than Milman at St Paul's. Stanley's approach to his role as Dean was founded in the Broad Church vision inspired by his mentor Thomas Arnold. He believed that 'whilst Westminster Abbey stands, the Church of England stands', and sought to ensure that it remained the sanctuary 'not of any private sect, but of the English people'.[71] Both Stanley and his biographer stressed that he was not proactive in formally offering the Abbey as a place of interment for public figures and, indeed, he was well aware of the limited space for further graves in the building. Nevertheless in appropriate cases he discreetly made it known to representatives of the deceased that were a request to be made it would be positively received.[72]

The first interment in the Abbey during Stanley's tenure of the deanery, that of Lord Palmerston in 1865, was made by authority of his successor as Prime Minister, Earl Russell, and so Stanley felt the 'responsibility of consenting' had been taken out of his own hands.[73] Nevertheless he evidently relished the link thus forged between the Abbey and the memory of a man whose political career had made him such a prominent focus of robust secular patriotism. *The Times* took the opportunity to reflect on the role of the Abbey as a national burying place. It regretted the fact that so much space was taken up with obscure individuals that there was little space left for 'men deserving every honour from their country'. It also bemoaned the 'narrow bigotry' that had denied interment there to Byron, who, though dead for forty years, was Palmerston's contemporary. Only on occasions such as Palmerston's funeral was the Abbey being devoted to its 'proper use'.[74]

Stanley probably needed little encouragement, but he took his cue. His criteria for admission to the Abbey related far more to evidence of an

[70] Ibid., Blomfield to Milman, 19 Nov. 1852.
[71] A. P. Stanley, *Historical Memorials of Westminster Abbey* (1882 edn.), 493.
[72] Westminster Abbey Muniments [WA], Dean Stanley's Recollections, fo. 22; R. E. Prothero, *The Life and Correspondence of Arthur Penrhyn Stanley, DD*, 2 vols. (1894), ii. 320–1; E. Carpenter (ed.), *A House of Kings: The History of Westminster Abbey* (1966), 303.
[73] WA, Stanley's Recollections, fo. 3. Correspondence in the Russell papers (PRO, PRO 30/22/15F, fos. 2, 145, 239–40) confirms Stanley's recollection that Russell confronted him with a 'fait accompli', but he does not appear to have objected in any way. See below Chapter 6.
[74] *The Times*, 25, 27 Oct. 1865.

individual's acknowledged national standing than to the personal morality or religious views of the deceased.[75] During the subsequent fifteen years interments represented a cross-section of national life, in respect of literature (Dickens, 1870; Bulwer-Lytton 1873), music (Sterndale Bennett, 1875), science (Herschel, 1871; Lyell, 1875); overseas expansion (Livingstone, 1874; Lawrence, 1879). Two great historians, Grote (1871) and Thirlwall (1875), representing respectively secular and Anglican traditions of scholarship, were buried in the same grave. Stanley's own sense of occasion and history combined with his own personal demeanour to render the funerals in the Abbey for which he was responsible very memorable occasions. He also used his sermons on the Sundays following a funeral to make explicit his own conception of the significance of the deceased.[76] Furthermore he facilitated subsequent pilgrimage to graves.

Two cases are worthy of particular note in demonstrating Stanley's inclusive attitude towards figures of acknowledged national status. When Charles Dickens died suddenly in June 1870, he was untroubled by the novelist's religious unorthodoxy and needed no prompting in offering burial in the Abbey.[77] In deference to the preferences of the deceased and the family, the funeral itself was private and unannounced, but, aware of the extensive public interest, Stanley asked that the grave be left open. He recalled that 'thousands' came to see it: 'Every class of the community was present, dropping in flowers, verses and memorials of every kind, and, some of them quite poor people, shedding tears.'[78] Preaching on the following Sunday, he applied the parable of the rich man and Lazarus to praise of Dickens's achievement in bridging gulfs of understanding between the poor and the wealthy. He also quoted approvingly from his will, in which the writer committed his soul to 'the mercy of God, through our Lord and Saviour Jesus Christ' and exhorted his children 'to try to guide themselves by the teaching of the New Testament in its broad spirit, and to put no faith in any man's narrow construction of its letter.'[79]

Second, when David Livingstone's body arrived back from Africa in 1874, his Christianity was not at issue, but he was not an Anglican. Stanley, however, took particular satisfaction in his interment in the Abbey, not only as an explorer and missionary hero, but also as a Scottish Nonconformist of

[75] WA, Stanley's Recollections, *passim*.

[76] Prothero, *Stanley*, ii. 317–20.

[77] *The Times*, 13, 15 June 1870; WA, Stanley's Recollections, fo. 10. Stanley's initial letter, however, went astray, and hence the matter was not settled until after *The Times* had published a leader also advocating interment in the Abbey (ibid., fos. 11–12).

[78] WA, Stanley's Recollections, fo. 17; Prothero, *Stanley*, ii. 324.

[79] A. P. Stanley, *Sermon Preached . . . in Westminster Abbey, June 19 1870 . . . being the Sunday Following the Funeral of Charles Dickens* (1870); *The Times*, 20 June 1870.

humble social origins who could be held to symbolize the inclusiveness of the national church.[80] Ten days after Livingstone's funeral, *The Times* reported that large numbers of people were visiting the grave and leaving spring blooms on it.[81]

Shortly before Stanley's own death in 1881, he was bitterly disappointed that Disraeli was not buried in the Abbey.[82] Under his successor George Granville Bradley, however, the sequence of notable funerals was maintained, in particular those of Darwin (1882), Shaftesbury (1885),[83] Tennyson (1892), and Gladstone (1898). By honouring Darwin the Abbey was expressing a general national consensus in which by 1882 the eminent scientist was no longer arraigned as a sceptic but hailed as a student of truth and a 'true Christian gentleman'.[84] At Lord Shaftesbury's funeral the enormous range of the dead man's philanthropic and religious interests, represented both in the Abbey and in the crowds outside, rendered the occasion one that decisively transcended both religious denomination and social class.[85] Tennyson's obsequies saw the introduction of a prominent patriotic reference, with the Union flag used as a pall, while the musical settings of two of his late works, 'Crossing the bar' and 'Silent voices' emphasized the poet's own faltering rather than orthodox Christian faith. Once again in the days after the funeral the grave drew thousands of pilgrims, to the extent that the Abbey authorities found themselves obliged to call in the police in order to regulate the crowds.[86] Gladstone, although a pillar of traditional Anglican belief, had been from the Church of England's point of view a politically ambivalent figure. Nevertheless, a sense of broad Christian and national duty continued to prevail over any tendency to narrow Anglican posturing. His funeral, like Darwin's and Tennyson's, was to be criticized as being over-formal and distancing the dead man from

[80] Stanley's readiness to inter a Nonconformist minister in the Abbey was criticized by at least one Anglo-Catholic periodical, but he was vigorously defended by the Evangelical *Record*, (20, 22 April 1874), not normally a supporter of the Broad Church Dean.

[81] *The Times*, 29 April 1874. For full discussion of the response to Livingstone's death see below Chapter 5.

[82] Prothero, *Stanley*, ii. 564.

[83] Shaftesbury was interred on his country estate after a funeral in the Abbey, a format unusual in the nineteenth century, but one that was to become more common in the twentieth century. For Iddesleigh (1887) and Bright (1889) memorial services were held in Westminster Abbey on the same day as the actual funerals, at Upton Pyne (Devon) and Rochdale respectively (*The Times*, 19 Jan. 1887, 1 April 1889). See below, Chapter 6.

[84] J. R. Moore, 'Charles Darwin Lies in Westminster Abbey', *Biological Journal of the Linnaean Society*, 17 (1982), 97–113.

[85] Hodder, *Shaftesbury*, iii. 516–20, 525–8.

[86] RA, VIC/R 44/12, Hallam Tennyson to the Queen, 13 Oct. 1892; 44/13, Canon Duckworth to the Queen, 16 Oct. 1892.

the more partisan springs of his popularity and identity, but this was the necessary corollary of using such occasions to affirm national consensus.[87]

Meanwhile St Paul's, having gained the great prize of Wellington in 1852, found itself somewhat subordinated to Westminster as a national burial ground for the rest of the Victorian period. It was not wholly eclipsed, however, and attracted some prominent interments, especially those of artists and of naval and military heroes, for example Picton (1859), Landseer (1873), Napier of Magdala (1890) and Leighton (1896).[88] Nevertheless, it was not until the years immediately before the First World War that St Paul's again began to rival Westminster Abbey as a focus for national mourning. It was to be the setting for the memorial services to the victims of the Titanic disaster in 1912, and Captain Scott's ill-fated polar expedition in 1913, as well as for the funerals of Lord Wolseley (1913) and Lord Roberts (1914).[89]

It is easy with hindsight to see the development of Westminster and St Paul's as inclusive national burying places to have been an inevitable process, but the French parallel should at least indicate the alternative potentialities that existed during the nineteenth century. The Panthéon in Paris had a variegated history, sometimes a church and sometimes secularized, but in 1885 the funeral of Victor Hugo provided the occasion for a final and decisive secularization.[90] Preaching in Westminster Abbey on the Sunday after Darwin's funeral, Harvey Goodwin, the Bishop of Carlisle, concurred in the judgement that 'Had this death occurred in France, no priest would have taken part in the funeral, or if he had, no scientific man would have been present.'[91] The Church of England, by burying its critics and dissenters alongside its committed friends, ensured that there was never any corresponding pressure in Britain for a secular or at least non-denominational national cemetery. Indeed during the later nineteenth century there were plans to build a major extension to Westminster Abbey in order to increase the number of interments that could take place there. The scheme was supported in Parliament, and considered by a Royal Commission set up in 1890. No action ensued, but inertia stemmed more from the inherent difficulty of finding a generally acceptable architectural solution for such an historic building, rather than from any opposition in principle.[92]

---

[87] R. B. Martin, _Tennyson: The Unquiet Heart_ (1980), 582–3; _Reynolds Newspaper_, 29 May 1898.
[88] For a full list of interments at St Paul's see W. M. Sinclair, _Memorials of St Paul's Cathedral_ (1909), 312–77 and 451–73, _passim_. Picton, who died at Waterloo, was reinterred.
[89] St Paul's Cathedral Library, Newbolt Scrapbook, Vol. VII.
[90] V-N. Jouffre (trans. A. Moyon), _The Panthéon_ (Rennes, 1996), 25.
[91] Quoted, Moore, 'Charles Darwin', 107.
[92] A. D. C. Hyland, 'Imperial Valhalla', _Journal of the Society of Architectural Historians_, 1962 (21/3), 129–39.

It is true that even the inclusiveness of Westminster Abbey had its limits: for example, in 1880, George Eliot's remains were relegated to Highgate Cemetery. Nevertheless Stanley would have been willing to countenance her burial in the Abbey, had there been sufficient support from influential opinion. Eliot's admirers, fearful of stirring controversy that would have dwelt on her unconventional private life as much as on her agnosticism, felt it wiser not to press the issue.[93] The funeral at Highgate was conducted by a Unitarian minister who spoke of her as 'profoundly devout' even though she did 'not accept a great deal of what is usually held to be religious belief'.[94] Thus her exclusion from the Abbey should not be seen primarily as an expression of confrontation between orthodoxy and scepticism. On the contrary it reflected, albeit in a negative sense, the same wish for accommodation between Christianity, heterodoxy, and scepticism in the commemoration of figures of national stature that was implicit in the admission of Dickens, Darwin and Tennyson. In this respect decisions regarding burials in Westminster Abbey served as an important symbolic microcosm of the distinctive cultural and religious history of later Victorian Britain.

The liturgical and musical content of prominent funerals remained very conservative, following the 1662 Book of Common Prayer Order for the Burial of the Dead, and largely using late seventeenth- and early eighteenth-century music. The Purcell and Croft settings of the scripture sentences and liturgical texts were consistently employed; Handel's anthem 'His body is buried in peace' was repeatedly used; and his 'Dead March' normally concluded services. The latter was not merely a final organ voluntary, but assumed a liturgical function, as a pause for solemn still reflection. When innovations were made, such as Goss's own anthems composed for the occasion at Wellington's funeral, or the playing of a Beethoven funeral march[95] at Palmerston's, these were added to the traditional framework rather than replacing any part of it.[96] Such continuity may have arisen from inertia and lack of rehearsal time between death and funeral, as much as from considered policy. Nevertheless it served the Church of England's purposes well in underlining its ongoing role as custodian of the national memory, and the impressive nature of its burial ceremonial was even acknowledged in Presbyterian Scotland.[97] The persistence in the use of the Purcell and Croft settings of the opening sentences was especially noteworthy, a reflection of the accessible but moving character of the music,

[93] F. Karl, *George Eliot: A Biography* (1995), 639–40.
[94] *The Times*, 30 Dec. 1880.
[95] Presumably an arrangement of the second movement of the 'Eroica' Symphony.
[96] *The Times*, 18 Nov. 1852, 28 Oct. 1865.
[97] *Scotsman*, 20 April 1874.

and an apparent tacit agreement that it was impossible to improve upon them.[98] Lord Shaftesbury's biographer recalled approvingly that 'the grand old music of Purcell and Croft' was sung at his funeral in 1885; a participant at Queen Victoria's funeral felt that they had 'in them something of the echo of all the dead'.[99]

Nevertheless funeral services were not unaffected by wider liturgical changes. The gradual improvement in general musical standards in the Church of England during the Victorian era served to ensure that the effect was genuinely impressive, even if the results were sometimes too elaborate for Evangelical taste.[100] At Westminster Abbey the tenure of Frederick Bridge as organist from 1882 to 1918 was a period of particular musical renaissance.[101] In the meantime, hymns, enormously popular in late Victorian England, also made their appearance even in otherwise very formal services in the Abbey. The decisive moment here appears to have been Livingstone's funeral, when Stanley, well aware of the need to offer some gesture to Nonconformists in the course of the Anglican liturgy, included Philip Doddridge's 'O God of Bethel'.[102] The precedent was followed at Shaftesbury's funeral eleven years later, when the congregational singing of Charles Wesley's 'Let all the saints terrestrial sing' was regarded as the emotional climax of the service.[103] Bishop Heber's 'Holy, Holy, Holy' was sung at Tennyson's funeral,[104] and at Gladstone's funeral, the text of Isaac Watts's 'O God our help' was prefaced on the service sheet by the rubric in bold type, 'It is earnestly requested that everyone present will join in singing it.'[105] Even if the instruction betrayed an uncertainty as to the enthusiasm of the distinguished guests for rousing hymn-singing, there was thus no doubt of the commitment of the Abbey authorities to such congregational participation. In the event, however, the congregation sang with such vigour that those in the street outside heard them and joined in.[106] Further endorsement came in 1904 when by the 'express desire' of the King, 'Onward Christian Soldiers' was sung at the funeral in the Abbey of his military cousin, the Duke of Cambridge.[107]

Royal attitudes to death and commemoration, as shaped and mediated

[98] I am indebted to Prof. Donald Burrows for this observation, and for other advice on the musical aspects of this section.

[99] Hodder, Shaftesbury, iii. 519; A. FitzRoy, Memoirs, 2 vols. (1925), i. 45.

[100] Record, 22 April 1874.

[101] Carpenter, House of Kings, 334–5.

[102] WA, Stanley's Recollections, fos. 42–3.

[103] Hodder, Shaftesbury, iii. 519.

[104] WA 63841B, Order of Service.

[105] WA 57697, Printed sheet.

[106] Lloyds Weekly Newspaper, 15 May 1910.

[107] WA, newspaper cutting.

by clergy close to Queen Victoria and Edward VII, became a significant impulse for liturgical change. Key clerical influences on the royal family were Dean Stanley himself, Gerald Wellesley, Dean of Windsor from 1854 to 1882, and, in the next generation, Randall Davidson, as Dean of Windsor (1883–91), Bishop of Rochester (1891–5), Bishop of Winchester (1895–1903), and Archbishop of Canterbury (1903–28).[108] The deaths of the Queen's mother, the Duchess of Kent, and of Prince Albert in 1861, brought decisively to an end a period when royal funerals in St George's Chapel had been largely routine observances, which surviving members of the family were content to have regulated by convention and precedent. The music for Albert's funeral itself contained significant innovations reflecting his German background, notably two chorales and Martin Luther's hymn 'Great God, what do I see and hear?' sung by the choir.[109] A. P. Stanley found it 'a profoundly mournful and impressive sight'[110] and it seems likely that the experience influenced his own subsequent stage management of funerals at Westminster. A year later in December 1862, Wellesley and Stanley were responsible, in response to royal command, for a series of private services to mark the anniversary of Albert's death and the consecration of his mausoleum at Frogmore.[111] These anniversary services were then continued in subsequent years, and their private and personal character permitted and indeed required a degree of liturgical flexibility and innovation, which might have been problematic in more public worship. Sir Henry Ponsonby, the Queen's private secretary, later recalled that 'Dean Wellesley used to tell her that the Frogmore service might be considered as prayers for the dead unless he arranged the Service carefully, which he did.'[112] When Davidson took over the task in 1883 he noted that 'I was directed . . . to introduce reference to the Duke of Connaught in India, successive deaths of Wellesley and Connor,[113] and above all J[ohn] B[rown][114], a very difficult task. But it must be done.'[115]

In the present context, the significance of these anniversary services is that during the 1860s and 1870s they accustomed the Queen and the royal family as a whole to expect funeral and memorial liturgy that expressed

---

[108] On Davidson, see W. M. Kuhn, *Democratic Royalism: The Transformation of the British Monarchy, 1861–1914* (Basingstoke, 1996), 82–111.

[109] PRO, LC 1/90, letter from S. J. Elvey (organist of St George's Chapel), 20 Dec. 1861.

[110] Prothero, *Stanley*, ii. 61.

[111] Ibid., ii. 123–5; *Services Held in Windsor Castle on the Anniversary of the Lamented Death of the Prince Consort, December 14 1862*; *Service in the Royal Mausoleum at Frogmore on 18th December 1862* (privately printed).

[112] LPL, DavP 4, fo. 45, Ponsonby to Davidson, 6 March 1885.

[113] Davidson's short-lived predecessor as Dean of Windsor.

[114] The Queen's highland servant who had died in March 1883.

[115] G. K. A. Bell, *Randall Davidson Archbishop of Canterbury*, 2 vols. (1935), i. 86.

and salved emotions of personal bereavement as well as fulfilling the traditional rituals of church and state. In this respect they were both reflecting and leading the contemporary trend in the country as a whole towards more sincerity and less hollow display in funeral ritual.[116] These trends found more public expression in the funerals of Prince Leopold, Duke of Albany, the Queen's youngest son, in 1884, and of her grandson, Prince Albert Victor, Duke of Clarence in 1892. Following Prince Leopold's death, Davidson was in close communication with the Queen and other members of the royal family, and she subsequently thanked him for the 'most touchingly beautiful services'.[117] The funeral had included two hymns, 'O God our help in ages past' and 'Lead kindly light', the work respectively of the Dissenter Isaac Watts and the Roman Catholic convert, John Henry Newman. Spohr's anthem, 'Blest are the departed' was sung, and funeral marches by Chopin and Beethoven were played, but not the Handel 'Dead March'.[118]

The bereaved mother, the Princess of Wales, chose the music for the Duke of Clarence's funeral herself.[119] It showed a further marked movement towards more contemporary composers, including settings by Samuel Sebastian Wesley, and Arthur Sullivan's anthem 'Brother thou hast gone before us'. Again a Chopin march was used in preference to Handel's 'Dead March'.[120] The choice of anthem appears to have led to some raised ecclesiastical eyebrows,[121] and The Times was unenthusiastic about the choice of the Chopin piece instead of 'Handel's sublime composition on the same theme.'[122] Under the circumstances, however, the royal family evidently felt themselves free to follow their own preferences rather than subordinate their feelings to convention. In the days after Clarence's funeral there were further private services at which popular hymns were sung, including 'My God and Father, while I stray', 'Just as I am, without one plea', and 'Lead kindly light'. The early loss of their son thus stimulated the Prince and Princess of Wales to follow the Queen's lead in seeking personal comfort as well as public show from memorial observance.[123]

[116] Jalland, Death in the Victorian Family, 194–203.
[117] St George's Chapel Archives, XVII.43, 'Memorandum as to the Queen's wishes in interview granted to Dean', 30 March 1884; DavP 4, fo. 33, Davidson to his father, 11 April 1884; Bell, Davidson, i. 81–2.
[118] The Times, 7 April 1884.
[119] DavP 30, fos. 307–8, Dalton to Davidson, 17 Jan. 1892.
[120] The Times, 21 Jan. 1892.
[121] DavP 30, fo. 309, Ponsonby-Fane to Davidson, Jan. 1892.
[122] The Times, 21 Jan 1892.
[123] Report of the Society of the Friends of St George's and the Descendants of the Knights of the Garter, 1968, pp. 382–4, printing letters from Dean Eliot to his mother, 21, 24 Jan. 1892.

Despite the diplomatic compromises with royal sensibilities that Wellesley and Davidson were obliged to make, it was nevertheless apparent that in the late Victorian period, churchmen were able to play a much more formative role in the shaping of funeral ceremonial than had been the case earlier in the century. There was also awareness of how such high profile occasions could shape the public image of the Church of England, with increasing pressure for it to be represented at the highest level.[124]

Within an hour of his mother's death in 1901 Edward VII was discussing arrangements for her funeral with Davidson, now Bishop of Winchester.[125] The resulting service showed a further move towards the music of the nineteenth century. Croft was now limited to the opening sentences and the only other pre-Romantic music was Felton's chant for Psalm 90, and Purcell's setting of 'Thou knowest Lord the secrets of our hearts'. 'Man that is born of woman' was sung to an S. S. Wesley setting, the Lord's Prayer sung to music by Gounod, and the anthems were Tchaikovsky's 'How blest are they' and Spohr's 'Blest are the departed'. The service concluded with a funeral march by Beethoven.[126] Davidson had prevailed on the royal family to drop their initial choice of an anthem from the Russian Kontakion for the faithful departed, 'Give rest O Christ to thy servant with thy Saints' because he feared it would be criticized as prayer for the dead. The incident well illustrated the tension between private preference and public image, and Edward VII agreed with Davidson in seeking to avoid potentially damaging controversy on 'a great national occasion'. The latter recalled:

> I had to keep on assuring them all that personally I had no objection to such petitions, and indeed that personally I believed in, and used such prayers, and should feel no sort of objection to their being sanctioned everywhere. At present, however, that had not been done, and I felt bound to remind them of the fact, reiterating that I was speaking merely in the interests of the King to avoid controversy. The King said repeatedly, 'I see. What you want to protect is the Nonconformist conscience.' I said he might put it so without being far wrong. Anyhow it was a near shave, and the blunder might have turned out to be a real misfortune for the Puritanical

---

[124] In relation to Prince Leopold's funeral, Davidson noted 'surprise' that the Archbishop of Canterbury took no part in the service; for the Duke of Clarence's he lobbied vigorously but unsuccessfully to have the Archbishop represented although he was unable to be present in person (DavP 4, fo. 33 Davidson to his father, 11 April 1884; 18, fo. 83, Davidson to Benson, 18 Jan. 1892).

[125] DavP 19, no. 101, fo. 23.

[126] RA, E&V QV's Death Esher volume, printed order of service.

and old-fashioned outcry wd have set back the hopes of our getting such prayers to be generally used.[127]

Official royal funeral ritual could serve to give direction to changes in public taste, but the royal family and the Church of England had a joint interest in ensuring that such events continued to command national sympathy, through a Broad Church civic ethos.

The actual funerals of Clarence and Victoria had not included any hymns, which were still felt too informal for the funerals of an heir presumptive and the sovereign herself. In relation to Victoria's funeral, however, the Bishop of Ripon, William Boyd Carpenter, confided to his diary that, 'I wish we could have had some old Hymn, which would have moved the heart.'[128] The initiative for the inclusion of two hymns at the funeral of Edward VII in 1910 came though from Queen Alexandra rather than from ecclesiastical sources. Her specific selections, Charlotte Elliott's 'My God and Father, while I stray' and John Ellerton's 'Now the labourer's task is o'er', were representative more of contemporary sensibilities than of long-term continuities. Sir Walter Parratt, the organist of St George's, complained to Davidson, now Archbishop of Canterbury, that this 'solemn national ceremony' was in danger of sinking 'into a Parish Church service'. He thought two hymns and one anthem to be out of proportion.[129] Worse still, the Dean of Windsor, Philip Eliot, considered that the Queen's choice of anthem, Sullivan's 'Brother thou art gone before us', which had been sung at her son's funeral in 1892, was inappropriate and might even 'provoke scoffing in some quarters'.[130] Davidson shared his concerns and tackled the new King on the subject. George V agreed with the Archbishop, but felt unable to override his mother's wishes. Nevertheless he encouraged Dav-

---

[127] DavP 19, no. 101, fos. 26–7. The offending piece was, however, used at the memorial service for the Queen at St Paul's Cathedral on the day of the funeral, without apparently arousing controversy (*The Times*, 4 Feb. 1901).

[128] BL, AddMS 46742, fo. 56.

[129] DavP 326, fo. 66, Parratt to Davidson, 12 May 1910.

[130] DavP 326, fos. 59, 78 Eliot to Davidson, 12, 13 May 1910. Eliot did not make fully explicit his objections, but the words of the first stanza alone could provide ample prompts for less innocent minds than Queen Alexandra's to make unfortunate links with the late King's life and the political situation at the time of his death:

> Brother, thou hast gone before us and thy saintly soul is flown
> Where tears are wiped from every eye and sorrow is unknown;
> From the burden of the flesh, and from care and fear released,
> Where the wicked cease from troubling and the weary are at rest.

Furthermore to the literal-minded the line 'So we lay the turf above thee now, and we seal the narrow bed', underlined in an MS copy in the Davidson Papers (DavP 326, fo. 61) seemed an inadequate description of interment in the royal vault.

idson to speak to her himself.[131] Even that master of ecclesiastical and courtly diplomacy found his encounter with the bereaved Queen to be a difficult one. She first said that a change was out of the question, but then when he urged her to 'sink her individual feelings for public advantage', she gave way. The traditional Handel anthem 'His body is buried in peace, but his name liveth for evermore' was substituted, thus balancing the hymns with a much more conservative reference.[132]

Nevertheless the inclusion of the hymns marked a culminating endorsement of the steady increase of their part in funeral liturgy during the half century since the death of Albert in 1861. Such recognition of popular religious sentiment was paralleled in 1910 by formal recognition of non-Anglican religious bodies through representation in the congregation, although not yet in active participation in the service.[133] There was a three-way creative tension between the personal sentiments of members of the royal family, the quest for inclusiveness, and the caution of the ecclesiastical and musical establishments, which produced services that successfully balanced civic and national dignity with a degree of popular appeal.

## Memorial Services

Obviously only a very small and privileged minority could be physically present at the central liturgical events of national mourning. Subsequent newspaper and magazine accounts provided lavish verbal description and sometimes pictorial illustration, but were still a poor substitute for the sense of personal participation, even for literate subscribers who were in a position to purchase and read such accounts. Hence arose the popularity of parallel commemorations in provincial churches on the day of the funeral, and also in London ones when the funeral itself was at Windsor or elsewhere outside the capital. Such services were often preceded by street processions that drew large crowds.

The precedent for such services had been set, albeit not without some dissent and controversy, at the time of Princess Charlotte's death.[134] Both

---

[131] DavP 581, fos. 24–5.

[132] DavP 581, fos. 26–9; *The Order of Service for the Burial of His Majesty King Edward VII* (1910).

[133] The invitation list for Edward VII's funeral included the Archbishop of Westminster, the Moderators of the General Assemblies of the Church of Scotland, United Free Church, and Presbyterian Church in Ireland, the President of the Free Church Council, the Great Archimandrite, and the Chief Rabbi (CA 160, Edward VII's Funeral III, fo. 130). It is not clear whether all the above actually attended.

[134] McCrie, *Free Thoughts*, 6–8, 34, 40–44, 62.

for her and for George III there were services in at least some Nonconformist chapels as well as in Anglican churches.[135] Jews too joined in the
commemoration and a dirge specially composed for the occasion was
chanted in the Great Synagogue in Aldgate.[136] During the subsequent three
decades, however, parallel memorial services were less numerous, while
funeral sermons were more likely to be preached on an appropriate Sunday
than at a special service. Nevertheless some instances of significant local
observance can be documented. At Newcastle-upon-Tyne there were
'prayers at all the Churches' on the day of the Duke of York's funeral in
1827, and for George IV's funeral in 1830 there was a civic procession to
St Nicholas' Church which 'was crowded to excess, many persons having
to retire for want of accommodation'.[137] Similar events took place in a
number of Yorkshire towns.[138] Wellington's funeral was the occasion for
larger and more numerous local commemorations than at any time since
1820. Services appear to have been limited to Anglican churches, but
members of other denominations participated.[139]

An emphasis on spectacle rather than piety was characteristic of such
local commemorations in the period between 1820 and 1860 and was
consistent with the elaborate secular ritual of private funerals in the same
period.[140] By the 1870s, however, simplicity and sincerity were increasingly
seen as desirable ends in the funerals of the aristocracy and middle classes,[141]
and this trend was mirrored, and arguably stimulated, by public responses
to the deaths of prominent individuals. In this respect the death of the
Prince Consort in December 1861 marked an important watershed. The
untimeliness of this bereavement seems to have evoked widespread, if
short-lived, feelings of shock and insecurity, both in relation to national
life and awareness of personal mortality. The clergy were given a golden
opportunity to focus and lead this mood through the chance of the Prince
dying late on a Saturday evening. Accordingly church services were the
main channel through which the grim news was spread on the following
day. The announcement was made in particularly dramatic form by the
Vicar of St John's, Leeds, who mounted the pulpit, gave out his text as 2
Samuel 3:38, 'Know ye not that there is a prince and a great man fallen

[135] *The Times*, 17 Feb. 1820.
[136] H. Hurwitz, *The Tears of a Grateful People, A Hebrew Dirge and Hymn Chaunted in the Great Synagogue, St. James's Place, Aldgate, on the Day of the Funeral of His Late Most Sacred Majesty King George III* (1820).
[137] Sykes, *Duke of York*, 23; Sykes *George the Fourth*, 23.
[138] *Leeds Mercury*, 15 July 1830.
[139] *Exeter Flying Post*, 25 Nov. 1852; *Leeds Intelligencer*, 20 Nov. 1852.
[140] Jalland, *Death in the Victorian Family*, 194–7.
[141] Ibid., 197–203.

this day in Israel?' delaying any explanation of what had happened until the body of his sermon.[142] Many clergy communicated the news in a liturgical context, in the Church of England by omitting the Prince's name from the prayer for the royal family and in other churches by explicit allusion in the prayers.[143] As the news spread many of those not already in church sought solace there: when the doors of Exeter Cathedral were opened for afternoon service the building was completely filled within two or three minutes 'and many were obliged to go away'.[144]

On the following Sunday unusually large congregations were again observed,[145] and one clergyman at least articulated in verse his perception that the shock of the Prince's death was drawing the people closer together and closer to God:

> Where a people's pent-up sorrow
>   For a Prince so good and rare,
> Finds fit utterance in the lesson
>   In the Psalm and in the Prayer
> In the Abbeys and Cathedrals,
>   Where the proud memorials stand,
> In the Churches and the Chapels
>   Thickly scattered o'er the land,
> Every crowding congregation
>   Finds it solacement to hear
> Of the virtues and the goodness
>   Of a prince all held so dear.
> O 'tis worth a Kingdom's ransom
>   Such a goodly sight to see,
> Where as one a people mourneth,
>   Loyal, loving, great and free![146]

On the day of the funeral itself services were much more numerous than they had been in 1852. In London a congregation of between three and four thousand people attended St Paul's, while the *Illustrated London News* asserted that throughout England there were services in all churches and

---

[142] *Leeds Intelligencer*, 21 Dec. 1861.

[143] Accounts of the reception of the news are widespread in local papers: see, for example, *Exeter Flying Post*, 18 Dec. 1861; *Scotsman*, 16 Dec. 1861. Anecdotal evidence relating to such events in living memory, for example the assassination of John F. Kennedy in 1963 or the fatal accident suffered by Diana, Princess of Wales in 1997, indicates that the context in which the news is received is very firmly lodged in the long-term memory of many people.

[144] *Western Times*, 21 Dec. 1861.

[145] *ILN*, 28 Dec. 1861, p. 676.

[146] J. Fletcher, *For the Prince Consort: A Lay* (n.d.).

most Nonconformist chapels.[147] The example of Leeds supports this claim. Here the *Leeds Mercury* had suggested a few days before that 'perhaps in no way could the inhabitants give a more fitting expression to their feeling than in the worship of God on such an occasion'.[148] Not only was the parish church packed with a congregation estimated at 4,000, but also its approaches and the processional route from the town hall were densely crowded with thousands of spectators. Services were also held in the other Anglican churches, in the Jewish synagogue, and in numerous Nonconformist chapels, 'though it was somewhat late before the general determination to adopt that course was arrived at'. Large congregations and 'full mourning costume' were everywhere observed, the latter perhaps an indication of the predominance of the more prosperous strata of society. In the evening there was a concert of 'sacred music' at the town hall, where the 'Dead March' was earnestly encored.[149] In Birmingham a nondenominational service in the town hall was similarly packed.[150] North of the Border, Presbyterian sensibilities again appear to have precluded fully-fledged memorial services, but the death was widely acknowledged in Sunday services, and prayer meetings were held on the day of the funeral in the Free Assembly Hall and in other churches in Edinburgh.[151]

The intensity and religious orientation of the mourning for Prince Albert were stronger than anything experienced since 1817, and were not to be repeated for a further generation. In the meantime funerals such as those of Palmerston, Disraeli, and Prince Leopold gave rise to observance in a more limited range of principal churches. These mid-Victorian years did however see two significant developments. First, up to the 1860s, the usual liturgical basis for Anglican services of this kind was the order for Morning or Evening Prayer, as applicable. The weight of specific funereal reference was carried by the choice of anthems and voluntaries and, above all, by the content of the sermon and any special prayers that might be added. By the 1880s, however, the burial service began increasingly to be used, a trend that appears contemporary with the somewhat declining emphasis on the funeral sermon. Second, fully-fledged memorial services began to be held in Scotland, notably on the occasion of the Duke of Albany's funeral, when a service at St Giles's Cathedral in Edinburgh drew a congregation of 3,000.[152]

Following the death of General Gordon at Khartoum in 1885, the

[147] *ILN*, 28 Dec. 1861, p. 676.
[148] *Leeds Mercury*, 17 Dec. 1861.
[149] Ibid., 24 Dec. 1861; *Leeds Intelligencer*, 28 Dec. 1861.
[150] Newspaper cutting in BL (1878.d.12).
[151] *Scotsman*, 14 Dec. 1861.
[152] *The Times*, 7 April 1884.

country experienced a need to focus collective emotion without having a body available for burial. Subsequent events well illustrate the potential sensitivities of the Church's position on such occasions. An approach was made to the Archbishop of Canterbury, Edward White Benson, by a committee of ladies, asking him to arrange for memorial services to be held at Westminster Abbey and St Paul's, including the psalms, lessons and prayers from the burial service. Benson was troubled both by the liturgical and theological issues raised, and by anxiety that the services should not appear to be political in character. He therefore attempted to consult both the Prime Minister (Gladstone) and the Queen, but was advised by their respective private secretaries that the decision was for him (the Archbishop) alone.[153] Accordingly Benson went ahead and circularized the bishops announcing the services in London and referring to public pressure for similar services in provincial cathedrals and 'possibly other Churches'.[154] Despite her own distress at Gordon's death, the Queen was 'rather surprised': she recalled ecclesiastical criticism of her Frogmore services, and was concerned that the Church itself should avoid any appearance of offering prayers for the dead on this occasion. Benson himself, however, rationalized the services as 'a simple devotional and national expression of the prayerful hearts of people for the army in danger, and for the remembrance of the fallen, just as if they could have been buried here.'[155] This interpretation appears to have been generally accepted. Certainly in the eyes of *The Times*, in the services held on 13 March 1885, the Church was doing no more than its duty in buildings interwoven with the history of the country, which had a national status uncompromised by the strength of Nonconformity. The lead of Westminster Abbey and St Paul's was followed in numerous cathedrals, including Canterbury which had an 'overflowing' congregation, Durham, which was 'crowded in every part', Bangor, where many Nonconformist ministers attended, and Manchester, where several hundred people overflowed into the churchyard.[156]

During the subsequent quarter of a century support for widespread parallel memorial services reached a peak. Archbishop Benson had in 1885 given an unprecedented official legitimacy to such observance and he and his successors became concerned that it should be properly regulated, at a period of ongoing tension over ritualistic innovations. When the Duke of Clarence died in 1892, Benson chanced to be out of the country, but the Archbishop of York (Maclagan), took it upon himself to issue special

[153] DavP 4, fo. 42, Benson to Davidson, 6 March 1885.
[154] DavP 4, fo. 31, circular from Benson to the bishops, 4 March 1885.
[155] DavP 4, fo. 42, Benson to Davidson, 6 March 1885; fo. 45, Ponsonby to Davidson, 6 March 1885.
[156] *The Times*, 14 March 1885.

prayers for memorial services.[157] The initiative was a personal one, but on the death of Victoria in 1901, there was a hurried scramble to issue forms of service with proper official sanction. Diocesan bishops and parochial clergy deluged Lambeth Palace with telegrams asking for guidance.[158] Archbishop Frederick Temple responded a little slowly, being hampered by the need to seek approval from the King at Osborne, who took 'a considerable interest in the subject'. In his letter submitting the proofs to the sovereign, Temple clearly indicated the pressure he was under and the pastoral basis of his response:

> The demands for such services is very widespread and it seems well to meet the wishes of the people in such a matter ... The Archbis of C. thinks that if such forms are issued by Order in Council it would be a great comfort to the mass of your Majesty's people to have such an opportunity of expressing before God the deep affection and admiration with which they regard the good and great Sovereign whom they have just lost.[159]

Two forms of service were issued. One simply prescribed the use of the Prayer Book liturgy of the litany and the burial service, with two concluding special prayers. The other drew material from the burial service and from Morning Prayer, with special versicles, responses and prayers. It suggested Goss's anthem 'And the King said', or 'some other suitable alternative', and the hymn 'O God our help in ages past'. The services were to be used 'either on the Day of the Funeral, or on the most convenient Day within the Octave'.[160] They were generally accepted, but it was probably inevitable that they should be criticized from both sides of the ritualistic divide. On the one hand, Protestant-minded clergy disliked the merest hint of prayer for the dead, which Temple defended as not differing from the language of the Prayer Book communion and burial services.[161] On the other hand, it was reported that 'many of her late Majesty's subjects' felt that there had been something lacking in the official proceedings', and some Anglo-Catholic churches sang requiems.[162] When Edward VII died nine years later the official format responded to this pressure by offering a third option of a communion service with a special collect and readings, but as in 1901 some

[157] *Yorkshire Post*, 18 Jan. 1892.
[158] LPL, Frederick Temple Papers 48, fos. 83–126, *passim*.
[159] Ibid., fo. 146, Temple to the King, 28 Jan. 1901.
[160] *Special Forms of Service in Commemoration of Her Late Majesty Queen Victoria* (1901).
[161] LPL, Temple Papers 48, fos. 183–4, F. Courtenay Burrough to Temple, 4 Feb. 1901; fos. 185–5, Thomas Houghton to Temple, 8 Feb. 1901 (with draft reply).
[162] DavP 506, fos. 78–88, requiem at St Matthew's Westminster; *South Wales Daily News*, 4 Feb. 1901, report on requiem at St Mary's, Cardiff. The latter church had also held a requiem for Clarence in 1892 (*South Wales Daily News*, 21 Jan. 1892).

clergy developed their own more overtly Catholic variants.[163] For example, at St Bartholomew's, Brighton, a 'solemn requiem' was held at the time of the funeral, containing an explicit prayer for the soul of the dead King.[164]

Outside England, there was a similar concern that the Established Churches should both lead and regulate observance. In 1901 the Bishop of St David's (Owen), a leading campaigner against disestablishment, urged Temple to provide a Welsh translation of the form of service. He confessed himself 'not sure as to precedents', but expected even the details would be 'watched with interest by Welsh-speaking church people'.[165] A Welsh text was hurriedly provided, but in 1910 the poor quality of the translation was to be a source of complaint.[166] Meanwhile the Church of Scotland now felt able positively to encourage observance. On the day after Victoria's death, the Moderator of the General Assembly, Norman MacLeod, issued a letter noting that he had already been asked for suggestions. He was sure that Sunday worship in every church would be a 'memorial service', and indicated that it would be appropriate as far as possible for further solemn services to be held in all churches on the day of the funeral. He urged every minister 'so to guide the thoughts and emotions of his people that the grief of these dark days may result in lasting benefit to this country'.[167] The Commission of the General Assembly subsequently endorsed the Moderator's lead.[168] On the death of Edward VII the then Moderator went a step further and sent a circular to all ministers 'respectfully suggesting' that they should hold memorial services at a convenient time, preferably at 1 p.m., the time of the funeral at Windsor.[169]

The ecclesiastical authorities were ready to support properly regulated memorial services because they were aware of their importance as a point of contact with larger than usual congregations. Such events were also significant in both stimulating and reflecting a trend towards stronger interdenominational co-operation and fellowship. In this respect the most pivotal event appears to have been the death of Gladstone in 1898, given the extensive religious as well as political associations that had become focused on the 'Grand Old Man'. Some genuinely interdenominational

---

[163] *Special Forms of Service in Commemoration of His Late Majesty King Edward VII* (1910).

[164] *St. Bartholomew's Church, Brighton. On the Occasion of the Funeral of His Late Most Gracious Majesty Edward VII, May 20th 1910. Solemn Requiem at 11.*

[165] LPL, Temple Papers 48, fos. 156–7, Owen to Temple, 28 Jan. 1901; P. M. H. Bell, *Disestablishment in Ireland and Wales* (1969), 263.

[166] LPL, Temple Papers 48, fo. 155, Eyre and Spottiswoode to Ridge, 30 Jan. 1901; *Cardiff and Merthyr Guardian*, 20 May 1910.

[167] *Scotsman*, 24 Jan. 1901.

[168] Ibid., 31 Jan. 1901.

[169] Ibid., 17 May 1901.

services were arranged, for example in Bradford and Batley.[170] In Leeds this proved impossible when the Vicar refused to allow Nonconformists to take any active part in the service in the parish church, and rejected a proposal from the deputation of Nonconformist ministers that a joint service should be held on neutral ground, such as the town hall. Nevertheless Nonconformist ministers were invited to join the congregation at the parish church, while their denominations joined together in a simultaneous joint service at the Brunswick (Methodist) Chapel.[171] In Exeter, however, a sourer note was struck when Nonconformist ministers were left to apply alongside members of the general public for tickets to the memorial service in the cathedral.[172] In Edinburgh the Free Church General Assembly was in session at the time of Gladstone's funeral, and seriously considered taking part in the Church of Scotland service in St Giles's. However, while stressing that they 'had no wish to separate themselves from other denominations in the matter', they decided, for practical reasons including awareness of the risk of overcrowding, to hold their own special service.[173]

The precedents thus set were developed on Victoria's death three years later. The president of the National Council of the Evangelical Free Churches wrote to Archbishop Temple proposing a joint service 'to illustrate the essential unity of Christians; as well as express a National sentiment'. Temple, however, stood by historic Anglican pre-eminence and declined to pursue the suggestion. He argued that the printed forms of service had been issued by authority of the nation, and expressed the hope that the Free Churches would be able to use these, and hence draw Christians together in a spirit of common observance.[174] Such official insistence that any formal co-operation should be on Anglican terms appears to have been replicated at local level, thus normally preventing Nonconformist participation (but not attendance) in Anglican services. Nevertheless there were reportedly cases in which clergy allowed a local Free Church minister to read the lesson or allowed church and chapel choirs to be combined for the occasion.[175] Certainly it was possible to hold united services on neutral ground, as in the 'memorial meeting' at Ipswich Public Hall on the evening

---

[170] *Leeds Mercury*, 26 May 1898.

[171] Ibid.; *Yorkshire Post*, 25, 28, 30 May 1898.

[172] *Western Times*, 30 May 1898.

[173] *Scotsman*, 28 May 1898.

[174] LPL, Temple Papers 48, fo. 152, Charles W. Kelly to Temple, 29 Jan. 1901 (with draft reply).

[175] DavP 326, fos. 79–80, R. N. F. Phillips to Davidson, 13 May 1910. Phillips, Vicar of Emmanuel, South Croydon, in seeking Davidson's sanction for such an arrangement in 1910, claimed that it had been done in many cases at Queen Victoria's funeral.

before the funeral, addressed by both the Mayor and the Anglican Rural
Dean. T. M. Morris, a former President of the Baptist Union, also spoke
at the gathering. He characterized it as a drawing together in the face of a
common loss, and hoped 'that Christian and God-fearing people would
cultivate a closer union in the future than have ever been accounted possible
in the past'.[176] Such a service, including active participation from Anglicans
as well as Nonconformists, appears still to have been somewhat ahead of
its time, but interdenominational services bringing all the Free Churches
together were widespread. In Edinburgh, meanwhile, the progress of
Presbyterian reunion was symbolized by the delivery of the opening
prayer at the memorial service at St Giles's by Robert Rainy, Moderator of
the General Assembly of the recently formed United Free Church [UFC].[177]

A similar pattern recurred in observance of the funeral of Edward VII.
In many English and Welsh towns Nonconformists gathered for large
united services, often in addition to services in their own chapels.[178] Archbishop Davidson, judging the circumstances 'altogether exceptional', now
gave his sanction to limited Nonconformist participation in Anglican
services. He thought such an arrangement was to be welcomed if it did
not offend local sensibilities, on an occasion 'when the national sorrow
draws Christian men together in an exceptional way'.[179] Newspaper reports
suggest that the implementation of this policy was still patchy, although the
presence of Free Church representatives in Anglican congregations was
often noted. The non-denominational Sunday School Union issued its own
form of service for use on the following Sunday, with a prayer which made
explicit aspirations for national religious harmony and spiritual regeneration:
'Do Thou sanctify this our sorrow to all throughout our land; turn the
hearts of all men to Thyself; and may we henceforth and ever abide in Thy
fear and love. Especially may we, the youth of this nation, grow up in the
knowledge of our Lord and Saviour Jesus Christ.'[180] In Scotland, interdenominational co-operation took a further step forward: the Church of
Scotland Moderator suggested that local services should be 'in union with
the congregations of other churches where that is thought possible and
advisable'.[181] At St Giles's, Edinburgh, not only did the UFC Moderator

---

[176] *The Proclamation of King Edward VII: An Account of the Ceremony at Ipswich on the XXV January MDCCCCI.*
[177] *Scotsman*, 4 Feb. 1901.
[178] See for example *Western Mail*, 21 May 1910; *Western Times*, 21 May 1910; *Yorkshire Post*, 21 May 1910.
[179] DavP 326, fo. 88, Memorandum by Davidson, 14 May 1910.
[180] *Sunday School Union: Form of Memorial Service, May 22nd 1910.*
[181] *Scotsman*, 17 May 1910.

again take part, but Episcopal clergy also joined in the procession wearing their vestments.[182]

Although steps towards genuinely interdenominational services were somewhat halting ones, the religious consensus behind local observance of national bereavements was by 1910 close to universal. Jews, like Nonconformists, were eager to demonstrate their sympathetic patriotism on such occasions. As Victoria's funeral chanced to take place on the Sabbath, synagogue services would have been held anyway, but these assumed a memorial character.[183] Edward VII's funeral was on a Friday, but special services were held, for example in Cardiff, where the rabbi addressed his congregation both as 'broken-hearted Jews and Jewesses' and as 'English [sic] men and women'. He stressed that they shared in the grief of the rest of the British people, while they rejoiced in the freedom and tolerance accorded to their co-religionists.[184]

Roman Catholics, although relatively very slow to identify with national grief by holding their own services, eventually followed the same pattern. In 1892 Canon Hobson, delivering his Sunday sermon at the Church of the Sacred Heart in Exeter, expressed sympathy with the royal family. He struck a discordant note, however, in comparing the manner of Clarence's death unfavourably with that of Cardinal Manning and urging his congregation 'to thank God that they were out of one church and into the other'.[185] Even in 1901, Roman Catholic observance appears to have been patchy and hesitant. Cardinal Vaughan, evidently anxious to pre-empt charges of disloyalty, issued a pastoral letter stating that 'none will mourn more sincerely than Catholics' for the Queen's death, and recalling how most of their grievances had been removed during her reign. He explained, however, that it was not proper for the Catholic Church to hold requiems for a non-Catholic and urged Catholics to join 'in the purely social and civil mourning'. The only recognition of the death in public worship was to be the addition of the collect *Deus, Refugium nostrum* at Mass.[186] In the Catholic Cathedral in Edinburgh a 'short memorial service' for Queen Victoria was tagged on to the liturgy for Candlemas Day and attracted merely 'a fairly numerous congregation'.[187] In 1910, by contrast, there was a 'full and imposing' High Mass presided over by the Archbishop of St Andrews and Edinburgh, with a crowded church and 'many of the congre-

---

[182] *Scotsman*, 21 May 1910.
[183] *South Wales Daily News*, 4 Feb. 1901; *Scotsman*, 4 Feb. 1901.
[184] *Western Mail*, 21 May 1910.
[185] *Western Times*, 18 Jan. 1892.
[186] *The Times*, 26 Jan. 1901.
[187] *Scotsman*, 4 Feb. 1901.

gation having to kneel in the aisles'.[188] At Westminster, Cardinal Bourne directed his clergy to recite the Litany of the Holy Name of Jesus at Mass or Benediction, to exhibit the Blessed Sacrament and invite prayers for the Empire and its rulers. He subsequently presided at a crowded memorial service, using the liturgy of Benediction.[189] A correspondent of the *Tablet* urged Catholics to take the opportunity to combine the public profession of their faith with demonstrations of national loyalty, thus gaining the goodwill of their compatriots.[190]

A further trend apparent from the 1890s was a somewhat patchy endeavour to take religious memorialization outside the confines of church buildings and thereby to achieve a point of contact with the unchurched working class. Gladstone's status as a popular hero gave a particular stimulus to such attempts in 1898. For example, in Edinburgh on the Sunday following Gladstone's death there was an overflowing crowd at Carubbers Close Mission and the memorial service held under the auspices of the West End Methodist Mission packed the United Presbyterian Synod Hall.[191] On the day of the funeral itself an open-air service drew a crowd estimated at 10,000.[192] Successful services in mission halls were again to be a feature of mourning in Edinburgh in 1901.[193] Meanwhile the Salvation Army was also marking major funerals with street processions and open air services.[194]

It was apparent that for many, whether in or out of church, music and, above all, the communal singing of hymns constituted a key focus for the expression of religiously orientated feelings of collective grief. Memorial concerts of 'sacred music' were popular occasions, providing an ecclesiastically neutral setting. They may well have drawn in some people who did not attend church services. The following account of a 'memorial musical service' at Leeds Town Hall on the afternoon of the Duke of Clarence's funeral gives a sense of the atmosphere on one such occasion:

> The people joined fervently and with remarkable effect in the four hymns which Dr. Spark [the Borough Organist] had included in his programme— 'Brief life is here our portion', 'Abide with me', 'A few more years shall roll' and 'Great God, what do I see and hear?' With only such lead as was afforded by the organ the people sang the hymns with a degree of precision which was only equalled by their extreme heartiness.[195]

---

[188] *Scotsman*, 21 May 1910.
[189] *The Times*, 9, 21 May 1910.
[190] *Tablet*, 14 May 1910, p. 775.
[191] *Scotsman*, 23 May 1898.
[192] *Scotsman*, 30 May 1898.
[193] *Scotsman*, 4 Feb. 1901.
[194] *Western Times*, 4 Feb. 1901; *Scotsman*, 21 May 1910.
[195] *Yorkshire Post*, 21 Jan. 1892.

The four hymns sung on this occasion were all repeated and popular choices. Other frequent selections were 'O God our help in ages past', 'When our heads our bowed with woe' and 'Nearer my God to thee'. The content of these hymns provides a clue to the nature of the appeal of such occasions: they emphasized the transience of human life and the reality of suffering and loss, alongside the expectation of hope, peace and union with God beyond the grave. Except in Martin Luther's apocalyptic 'Great God, what do I see and hear?', the less comforting judgmental side of traditional Christian teaching received little attention. Although the content of the hymns spoke of personal faith and encounter with death, the context in which they were sung asserted the collectivity of the bereaved national community.

Local and national newspapers gave consistent testimony to the large crowds drawn to memorial services. A few examples drawn from different towns and dates will provide initial illustration of a point that will be further developed in the next chapter. On the day of the Duke of Clarence's funeral St Giles's Cathedral in Edinburgh was 'besieged'. Many who wished to attend the service were disappointed and a large crowd remained around the door. At St Mary's Episcopal Cathedral a congregation estimated at over 3,000 occupied every inch of standing room.[196] In Cardiff on the Sunday following Queen Victoria's death 'the attendance at places of worship, notwithstanding the gale that raged, was far greater than the average'.[197] On the day of her funeral St John's Church was filled to capacity while the police struggled to keep the roadway outside clear from the crowd who could not get in. At Llandaff Cathedral, 'every available space was occupied large numbers standing in the aisles and in front of the rails of the Communion table'. The Free Church service at the Park Hall could have been filled 'half-a-dozen times over' with the crowd outside.[198] In Leeds on the same day there were full services at many places of worship, despite a tram-drivers' strike and thoroughly inclement weather.[199] For Edward VII's memorial service, Exeter Cathedral received 20,000 applications for 4,000 seats, and attempted to meet the demand by holding a second service in the evening. A 'reverent' and 'orderly' crowd gathered outside.[200] Even packed churches did not of course equate with universal participation in religious observance, and one might surmise that many of the working classes especially did not do more than join crowds in the streets at most. Nevertheless, churches and religious services served in the 1890s and 1900s

[196] *Scotsman*, 21 Jan. 1892.
[197] *Cardiff Times*, 2 Feb. 1901.
[198] *South Wales Daily News*, 4 Feb. 1901.
[199] *Leeds Mercury*, 4 Feb. 1901.
[200] *Western Times*, 20, 21 May 1910.

as the pre-eminent foci for national mourning, and drew in congregations that extended far beyond their regular Sunday attendance.

The religious dimensions of national response to death reflected wider theological and liturgical changes. At the same time, however, the churches became increasingly responsive to strong currents in the popular mood. The Church of England led the way in asserting its own national role and seeking to meet and build upon perceived pastoral needs. In so doing it demonstrated an increasing liturgical flexibility. Other churches were not far behind, but in general saw themselves as complementing Anglican services rather than competing with them. Genuinely interdenominational services were not yet possible, except in Scotland. Nevertheless the shared expression of communal grief was a notable stimulus to a more consensual spirit in which the Established Churches were seen as legitimate leaders of a process of commemoration with which the great majority of Christian and Jewish congregations came to associate themselves. The indications, moreover, are that many of those normally on the fringes of organized religion found the combination of patriotism, a sense of occasion, and emotional hymn-singing, a powerful magnet drawing them to relatively unaccustomed participation in public worship. The impact of such occasions needs to be taken into account in any overall assessment of the religiosity of late Victorian and Edwardian Britain.

# 4

# *Death and the City:* Commemoration, Identity and Religiosity

> We have our divisions—only too many of them in this great centre
> of industrial life ... but yesterday every sound not only of strife, but of
> difference was hushed ... There are sublime moments in which there
> vibrates through a great community the chord of admiration for a nature
> of noble quality—moments in which men realize their common possibilities
> for good, and are touched in common by an inspiration to self-sacrificing
> endeavour.[1]

The reflections of the *Leeds Mercury* on the funeral of its own proprietor
and former editor, the leading Nonconformist and erstwhile Liberal MP
for Leeds, Sir Edward Baines, may well have contained an element of
hyperbole, but they nevertheless provide a suggestive text. Both in the
funerals and memorials of their own most distinguished and prominent
members, and in the commemoration of national figures, the towns and
cities of Victorian and Edwardian Britain more or less consciously sought
to assert their essential unity and status as communities. Such concerns
mingled with often sincere expressions of public grief to produce very
extensive local observance at times of prominent bereavements. A comprehensive examination of this phenomenon would be an impossible task, but
in the endeavour to explore some of its dimensions and significance, this
chapter adopts a case-study approach, examining five towns and cities in
different parts of the United Kingdom: Exeter, Leeds, Cardiff, Edinburgh
and Dublin. The choice of examples has been made with a view to exploring
not only civic life, but also regional and national similarities and variations
in the official and popular response to major deaths. The selection also
provides an appropriate context in which to discuss deaths and funerals
that had a much wider significance in relation to Scottish and Irish history

---

[1] *Leeds Mercury*, 7 March 1890.

respectively, those of Thomas Chalmers in Edinburgh in 1847 and of Daniel O'Connell and Charles Stewart Parnell in Dublin in 1847 and 1891 respectively.

In the previous chapter there has already been discussion of such local observance in the context of an examination of the role of organized Christianity in national mourning. In what follows the conceptual field of vision will be widened to consider interaction between official Christianity and the quasi-religion of civic consciousness. The distinction between these two categories is analogous to that made by Robert Bocock between *religious* ritual, involving some sense of contact with the transcendent; and *civic* ritual, which merely affirms group consciousness. Bocock, criticizing Durkheim, sees the analytical distinction as crucial, but recognizes that empirically many rituals combine the two.[2] Such overlap and association is inherent to the material to be surveyed in this chapter, which ranges from explicitly mainstream religious activities as such church services, to primarily secular ones such as the erection of statues. In examining such a spectrum of events in response to prominent deaths, it is intended to illuminate the role of religion in Victorian and Edwardian cities from a fresh perspective.

## Exeter

At the time of the death of the Duke of Wellington, Exeter was a city of some 33,000 people, a relatively stable community with a slow rate of population growth: in 1901 numbers had increased only to 47,000. The shift of the textile trade from the west country to the north had shattered its previous economic importance, but as an episcopal see and the county town of Devon it was still a place of considerable consequence and even greater pretensions. Socially it was very diverse, graced by county society and prosperous middle-class suburbs, but also having grim and crowded slums on the lower ground close to the river Exe. The cholera epidemic in 1832 and municipal reform in 1835 served as spurs to some improvement during the 1840s, but even in the 1860s the city was still a smelly place with over-crowded working-class districts. Problems of destitution and unemployment were reflected in bread riots in 1847, 1854 and 1867. Politically the council was dominated by Conservatives, but with a strong Nonconformist and Liberal minority. The latter gained control for short periods in the late 1830s and early 1880s and for seven years from 1900. In general though, 'the tone of the city, what is called its respectability, is

---

[2] R. Bocock, *Ritual in Industrial Society: A Sociological Analysis of Ritualism in Modern England* (London, 1974), 60–62.

decidedly Tory'.[3] The 1851 Census of Religious Worship showed total congregations in the Exeter registration district amounting to 84.5% of population compared to the national average of 60.8%. Of these attendances 64.7% were Anglican, whereas the national average was 48.6%.[4] It was thus comparatively a highly religiously observant and Anglican district, although the authoritarian high-churchmanship of the bishop, Henry Phillpotts, had contributed to it becoming a battleground for conflict within the Church of England over allegedly Tractarian innovations, most notably in the surplice riots of 1845.[5]

Initial reaction to Wellington's death was muted. Church bells were tolled and it was claimed that the event produced a 'profound' public feeling, but little further specific action was forthcoming for some time.[6] Indeed, it was not until the very week of the Duke's state funeral that any steps were taken to arrange a parallel commemoration in Exeter. On Monday 15 November a committee of the council met in response to a requisition, recommended the closing of shops on the Thursday, and announced that there would be a procession through the streets to the cathedral. The arrangements on the Thursday bore the marks of haste: one of the military detachments was only given a few hours' notice that their presence was required.[7] The hurried nature of the arrangements was all the more striking in view of the long interval between the Duke's death and his funeral: it therefore seems likely that the local commemorations were inspired primarily by last-minute public pressure and a desire to emulate other towns.

Nonetheless the commemoration in Exeter was an imposing spectacle. The procession gathered at the Royal Subscription Rooms at the opposite end of the High Street from the cathedral. It was headed by the military detachments with a band playing the 'Dead March'. These were followed by the Improvement Commissioners, the Corporation of the Poor and a substantial body of 'reputable citizens of all classes', including men of diverse political opinions. The clergy, the police and the Mayor, aldermen

[3] Quoted in R. Newton, *Victorian Exeter 1837–1914* (Leicester, 1968), p. xvii; R. S. Lambert, *The Cobbett of the West: A Study of Thomas Latimer and the Life of Exeter* (1939).

[4] B. Coleman, 'The Nineteenth Century: Nonconformity', in N. Orme (ed.), *Unity and Variety: A History of the Church in Devon and Cornwall* (Exeter, 1991), 137–141. The figures given here for attendances, as for the other cities below, represent total congregations on the census Sunday, among which many individuals might well have been counted twice or even three times at different services. They therefore overstate religious observance when taken in isolation, but are useful for comparative purposes.

[5] J. A. Thurmer, 'The Nineteenth Century: The Church of England', in Orme, *Unity and Variety*, 121–2.

[6] *Western Times*, 18 Sept. 1852; *Exeter and Plymouth Gazette*, 18 Sept. 1852.

[7] *Exeter Flying Post*, 18, 25 Nov. 1852.

and town council brought up the rear. The procession extended about two hundred yards along the High Street, where it passed through a dense crowd. At the cathedral there was a considerable press of spectators and some difficulty was experienced in keeping the way clear for the procession. Only after it had entered the cathedral was the general public admitted, and a numerous crowd milled around in the nave while the choral service was sung in the choir. Following a sermon, the congregation left to the strains of the 'Dead March' on the organ, a procession re-formed, and the Mayor, magistrates and others proceeded to the guildhall while the 'British Grenadiers' was played by a cavalry band. Wine and biscuits were served in the council chamber, toasts were proposed to Wellington's memory and three cheers given for the Queen, the army and the navy. A vote of thanks was given to the Dean and Chapter and, responding to a toast to his own health, the Mayor avowed his own sense of duty in maintaining 'the Church and State of this nation, as the illustrious Duke had always so earnestly done'.[8] Despite the mournful pretext for the event, there was therefore a significant element of celebration in the occasion, especially after the cathedral service had provided a symbolic interment of the Duke. The emphasis was on communal consensus and dignity in the recognition of a great national hero.

The death of Prince Albert nine years later gave rise to more intense feelings, reflected initially in both Anglican and Nonconformist church services on the Sunday when the news was received,[9] and then in a special meeting of the town council followed by a gathering of citizens. An attempt by a Liberal alderman to make political capital out of the occasion by suggesting that the Prince's career would have been more beneficial had he taken John Bright into his confidence, was seen as inappropriate even by the Radical *Western Times*.[10] The emphasis was again on consensus, expressed in the explicitly religious language of an address of condolence to the Queen, which trusted that she would be comforted 'by the Divine Mercy and the universal sorrow of the Nation'.[11] Again the centrepiece of local mourning was a procession to the cathedral on the day of the funeral in which 'men of all sects and parties' joined, and which was watched by a crowd 'of people of all grades, down to the lowest'. An unfortunate incident revealed, however, some limitations to the professed harmony in grief: some of the onlookers had been admitted to the cathedral and, when the procession

[8] *Exeter Flying Post*, 25 Nov. 1852; *Exeter and Plymouth Gazette*, 20 Nov. 1852; *Western Times*, 20 Nov. 1852.
[9] *Western Times*, 21 Dec. 1861.
[10] Ibid., 28 Dec. 1861.
[11] Devon Record Office, Minute Book of the Exeter Chamber (Council) [MEC] B2/35, 21 Dec. 1861.

arrived, it was found that there was not sufficient space in the building for all the worthy participants. The *Western Times* described the scene:

> Gentlemen felt that they had been broken faith with; that they had been done in a most shameful manner, part of the rabble had been allowed to enter the Cathedral to their exclusion; and the other part had been left outside to laugh at their disappointment and augment their chagrin. They had gone, as they understood at the wish of the Mayor, to give form and presence to the gathering, and they found themselves now the victims of an inconsiderate arrangement.[12]

It can be inferred that in the context of the insecurity stirred by national bereavement, such an inversion of the normal social order was seen as doubly offensive.

Civic pride in local distinctiveness was closely bound up with the process of commemoration. Exeter was concerned on such occasions to express its sense of loyalty to the wider national whole, but such identification had its limits: initial enthusiasm for erecting a statue to Wellington appears quickly to have dissipated, and when a few years later the corporation accepted the gift of an equestrian portrait of the Duke for the guildhall, it offended the donor by hanging it in a passageway rather than giving it a prominent place in the main hall.[13] Meanwhile, some Waterloo cannon shipped to Exeter and intended for the Wellington monument in Somerset, were left to languish on the quay for many decades.[14] By contrast, however, considerable interest and pride had been focused in 1861 on the erection of a statue to the local landowner, politician and philanthropist, Sir Thomas Dyke Acland.[15] Following Prince Albert's death, interest in a permanent commemoration was channelled not, as in many cities, into the erection of a outdoor statue, but rather to the building of a tangible civic improvement, the Royal Albert Memorial Museum, which had already been under active consideration before December 1861.[16] After Queen Victoria's death, funds were similarly directed to the development of the Royal Albert Memorial College, and the Lord Mayor of London was informed that Exeter therefore was not in a position to assist the national appeal for a metropolitan memorial 'to any material extent'.[17] No statues to figures without strong local associations were erected on the streets of Exeter

[12] 28 Dec. 1861.

[13] MEC B2/35, 14 Dec. 1859, 13 Feb. 1861; B2/36, 9 July 1862.

[14] MEC B3/41, 10 Dec. 1890.

[15] *Exeter Flying Post*, 23 Oct. 1861; *Western Times*, 26 Oct. 1861.

[16] G. T. Donisthorpe, *An Account of the Origin and Progress of the Devon and Exeter Albert Memorial Museum* (Exeter, 1868), 7, 9, 12; E. Darby and N. Smith, *The Cult of the Prince Consort* (New Haven, Conn. & London, 1983), 85–6.

[17] MEC B3/43, 13 March 1901; Newton, *Victorian Exeter*, 233–4.

during this period: it was as if a city proud of its motto *semper fidelis* felt that its loyalty was sufficiently self-evident not to require further symbolic expression.

Indeed for a generation after 1861 little further occasion was found for public observance of major deaths. Responses to the deaths of Palmerston in 1865 and Disraeli in 1881 were muted, with some shuttering of shops, but no recorded processions or special church services. The *Western Times* characterized the national response to Disraeli's death as a 'factitious expression of woe', worked up by the Tories for political purposes. The council passed a resolution of regret at his death, but several members abstained on the vote.[18] In 1885 Exeter Cathedral stood aloof from the wave of memorial services held in cathedrals across the country for General Gordon: according to the *Exeter Flying Post*, 'the Dean slumbered and the Chapter slept, and all the Prebendaries nodded in their stalls to the usual "Dearly beloved brethren" and the market-day anthem'.[19]

In 1887, however, the sudden death of Stafford Northcote, Earl of Iddesleigh, stirred a strong local response. Iddesleigh had been Disraeli's Chancellor of the Exchequer and leader of the Conservative Party in the Commons, but probably more significant in the eyes of the people of Exeter was the fact that he was a 'Devonshire gentleman who served his Queen right loyally',[20] and a Freeman of their city. His country seat, Pynes, was close at hand. In contrast to 1881, the mood was strongly consensual: the council passed an address of sympathy to the family, stressing the local associations of the deceased, as well as personal qualities that transcended politics.[21] A speaker claiming to represent the working men of Exeter stated that 'Although they differed in many respects from the deceased statesman, yet they all admitted his true nobility of character, his genuineness of purpose, his high-toned morality, and the kindly nature which endeared him to all.'[22] Iddesleigh's funeral took place at the village church of Upton Pyne on 18 January 1887. Large crowds turned out to watch the body being taken from the station on its arrival from London. At the Mayor's instigation there was a simultaneous memorial service in the cathedral, with a civic procession, which in contrast to arrangements in 1852 and 1861 was limited to men with an elective or representative function rather than including all substantial citizens who chose to attend. The service, however, was held in the nave rather than the choir, thus affording a stronger sense of congregational participation than had been the case in the past. It drew large

[18] *Western Times*, 24, 31 Oct. 1865, 28, 29 April 1881.
[19] *Exeter Flying Post*, 18 March 1885.
[20] The Dean of Exeter quoted in *Western Times*, 17 Jan. 1887.
[21] MEC B3/40, 17 Jan. 1887.
[22] *Western Times*, 18 Jan. 1887.

numbers, while many more gathered outside. Meanwhile, despite unpleasant winter weather, a further large crowd made its way out of the city and travelled the four miles to Upton Pyne, often on foot. They lined the road between the country house of the deceased and the church, surrounded the graveyard, and stood patiently and reverently in the rain while the service proceeded. The atmosphere appears to have been a sombre one of genuine mourning.[23]

In contrast to the two decades after 1861, in the 1890s and 1900s national bereavements proved fully weighty enough to stir strong reactions in Exeter. The most salient feature of the aftermath of the deaths of Clarence, Gladstone, Victoria and Edward VII in Exeter was the prominence of official Christian reference and association. The immediate response of many was to go to church. Congregations were reported as 'unusually large' on the Sunday after Clarence's death, and the *Western Times* judged that people devoutly 'sanctified their condolence with the relatives of the Prince, by perfect trust in the power of religion to afford consolation to the soul suffering from bereavement'.[24] When Gladstone died, public expectations of an immediate observance in the cathedral were disappointed,[25] but on Victoria's death the Chapter reacted quickly, holding a special service at noon on the following day (a Wednesday), for which the nave was crowded, despite the short notice.[26] On the following Sunday both Anglican and Nonconformist church services gave focus to mourning, a crowd gathered outside the cathedral before the doors were opened for afternoon service, and a very large congregation also attended in the evening.[27] Church congregations were similarly unusually large on the Sunday after Edward VII's death.[28]

Council addresses of condolence were also suffused with religious language. On Clarence's death they referred to 'God in His Almighty and Infinite Wisdom . . . at whose Decree this has happened' and prayed that 'the Creator of all Men will comfort your Royal Highnesses and assuage your grief as He alone in His Almighty Power can well do'.[29] In relation to Victoria they trusted and prayed 'that the light of God may shine on her for ever', and that 'under Divine guidance and protection' the progress and

[23] *Western Times*, 21 Jan. 1887; RA, VIC/R 42/40, Sir J. McNeill to the Queen, 19 Jan. 1887.
[24] *Western Times*, 18, 19 Jan. 1892.
[25] Ibid., 20, 23 May 1898.
[26] Ibid., 24 Jan. 1901.
[27] Ibid., 28 Jan. 1901.
[28] Ibid., 9 May 1910.
[29] MEC B3/41, 20 Jan. 1892.

development of the Empire might be continued.[30] For Edward VII they offered their 'fervent prayer' that the grief of his successor might 'be relieved by the mercy of Almighty God . . . and that it may be reserved for you under His divine guidance to rule for many years over a peaceful and contented Empire'.[31]

Cathedral and church services also consolidated their place as central features of local observance on funeral days. Civic processions gathered at the guildhall and walked to the cathedral. For Clarence in 1892 the cathedral was filled to 'utmost capacity' and there was some disorder when more attempted to squeeze in.[32] Lessons were evidently learnt, because tickets were issued for Gladstone's memorial service in 1898, hailed as a 'beautiful, . . . solemn and sympathetic' occasion which enabled 'the citizens of Exeter of all classes to join in spirit with those . . . within Westminster Abbey'.[33] For Victoria and for Edward VII demand was such that two services were held.[34] In 1910, moreover, the Dean sought to prevent any tendency for the occasions to become merely an expression of civic and corporate dignity. He indicated that the cathedral would primarily be allocating tickets to private individuals rather than to representatives of organizations. 'It will be far more touching', he wrote, 'to all to see the citizens flocking in twos and threes as individual mourners, and less distracting than to see the formal organised processional demonstrations of different societies, suitable on other occasions, but not on the day when the people are mourning as one for one.'[35] In contrast to the essentially non-participatory observance held for Wellington sixty years before, the service for Edward VII sought to engage the feelings of the whole congregation: in the eyes of the *Western Times* the high point was reached when the four thousand people present joined with 'heartiness and deep meaning' in the singing of 'O God our help in ages past'.[36] Furthermore, for both Victoria and for Edward VII services on the day of the funeral were held in most, if not all, other churches in the city, at which large and fervent congregations were also reported. The combined evening gathering for the Free Churches held at the Mint Wesleyan Chapel in 1901 was repeated in 1910 when it had to be supplemented by an overflow meeting at Bartholomew Street Baptist Church. In 1910 the *Miserere* was sung at the Roman

---

[30] MEC B3/43, 23 Jan. 1901.
[31] MEC B4/47, 7 May 1910.
[32] *Western Times*, 21 Jan. 1892.
[33] Ibid., 30 May 1898.
[34] Ibid., 4 Feb. 1901, 21 May 1910.
[35] Ibid., 12 May 1910.
[36] Ibid., 21 May 1910.

Catholic Church.[37] Meanwhile there was more detailed planning and regulation than in the past. Only a limited number of non-ticket holders were
even admitted to the Cathedral Close. Barriers were erected to keep the
streets clear for the procession, and extra police drafted in from country
districts.[38]

   In Exeter reactions to prominent deaths were refracted through the
prism of a strong sense of local pride, tradition, and distinctiveness. In a
religiously observant and Anglican-dominated city, it seemed natural for
cathedral services to provide the pre-eminent focus for civic mourning,
supplemented as necessary by services in other churches and chapels, which
were emphatically seen as complementary rather than competing events.
The role of organized religion became, if anything, more central and extensive as the period went on, while a growing concern for regulation reflected
anxiety to avoid any disruption of the outward fabric of community solidarity at times of national grief.[39]


## Leeds


On the face of it, Leeds presented a strong contrast with Exeter, in respect
of its social, political and religious life. Not only was it much larger, with a
population in 1851 of 172,270 in the borough, and 101,343 in the main
township, but it was also growing much faster. In 1901 the populations of
borough and township had increased to 428,968 and 177,920 respectively.
It held its position as the fifth largest town in England, whereas Exeter's
relative position declined rapidly.[40] Economically it was at the cutting edge
of industrialization: having established its wealth and employment opportunities on the basis of textile production, it diversified during the Victorian
period, with the development of the clothing and engineering industries.[41]
Its social pyramid had a considerably broader bottom than Exeter's, being
numerically dominated by the working classes, generally inhabiting over-
crowded back-to-back housing. Nevertheless over a fifth of the population
had a middle-class economic status[42] and at the pinnacle of town life were


[37] Ibid., 4 Feb. 1901, 21 May 1910.

[38] Ibid., 21 May 1910.

[39] Robert Newton (*Victorian Exeter*, 319, 323) judged that in 1914 Exeter was 'still Christian
in practice as well as by descent' and characterized it as a 'small relatively homogenous city'.

[40] C. J. Morgan, 'Demographic change, 1771–1911', in D. Fraser (ed.), *A History of Modern
Leeds* (Manchester, 1980), 47–52.

[41] E. J. Connell and M. Ward, 'Industrial Development, 1780–1914' in Fraser, *Modern Leeds*,
156–7.

[42] R. J. Morris, 'Middle-class Culture, 1700–1914' in Fraser, *Modern Leeds*, 200.

a wealthy élite of manufacturers and professional men. Local politics in Leeds were almost a mirror image of those in Exeter, with Liberal and Nonconformist domination for much of the period. There was, however, a strong Tory minority that came close to gaining control of the council in the early 1840s, and retained important influence in subordinate agencies of local government. It eventually was in power from 1895 to 1903 and thereafter remained a major player in a period of instability.[43] In religious observance too there was a very marked contrast: attendances on 30 March 1851 amounted to only 47.4% of the population of the borough, little more than half the proportion in Exeter, and of these only 34.5% were Anglican. Of the remainder much the greatest proportion, 41.7% of the total attendances, were Methodist, with the other significant groups being Independents (7.4%), Baptists (5.6%) and Roman Catholics (6.1%), the last arising from the migration to the town in recent decades of over 10,000 Irish. The Irish Roman Catholic population continued to grow in the 1850s, and in the late Victorian period, Jewish migration from Eastern Europe gave the city another substantial religious minority, amounting to up to 20,000 in the early twentieth century.[44] A further noteworthy difference lay in the physical development of public buildings: whereas Exeter's civic and religious life continued to be centred on its medieval cathedral and guildhall, Leeds Parish Church had been totally rebuilt between 1838 and 1841, and the opening of the town hall in 1858 provided a new secular focus and source of pride and dignity for the community.[45]

Despite such differences of context there was significant common ground with Exeter in local observance of prominent deaths. On Wellington's death, local Liberal opinion, as represented by the *Leeds Mercury*, showed itself quite prepared to bury the political hatchet in the cause of honouring a man who had accepted the changes he had opposed and had always taken 'a rigid view of his duty to his sovereign and the country'.[46] The day of Wellington's funeral was kept as a local holiday and there was a civic procession from the courthouse in Park Row to attend service at the parish church. It was watched by a crowd estimated by the *Leeds Mercury* at between 20,000 and 30,000. The mood was respectful and the police restrained, although sheer press of numbers presented them with some difficulties. The parish church and its precincts were densely crowded and many would-be attenders were unable to get into the service. W. F. Hook

---

[43] D. Fraser, 'Politics and Society in the Nineteenth Century' in Fraser, *Modern Leeds*, 282–5; T. Woodhouse, 'The Working Class', in Fraser, *Modern Leeds*, 363.

[44] B. I. Coleman, *The Church of England in the Mid-Nineteenth Century* (1980), 41; Morgan, 'Demographic Change', 61–2.

[45] A. Briggs, *Victorian Cities* (1963), 139–83.

[46] *Leeds Mercury*, 18 Sept. 1852.

portrayed the ceremonial not only as patriotic, but also as socially cohesive, on the grounds that the expenditure assisted the poor and gave them work. 'It may be necessary', he said, 'to exhort the wealthy to give, but it is even more necessary to entreat them to spend.' As in Exeter, a mood of not wholly subdued festivity was evident in the adjournment of the council and the military officers at the end of the proceedings for a sumptuous lunch at Fleischmann's Scarborough Hotel.[47]

A similar ritual was observed on the day of Prince Albert's funeral. If anything, the crowds on the streets were larger, and attendance at the parish church by the town council, forty-nine out of sixty-four members, was even more impressive. The Vicar, James Atlay, followed the example of his predecessor in preaching a sermon sensitive to the Liberal and Noncon-formist element in the congregation. In response Edward Baines expressed his 'admiration of the very proper and judicious discourse' they had heard. Indeed the mood appears to have been rather more harmonious than in Exeter where the inadvertent exclusion of some of the worthy citizenry from the cathedral service had marred the occasion. Meanwhile, however, the widespread holding of well-attended services in Methodist and other Nonconformist chapels in Leeds was a contrast with Exeter, illustrating the manner in which Nonconformity had already assumed the status of a quasi-co-establishment in local life. Summing up the day's proceedings, the *Mercury* referred to 'the strong religious feeling which pervaded all ranks, sects and parties. It was a solemn occasion solemnly observed, and the religious character of the proceedings gave to them an importance and value which it would have been impossible to secure in any other way.' [48] That religious tone was also strongly apparent in the town council's address of sympathy to the Queen which ended by praying 'above all, that your Majesty may have Divine strength and consolation'.[49]

During the subsequent three decades Leeds was perceptibly more assiduous than Exeter in memorial observance and commemoration. Indeed the movement that resulted in the building of the town hall had been initially linked to the memory of Sir Robert Peel, following his death in 1850.[50] Subsequently, whereas Tory Exeter had looked the gifthorse of Wellington's equestrian portrait in the mouth, Liberal Leeds erected a statue to him in 1858.[51] Following Albert's death, the Mayor and Vicar found common cause in leading a committee responsible for providing a memorial

---

[47] *Leeds Intelligencer*, 20 Nov. 1852; *Leeds Mercury*, 20 Nov. 1852.

[48] *Leeds Mercury*, 24 Dec. 1861; *Leeds Intelligencer*, 28 Dec. 1861.

[49] Leeds City Archives [LCA], File Case 32.

[50] Briggs, *Victorian Cities*, 156.

[51] This is the date carved on the pedestal of the statue (by Marochetti), now on Woodhouse Moor.

to him, which resulted in 1865 in a marble statue in the vestibule of the town hall.[52] Palmerston's death, also in 1865, was marked by a council resolution of sympathy, tolling of bells at the town hall and at churches, and an almost complete suspension of business at the time of the funeral.[53] On Disraeli's death in 1881, Leeds Liberals showed greater magnanimity than their Exeter counterparts: the Radical Nonconformist Mayor had the town hall bell tolled and the flag flown at half-mast, while the *Mercury*, although not denying what it saw as 'grave public errors', praised the deceased's 'eminent private virtues and brilliant intellectual gifts'.[54] Although there was no civic procession, a number of Leeds churches held special services on the afternoon of the funeral and the normal weekday services at the parish church were adapted to the occasion and drew abnormally large congregations. There was also a memorial organ recital at the town hall in the evening, which was crammed with more than 2,500 people, who sang the hymn 'Brief life is here our portion' with 'intense sympathy'. The borough organist, Dr Spark, composed and played a funeral march of his own for the occasion.[55] Similar organ recitals with hymns and funeral music were to be held at the town hall on the deaths of Prince Leopold (1884), Iddesleigh (1887), Bright (1889), Baines (1890) and Clarence (1892). They evidently served as a significant focus for a non-denominational, but still religious, response to public bereavement.[56]

The death and funeral of Edward Baines, which took place in Leeds in March 1890, can be compared with local events in Exeter on the death of Lord Iddesleigh three years earlier. Baines similarly maintained very strong local ties while achieving national prominence, and his personal worth, piety and substantial contribution to the life of his native town were praised even by political opponents.[57] Baines's funeral on 6 March, however, provides a significant example of public mourning centred not on an Anglican church, but on a Nonconformist building, East Parade Congregational Chapel. Outside the chapel a gathering 'mainly composed of working people' was reported as many times outnumbering the packed congregation within. From there a procession half a mile long continued through streets lined with spectators to Woodhouse Lane Cemetery where

---

[52] LCA, Town Hall Committee Minutes 17 April 1862; J. Darke, *The Monument Guide to England and Wales* (1991), 224.

[53] LCA, Council Minutes 25 Oct. 1865; *Leeds Mercury*, 19, 20, 25, 28 Oct. 1865.

[54] *Yorkshire Post*, 20 April 1881; *Leeds Mercury*, 26 April 1881.

[55] *Leeds Mercury*, 27 April 1881; *Yorkshire Post*, 27 April 1881.

[56] *Leeds Mercury*, 31 March 1884, 19 Jan. 1887, 1 April 1889, 10 March 1890, *Yorkshire Post*, 21 Jan. 1892.

[57] On the role of the 'Bainesocracy' in the civic and religious life of Leeds see C. Binfield, *So Down to Prayers: Studies in English Nonconformity 1780–1920* (1977), 54–100.

it was met by the Mayor and corporation. The *Mercury* saw the funeral procession as symbolic of the significance both of Baines's own educational work and of the civic achievements to which he had contributed:

> The route by which his mortal remains were . . . borne from the sanctuary in which he worshipped to the grave illustrates in a sufficiently striking manner much of the work on which he has been engaged in the England of VICTORIA: on that route lie the School Board Buildings, the Higher Grade Board School, the Mechanics Institute . . . and the Yorkshire College.

Six Anglican clergy, headed by the Vicar of Leeds (Edward Talbot) had joined the procession together with thirty-six Nonconformist ministers.[58] In his sermon at the parish church on the following Sunday Talbot referred to the 'singularly united and genuine feelings of affection and respect' that had been expressed, and praised Baines as a high example of Christian citizenship.[59]

Observance in Leeds of national bereavements in the 1890s and early twentieth century further expressed interlinked concerns to affirm religious harmony and assert civic dignity. The town was given the status of a county borough in 1889, it became a city in 1893, and its chief magistrate was given the status of Lord Mayor in 1897.[60] The laying out of City Square at the turn of century gave physical expression to this enhanced status. Among the statues of men with historic associations with Leeds, both Nonconformity and Anglicanism were represented, in the persons of Joseph Priestley and W. F. Hook.[61] There was an ongoing punctiliousness in ensuring that prominent deaths were marked in a dignified and consistent manner.[62] Civic processions from the town hall to the parish church took place in 1892, 1898, 1901 and 1910, and the town hall bell was tolled on all these occasions. In January 1901 there were two such observances, one on the Sunday after Queen Victoria's death, and the other on the day of her funeral.[63] These processions, unlike their counterparts in Exeter, where the guildhall was only a hundred yards or so from the cathedral, had to travel a distance approaching a mile, traversing the main commercial and business district of the city. Normally the town hall and the parish church were competing focal points for Leeds public life, but on such occasions

---

[58] *Leeds Mercury,* 7 March 1890.

[59] Ibid., 10 March 1890.

[60] *Victoria RI, Queen and Empress. Official Programme and Illustrated Souvenir of the Unveiling of the Queen Victoria Memorial Statue* (Leeds, 1905), 10–11.

[61] Darke, *Monument Guide*, 223–4.

[62] LCA, File Case 32 contains records of local observances on the deaths of prominent members of the royal family, indicating that from the 1890s care was being taken to record precedents and then follow them as closely as possible.

[63] LCA, File Case 32, *passim;* *Yorkshire Post,* 23, 30 May 1898.

they were linked in public spectacles that could be viewed by thousands of spectators in the main streets. Throughout there was a strong emphasis on consensus, expressed in the full range of observance and events marking national bereavements.

News of Queen Victoria's death reached Leeds at seven o'clock in the evening when performances had already started at two theatres. Crowds gradually gathered outside and loudly demanded that the entertainment cease. At the Grand Theatre the police had to prevent people from forcing their way in. The management of both theatres duly complied.[64] There was subsequent uncertainty as to whether all shops should be closed on the day of the funeral, but a firm lead from the Lord Mayor in favour of closure was generally complied with, except in poorer areas where opening was condoned as sparing inconvenience to inhabitants.[65] The *Leeds Mercury* saw the suspension of business as 'a solemn rite' in which everyone felt they must take part. Two discordant notes, however, were struck by publicans who only closed in the middle of the day, and by tram drivers who went on strike, arguing that as the King had declared a day of mourning they should not be required to work.[66] The civic procession on Sunday 27 January was watched by a large and orderly crowd,[67] and that on the funeral day by a 'dense mass' of people, despite unpleasant weather and the transport difficulties. Again the parish church was packed. Similarly crowded services were held in many other Anglican and Nonconformist churches.[68]

Although Leeds already had a statue of Queen Victoria, erected in 1858 in the vestibule of the town hall, it was decided following her death to commission a further monument to her. The link between national grief and civic pride was well illustrated in the 'expectation that it will be one of the finest and largest statues of the Queen, and will take its place in the first rank of the statuary of the Kingdom'. The iconography of the monument, erected by voluntary subscription, linked the arms of Leeds and symbols of its industries to the larger whole represented by emblems of empire and the image of the Queen herself.[69] It was unveiled in 1905 in an impressive ceremony in a prominent location outside the town hall, but after barely thirty years the decline of the kind of civic culture it represented was reflected in a decision in 1937 to move it to a relatively inconspicuous position on Woodhouse Moor.

In the meantime however, the Edwardian era in Leeds found its apothe-

[64] *Yorkshire Post*, 23 Jan. 1901.
[65] Ibid., 31 Jan., 1 Feb. 1901.
[66] *Leeds Mercury*, 4 Feb. 1901.
[67] *Yorkshire Post*, 28 Jan. 1901.
[68] Ibid., 4 Feb. 1901; *Leeds Mercury*, 4 Feb. 1901.
[69] *Queen Victoria Memorial Statue*, 11–13.

osis in impressive and well-regulated mourning for the King. The principal
service in the parish church was now, as in Exeter Cathedral, made an all-
ticket occasion, but it was repeated in the evening. The Lord Mayor and
the Vicar processed together to the church, as they had done in 1901,
accompanied now by representatives of the recently established university,
in front of great crowds of soberly dressed people who rendered the
pavements almost impassable. Many children were present. After the service
military bands led the procession back to the town hall, now playing a
quickstep, a reminder that the service itself was felt to provide a close to
the mournful mood, and that reaffirmation of ongoing normal life was now
considered appropriate. In the meantime dense overflowing congregations
were observed at the other Anglican churches; the Free Churches gathered,
as they had done on Queen Victoria's death, for a united service at Oxford
Place Chapel, but this was complemented by services in numerous other
places of worship both in the city centre and the suburbs. Special masses
were said in the Roman Catholic churches, and there was an overflowing
congregation at St Anne's Cathedral. Jews also joined in the observance:
New Briggate Synagogue in the city centre was packed with a congregation
of over a thousand, with hundreds reportedly unable to get in. The memorial
concert at the town hall was similarly overwhelmed.[70]

When Leeds is compared with Exeter, there is seen to be a striking
similarity in respect of the prominence of official Anglican observance at
the centre of well-supported civic and popular mourning, a resemblance
which is all the more remarkable when one considers the very different
political composition and religiosity of the two cities. The contrasts were
more subtle ones, reflecting the fact that whereas in Exeter the dominant
Anglican tone of local culture could be assumed, the reality of life in Leeds
was much more variegated and divided. The cathedral clergy in Exeter
appear, almost to the end of the nineteenth century, to have taken it for
granted that congregations would come to them, but successive Vicars of
Leeds followed the example of W. F. Hook in recognizing that the parish
church had to be proactive in asserting its role in local life, and also sensitive
to the predominantly Nonconformist loyalties of the Liberal-dominated
muncipality. The corporation, for its part, was fully prepared to collaborate
in rituals that affirmed local solidarity and dignity in the face of national
grief. Nonconformist chapels and the town hall itself provided alternative
points of focus for public mourning, but complemented rather than superseded the Anglican dimension centred on the parish church.

The sheer size of Leeds by the end of nineteenth century renders it
unlikely that all the population could have felt a sense of active participation
in public civic mourning in the way that might well have been possible in

---

[70] *Yorkshire Post*, 21 May 1910.

smaller communities. Even if the newspaper reports of packed churches and crowds amounting to tens of thousands on the streets are taken as accurate, the numbers involved would have represented only a minority of the population of the borough. There were occasional hints of the limits to popular consensus, such as the tram-drivers' strike on the day of Queen Victoria's funeral and complaints at the continuing opening of public houses. Nevertheless, protest by the crowd at theatre-going serves as an indication that any such fissures did not necessarily occur simply on class lines. Although the tram drivers were censured in the press for inconveniencing the public, they themselves claimed respectful motives in not wishing to run their vehicles while the funeral was actually taking place.[71] Moreover, whatever private thoughts and alternative activities might have been, the remarkable harmony of publicly expressed sentiment left little scope for open dissent.

## Cardiff

The development of Cardiff in the Victorian and Edwardian eras presents a further distinctive context. Whereas both Exeter and Leeds were substantial and established towns well before the nineteenth century, in the census of 1801 Cardiff was still only, in effect, a large village, with a population of 1,870. Even in 1851, although its population had increased nearly tenfold in fifty years, it was still a relatively small place with a population of 18,351. By 1901, however, continued vigorous growth combined with an extension of the borough boundaries in 1875, to produce a further massive increase to 164,333, a proportionate rate of expansion in the later nineteenth century that was second only to Middlesbrough among major British towns. Cardiff's growth was founded on its role as the major port and commercial centre serving the South Wales coalfield, with an occupational structure dominated by workers in transport and manufacturing, but also with a substantial prosperous middle-class element.[72] When Victoria came to the throne, it was a small pocket borough strongly under the influence of the second Marquess of Bute (1793–1848), whose development of the docks laid the foundations of its subsequent boom. By the time she died it had become a proud and independent-minded place, recognized as a city in 1907, and increasingly regarded, as least by its own citizens, as the *de facto* capital of Wales. Its own development was thus bound up with the process that Kenneth Morgan has characterized as the 'rebirth of a nation' in the

---

[71] *Leeds Mercury*, 4 Feb. 1901.
[72] M. J. Daunton, *Coal Metropolis: Cardiff 1870–1914* (Leicester, 1977), 1–14, 182.

principality.[73] The town council, which had been a passive and inactive institution in the years of the Bute ascendancy, became in the late 1860s a focus for more active local politics. It was dominated by Liberals for much of the late nineteenth century, although the Conservatives were to gain control between 1904 and 1909.[74] Attendances at religious worship in 1851 amounted to an estimated 56.3% of population, significantly more than in Leeds, but much less than in Exeter. Of these attendances only an estimated 20.5% were Anglican (although the proximity of Llandaff Cathedral, then outside the borough, somewhat strengthened the Anglican presence in the area as a whole) while 14.0% were Roman Catholic, reflecting the large Irish immigration into South Wales in the preceding decade. Nonconformists accounted for 59.2% of attendances, the balance being accounted for by one congregation of Latter Day Saints.[75]

Whereas Exeter found a natural focus in its traditional Anglicanism for civic ritual following prominent deaths, and Leeds used such occasions to express a sense of civic unity and dignity that transcended denominational division, it is much less easy to discern a consistent theme in Cardiff's responses. The town was changing so fast that past precedents were as frequently discarded as followed. Lord Bute's sudden death in March 1848 was a major landmark in the history of the town, which had a sense that it was mourning its own creator. The crowd that turned out to watch the lengthy procession taking the body from the castle to the pier was estimated as being double that present at local observance of the funerals of George IV and William IV. The tone of the proceedings reflected the Tory Anglicanism of which Bute himself had been so influential an exponent, but it was to a significant extent the apotheosis of a religious and political era as well as of an individual.[76]

[73] Ibid., 17–18; J. Davies, *Cardiff and the Marquesses of Bute* (Cardiff, 1981), 143; K. O. Morgan, *Rebirth of a Nation: Wales 1880–1980* (Oxford, 1981), 126–7.

[74] Davies, *Cardiff,* 106–37; Daunton, *Coal Metropolis,* 170–1.

[75] I. G. Jones and D. Williams (eds.), *The Religious Census of 1851: A Calendar of the Returns Relating to Wales,* 2 vols. (Cardiff, 1976, 1981), i. 137–40. This calculation for Cardiff depends on an estimated figure for one of the two Anglican churches (St John's), which failed to make a return of attendance. It has been assumed that attendance there was in the same proportion to seating capacity as at the other Anglican church (St Mary's), but if it was actually lower, then the Nonconformist predominance was even greater than the stated figures suggest. Figures returned to the Welsh Church Commission in 1906 would put total adult church affiliation at that date at 45.4% of population, with Nonconformist Sunday scholars amounting to a further 17.4%. Nonconformists made up 63.8% of the adult total, Anglicans 25.5% and Roman Catholics 10.7%. All these figures should be treated with caution, but are indicative of substantial ongoing Nonconformist predominance.

[76] *Cardiff and Merthyr Guardian,* 25 March, 1 April 1848; Glamorgan Archive Service [GAS], Cardiff Borough Council Minutes [CBCM] B/C 4/2, 3 May 1848.

Shortly before the Duke of Wellington's death, Cardiff had in a hard-fought contest elected as its Liberal MP Walter Coffin, a Unitarian coalmaster and railway proprietor, thus defeating the interest of the Bute family.[77] In this context the question of how to mark the Duke's funeral was a matter of some debate in the town council. Alderman Morgan referred to the precedent of Princess Charlotte's death and proposed a procession to church, but Coffin himself seemed much more uncertain as to the appropriate means of commemoration. John Batchelor, a leading opponent of the Bute influence, opposed the closing of shops on the day of the funeral.[78] The eventual resolution was an open-ended one: 'That some mark of respect should be paid by the Council to the memory of the late Duke of Wellington on the day of his Funeral which was left to the Mayor to carry out in the best manner he should think fit.'[79] The Mayor opted for a strongly Anglican observance, attending St Mary's Church on the morning of the funeral, and 'respectfully' inviting his fellow townsmen to join him in a procession to the other Anglican church, St John's, in the afternoon. The latter event attracted substantial crowds, but the indications are that the form it took expressed something less than the general consensus apparent in Exeter and Leeds.[80]

The people of Cardiff appear initially to have been as profoundly moved by Prince Albert's death as those of other towns: flags were half-masted, minute guns fired and bells tolled. Many were observed to be in tears when the news was communicated by clergy and ministers at the Sunday services on the following day.[81] A correspondent of the *Cardiff Times* suggested that the day of the funeral would be a fitting occasion for an interdenominational service of 'prayer and humiliation'.[82] Such an event did not materialize, but most places of worship held special services or prayer meetings, and there were military processions to Llandaff Cathedral and St John's Church. Significantly, however, the council, although later passing an eloquent address of sympathy to the Queen, does not appear to have participated in any official way in these Anglican services, and the involvement of the military at St John's gave rise to 'many criticisms'.[83] A subsequent attempt to raise money for a local memorial to Albert fell flat, an indication that in Cardiff there was not yet the sense of civic identity associated with

[77] Davies, *Cardiff*, 133–4.
[78] *Cardiff and Merthyr Guardian*, 25 Sept. 1852. On Batchelor see Daunton, *Coal Metropolis*, 169–70.
[79] GAS, CBCM B/C 4/2, 20 Sept. 1852.
[80] *Cardiff and Merthyr Guardian*, 20 Nov. 1852.
[81] Ibid., 21 Dec. 1861.
[82] *Cardiff Times*, 20 Dec. 1861.
[83] Ibid., 27 Dec. 1861; GAS, CBCM B/C 4/3, 30 Dec. 1861.

commemoration that translated immediate grief into a statue in Leeds and in Exeter led to the Prince's name being linked to the new museum.[84]

Indeed in the mid-nineteenth century, Cardiff's response to national mourning failed to manifest the degree of collective self-consciousness already apparent elsewhere in 1852 and 1861. The Liberal *Cardiff Times* did not record any local commemoration at all for Palmerston in 1865. Disraeli's death in 1881 was noted in some Anglican Sunday sermons, and the Tory *Western Mail* claimed that 'even the most fierce Radical' expressed respect for him, but observance on the day of the funeral was limited to half-masted flags and the ringing of a muffled peal at St John's.[85] Llandaff Cathedral and several other Anglican churches held memorial services for General Gordon, attracting large congregations, but no civic recognition.[86]

From the 1890s, however, Cardiff rapidly made up lost ground, in a manner which reflected its own predominant Nonconformity, though articulation of a Welsh identity remained limited. On the day after Clarence's death in 1892 there were a succession of speeches of condolence in the General Purposes Committee of the council and an agreement to invite the people of Cardiff to join in mourning on the day of the funeral. The Mayor though said that they 'had no desire to appear to dictate to the public in the matter'. The *Western Mail* took satisfaction in a perceived unity of Radical and Tory in grief and loyalty to the throne.[87] On the following Sunday funeral sermons were preached at numerous churches and chapels. A special interdenominational service at the Park Hall had a reported attendance of more than 3,000.[88] On the day of the funeral thousands of people were observed on the streets wearing mourning insignia, and a packed memorial service at the recently-enlarged St John's was attended by the Mayor and a large number of the corporation. In his sermon the Vicar, Charles John Thompson, under whose ministry since 1875 the church in Cardiff had enjoyed a notable renaissance, took the opportunity to flatter the corporation.[89] He regretted that the town's growing importance was receiving inadequate recognition and suggested that Clarence (who would have become Prince of Wales had he lived) would have had a life bound up with 'something of the fulness of the future of Cardiff'. On the other hand the limits to the preacher's Welsh identification were very evident

---

[84] *Cardiff Times*, 14, 21 Feb. 1862.

[85] *Western Mail* , 25, 27 April 1881.

[86] *Western Mail*, 16, 17 March 1885.

[87] Ibid., 16 Jan. 1892; Cardiff Central Library [CCL], CBCM 1891–2, pp. 155–6 (15 Jan. 1892).

[88] *Western Mail*, 18 Jan. 1892.

[89] On Thompson and St John's see J. C. Read, *A History of St John's Cardiff and the Churches of the Parish* (Bridgend, 1995).

when he went on to describe the deceased as English to his 'heart's core', which was obviously intended as a compliment.[90] Even in Nonconformist Sunday sermons there was no articulation of a consciously Welsh response to Clarence's death, and copious inclusive references to 'England' were made without any apparent sense of incongruity.[91]

When Gladstone died six years later, the council, on which the parties were then finely balanced, passed a particularly effusive but politically and religiously neutral resolution of regret and sympathy. They noted that he had been 'an Honorary Freeman of this ancient Borough'; praised his 'disinterested public service' and 'broad-minded statesmanship'; and expressed gratitude for his 'noble example of sublime Christian faith and calm resignation in the hour of death'. Whereas in 1892 the corporation's attendance at St John's had appeared to favour the Anglican church, it now adopted an impartial stance, noting with satisfaction that both Anglican and Nonconformist services were to be held and resolving that its own members 'should attend such place of worship as they may desire'.[92] A number of councillors were present at St John's, but the deputy Mayor was among the platform party at a joint Nonconformist memorial service at the Park Hall, which was reportedly broadly representative of all denominations and of 'officialdom, . . . the tradespeople and the masses'.[93]

When news of Queen Victoria's death reached Cardiff and was communicated to the town by the sounding of the *Western Mail* siren, a large crowd rapidly gathered in St Mary Street. At the Empire Theatre a picture show was suddenly interrupted with the news, and a portrait of the Queen projected on the screen while the band started to play the 'Dead March'. Unfortunately boys in the gallery had not heard the announcement and started to cheer, but were quickly 'shushed' by the adults, and the whole audience rapidly subsided into a sombre silence broken only by the band.[94] The next day a special meeting of the full town council recorded unanimously its 'most profound and heartfelt grief at the death of the most illustrious and venerable Sovereign who has ever adorned the British throne'.[95] On the following Sunday morning church and chapel services generally assumed a memorial character, and were unusually well attended.[96]

Official arrangements for the day of the funeral were again left to the personal discretion of the Mayor, who this time formally announced that

[90]  *Western Mail*, 21 Jan. 1892.
[91]  Ibid., 18 Jan. 1892.
[92]  CCL, CBCM 1897–8, p. 565 (23 May 1898); *Cardiff Times*, 28 May 1898.
[93]  *Cardiff Times*, 4 June 1898.
[94]  *Western Mail*, 23 Jan. 1901.
[95]  CCL, CBCM 1900–1, p. 189, 23 Jan. 1901.
[96]  *Cardiff Times*, 2 Feb. 1901.

he would be attending service at St John's and 'kindly asked' members and officials of the corporation to join him.[97] An unspecified number duly did so. A civic procession was formed and made its way to a packed church in front of a large, orderly, and solemn crowd. Meanwhile a service at Llandaff Cathedral was similarly filled to capacity, and Volunteer companies paraded for a service at their own drill hall, while others marched to St Andrew's Church. Nevertheless, the largest congregations of all were to be found at Nonconformist services, notably at the Park Hall and at Wood Street Congregational Church. The Welsh Church, Dewi Sant, also held a service, as did the synagogue, but no Roman Catholic services were recorded. It was observed that 'every place where services were announced were [*sic*] crowded out long before the hour of service'. Indeed it would appear that this was an occasion when the supply of religious observance in Cardiff was generally insufficient to meet the public demand. The one exception was St Mary's Church where the choral requiem service only drew between 500 and 600 people, less than half the capacity of the building. In Cardiff at least, more Protestant expressions of mourning had a much greater appeal.[98]

Edward VII's death gave rise to a similarly intense public mood, finding expression in widespread and well-attended religious observance. Events on the day of the funeral showed a swing back to greater official recognition of the predominance of Nonconformity in the life of Cardiff, while also seeking to convey a sense of underlying solidarity. Following a military parade in Cathays Park, which then marched to attend a brief service at St John's, the civic and official procession walked from the City Hall to the Free Church service at the Park Hall. The crowd watching the proceedings in Cathays Park was estimated at 50,000, more than a quarter of the population of the city. Simultaneous services were held at St John's, Llandaff Cathedral, and at Pembroke Terrace Chapel, for Welsh-speaking Nonconformists, the latter addressed by the Archdruid of Wales. Later in the day there were two further processions to St John's, by the Masons in the afternoon and by the Boys' Brigade, Church Lads' Brigade and Boy Scouts in the evening. Meanwhile, services were held at the synagogue, and various other churches and chapels, this time including crowded Roman Catholic ones. 'It will thus be seen', concluded the *Western Mail*, 'that all sections of the religious, civic, and military life of Cardiff united with one accord in giving expression to that sense of irreparable loss which is felt by the whole of the civilised world.'[99]

By this time Cardiff was showing an increasing consciousness of its status as 'the metropolis of Wales', a phrase first appearing in connection

[97] CCL, lithographed notice, 30 Jan. 1901.
[98] *South Wales Daily News*, 4 Feb. 1901.
[99] *Western Mail*, 21 May 1910.

with commemorative observances in 1898. In July 1898 the Public Works Committee of the council received a circular proposing the erection of monuments to Gladstone 'in the capitals of England, Scotland and Ireland' and responded with an unanimous resolution to the effect that a similar memorial should be erected in Cardiff 'as the capital of Wales'.[100] Local comment in 1901 and, more particularly 1910, reflected a similar sense of a developing Welsh identity linked to growing local pride. Such identity presented itself as fundamentally consistent with wider loyalty: the 'good government' of Victoria, had, according to the *Cardiff Times*, 'finally won the reverence and love of the Welsh people for the British throne'.[101] On Edward VII's death his long association with the principality as Prince of Wales was recalled and he was praised as having been 'always a friend of Wales'.[102] Local observance of his funeral was described as 'inspiring . . . evidences of the universal and deep-rooted loyalty of Wales to the Throne.'[103] The presence of the Lord Mayor of Cardiff at the funeral itself at Windsor was perceived as an honour in which the 'Welsh nation' as a whole was sharing.[104] Subsequently a conference with representatives from all parts of Wales was held at Cardiff City Hall to initiate a movement for a national memorial to the King. One suggestion given a prominent airing well illustrates the manner in which civic pride, national identity and loyalty to the Crown were becoming woven together in the process of mourning and commemoration. It was proposed 'that the University Gardens, Cathays Park, should be transformed into a "Forum" in which representations of all that was greatest and most inspiring in Welsh History, grouped with gardens round the personality of the late King, and blended with architectural adornments, should form a fitting image of Welsh Nationality.'[105]

Cardiff was thus becoming increasingly confident in finding forms of commemoration that reflected its own distinctive sense of civic community. The continuing tone of caution and experimentation indicates, however, that the development of such ritual, seemingly uncontentious in Exeter, and even in Leeds, was here much more uncertain. Nevertheless beneath various attempts to bridge the religious and cultural divisions of the town and to express a sense of unity in bereavement lay recognition of the

[100] CCL, CBCM 1897–8, p. 727 (28 July 1898).
[101] *Cardiff Times*, 26 Jan. 1901.
[102] *Western Mail*, 7 May 1910.
[103] Ibid., 21 May 1910.
[104] *Western Mail*, 20 May 1910.
[105] CCL, Cardiff City Council Minutes 1910, p. 249 (13 July 1910). The scheme does not appear to have got off the ground, and the site apparently envisaged was subsequently used for the Welsh National War Memorial. The central roadway in the monumental development of Cathays Park was, however, named King Edward VII Avenue.

widespread fundamental religiosity of public attitudes. If civic ritual was to have any prospect of achieving an overall sense of group consciousness, it had to build upon religious ritual rather than attempt to replace it. Cardiff's eventual success in establishing forms of collective mourning that expressed a wider consensus was a necessary corollary of its own gradual emergence during this period as the acknowledged capital of Wales.

## Edinburgh

Edinburgh, in contrast to Cardiff, had long enjoyed the status of a capital city, and its response to prominent deaths reflected a self-conscious aware-ness of its wider representative function in relation to Scotland as a whole. The population (including Leith) was 194,000 in 1851, making it slightly larger in overall size than Leeds at the same date, although in Edinburgh people were more concentrated in the crowded central districts. Subsequent growth, however, was slower, and in 1901 Edinburgh, with 395,000 people, had been overtaken by Leeds.[106] A further contrast lay in occupational and social structure: Edinburgh had a particularly numerous legal, commercial, academic, and ecclesiastical middle class, in 1881 employing 20.51% of the occupied population in domestic service, compared with the comparable figure for Leeds of 10.1%. The working classes were spread among a wide variety of small-scale artisan and service industries. There were great extremes of wealth and poverty: between the splendid Georgian terraces of the New Town, and the more recent middle-class developments of Morningside and Newington, lay the crowded slums of the Old Town, with their population swelled by a significant recent Irish influx.[107] Liberalism was politically dominant until the Home Rule split of 1886, but the Tories were not wholly eclipsed.[108] Church attendance on 30 March 1851 amounted to 55.4% of population, of which only 16% of the total were at Church of Scotland services. The massive impact of the Disruption in 1843 was apparent in the 33% of attendances at the Free Church, while the United Presbyterian Church, at 27%, also substantially exceeded the Established Church. The largest contributors to the balance were the Congregationalists, the Episcopal Church and the Roman Catholic Church, all with 5% of attendances apiece.[109] The membership of the town council in 1856 com-

[106] Mitchell, *British Historical Statistics*, 24–5.

[107] R. Q. Gray, *The Labour Aristocracy in Victorian Edinburgh*, (Edinburgh, 1976), 9–27.

[108] W. H. Marwick, 'Municipal Politics in Victorian Edinburgh', *The Book of the Old Edinburgh Club*, 33(1) (1969), 31–5.

[109] C. G. Brown, *Religion and Society in Scotland since 1707* (Edinburgh, 1997), 45, 59.

prised only seven members of the Church of Scotland, but seventeen members of the Free Church, fourteen Dissenters, and one Episcopalian.[110]

Responses to the death of Sir Walter Scott in 1832 well illustrated the complexities of a frame of mind that Graeme Morton has recently termed 'unionist nationalism'. Scott was mourned simultaneously as a universal genius, as a literary figure of British and European stature and as an articulator of Scottish identity and history, but never as a symbol of Scottish political independence. In fundraising for the grandiose monument in Princes Street, erected between 1840 and 1844, the author's Scottishness was not particularly emphasized. 'Rule Britannia' was played at the laying of its foundation stone.[111]

Parallel ambivalences were already apparent in memorial observance. In John Knox's *Book of Common Order*, the basis on which the worship of the Church of Scotland originally developed, it was stated that 'the corpse is reverently brought to the grave, accompanied with the congregation, without any further ceremonies'.[112] A traditional Scottish funeral therefore proceeded straight from prayers at the house of the deceased to the place of interment, without any intervening service in church. If prayers were held in church this was a matter of convenience rather than liturgical necessity. In a contribution to a pamphlet controversy generated by the services held in Scotland on the day of Princess Charlotte's funeral in 1817, Thomas McCrie, a Presbyterian Dissenter and church historian, had therefore argued that burial services (and by implication parallel memorial services) had been condemned by the Church of Scotland at the Reformation, and remained inconsistent with true Presbyterianism. According to McCrie, they were a superstitious practice, unknown to early Christianity, and their retention by the Church of England was but one symptom of how vestiges of 'Popery' remained south of the Border.[113] Even in 1817, as McCrie noted with concern, the 'highly excited sympathy' of the people,[114] had led the Scottish churches into compromising the consistency of this position: the subsequent development of observance of this kind in Scotland is therefore a revealing touchstone of the erosion of a traditional Presbyterian stance in favour of broader religious expressions of Scottish identity.

A distinctively Presbyterian and Scottish tone was, however, evident in

---

[110] Marwick, 'Municipal Politics', 35. For further analysis of the social and political fabric of early Victorian Edinburgh see G. Morton, *Unionist Nationalism: Governing Urban Scotland 1830–1860* (East Linton, 1999).

[111] Ibid., 156–72.

[112] Quoted in A. I. Dunlop, 'Burial', in N. M. de S. Cameron (ed.), *Dictionary of Scottish Church History and Theology* (Edinburgh, 1993), 110–11.

[113] McCrie, *Free Thoughts*, 9–23.

[114] Ibid., 36.

the funeral in Edinburgh on 4 June 1847 of Thomas Chalmers, social
reformer and leader of the Free Church of Scotland. All shops closed for
the day. The proceedings began with a procession headed by the General
Assembly of the Free Church to the home of the deceased at Morningside
in the southern suburbs of the city. As the procession passed along the
Lothian Road numerous other groups fell in, including the magistrates,
town council, and large numbers of other clergy, including some from other
denominations. At the house devotions were conducted. The body was
then brought out and taken in procession back through the city and past
the university on its way to the recently-opened Grange cemetery which,
in the opinion of the *North British Daily Mail*, was thereby being established
as the '*Père la Chaise* of the Modern Athens'. Although this place of burial
was less than a mile from the house, the chosen circuitous route was some
three miles long, and was evidently intended to enhance the impact of the
spectacle. Numbers in the procession were estimated at 2,000 and it was
calculated that there were as many as 100,000 spectators. The Free Church
General Assembly organized the proceedings, and the whole impressive
spectacle held great significance for them. The Free Church had been in
existence for only four years at the time of Chalmers's death: the loss of
its greatest leader was a cause of great emotional distress and insecurity,
but it also provided an opportunity for a very public show of strength and
demonstration of status and support.[115] The Free Church newspaper, the
*Witness*, claimed that 'It was the dust of a Presbyterian minister which
the coffin contained, and yet they were burying him amid the tears of a
nation, and with more than kingly honours.'[116] Another newspaper report
described the occasion as a 'protestant pilgrimage'.[117]

    At the same time Chalmers was seen as a figure representative both of
Scotland and of a more universal Christendom. In the opinion of the
*Scotsman*, he 'was a man whom Scotchmen of all opinions and of many
coming generations will regard with pride and reverence as one of their
country's great names'.[118] One poetic tribute linked grief for Chalmers to
evocation of the landscape and history of his native country, visualizing

> The picturesque Clyde, her Ocean lochs and Firth,
> The fields where patriots fought, and martyrs bled, . . .

[115] New College Library, Edinburgh [NCL], Chalmers Papers, CHA.6.26.86, *Programme of
Arrangements of the Funeral of the Rev. Dr. Chalmers*; Anon., *Funeral of Dr. Chalmers, in a Letter
to a Friend by an Englishman* (1847); *North British Daily Mail*, 5 June 1847. On Chalmers see
S. J. Brown, *Thomas Chalmers and the Godly Commonwealth in Scotland* (Oxford, 1982).
[116] Reprinted in *Free Church Magazine*, 42 (June 1847), 187.
[117] Cutting from *People's Journal* in collection of tributes to Thomas Chalmers, NCL, X13b
4/1.
[118] *Scotsman*, 2 June 1847.

> The hills of Lanark, and secluded scenes,
> Where Covenanters struggling learn'd to die,

all as mourning with deep emotion and agitation.[119] The *Inverness Courier* saw the death of Chalmers, 'the pride of a Presbyterian Scotland', as a striking counterpoint to the recent demise of Daniel O'Connell, 'the champion of Ireland and of Catholic Europe'.[120] Its suggestion that 'an important cycle of time had been completed' proved, however, to be more perceptive than it realized, in that the kind of extensive posthumous national and religious cult confidently foreseen for Chalmers in 1847 did not materialize. Once the immediate shock of his death had passed, but while memories of his life were still relatively fresh, he was in reality too divisive a figure to serve as a national symbol. No statue to him was erected in Edinburgh until the 1870s, and the eventually successful campaign to remedy the omission stemmed primarily from embarrassment that such an eminent figure should have been left without a public monument for so long.[121]

The Scottish religious patriotism evoked by Chalmers's death and funeral was to prove a less characteristic response to prominent deaths than did endeavours to express local dignity and status in the context of a wider British whole. At the time of Wellington's death, however, local civic or religious responses of any kind were relatively very limited. The town council's assertion of precedence over Dublin at St Paul's 'on the ground of their being the older Corporation of the two, and also as representing Scotland which was united with England nearly a century before the Union with Ireland', was indicative of a mentality in which events in London were seen as more important than those in Edinburgh.[122] They recommended the closing of places of business on the day of the funeral, and there was general compliance in the centre of the city, although not in the suburbs. Otherwise in noticeable contrast with the processions and church services widely held south of the Border, Edinburgh's formal tribute was limited to the firing of minute guns from the castle and the tolling of church bells.[123] Traditional Presbyterian suspicion of memorial services and the impossibility, in the aftermath of the Disruption, of finding a location and format

[119] NCL, Chalmers Papers, CHA6.26.56, MS tribute by John Gemmel, fo. 3.

[120] Reprinted in *Free Church Magazine*, 42 (June 1847), 189–90.

[121] *Proposed National Monument to Dr. Chalmers*, printed report of meeting on 30 Nov. 1869 (NCL, Chalmers Papers, CHA 6.26.87). The statue, by John Steell, was eventually erected at the intersection of Castle Street and George Street in 1878 (M. T. R. B. Turnbull, *Monuments and Statues of Edinburgh* (Edinburgh, 1989, 48–9)).

[122] Edinburgh District Council Archives, Town Council Minutes [ETCM] 258, pp. 426–8 (1 Nov. 1852); 259, pp. 121–4 (28 Dec. 1852).

[123] *Scotsman*, 20 Nov. 1852.

that would have commanded general support were no doubt unspoken factors behind this relative passivity.

During ensuing decades there was a continued pattern of limited response in which civic and ecclesiastical strands were kept more distinct than south of the Border. On Prince Albert's death the council passed an eloquent address of condolence, and on the subsequent Sunday the Lord Provost and members attended St Giles's Cathedral in official robes. Participation in a Church of Scotland service on this occasion indicates that in Edinburgh, as in Leeds, Free Church and Dissenting councillors were now prepared to acknowledge the national role of the Established Church at such times. On the day of the funeral itself, however, public observance was again limited to the tolling of bells and the firing of minute guns, and the churches held prayer meetings rather than full services. Subsequent council discussion of monuments to the Prince well illustrated their wish to uphold Scottish distinctiveness within a framework of underlying loyalty: they gave moral support to plans for the London memorial, but noted that before they had even heard of this,

> steps had been already taken to provide by subscription for a Memorial in Scotland, and, while they are confident that the wealth of England will enable her to dispense with contributions from this part of the Country, they have no doubt that a Memorial will also be provided in Scotland not unworthy of the Prince to whose Memory it is to be erected or of this portion of the Kingdom which desires to give expression in this form to its profound and universal feeling.[124]

The subsequent process of raising money and erecting the monument was involved and protracted, but it was eventually unveiled in Charlotte Square in 1876.[125]

In the meantime Palmerston's death in 1865 was followed by a resolution of sympathy, but no recorded public observance, although the council was concerned that the Lord Provost should represent it at the funeral at Westminster.[126] In 1881 muffled peals were rung for Disraeli from St Giles's and the Tron, and for the Duke of Albany in 1884 minute guns were also fired.[127] Meanwhile James Cameron Lees, who had been appointed Minister of St Giles's in 1877, led the restoration of the cathedral's fabric and sought to develop its role in Scottish national life, in a manner modelled on the work of Dean Stanley at Westminster Abbey.[128] Following Lord Iddesleigh's

---

[124] ETCM 283, p. 393 (4 Feb. 1862).
[125] Darby and Smith, *Cult of the Prince Consort*, 67–70.
[126] ETCM 291, pp. 226, 291 (24, 31 Oct. 1865); *Scotsman*, 28 Oct. 1865.
[127] *Scotsman*, 27 April 1881; *The Times*, 7 April 1884.
[128] N. Maclean, *The Life of James Cameron Lees* (Glasgow, 1922).

death in 1887 he initiated a service at St Giles's on the day of the funeral, prompted particularly by the deceased's personal association with Edinburgh as Rector of the University. In his address Lees well articulated a sense of participation in a wider national community:

> We are met to-day, brethren, in this house of prayer, to join our devotions with those, and to express our deep sympathy with those, who at this hour in far-off Devonshire are laying in the grave the remains of that honoured statesman who was personally known to so many of us, and whose death has caused a thrill of sadness to vibrate throughout the whole land.[129]

Such a sense of seamless solidarity with Anglican mourners implied a significantly different blend of civic, national, and ecclesiastical sentiment from that apparent earlier in the century.

Indeed, during the period between 1890 and 1910 observance of mourning and funerals in Edinburgh began strongly to resemble the practice of major English towns and cities. The Duke of Clarence's death stirred an 'immense sensation' in the Scottish capital.[130] The Lord Provost and magistrates met to decide what form local ceremonies should take, an indication that there was now demand for more extensive public display than hitherto, but that both precedent and appropriate practice were still uncertain. The *Scotsman* reported that 'it seems to be the feeling that a funeral service in St Giles' should form the central feature of the celebration',[131] a scheme that was duly implemented simultaneously with the ceremony at Windsor. The council first met to adopt addresses of condolence and then proceeded in state to a service at St Giles's, to hear an address in which Lees dwelt on the closeness of the royal family to the life of the people of Scotland, and an anthem by John Stainer, the organist of St Paul's Cathedral. Meanwhile businesses were closed, blinds drawn and minute guns fired.[132] Cameron Lees wrote: 'I never saw anything like the feeling Scotland has displayed. Edinburgh . . . was a sight I will never forget . . . Thousands went away who could not get into the church [St Giles's] and the whole scene was most impressive.'[133]

When Gladstone died, the Lord Provost delivered an eloquent speech to the council, placing particular stress on the local and Scottish connections of the deceased, and suggesting that there was a temporary hushing of 'the strife of tongues' in the face of 'the great fact of his departure'.[134] He asked

[129] *Scotsman*, 19 Jan. 1887.
[130] *Scotsman*, 15 Jan. 1892.
[131] *Scotsman*, 16 Jan. 1892.
[132] ETCM 1891–2, pp. 115–6 (20 Jan. 1892); *Scotsman*, 21 Jan. 1892.
[133] RA, VIC/Z 93/59, Cameron Lees to Miss McNeill, 21 Jan. 1892.
[134] ETCM 1897–8, pp. 379–81 (24 May 1892).

St Giles's to hold a service on the day of the funeral and the cathedral duly obliged with a format intended to be 'as simple and non-official as possible'. Nevertheless the council attended in their robes.[135] Meanwhile in parallel with their emphasis on consensus and their increasing acceptance of English-influenced ceremonial, they continued jealously to uphold their claims to precedence over Dublin in Westminster Abbey, seeing it as a question of 'precedency between countries represented by their capitals'.[136] Scottish national status was asserted within the framework of the Union.

The increase in ceremonial and the assimilation between civic and ecclesiastical ritual reached its culmination in 1901 and 1910. Following the deaths of both monarchs the council held special meetings, which were opened in prayer by the Minister of St Giles's, after which the Lord Provost moved an address of condolence.[137] Large formal services were held in St Giles's on both the funeral days, and seen as representative of a cross-section of local and national Scottish life. Lees, still in harness in 1901 and recalled from retirement in 1910, gave both memorial sermons, eloquently evoking his idealized perception of common feeling and sentiment between the royal family and the Scottish people. Mourning draperies were widely displayed by businesses, and sombre, reverent crowds gathered outside the cathedral and in other public places. On both occasions a general consensus was perceived by the *Scotsman*, which noted in 1901 that people turned out in large numbers, not only for the pageantry of St Giles's, but also for the 'quiet unostentatious services' in suburban and working-class districts. During the day the local police had made only two arrests, whereas the average Saturday figure was 'about 80 or 90'. Even if this circumstance was in part attributable to the closure of public houses, it was still suggestive of far-reaching acceptance of the consensual mood that the circumstances required a particularly decorous standard of behaviour. Nine years later, at one o'clock, the time of Edward VII's funeral at Windsor, all the trams were stopped for a quarter of an hour and a solemn stillness descended on the city's normally bustling streets, broken only by the sound of psalm singing from the churches and by the tolling of bells.[138]

Thus at the beginning of the twentieth century, in Edinburgh, as elsewhere, the forms and symbols of official religiosity constituted the dominant expression of the mood of communal grief. If Presbyterian suspicion of such rituals lingered at all, it was overwhelmed by the public pressure to express grief in a manner that since the mid-nineteenth century

---

[135] *Scotsman*, 26, 27, 30 May 1898.

[136] ETCM 1897–8, pp. 431–3 (14 June 1898).

[137] ETCM 1900–1, pp. 161–2 (24 Jan 1901); 1909–10, pp. 427–8 (9 May 1910); *Scotsman*, 25 Jan. 1901, 10 May 1910.

[138] *Scotsman*, 4 Feb. 1901, 21 May 1910.

had moved much closer to English norms. The Scottish capital remained very conscious of its own civic dignity and its wider national role, but in the context of a wider British whole in which thoughts were drawn inexorably to the invisible ceremonies in London and Windsor. These events were a continuing and developing expression of 'unionist nationalism'.[139]

## Dublin

Nineteenth-century Dublin has been generally perceived as a city in decline, suffering both politically and economically from the loss of the Irish Parliament in 1800, and further ravaged by the devastating demographic and social impact of the Great Famine of the 1840s. Certainly it was faced by problems of poverty and public health that were more extreme even than those of contemporary British towns, and the population within the old city boundaries was almost unchanged during the second half of the nineteenth century, at 258,389 in 1851 and 260,035 in 1901. When the suburbs are taken into account, however, there was a rising trend, from 317,837 in 1851 to 381,492 in 1901, but the rate of growth was still proportionately much the lowest of the five cities under consideration in this chapter. Nevertheless the modest increase in Dublin's population in the later nineteenth century was contrary to the decline of the Irish population as a whole in the decades after the famine. It indicates that the capital (together with its great rival Belfast) was assuming increasing demographic and economic importance in relation to the rest of Ireland. Moreover in the face of the abject poverty of many, the city had a significant professional and commercial middle class, and remained the cultural, administrative, and political focus of Irish life, being both the seat of the vice-regal court and a centre of nationalist activity.[140] In religious terms Roman Catholicism was numerically dominant, constituting 77 per cent of the city's population in 1861, rising to 83 per cent in 1911,[141] but the Protestant minority was more substantial than in any other part of Ireland outside Ulster, and was over-represented among the middle and upper classes. In Dublin, in contrast to Ulster, the great majority of Protestants were Anglicans. The city's religious

---

[139] Cf. Morton, *Unionist Nationalism*, 189–200. Morton argues that the high point of this state of mind occurred in the middle years of the century, and (196–7) that the foundation of the Scottish Home Rule Association (SHRA) in 1886 marked a 'fundamental shift' away from it. The SHRA, however, was devolutionist rather than separatist in its objectives, and the mere fact of its existence proves little about wider public attitudes.

[140] A. MacLaren, *Dublin: The Shaping of a Capital* (1993), 37–40; M. E. Daly, *Dublin, the Deposed Capital: A Social and Economic History 1860–1914* (Cork, 1984), 1–5, 18–19.

[141] Ibid., 122.

and political divisions were reflected in the composition of its municipal council, which in the decades following the reform of the Irish corporations in 1840 consistently had a Catholic and nationalist majority and a Protestant and unionist minority. These blocks, however, were not monolithic: Protestants included Liberals as well as Conservatives and in the latter part of the century the nationalists were exposed to the same fragmentation as their counterparts in the country as a whole. Indeed, the Dublin municipal council at times came close to itself assuming the role of a surrogate parliament, debating issues that went far outside its own direct responsibilities.[142] In this context its responses to prominent deaths, alongside the wider cultural and religious pattern of reaction in the city as a whole provides a revealing microcosm of Irish attitudes to British rule and nationalist aspiration.

Daniel O'Connell, who died in May 1847, was not only the hero of Catholic Ireland as a whole, but had also in 1841 been the first Catholic Lord Mayor of Dublin since the Reformation. His death at Genoa on the way to Rome was symbolic of his Catholic as well as Irish sense of identity and status, and his heart was conveyed onwards for interment in the Eternal City. Meanwhile back in Ireland there was a great outpouring of grief at the loss of O'Connell at a time when the country's need for the charismatic leadership he had offered had never seemed greater. Such sentiments were notably expressed in poems and ballads, which, like Scottish counterparts for Chalmers, linked mourning for the deceased to the evocation of the national landscape and history:

> Oh Erin, darling, both night and morning,
>    Your grief's alarming as may be seen;
> Your hills and mountains—your silver fountains
>    From sweet Killarney to College Green
> Thro' Groves and vallies [*sic*]—thro' lanes and allies
>    Oh bid your children to deplore
> In lamentation, throughout the nation,
>    Brave O'Connell he is no more. . . .
>
> In mournful strains, his dear remains
>    Will be convey'd to his native place,
> Where there reverr'd he will be interred
>    With honor bright, and immortal grace.
> A noble statue will be erected,
>    With golden letters, enscribbed [*sic*] all o'er

---

[142] Ibid., 203–21.

That Granua's children in future ages,
Will pray for O'Connell on the Irish Shore.[143]

These aspirations began to be fulfilled on 2 August 1847, when a steamer carrying O'Connell's body arrived in Dublin Bay. Surrounding vessels, reportedly irrespective of the political or religious opinions of the owners, lowered their colours to half-mast, while the emigrants crowding the deck of an outbound steamer all removed their hats and began keening.[144] The coffin was brought on shore in front of an enormous crowd, of whom 'not one remained standing where room was left to kneel, to offer a prayer up to Heaven for the eternal repose of Ireland's liberator'. A French observer felt the mood to be more intense even than that prevailing in Paris when Napoleon's remains had returned there in 1840.[145]

The body was taken through crowded but silent streets to the Catholic pro-cathedral where it was received with elaborate ceremonial and lay in state with large crowds milling around outside.[146] On the following day, Tuesday 3 August, a continuous stream of mourners passed though the church paying their respects.[147] On Wednesday 4 a pontifical High Mass was celebrated, with two archbishops (Murray of Dublin and MacHale of Tuam), sixteen bishops and over a thousand clergy present.[148] In his sermon, Fr John Miley, who had accompanied O'Connell on his last journey and had escorted the body home, characterized the service as an 'august solemnity in which the whole Church and nation of the Irish people are represented'.[149] He recalled O'Connell's contribution to the Irish national cause, while holding that 'his love of country was grand and invincible because it was sanctified by his love of religion.'[150] Absolution was pronounced over the body in a form normally used only for a bishop or prince, thus setting the seal on the Catholic Church's posthumous endorsement of O'Connell and its readiness to lead funeral observances in which Christian devotion blended imperceptibly into nationalist fervour.[151]

In his sermon Miley had advocated that O'Connell should be buried at his home, Derrynane on the Atlantic coast of County Kerry, in the hope

---

[143] Trinity College Dublin Library [TCD], Irish Ballads Collection, vol. 1, no. 142 (see also vol. 1, nos. 141, 143, 167, 176, 187, 188; vol. 2, nos. 61, 123, 250).

[144] W. B. MacCabe, (ed.), *The Last Days of O'Connell* (Dublin, 1847, reprinting newspaper reports), 206–7.

[145] Ibid., 208.

[146] Ibid., 208–9.

[147] Ibid., 210.

[148] Ibid., 211.

[149] Ibid., 123 [*sic*, misprint for 223].

[150] Ibid., 237.

[151] Ibid., 215.

that this remote location would become a focus of both national and religious pilgrimage.[152] In the event, however, it was decided to inter the body at Glasnevin Cemetery in the northern suburbs of Dublin, thereby retaining its powerful symbolic and emotional associations for the capital. The Liberator's elaborate apotheosis accordingly concluded on 5 August with a lengthy street procession. As on previous days nationalistic and Catholic motifs were freely combined: the procession itself was preceded by acolytes bearing torches, and consisted of religious confraternities, clergy and bishops, as well as numerous secular dignitaries and the trades of Dublin. Many knelt in the streets as the coffin passed, and accompanied its progress with wailing and lamentation; others believed that O'Connell would be canonized and hence sought healing from their disabilities.[153] As with Chalmers's funeral in Edinburgh, the procession took a circuitous route to the cemetery. It first set out from the pro-cathedral in the contrary direction, crossing the river Liffey, passing though College Green, Merrion Square (where O'Connell had lived) and St Stephen's Green, and proceeding almost to the southern outskirts. Only then did it turn north, passing again through the heart of the city, before eventually recrossing the Liffey and taking the direct route to Glasnevin.[154] The interment, like the funeral, was characterized by the presence in force of the Catholic hierarchy.[155]

During subsequent decades the impulse to commemorate O'Connell remained a significant factor in the political life of Dublin and had a lasting impact on the physical fabric of the city. A movement to erect a memorial to him in the centre of the city was initiated in 1862, and the foundation stone was laid in 1864 amidst impressive ceremonial.[156] The O'Connell Monument Committee was a seedbed for the National Association, also launched in 1864, which provided a focus in subsequent years for constitutional nationalist politics both in the Dublin municipal council and in the country as a whole.[157] The building of the monument itself made only slow progress during the subsequent two decades, but 1869 saw the completion of a parallel scheme for the building of a memorial crypt, blending Catholic and patriotic iconography, under a symbolic Irish round tower close to the entrance of Glasnevin cemetery. This arrangement necessitated the reinterment of the body, providing an occasion for further religious ceremonial and a powerful oration by the Very Revd Thomas Burke, who

---

[152] Ibid., 238.

[153] Ibid., 243–4; *The Times*, 7 Aug. 1847.

[154] MacCabe, *Last Days of O'Connell*, 244–9.

[155] Ibid., 252.

[156] J. O'Hanlon, *Report of the O'Connell Monument Committee* (Dublin, 1888), p. xlvii.

[157] Daly, *Dublin*, 211; Dublin City Hall, Minutes of the Municipal Council of the City of Dublin [MCCD] 6 Oct. 1862; *O'Connell Centenary Record* (Dublin, 1878), 2.

emphasized the ties between Irish national history and the Catholic faith.[158] In August 1875 the centenary of O'Connell's birth was celebrated on a grand scale: a pontifical High Mass was attended by the great majority of the Catholic hierarchy, while the subsequent procession through Dublin reportedly comprised 55,000 people, and was watched by up to half a million more. The procession included Dublin trades, religious bodies and political associations, and followed a seven-mile route through the city passing numerous sites of historic and national significance.[159] A further high point in the posthumous cult of O'Connell came with the eventual unveiling of the elaborate statue in August 1882. It was (and is) very prominently located, combining national motifs and allusions with the commemoration of the Liberator himself.[160]

During the same period, the tensions and ambivalences in Ireland's attitudes to British rule were reflected in Dublin's responses to the deaths of the Duke of Wellington and Prince Albert. Nationalist hostility towards Wellington as an instrument of perceived oppression was softened by recollection of his Irish origins. The *Freeman's Journal* lambasted the Duke for his 'hatred of his own land', but still took an ironic pride on the day of his funeral in the spectacle of the 'proudest race in the world' weeping 'over the bier of an Irishman'.[161] There was also lively local debate as to whether the Duke had in fact been born in Dublin or at the family seat of Trim in County Meath.[162] As one lampoonist put it:

> Dublin and the County Meath will have a gallant fight
> To see which of them will prosper best on Arthur's cradle-right.[163]

Anti-British sentiment did not prevent the council from resolving by a majority of twenty-six to eight that it was 'desirous to unite in the National demonstration of respect for their illustrious Countryman and fellow Citizen',[164] nor from sending a numerous deputation to the funeral in London, and using the occasion to pursue their simmering dispute with Edinburgh as to which city should take precedence in a United Kingdom context.[165] In Dublin itself, however, observance on the day of the funeral was limited: some bells were tolled, there was a special choral service at

[158] Ibid., 251, 520–3; J. Sheehy, *The Rediscovery of Ireland's Past: The Celtic Revival 1830–1930* (1980), 58–60.
[159] *O'Connell Centenary Record*, 79ff.
[160] O'Hanlon, *O'Connell Monument*, pp. lxix–lxxi; Sheehy, *Ireland's Past*, 50–53.
[161] *Freeman's Journal*, 16 Sept., 18 Nov. 1852.
[162] J. Murray, *Wellington: The Place and Day of his Birth Ascertained and Demonstrated* (Dublin, 1852).
[163] TCD, Irish Ballads Collection, vol. 2, no. 230.
[164] MCCD, 27 Oct., 1 Nov. 1852.
[165] See above, 38.

Christ Church Cathedral, and some public offices were closed, but the Bank of Ireland, Custom House and Post Office were open as usual and no shopkeepers or tradesmen observed any outward marks of respect on their premises.[166]

Nine years later the human tragedy of Prince Albert's death was met with a unanimous resolution of sympathy from the council[167] and a general mood of 'deep sorrow' in the city.[168] The *Freeman's Journal* felt obliged to explain that its failure to appear with mourning rules was due to technical problems rather than an absence of sympathy for the bereaved Queen or a lack of loyalty.[169] On the day of the funeral signs of mourning were widely apparent.[170] Once the initial shock had passed, however, tensions founded in Irish national and local civic sentiment began to surface. In February 1862 a letter from the Lord Mayor of London soliciting support for the Albert Memorial gave offence both because it was addressed to the 'Worshipful the Mayor [rather than Lord Mayor] of Dublin' and because it appeared to treat Dublin like an English provincial town.[171] Nevertheless the council was quite prepared to promote the movement to commemorate Albert in Dublin itself, identifying itself with the 'very strong feeling that all the subscriptions in Ireland should be used, not for an imperial, but for an Irish national monument'.[172] Two years later the statue became more controversial when a plan emerged to erect it on a prime site on College Green directly outside Trinity College and the former Parliament House.[173] This suggestion was too much for more committed nationalist opinion, which held that such a location was quite inappropriate for a 'foreign prince'. Advocates of the College Green site then raised the stakes by suggesting that their opponents were disloyal to the Queen and were insulting the Prince's memory, charges that were angrily denied.[174] Controversy continued to rage for several months, being further fuelled by a hastily organized counter request that the College Green site should be allocated for a statue of Henry Grattan.[175] Initially Albert's cause triumphed in the council, but in 1865 the committee promoting the statue itself diplomatically took the initiative in asking the Queen to agree to a change of site to a

[166] *The Times*, 20 Nov. 1852.
[167] MCCD, 16 Dec. 1861.
[168] *Freeman's Journal*, 17 Dec. 1861.
[169] Ibid.
[170] Ibid., 24 Dec. 1861.
[171] Ibid., 4 Feb. 1862; *Irish Times*, 4 Feb. 1862.
[172] MCCD, 3 Feb. 1862; *Freeman's Journal*, 24 Feb. 1862.
[173] MCCD, 8 Feb. 1864.
[174] *Freeman's Journal*, 9 Feb. 1864.
[175] MCCD, 15 Feb., 4 April, 2 May 1864; *Freeman's Journal*, 24 Feb., 5 April, 3 May 1864 and *passim*.

new public garden to be erected behind Leinster House. The statue was eventually inaugurated in 1872.[176] The advocates of the Grattan statue waited until 1868 before seeking to further their cause, but then launched an appeal, in which they aimed to bring together 'Irishmen of all classes, all creeds, and all parties'. They achieved their object with the unveiling of a statue to the great orator on College Green in January 1876.[177]

For the Dublin municipal council the consideration of resolutions of condolence, of the kind that usually passed unanimously in British corporations, became a matter of political contention. When Palmerston died in 1865 a move to suspend standing orders so as to permit an immediate resolution was prevented.[178] Although it was passed unanimously the following week, critical views towards the deceased were expressed and applauded by the public, reflecting a feeling that he, like Wellington, had been less than true to his Irish blood and origins.[179] Meanwhile the unionist *Irish Times* took consolation from the Lord Mayor's attendance at the funeral at Westminster, which it felt saved the city 'from an indelible disgrace'.[180] Similar tensions were apparent in 1881 when a scrupulously non-political attempt to persuade the Council to record its sense of loss at Disraeli's death was again foiled by resort to standing orders.[181]

The two decades after 1890 saw national mourning and commemoration in Dublin continuing to reflect the tensions in the city's political and religious identity. On 11 October 1891 the body of Charles Stewart Parnell, who had died the previous week in Brighton, arrived back in the Irish capital, for a large-scale funeral that inevitably evoked comparison with O'Connell's obsequies over forty years before. There were indeed some superficial similarities: both great nationalist leaders had died outside Ireland at a time when their political fortunes had appeared to be in decline,[182] and were eventually buried in proximity to each other at Glasnevin after processions that traversed the streets of Dublin for many hours. A fundamental contrast lay, however, in the attitude of the Roman Catholic Church. It had used O'Connell's funeral to express a powerful sense of identification between Catholicism and nationalism, but now entirely abstained from any participation in Parnell's, so as to reinforce its disapproval of the adultery

---

[176] Darby and Smith, *Cult of the Prince Consort*, 70–73. In a rich irony, the subsequent adoption of Leinster House as the seat of the parliament of independent Ireland gave a wholly unintended prominence to the new site, where the statue still stands.

[177] TCD, MS 1703, The Grattan Statue, fos. 12–13 and *passim*.

[178] *Irish Times*, 24 Oct. 1865.

[179] Ibid., 31 Oct. 1865.

[180] Ibid., 27 Oct. 1865.

[181] Ibid., 26 April 1881.

[182] For detailed analysis of the political background to Parnell's death see F. Callanan, *The Parnell Split 1890–1891* (Cork, 1992).

that had split his party and led to his political downfall. Priests urged their congregations not to attend the ceremony.[183] To the extent that a Christian dimension was present at all, it was (in conformity with the nominal allegiance of the deceased) a Protestant rather than Catholic one: the procession halted for a Church of Ireland funeral service at St Michan's Church, and two Anglican clergymen officiated at the graveside.[184] Meanwhile bands in the procession played *Adeste Fideles* and other hymn tunes together with the 'Dead March', thus diffusing something of a devotional tone among the crowd.[185] Nevertheless, whereas O'Connell's funeral might well be judged to have been the most fervently religious of any such major occasion in Britain or Ireland during the nineteenth century, Parnell's assumed a predominantly secular tone, even though it chanced to take place on a Sunday.

When news of Parnell's death had reached Dublin, crowds had gathered on the streets and the municipal council held a special meeting to record its sorrow, political differences being transcended in mourning for 'a great and distinguished Irishman'. The council resolved to attend the funeral in state.[186] Magnanimity was apparent in the stance of the *Irish Times*, which felt that the circumstances required a suspension of controversy. On the other hand, advocates of Catholic and anti-Parnellite nationalist opinions were by no means so restrained and the funeral accordingly became a partisan demonstration by Parnell's supporters whose greatest remaining strength lay in the Dublin area. The body arrived at Westland Row railway station early in the morning of 11 October and was immediately taken by way of St Michan's Church to the city hall where it lay in state for several hours. An enormous throng, estimated at around 30,000 people, passed through the building. The procession then formed up, the hearse being escorted by Parnellite members of Parliament, and followed by the Gaelic Athletic Association, the Dublin corporation, and numerous deputations from all parts of Ireland. Participants were estimated to number 20,000. The procession made a lengthy circuit to the west of the city hall before returning to its starting point, thereby nearly overlapping itself. It then continued past Trinity College, and up Sackville Street (now O'Connell

---

[183] E. Larkin, *The Roman Catholic Church in Ireland and the Fall of Parnell 1888–1891* (Liverpool, 1979), 284–5.

[184] *Irish Times*, 12 Oct. 1891. One of the officiating clergymen, the Revd Mr Vincent, Chaplain of the Rotunda Hospital, defended his decision to take part with an analogy that suggests he did not approach the duty with any enthusiasm: 'If he were chaplain of a jail he might be required to read the service for the burial of the dead even over the grave of one executed for murder.'

[185] *Irish Times*, 12 Oct. 1891.

[186] Ibid., 8 Oct. 1891; MCCD, 8 Oct. 1891.

Street) on its roundabout course to Glasnevin. The *Irish Times* reported consistently thronged streets and noted that the 'populace regarded the funeral with reverential awe', even if their demeanour was not always shared by the more prosperous spectators who gained access to windows and rooftops.[187] A government observer thought that the total size of the crowd amounted to nearly 100,000, and saw the evident popular defiance of the Roman Catholic Church's stance as a significant defeat for priestly influence. He found the spectacle 'most imposing' and 'unique', and was struck by the 'sad stern look' on the faces of the participants. The authorities kept the police and the military out of sight and allowed the Fenians to regulate the crowd. The spectacle was 'entirely composed and controlled by the lower classes'.[188]

Even though the funeral was, as the *Irish Times* put it, 'a ceremony conducted by Mr. Parnell's fragment of the party alone', it would still, it accurately prophesied, 'prove ineffaceable from the minds of all, young or old, who witnessed it, and in a generation to come may be looked back upon, under greatly altered circumstance, just as some now recall every feature of the dismal forenoon when the remains of the first great tribune whose heart was broken were deposited in Glasnevin'.[189] The *Freeman's Journal* judged that the occasion 'stands unequalled' as an expression of national sorrow and considered that ' "I was at Parnell's funeral" shall be a proud yet melancholy boast in days to come'.[190] In subsequent years the cult of Parnell, like that of O'Connell before him, was stimulated by a project for an elaborate memorial in Dublin, unveiled in October 1911 by his successor John Redmond.[191] As memory of Parnell's actual career and political beliefs receded, the recollection of his death and apotheosis continued to fuel the powerful mythologies of twentieth-century Irish nationalism. This development of the Parnell legacy was already foreseeable in 1891: 'The extremists will now canonize Parnell, he will be credited with all sorts of extreme views and intentions and they will benefit more by Parnell dead than by Parnell living.'[192]

While the death of the greatest Irish political leader of the later nineteenth century exposed the continuing deep divisions among his

---

[187] *Irish Times*, 12 Oct. 1891.
[188] BL, AddMS 49812 (Balfour Papers), fos. 187–9, Ridgeway to Balfour, 12 Oct. 1891; cf. Larkin, *Fall of Parnell*, 285–6.
[189] *Irish Times*, 12 Oct. 1891.
[190] 12 Oct. 1891.
[191] *Souvenir of the Unveiling of the Parnell Monument* (Dublin, 1911).
[192] BL, AddMS 49812, fo. 186, Ridgeway to Balfour, 10 Oct. 1891. The ambivalent legacies of the Parnell myth were to be brilliantly evoked by W. B. Yeats in his poem 'Parnell's Funeral', published in 1935 (*Collected Poems* (1950), 319–20).

countrymen, the death a few months later of a British prince was met with
an apparent consensus of mourning in Dublin. In January 1892, the council
unanimously passed a resolution of condolence and sympathy with the
royal family on the loss of the Duke of Clarence. One speaker hoped that
in the future their differences with each other 'might be somewhat lessened
and softened by the recollection of occasions such as that, when the ties
of common human interests overbore all thoughts of difference whatever'.[193]
The *Freeman's Journal*, not predisposed to write up apparent indications of
loyalist sentiment, reported that popular sympathy was general, and noted
the dispatch of telegrams of condolence on behalf of the Roman Catholic
hierarchy.[194] The Church of Ireland demonstrated that disestablishment was
no bar to providing a focus for official Protestant mourning. It held a
crowded memorial service on the day of the funeral at St Patrick's Cathedral
attended by the Lord Lieutenant. Services were also reported at Christ
Church Cathedral, and Blackhall Place Methodist Church, and a prayer
meeting was held at the Christian Union Buildings.[195]

A similar apparent consensus followed Gladstone's death. At a special
meeting the council recorded its 'recognition of his well-intentioned efforts,
strenuous labours, and life-long devotion to the cause of Ireland, of freedom
and of justice' and resolved that its officers should attend the funeral at
Westminster. Even if a somewhat discordant note was then struck by
renewed agitation of the precedence dispute with Edinburgh, that itself
indicated that the council remained concerned to assert its dignity within
an imperial framework.[196]

Mourning for Queen Victoria proved, however, to be more contentious.
The nationalist majority in the council felt that its courtesy the previous
year in offering an address of welcome to the Queen on her visit to Dublin
had been construed as acceptance of the present constitutional situation of
Ireland. It was accordingly concerned that a vote of condolence should not
be similarly misinterpreted. Hence they refused to allow such a resolution
to be proposed at the beginning of the routine meeting held on the day
following the Queen's death. When the matter recurred at the end of the
meeting, an amendment was proposed by Councillor Harrington who had
just been elected Lord Mayor for the following year, to the effect that an
expression of sympathy was not a demonstration of loyalty. After heated
debate, in which moderate nationalists concurred with unionists in seeing
the issue as non-political, the amendment was defeated but only by a margin

[193] *Irish Times*, 19 Jan. 1892.
[194] *Freeman's Journal*, 15, 16, 21 Jan. 1892.
[195] *Irish Times*, 21 Jan. 1892.
[196] MCCD, 24 May 1898; *Irish Times*, 25 May 1898.

of thirty votes to twenty-two.[197] Meanwhile the *Freeman's Journal* perceived the late Queen as disastrously alienated from the cause of religious and social emancipation in Ireland, and with double-edged charity hoped that 'may her virtues be remembered; and may her mistakes be blotted out in the waters of an Infinite Mercy'.[198] Nevertheless wider public sentiment at least quietly acquiesced in the strong manifestations of mourning apparent among the Protestant community. On the night of the Queen's death large crowds gathered in the streets;[199] both on the following Sunday and on the day of the funeral itself unusually numerous congregations attended the Church of Ireland cathedrals and other Protestant places of worship.[200] The Unionist outgoing Lord Mayor, Sir Thomas Pile, and a minority of the council attended the memorial service at St Patrick's.[201] Roman Catholics and nationalists might hold themselves aloof from such official commemorations, but the sombre appearance of the streets during the days following the Queen's death, and almost universal wearing of black indicates that they felt it right to respect the mood of the moment.[202] Indeed many went further insofar as it was reported that 'the evening tramcars on Sunday were filled not only with Protestants but with many poor Catholics who had been to hear a requiem or say a prayer for the Queen'.[203]

Edward VII was widely perceived as a friend of Ireland,[204] and accordingly his death was followed by a more universal expression of grief and regret. On the following Sunday the 'Dead March' was played as a tribute in some Roman Catholic churches as well as in Protestant ones, and Catholic dignitaries and organizations sent messages of sympathy.[205] In the council Sinn Fein members attempted to move an amendment to the vote of condolence, but the Lord Mayor, Michael Doyle, himself a nationalist, insisted that the matter was felt to be a non-political one by seven-eighths of the people. The substantive motion was carried by thirty-two votes to seven.[206] Doyle subsequently accepted an invitation to the funeral itself, 'simply as a mark of respect to a Sovereign who was regarded as friendly to the national aspirations of the Irish people'.[207] On the day of the funeral,

[197] MCCD, 14 March 1900, 23 Jan. 1901; *Irish Times*, 24 Jan. 1901; *Freeman's Journal*, 24 Jan. 1901.
[198] *Freeman's Journal*, 23 Jan. 1901.
[199] *Irish Times*, 23 Jan. 1901.
[200] *Irish Times*, 28 Jan., 4 Feb. 1901.
[201] Ibid. (both dates).
[202] *Irish Times*, 26 Jan. 1901; *Freeman's Journal*, 4 Feb. 1901.
[203] *Irish Times*, 4 Feb. 1901.
[204] *Freeman's Journal*, 7, 14 May 1910.
[205] *Irish Times*, 9, 10 May 1910.
[206] MCCD, 12 May 1910; *Irish Times*, 13 May 1910.
[207] *Irish Times*, 19 May 1910.

the continuing national status of the Church of Ireland in the eyes of the government was again endorsed by the attendance in state of the Viceroy and the military at a grandiose service at St Patrick's Cathedral. Memorial services were also held in numerous other Church of Ireland churches, at the Jewish synagogue, and by the Congregationalists, Methodists and Presbyterians. In an unprecedented and noteworthy development, a votive Mass was also offered at the Roman Catholic pro-cathedral, drawing a numerous congregation of official representatives as well as a large crowd outside. The Lord Mayor and the council were represented both there and at St Patrick's by members of the appropriate religious tradition, and care was taken to have the civic insignia transported from one location to the other so that they could be carried in both services. Conversely the Viceroy and the armed services were represented at the Catholic service. The *Irish Times* was understandably gratified at such evidence of Catholic and nationalist readiness to share in grief for the King, and to respect the feelings of the Protestant minority. It counselled though against unionist triumphalism: nationalist courtesy and chivalry on this occasion should not be misconstrued as constituting an abandonment of their essential political position.[208] Nevertheless it allowed itself to hope that the mood of May 1910 might be indicative of an unrealized potential for reconciliation in Ireland: 'It would be the greatest tribute which Ireland could pay to the memory of the dead King if his death were to bring an assuagement of bitterness between man and man ... Let us forget the disputes of our grandfathers, and apply ourselves to bettering the conditions of life for our grandchildren.'[209]

With the luxury of hindsight it is all too easy for the historian to dismiss such aspirations as wholly unrealistic. The events of the ensuing decade were indeed to transform, polarize and embitter Irish life in a manner that cast a long shadow across the remainder of the twentieth century. In the context of this book, however, three points merit consideration. First, in 1910, Dublin, despite its divided political allegiances, appeared to be feeling its way towards forms of shared expression of grief that recognized its own diversities and were perceived as consensual and universal rather than partisan and exclusive. In particular, civic authorities recognized a responsibility to seek to bridge religious divisions, and found that the emotional and spiritual reactions stirred by death gave them an opportunity to do so. In this respect the trend in Dublin was similar to that observed in the British cities discussed earlier in this chapter, even if the local circumstances were more extreme and the degree of harmony achieved accordingly more transient and fragile. Second, after 1916, the

---

[208] *Irish Times*, 21 May 1910; *Freeman's Journal*, 21 May 1910.
[209] *Irish Times*, 20 May 1910.

ongoing power of response to death in Irish politics and culture was to be demonstrated in the radicalization of nationalism following the British suppression of the Easter Rising and the execution of its leaders. Padraic Pearse's explicit use of the imagery of blood sacrifice was to inspire the 'terrible beauty' of which Yeats wrote.[210] Then, as in reactions to Parnell's death, such emotions proved to be partisan and divisive. Nevertheless the experience of 1910 suggests that alternative potentialities still remained in early twentieth century Ireland if death could be used to affirm consensus rather than to shatter it.

Finally, when the British cases are themselves reviewed in the light of Dublin's experience, the force of underlying consensus in the other cities is highlighted. Elsewhere votes of condolence were seldom contested, and if there was dissent from the official response represented in church services and processions, it seldom went beyond quiet abstention of the kind that leaves no trace on the historical record. The underlying concern was to assert a sense of local participation in a greater whole, through appropriate formal actions and ritual observance. National mourning might frequently be refracted through the prism of local circumstances and consciousness, but its underlying validity and importance was uncontested.

[210] Cf. S. Gilley, 'Pearse's Sacrifice: Christ and Cuchulain Crucified and Risen in the Easter Rising, 1916' in J. Obelkevich, L. Roper and R. Samuel (eds.), *Disciplines of Faith* (1987), 479–97.

# 5

# *Martyrs of Empire:*
# Livingstone and Gordon

> Thou dauntless soul thou soldier of the cross,
> Our love is cold set side by side with thine. . . .
> Thy body in the ancient abbey's shade:
> Thy spirit with the martyred ones, who cry
> From heaven's high altar for the Advent dawn. . . .
> And thou, dear martyr of His sacred cross,
> The loving servant of the crucified . . .[1]

In April 1874, as David Livingstone's body was being interred beneath the centre of the nave of Westminster Abbey, an anonymous poet thus reflected on his life as having followed the example of Christ, the suffering servant. Similar language readily recurred with reference to the death of General Charles Gordon at the fall of Khartoum in January 1885. According to the *Leeds Mercury*, 'That he should have closed his noble life of heroic effort by this martyr's death will strike all among us with a sense of fitness.'[2] Hensley Henson, the future Bishop of Durham, took to lecturing on Gordon in working-men's clubs, judging that 'he lived the life of a Christian saint' and dwelling on his 'never-dying example'.[3]

There were strong links of influence and perception between these two larger-than-life figures. Livingstone stood in a tradition of missionary heroes,[4] and Gordon in a succession of military ones,[5] but their shared

---

[1] W. J. H. Y., *David Livingstone. A Missionary Poem: In Memoriam* (1874), 8–11.

[2] *Leeds Mercury*, 12 Feb. 1885.

[3] H. H. Henson, *Gordon: A Lecture* (Oxford, 1886), Preface, 10, 30.

[4] In addition to the recent case of Patteson noted below, the death of John Williams in the South Seas in 1839 had given impetus to the image of the missionary hero (B. Stanley, *The Bible and the Flag: Protestant Missions and British Imperialism in the Nineteenth and Twentieth Centuries* (Leicester, 1990), 78–9.

[5] O. Anderson, 'The Growth of Christian Militarism in Mid-Victorian Britain', *English Historical Review* 86 (1971), 46–72; C. I. Hamilton, 'Naval Hagiography and the Victorian Hero', *Historical Journal*, 23 (1980), 381–98.

Christian professions and endeavours to spread British influence constituted substantial common ground. Gordon admired Livingstone and, during the decade between the explorer's death and his own, was hailed as the heir to his leadership of the crusade to free central Africa from the ravages of the slave trade. Comment on Gordon frequently linked the two together as 'the greatest heroes of this generation'.[6] Dean Bradley hoped that their bodies might eventually rest side by side in Westminster Abbey.[7] Gordon's death inspired Elizabeth Charles to write a book entitled *Three Martyrs of the Nineteenth Century*, linking him not only to Livingstone but also to the missionary bishop John Coleridge Patteson who had been killed by Pacific islanders in 1871. She presented all three men as standing in the great historic tradition of Christian sacrifice and martyrdom, still as vibrant as it had ever been. Moreover she regarded them as also patriotic and chivalrous heroes, imbued with the spirit of King Arthur and King Alfred, and of Francis Drake as well as Francis of Assisi. Patriotism and piety could unite in the veneration of these contemporary martyrs, just as they could in the remote memory of Alban and Boniface, commemorated with Patteson on the pulpit of Exeter Cathedral.[8]

The deaths of Livingstone and Gordon both contrast with the majority of the cases selected for examination in this book, in that they did not remove perceived pillars of the constitutional or political fabric of national life. Ironically too, both men—unlike, say, Nelson—had died in circumstances of failure: Livingstone did not find the source of the Nile; Khartoum was lost with Gordon. The aftermath of their deaths also lacked the sharply defined liminal phases that followed deaths in Britain. Their distinctive impact thus rests on other factors. While still living, both men had acquired heroic status and had been in a mysterious environment of perilous remoteness that provided a psychological prelude to their actual deaths. After they died there was then a further long transitional phase, as news filtered through to Britain. In Livingstone's case this period was eventually brought to a visible conclusion by the return of the body itself and the funeral at Westminster Abbey, but in Gordon's the lack of a body or clear information regarding the exact circumstances of his death meant that liminality could

---

[6] J. Macaulay, *Gordon Anecdotes: A Sketch of the Career, with Illustrations of the Character of Charles George Gordon*, RE (1885), 131; *Who is the White Pasha? A Story of Coming Victory* (1889), 208; D. O. Helly, *Livingstone's Legacy. Horace Waller and Victorian Mythmaking* (Athens, Ohio, 1987), 261–320. Cf. J. M. MacKenzie, 'Heroic myths of empire' in J. M. MacKenzie (ed.), *Popular Imperialism and the Military 1850–1950* (Manchester, 1992), 109–38.

[7] *The Times*, 14 March 1885.

[8] E. Charles, *Three Martyrs of the Nineteenth Century: Studies from the Lives of Livingstone, Gordon and Patteson* (1885), pp. v–ix, 390. The book, published by SPCK, sold many thousands of copies and was still being reprinted in the 1920s.

never be fully resolved. Such circumstances added intensity and persistence to strong public feeling centred around perceptions of heroic sacrifice, to which the language of martyrdom was readily applied. Consideration of these instances therefore adds important further dimensions to our analysis as a whole.

## Livingstone

The subsequent wide appeal of the Livingstone cult owed much to two circumstances, its hero's genuinely humble origins in a Blantyre tenement in 1813, and the non-sectarian character of his profound Christian commitment. He was baptized a Presbyterian, lived a Congregationalist, and was buried by Anglicans.[9] He went to southern Africa as a missionary doctor, but in terms of conversions his career must be judged a failure. His fame was made by his epic journey of exploration across central Africa between 1849 and 1856, but his reputation was seriously damaged by the disaster of the Zambezi expedition of 1858 to 1864. The last phase of his life saw his incessant and seemingly futile wanderings in search of the source of the Nile, the famous meeting with Henry Morton Stanley at Ujiji in October 1871, and his lonely death in a hut at Ilala south of Lake Bangweolo during the night of 30 April 1873. It was an ambiguous martyrdom: he died as an explorer not as a preacher, and was killed by dysentery and exhaustion[10] not hostile natives. Even the famous image of him passing away while in prayer for Africa is dependent on a colourful and pious reading of the evidence.[11]

Nevertheless, Livingstone's death occurred at a time when the memory of the meeting with Stanley was still fresh, and when there was great public interest in his fate.[12] Subsequent events were to imbue his death with the mythic qualities that already surrounded his life. Rather than bury him immediately, his African followers, led by James Chuma and Abdullah Susi, first removed and buried the internal organs and preserved the body with salt. They then carried it with Livingstone's personal effects back to the coast, a journey that took nine months, and involved considerable risks and hardships. Initial British reaction was ungracious. At Unyanyembe in

---

[9] J. M. MacKenzie, 'David Livingstone: The Construction of the Myth', in G. Walker and T. Gallagher (eds.), *Sermons and Battle Hymns: Protestant Popular Culture in Modern Scotland* (Edinburgh, 1990), 31–2; T. Jeal, *Livingstone* (1973), 7–14, 109 and *passim*.

[10] WA, certificate by Sir William Ferguson, 17 April 1874.

[11] Helly, *Livingstone's Legacy*, 108–12.

[12] H. M. Stanley had returned to England on 1 August 1872, and his story attracted very extensive coverage in the newspapers (Jeal, *Livingstone*, 351).

October 1873 the party met an expedition sent by the Royal Geographical Society [RGS] in support of Livingstone. Its leader, Verney Lovett Cameron, advised the Africans to bury the body there, but Chuma and Susi refused and pushed on to Bagamoyo on the Indian Ocean coast, which they reached in February 1874.[13] Meanwhile Cameron's report of Livingstone's death had been relayed back to Britain on 27 January by W. F. Prideaux, the acting consul-general in Zanzibar.[14] Incredulous comment at home seized on the implausibility of 'negroes' carrying a dead body for hundreds of miles.[15] Livingstone's own sister doubted the report, thinking that he would have been far more anxious about his papers than the disposal of his body and would have wished to have been quietly buried where he died.[16]

Prideaux had the body brought to Zanzibar, and the fifteenth Earl of Derby, Foreign Secretary in the newly elected Disraeli government, then instructed him to send it on to England.[17] Initially the government planned to do no more than hand the body over to the relatives when it reached Southampton.[18] In the meantime, however, public interest was gathering momentum. Dean Stanley wrote to the RGS to indicate that, if asked, he would be glad to provide a grave in Westminster Abbey.[19] Sir Bartle Frere, President of the RGS, lobbied the government to induce them to give a grant towards funeral expenses, but Derby and Disraeli were adamant that their involvement would end at Southampton.[20] On 31 March, Russell Gurney, a leading Conservative back bencher and MP for Southampton, raised the matter in the Commons. Gurney noted the general desire for interment in Westminster Abbey, and the lack of means to pay for such a funeral without public support. In response Disraeli was non-committal, but denied that the government had any 'deficiency of respect for the name or *manes* of Dr Livingstone'.[21]

The government's hesitation stemmed primarily from its scepticism as to whether the body then being conveyed through the Mediterranean aboard the SS Malwa really was Livingstone's, and their consequent fear of becoming implicated in a hoax. Its hand was forced on 9 April when an

[13] Jeal, *Livingstone*, 368–9.
[14] *The Times*, 28 Jan. 1874.
[15] Ibid., 3, 13, 19 Feb. 1874.
[16] National Library of Scotland, Edinburgh [NLS], MS 10779 (12a), fos. 290–2, Janet Livingstone to John Murray, 13 Feb. 1874. There is indeed no evidence that Livingstone himself had wished his body to be brought back to Britain.
[17] *The Times*, 10 March 1874.
[18] BodL, Dep.Hughenden 55/3 (Disraeli Papers), fos. 61–84, Notes by Derby and Disraeli, 30 March 1874.
[19] WA, Stanley's Recollections, fos. 36–7; *The Times*, 25 Feb. 1874.
[20] BodL, Dep.Hughenden 55/3, fos. 61–84.
[21] *Hansard* third series, 218, cols. 486–8.

unauthorized report appeared in *The Times* to say that the government had agreed to defray the cost. In fact no such decision had yet been taken and Stafford Northcote, the Chancellor of the Exchequer, convened a crisis meeting to decide what to do.[22] Northcote wrote to Derby that 'Grave doubts are entertained as to whether the body is Livingstone's at all, and whether he must not be regarded as a sort of posthumous Arthur Orton, invented by Mr Gordon Bennett and Mr Stanley, and now killed and to be buried by them.'[23] Disraeli also suspected a 'swindling transaction'.[24] Such fears confirmed the government's disinclination to hold a formal 'public' funeral, which was in any case an honour limited by precedent to statesmen and outstanding military and naval commanders.[25] Accordingly Northcote compromised by offering the RGS a grant of £250 on the understanding that the society would take responsibility for the funeral. The offer was accepted and the subsequent arrangements were made by the RGS in conjunction with Dean Stanley, representatives of the family, and Southampton Town Council.[26]

Livingstone's impressive funeral was thus the product not of government initiative, but of press-inspired public interest and pressure. It also reflected the convergent interests of the RGS and of Dean Stanley in bringing the great explorer's remains to Westminster Abbey, to dignify the cause of African exploration and to extend the role of the Abbey as a national shrine.[27] When the body arrived at Southampton on 15 April large crowds turned out to witness an imposing procession in which the Mayor and corporation, clergy of all denominations and representatives of public bodies and professions accompanied it from the quayside to the railway station.[28] The remains were taken by special train to London, and then to the RGS's headquarters in Savile Row. The distinguished surgeon Sir William Fergusson examined the body that evening. He confounded the sceptics by giving a conclusive identification on the basis of a deformed bone in the left arm that was consistent with the injuries sustained by Livingstone when

---

[22] *The Times*, 9 April 1874; BL, AddMS 50016 (Iddesleigh Papers), fos. 209–10, Northcote to Disraeli, 9 April 1874. I am indebted to Professor James Sack for this reference.

[23] DerP (15th Earl) 16/2/6, Northcote to Derby, 10 April 1874. Arthur Orton was the Tichborne claimant; James Gordon Bennett was the proprietor of the *New York Herald* who had sent H. M. Stanley in search of Livingstone.

[24] BL, AddMS 50016, fos. 211–2, Disraeli to Northcote, 9 April 1874.

[25] Ibid., fos. 209–16.

[26] *Proceedings of the Royal Geographical Society [RGS]*, 18 (1873–4), 445, 449–50, 511.

[27] On Stanley's perspective, see also above Chapter 3.

[28] *The Times*, 16 April 1874; A. Hyde, F. C. Bliss and J. Taylor, *The Life and Life-Work of Dr David Livingstone* (Hartford, CT, 1875), 659.

he had been mauled by a lion in 1844.[29] The coffin rested in the map room at the RGS on 16 and 17 April, and although this was not a fully-fledged lying-in-state, it was visited 'by a large number of the Fellows [of the RGS] and the public'.[30]

Demand for tickets for the funeral on Saturday 18 April greatly exceeded supply, and a 'large concourse' of people gathered in the streets to witness the procession to the Abbey along Pall Mall and Whitehall.[31] Dean Stanley believed that, with the exception of the funeral of his own wife, on which he was hardly an objective commentator, it 'called forth a greater amount of popular feeling than any other in which I ever took part'. On the other hand he was struck by lack of participation from the aristocracy. The Queen had sent a representative, and Lord Shaftesbury and Lord Houghton (Richard Monckton Milnes) attended the service, but apart from these two individuals with special interests in Livingstone he could not recall the presence of any other peers or leading churchmen. On the other hand 'the middle class of society' were 'represented by Nonconformist ministers in great numbers'.[32] Stanley's memory deceived him somewhat: newspaper reports also mentioned the presence of the Bishop of Lincoln (Wordsworth), the Dukes of Sutherland and Manchester, several other peers, the Lord Mayor of London, and several representatives of foreign powers.[33] Other sources though confirm Stanley's impression that a wide cross-section of society attended the funeral: according to the *Illustrated London News*, Livingstone drew 'a throng of mourners as diverse and unique as was ever collected around an open grave'.[34] The prominent position of the grave added to the sense of occasion. Stanley recalled:

> The place for the burial, after some doubt, was chosen in the centre of the nave near the spot where, on the one hand, there were interred two very humble mechanicians who, like Livingstone, had risen to high eminence in their department—Tompion and Graham, watchmakers, and where on the other hand Rennell, the founder of the Society for African Exploration, was deposited. It so happened that this juxtaposition also imparted to the grave a central place which converted the funeral into a most august ceremonial.[35]

[29] J. M. MacKenzie and J. Skipwith (eds.), *David Livingstone and the Victorian Encounter with Africa* (1996), 212–3. Casts of the bone thus served as proof of identification as well as relics and medical curiosities.
[30] *Proceeedings of the RGS*, 18 (1873–4), 449; *The Times*, 17 April 1874.
[31] *The Times*, 17, 20 April 1874.
[32] WA, Stanley's Recollections, fos. 39–41.
[33] *The Times*, 20 April 1874; *Glasgow Herald*, 20 April 1874.
[34] *ILN*, 25 April 1874, p. 382.
[35] WA, Stanley's Recollections, fos. 39–40.

There was also a strong echo in Scotland of events in Southampton and London. In Edinburgh it was decided in mid-April 1874 to erect a statue to Livingstone, which was very swift action, when compared with the belated decisions at the same period to commemorate Knox who had been dead for three centuries, and Chalmers who had been dead for nearly three decades. There was immediate pressure for a similar monument in Glasgow. Mrs D. O. Hill's design for the Edinburgh statue was greeted with enthusiasm. It was held effectively to encapsulate the popular image of the man, 'with his pistol in his belt, and his Bible in his hand, and altogether like a fellow marching through the jungle, trusting in God and his own native Scottish muscle' (See Plate 3).[36] There were some hints of regret that Livingstone's body was not to lie 'under the shadow of the green hills of his native Clydesdale', but there was nevertheless appreciation of the tribute paid at Westminster to the remains of a great Scotsman.[37] Both on the day of the funeral and on the following Sunday memorial services were held in Hamilton.[38]

A powerful chord in popular consciousness had indeed been struck. In December 1874 Francis Kilvert recorded visiting a diorama on Livingstone's life displayed in Chippenham, with a party of children who particularly appreciated a cleverly contrived image of the funeral in which the burial party was imposed on an initially empty Abbey.[39] Cheap publications on Livingstone enjoyed an extensive sale among the working classes.[40] Meanwhile Lord Derby was pressing his Cabinet colleagues to agree to a pension for Livingstone's family: 'The Livingstone enthusiasm is just now so strong and so widely diffused, that I believe we cannot prudently refuse to do something in the sense demanded. It will be a popular move generally, but especially in Scotland.'[41] A sum of £3000 was granted.[42] The government also decided, in the light of the public mood, to defray the total costs of the funeral. These amounted to more than double the £250 it had initially granted to the RGS.[43] Nevertheless, despite such belated support, it was apparent that at this stage the Disraeli administration saw itself as doing the minimum consistent with the public mood, and had no aspirations itself further to encourage veneration for Livingstone.

Livingstone could readily be portrayed as an inclusive figure. In his

[36] *Glasgow Herald*, 15, 18 April 1874.
[37] *Scotsman*, 15, 20 April 1874.
[38] *Glasgow Herald*, 20 April 1874.
[39] W. Plomer (ed.), *Kilvert's Diary 1870–1879* (1986), 217 (14 Dec. 1874).
[40] NLS, MS 10779 (12a), fo. 470, Thomas Livingstone to John Murray, 5 Oct. 1875.
[41] DerP 17/2/6, Derby to Northcote, 24 April 1874.
[42] DerP 16/2/6, Northcote to Derby, 11 June 1874.
[43] *Proceedings of the RGS*, 18 (1873–4), 450.

sermon in the Abbey on 19 April Dean Stanley made explicit his co-option of this Scottish Nonconformist into his own liberal Anglican vision of a national church providing the moral and spiritual fibre of Empire. He dwelt on the spiritual dignity and significance of Livingstone's restless explorations in unveiling God's handiwork, and emphasized the comprehensiveness of his Christianity: 'Followed to his grave by the leading Nonconformists of England and the staunchest Presbyterians of Scotland, yet we feel that all the Churches may claim him as their own; that all English-speaking races may regard him as their son.'[44] Meanwhile in Hamilton the Revd H. M. Hamilton was citing Livingstone's example as stimulating the church at home as well as in Africa to 'a broader view of what true mission must embrace'.[45] The Nonconformist *British Quarterly Review* saw Livingstone as having taught the world 'that religion is not a speciality of dogmas and ceremonies, but a great sanctifying influence, catholic enough to embrace all forms of fruitful labour, and intense enough to touch them all with the peculiar energy of inspiration.'[46] Livingstone moreover was presented as a democratic as well as an ecumenical ideal: Dean Stanley reminded 'artisans or craftsmen from the loom or the factory' that Livingstone was especially one of them. He was an inspiration to all and sundry to achieve their full potential and to carry on the work in which he had given his life.[47] He also had an international appeal, reflected not only in the published tributes that rapidly began to appear in North America[48] but also in the sentiments of the French composer Charles Gounod who set to music Lord Houghton's poem on Livingstone's death. In Gounod's view 'La mort d'un grand homme n'est pas seulement un deuil national, c'est un deuil universel.'[49]

Grief for Livingstone was rapidly translated into enhanced inspiration for missionary endeavour and cultural imperialism in Africa. The *Wesleyan Methodist Magazine* saw Livingstone's death as an irreparable loss, and regretted that the public had been denied the pleasure of welcoming home a living hero. Nevertheless it saw his grave as making a silent appeal for mission in Africa, reinforced by the devotion of the Africans who had carried his body for a thousand miles.[50] Interest in Africa was further stimulated by the attendance at the funeral of Jacob Wainwright, 'the

---

[44] A. P. Stanley, 'The Mission of the Traveller', in *Sermons on Special Occasions* (1882), 173, 179–80.

[45] *Glasgow Herald*, 20 April 1874.

[46] *British Quarterly Review*, 59 (1874), 513.

[47] Stanley, *Sermons on Special Occasions*, 181–3.

[48] For example see Anon., *The Last Years of Livingstone* (Toronto, 1874); Hyde, Bliss and Taylor, *Life of Livingstone*.

[49] NLS, MS 10755, Photocopy of autograph score.

[50] *Wesleyan Methodist Magazine* fifth series, 20 (1874), 315, 520.

manumitted and Christianized young African whose presence symbolized the beneficent work of the master whom he tended so faithfully to the last'.[51] The evocation of Livingstone's lonely death confirmed links of imagination between Africa and Britain while heightening the aura of his own self-sacrifice. Lord Houghton visualized the dying man recalling his homeland as he lay in his remote hut at Ilala; a schoolboy poet evoked his call from a peaceful village to bring tidings of salvation to Africa, until the 'dying Scottish martyr's weary head' was laid down for the last time.[52] Within months of the funeral, Horace Waller, an Anglican clergyman, published his edition of Livingstone's *Last Journals*, with selections and revisions designed to convey the image of a saintly self-sacrificing man, who had died on his knees in prayer. The illustrations both reinforced the sense of Livingstone's martyrdom and conveyed an image of noble but primitive Africans.[53]

In a sermon on the day after Livingstone's funeral, Edmund Lane, curate of St George the Martyr, Southwark, articulated his sense of 'Hope for Africa'. He visualized an angel bearing the gospel flying over the continent, and asserted that God's hand lay behind the growth of British and American influence there. He looked forward to a future in which Africa would speak English, be governed by English laws and institutions, and civilized through the work of 'Christian patriots and philanthropists'. Livingstone himself had died without achieving his grand design, but he 'gave his life to kill slavery' and the fruit of his labours would be seen in the future. Lane concluded by dwelling on death itself as both the end of this life and the beginning of eternity, and calling on his hearers to give themselves to Christ.[54]

Rhetoric of this kind with its seamless blending of spiritual and secular aspirations and its linking of missionary vision to the spiritual needs of Britain itself was a characteristic response to Livingstone. In 1889 the veteran writer and social reformer Thomas Hughes looked back on the years since 1873. According to Hughes, Livingstone had died believing himself a beaten man, and this was indeed the common experience of martyrs. In the event though, Hughes considered his death to have been the seed from

---

[51] *The Times*, 20 April 1874. Wainwright's passage to Britain had been paid by the Church Missionary Society, which had educated him. The effect of choosing a CMS convert rather than Livingstone's more longstanding employees Susi and Chuma was to accentuate the Christianizing image of his work (cf. *The Times*, 31 March 1874, letter of Horace Waller).

[52] *The Times*, 20 April 1874; A. E. Campbell, *Livingstone* (1875).

[53] MacKenzie, 'Livingstone: The Construction of the Myth', 28–9; T. Barringer, 'Fabricating Africa: Livingstone and the Visual Image, 1850–1874' in MacKenzie and Skipwith, *David Livingstone*, 194–7.

[54] E. Lane, *Hope for Africa; or a Memorial to Dr Livingstone* (1874).

which much missionary and commercial endeavour had sprung.[55] This contemporary judgement is confirmed by the recent scholarship of John MacKenzie who both notes the intensity of the zeal with which Livingstone posthumously inspired his contemporaries, and suggests that he became in effect that most paradoxical of religious figures, a Protestant saint. His funeral had an immediate impact in stirring the Scottish churches to begin missionary activity in the Lake Malawi region, while other missionary societies also felt inspired to expand their work in east and central Africa.[56] From the early 1880s onwards commercial and eventually political involvement followed the missionaries. Livingstone also had a powerful and enduring impact at home: in the 1920s and 1930s his birthplace at Blantyre was to become a 'shrine' and a focus for Scottish national reawakening.[57] Such later developments fall outside the scope of this book, but their seeds were indeed sown in the immediate context of Livingstone's death and funeral. A process that too readily appears inevitable in retrospect owed much in reality to specific circumstances. In particular these included the perceived tragic heroism of Livingstone's last journey, the return of the body to provide a physical focus for mourning and ceremonial, the popular demand for such observance, and the readiness of the RGS and Dean Stanley to organize an impressive funeral. Livingstone's enormous reputation meant that his death would inevitably have made some impact, but had he either lived to return to Britain or been speedily buried under the trees at Ilala, it is probable that the form and extent of the response would have been very different.

## Gordon

Responses to Livingstone's death established the preconditions for powerful reactions to Gordon's: the model of the great hero standing and dying alone in the face of the natural and human perils of Africa had now been firmly anchored in the public mind. Charles Gordon made his military reputation in the early 1860s when he was seconded to lead the 'Ever Victorious Army' in the suppression of the Taiping rebellion in China. From 1874 to 1880 he was in the service of the Egyptian government, first as governor of Equatoria and then as governor-general of the Sudan. During this period he made considerable efforts to suppress the slave trade.

[55] T. Hughes, *David Livingstone* (1889), 191–208.
[56] J. M. MacKenzie 'David Livingstone and the Worldly After-Life: Imperialism and Nationalism in Africa' in MacKenzie and Skipwith (eds.), *David Livingstone*, 203–16; Stanley, *Bible and the Flag*, 123.
[57] MacKenzie, 'Livingstone: The Construction of the Myth', 32–40.

In the meantime his philanthropic interests, moral zeal, and profound, albeit unconventional, Christian faith imbued him with an aura of sanctity. Even before his death he was being extolled as a model man of faith.[58] As well as being perceived as Livingstone's successor in the endeavour to bring Christianity and 'civilization' to Africa, he was also seen as the leading living representative of the ideal of the Christian soldier, as established by men such as Captain Hedley Vicars in the Crimea and Sir Henry Havelock in India.[59] In January 1884 the Gladstone government made its fateful decision to send Gordon back to the Sudan to oversee the evacuation of the territory, which had slipped from Egyptian control in the face of the revolt led by Mohammed Ahmed, the self-proclaimed Mahdi. Gordon, however, aspired, in disregard of his instructions, to hold on to Khartoum and the Nile valley, and as he deferred evacuation, in May 1884 the Mahdists cut off his line of retreat to Egypt. As hostile forces surrounded Khartoum and at home public pressure mounted for action to relieve Gordon, political and military indecision ensued, and it was not until October that an expedition eventually started out. When the first British troops reached Khartoum on 28 January 1885, they found that the town had fallen to the Mahdists two days before, and Gordon himself had been killed.

Three distinctive circumstances should be borne in mind in understanding the reaction to Gordon's death. First, the body was never recovered. Accordingly there was a sense of incompleteness, reflected both in heightened feelings of outrage and indignity, and in suggestions even several years later that perhaps Gordon was after all still alive.[60] A second and related issue was a lack of conclusive information about the exact circumstances of his death. Accordingly the event could readily be visualized in terms of Christian heroism. In the longer term writers from F. R. Wingate to Winston Churchill constructed the compelling image of Gordon confronting his assailants at the top of the palace steps, disdaining to fight them and thus 'marching in all the pride of faith . . . to a martyr's death'. In reality the weight of the evidence points to the conclusion that Gordon was shot, perhaps by accident, and certainly without any dramatic confrontation with his assailants.[61]

[58] See for example W. Frith, *General Gordon or the Man of Faith* (1884?); C. C. Long, *The Three Prophets: Chinese Gordon, Mohammed-Ahmed (El Maadhi), Arabi Pasha* (New York, 1884).
[59] Anderson, 'Growth of Christian Militarism'; K. E. Hendrickson, *Making Saints: Religion and the Public Image of the British Army 1809–1885* (1998).
[60] *Who is the White Pasha?*
[61] D. Johnson, 'The Death of Gordon: a Victorian Myth', *Journal of Imperial and Commonwealth History*, 10 (1982), 285–310. Johnson is misleading in positing a dichotomy between soldierly and saintly constructions of Gordon's death. Religious interpretations of the event were prominent from the outset, and were blended with military ones through the concept of a 'soldier of Christ' (see, for example, *In Memoriam: Epitaphs on C. G. Gordon* (1885), 19).

Above all, Gordon's death was distinctive in its political implications, in that it was perceived as having been avoidable, and Gladstone and his ministers were widely held to be responsible for it. Such sentiment was led by the Queen herself who on 5 February in her fury and distress at the news of the fall of Khartoum fired off her celebrated *en clair* telegram to Gladstone, lamenting the tardiness of the efforts to save Gordon.[62] Gladstone unwisely reinforced the impression that he was insensitive to Gordon's fate by persisting with a planned visit to the theatre on February 10 as accounts of the General's death were first reaching London.[63] A Tory poet linked the recollection of Disraeli with that of Gordon:

> O for the heart and eye of Beaconsfield!
> The kindly heart that felt another's pain—
> The keen far-seeing eye that scann'd the world
> And realised our England's destiny . . .
> Then had we not been weeping this dark day
> Our noblest hero's painful, Christ-like death . . .[64]

The government narrowly survived a vote of censure and was to fall in June.

Specifically party-political reaction to Gordon's death overlaid a wider consensus of adulation for the deceased, the expression of which proved to be a satisfying mode of assuaging grief and anger. In some ways it transcended the immediate controversy over responsibility for the fall of Khartoum, although differences of emphasis are still suggestive. Gladstone himself set the tone in the Commons on 23 February when he acknowledged that Gordon's death was a great loss, but claimed that 'such examples are fruitful in the future, and I trust there will grow from the contemplation of that character and those deeds other men who in future time will emulate his noble and most Christian example'.[65] Nonconformists sympathetic to the government similarly preferred to dwell on Gordon's life as a whole and were ambivalent about the final Khartoum episode. The *Baptist Magazine* admired Gordon, but thought he was largely responsible for his own downfall: now that he was dead, speedy withdrawal from the Sudan was the only appropriate course.[66] In the opinion of the *British Quarterly Review*,

---

[62] The Queen's private secretary subsequently claimed that her failure to cipher the telegram was a consequence of her impulsive anger rather than arising from any calculated intention of making her displeasure public (BL, AddMS 48603A (Hamilton Papers), fos. 220–2, Ponsonby to Hamilton, 7 Feb. 1885).

[63] D. W. R. Bahlman, *The Diary of Sir Edward Walter Hamilton 1880–1885*, 2 vols. (Oxford, 1885), ii. 794–5 (11 Feb. 1885).

[64] J. Rutter, *Gordon Songs and Sonnets* (1887), 114.

[65] *Hansard* third series, 294, col. 1080.

[66] *Baptist Magazine*, 78 (1885), 228–30.

the sense of panic that had gripped London on receipt of news of the fall of Khartoum was an unjustifiable loss of national dignity stemming from excessive adulation for Gordon.[67] The *Congregationalist* greatly reverenced Gordon, stressing his powerful faith in God and his dedication to the welfare of his fellow human beings, as manifested particularly in his philanthropic and evangelistic activity while stationed at Gravesend between 1865 and 1871. It suggested that those qualities manifested by Gordon in the life of a soldier should be an inspiration to others to work for the conversion of men.[68] Dr Hiles Hitchens, preaching at Eccleston Square Congregational Church on 15 February, held Gordon up as a model of piety and moral virtue. His audience might not have to fight literal battles, but they were called to war 'with intemperance, with indifference, [and] with infidelity'. Chivalry was needed in the lives of everyone.[69]

For others, especially Anglicans, Gordon was perceived as a martyr whose death had purpose, and moral and spiritual significance. Elizabeth Charles recorded a report that his attackers had offered him a choice between death and conversion to Islam, and hence he had been in the most literal sense a martyr 'for the faith of Christ'. She thought, however, that such 'details' mattered little.[70] For the newly-appointed Dean of Gloucester, Henry Montagu Butler, it was Gordon's 'lonely martyrdom' that was the 'very symbol of [his] unworldliness and self-sacrifice', crowning a Christ-like life with a Christ-like death.[71] Preaching at Holy Trinity, Coventry, Brooke Lambert pursued further this ultimate precedent for martyrdom, suggesting that although Gordon's end appeared to be a failure, the Cross of Christ itself was both the greatest success as well as the greatest failure in world history.[72] Similarly, for Hensley Henson, although Gordon's life did offer much that his hearers might seek to emulate, it was his end that was his finest hour. There was, he said, 'nothing wanting to the moral splendour of that long martyrdom. It was lonely, it was unselfish, it was voluntary; and when we look more closely at the hero as he endures, we can, methinks form some faint glimmering of the power of faith. The secret source of that noble courage, that self-suppression, that martyrdom, was his faith in God.'[73]

A contrasting Anglican view came from William Sinclair, Vicar of St Stephen's, Westminster, who idealized Gordon's qualities in life as 'a great

[67] *British Quarterly Review*, 81 (1885), 417–18.
[68] *Congregationalist*, 14 (1885), 308–13.
[69] H. Hitchens, *On the Death of General Gordon* (1885).
[70] Charles, *Three Martyrs*, 284.
[71] Quoted by A. Besant, *Gordon Judged Out of His Own Mouth* (1885), 4.
[72] *The Times*, 14 March 1885.
[73] Henson, *Gordon*, 30–1.

Christian hero', with faith that could move mountains and complete self-surrender to Christ. Sinclair also regarded him as possessed of unequalled courage, enormous military skill, and inspired judgement. His death, however, was portrayed not as a martyrdom, but as a pointless waste. Moreover it was the responsibility of the nation as a whole, which had too readily acquiesced in the inertia of its leaders. The catastrophe was a sign that the nation was 'unfit any longer to carry out those high destinies with which God had at one time entrusted us'.[74]

Other comment blurred the distinction between Christian conviction and patriotic enthusiasm. Preaching in Balliol College Chapel, Benjamin Jowett judged that no 'public calamity' had ever so deeply affected the 'hearts and minds of England'. According to Jowett, Gordon's true greatness lay in his vision of the 'Eternal and Unchangeable', but the inspiration of his example was seen in more material terms as stirring his compatriots to fulfil their God-given national destiny.[75] A short illustrated life published by the SPCK bracketed Gordon with Nelson, who could hardly be presented in the same way as a model for the life of faith. Gordon, according to the writer, was a 'richly-gifted Christian Hero who held on high once more the supremacy of his race'.[76] A preacher in front of the Prince of Wales in 1891 was to visualize Gordon looking from the ramparts of Khartoum 'to the England for whom he lived and for whom he was about so soon to die'.[77]

The spectrum of perception is completed by the straightforwardly secular approach of *The Times*'s leader on Gordon's death, which hailed his life as a reminder that chivalry was not dead and as proof that 'the English race is in no sense degenerate'.[78] In similar vein Reginald Brett (later Viscount Esher) judged that his heroic life and death had been 'good for the nation', stirring 'men of all classes' to a nobler sense of responsibility.[79] Edward Hamilton, Gladstone's private secretary, judged that 'Gordon was certain[ly] a hero—the very embodiment of British chivalry and pluck'.[80]

In default of the opportunity to hold a funeral, the memorial services held in Westminster Abbey and in many cathedrals on 13 March 1885 provided some focus and conclusion for public mourning.[81] Large attendances and apparently sincere expressions of feeling supported an appearance

---

[74] W. M. Sinclair, *Gordon and England* (1885), 5, 20 and *passim*.
[75] O. S., *The Hero Sacrificed: Stray Cuttings from the Portfolio of an Old Soldier* (1885), 106–10.
[76] W. J. G., *Gordon: A Life of Faith and Duty* (1885), 35–6.
[77] T. T. Shore, *General Gordon* (1891), 6.
[78] *The Times*, 12 Feb. 1885.
[79] M. V. Brett (ed.), *Journals and Letters of Reginald Viscount Esher*, 4 vols. (1934), i. 109.
[80] Bahlman, *Hamilton*, ii. 793 (11 Feb. 1885).
[81] See above, Chapter 3.

of consensus, although the cathedral services do not appear to have been emulated in parish churches or in Nonconformist chapels.[82] Nevertheless a goodly turnout of peers indicated that Gordon had captured the imagination of the aristocracy to an extent that Livingstone had failed to do. The presence of substantial military contingents seemed to bear out the view expressed by more than one preacher that 'the life of Gordon told plainly that the military spirit could exist together with the most intense devotion to Christ'.[83] A further focus for mourning was provided by the memorial fund in which the Prince of Wales took an active role, and which enjoyed cross-party and interdenominational support.[84]

The response to Gordon's death boosted the tendency already apparent in the response to Livingstone's for a Christian concept of martyrdom to blend almost imperceptibly into a more diffuse ideal of dying for the cause of the nation and the Empire. Nowhere was this trend more apparent than in the lavishly produced address presented to Gordon's sister, which was numerously signed by princesses, peeresses, and the wives of bishops and MPs 'as representing the women of the United Kingdom'. The address affirmed that Gordon 'sacrificed his life to uphold the honour of his country', and left 'an undying legacy of self denying faith, and of devotion to duty and to God'. In the future 'British Mothers' would hold up General Gordon as a role model for their sons. The embossed front cover carried St Paul's archetypal reflection on the Christian life, which in the context appeared highly ambiguous in its implications: 'I have fought the good fight. I have finished my course. I have kept the faith.'[85] Such willingness on the part of women to associate themselves with veneration for Gordon was somewhat ironic in view of the late hero's notorious misogyny. His martyrdom, like Livingstone's, had been a robustly masculine one. Nevertheless the address to Miss Gordon signalled the anxiety of women to identify with self-sacrifice in the cause of God and Empire. Moreover it represented a further noteworthy link with the Queen herself. Her staff had been consulted at an early stage in the collection of signatures,[86] and the readiness of her daughters, daughters-in-law and granddaughters to sign it indicated that she adhered to its sentiments.

There were, however, limits to the chorus of adulation. Charles C. Coe maintained that Gordon had been the 'least fit of all men to accomplish the evacuation of the Soudan' and it was 'a curious moral phenomenon' that he was now venerated as an 'incarnation of all the virtues and pieties'.

---

[82] Nor did every cathedral participate: for Exeter's abstention see above, 99.
[83] *The Times*, 14 March 1885.
[84] *The Times*, 23, 25 Feb., 16 March, 1 June 1885.
[85] BL, AddMS 34482.
[86] RA, PP/VIC/1885/2526, Note by Ponsonby, 7 March 1885.

If Gordon was worthy of emulation at all it was not as a soldier, but as an advocate of peace.[87] In a telling pamphlet, the freethinker Annie Besant argued that Gordon was no more than a straightforward, brave soldier of fortune, who happened to have eccentric religious beliefs. He took a much more down-to-earth view of his own work than his admirers attributed to him. In short he was a far more plausible human being than 'the impossible hybrid of heroism, saintliness, St Michael-and-the-dragonism, and pietism that has been held up for the homage or the derision of the world'.[88] His death was no martyrdom but rather the consequence of his own 'fanatical imprudence and self will'. Besant hoped that the 'rebuking voices' of English workers would check the statesmen and pressmen who were using Gordon's name 'as the fiery cross to gather an army of revenge'.[89] It is indeed arguable that although Gordon's death inspired a stronger reaction than Livingstone's among the social and political élite, the converse was true among the middle and lower classes. Significantly Edward Hamilton specifically attributed the hostility to Gladstone to 'London Society'.[90] As we have seen, Nonconformist journals were relatively lukewarm in their reactions, and no explicit evidence has been found of demonstrably popular manifestations of mourning.

The impression that sentiment was strongest among the upper classes is confirmed by the measures taken to commemorate Gordon. Plans were made in May 1885 for a Gordon League to elevate the moral condition of the working class, so as to lay the foundations for Christian commitment. It was intended that 'ladies and gentlemen' would run halls for 'working men' offering a variety of social support and short religious services.[91] This initiative does not appear to have gained much momentum, but similarly paternalist attitudes were implicit in the main memorial scheme under which homes were set up for orphaned and neglected boys. Donations came predominantly from the wealthy. Although the organizers proudly reported that a collecting box containing £29 4s 6d represented the small contributions of the poor, its location outside the Mansion House in the City of London must cast some doubt over this supposition.[92]

[87] C. C. Coe, *General Gordon in a New Light: the Cause of War, and the Advocate of Peace* (Bolton, 1885).

[88] Besant, *Gordon Judged*, 3, 5ff. For scholarly analysis of the disjunction between the popular image of Gordon and the seriously flawed reality see Hendrickson, *Making Saints*, 134–9.

[89] Besant, *Gordon Judged*, 16.

[90] Bahlman, *Hamilton*, ii. 794.

[91] *The Gordon League: How to Organize a Gordon Hall* (Printed leaflet in RA, PP/VIC/1885/2526).

[92] *The Times*, 16 March 1885. The boys' home scheme reflected the wishes of Gordon's sister.

Meanwhile the Gordon literature rapidly assumed a didactic dimension. The Revd S. A. Swaine targeted his biography at children for whom, he suggested, the heroic had a particular appeal. There could be no better example, he wrote, than Gordon's in inspiring them to grow up 'brave, and good, and true'. Swaine emphasized a practical rather than devotional Christianity and asserted that 'Englishmen' would be richer and nobler for Gordon's example. He lived and died for others, and deserved to be called 'not only the Hero, but the Martyr of Khartoum'.[93] In similar vein Abraham Kingdon expounded Gordon's moral and practical qualities as suitable for emulation by the young. He was a man who had spent his life rescuing others, but for him in his own hour of need deliverance came late.[94] An Australian preacher contrasted the enthusiasm of his countrymen with the lukewarm response he perceived among the masses at home, and urged that the tale of 'saintly heroism' should be 'told again and again in our children's ears'. If need be, now that an Australian detachment was sailing for Egypt, 'let Australian blood flow on Nubian sands for Christ and British honour'.[95]

The Gordon cult remained vigorous for a generation. There continued to be varieties of emphasis, ranging from devotional tracts to primarily secular portrayals of patriotic heroism.[96] The dominant flavour, however, was a combination of Christian and patriotic reference. Gordon was acclaimed an examplar of the practical power of Christian faith, as a great Englishman who contributed to the building of Empire, and as a martyr who laid down his life for his country, his fellow human beings and his God. The image was sustained in regular published sermons, preached in front of the Prince of Wales, in aid of the Gordon Boys' Home and encapsulated in the inscription on Gordon's monument in St Paul's Cathedral. It stated that he

> at all times and everywhere gave his strength to the weak, his substance to the poor, his sympathy to the suffering, his heart to God. . . . He saved an Empire by his warlike genius, he ruled vast provinces with justice, wisdom, and power. And lastly, obedient to his Sovereign's command, he died in the

---

[93] S. A. Swaine, *General Gordon* (1885), 5, 127.

[94] A. Kingdon, *Gordon the Christian Hero: A Book for the Young* (1885), 96 and *passim*.

[95] H. F. Tucker, *A Tribute to the Memory of General Gordon* (Melbourne, 1885), 9–11. For another Australian tribute see G. Welch, *Life of General Gordon* (Melbourne, 1885).

[96] For two examples illustrating the range of the spectrum see H. C. Wilson's edition of Joseph Hall, *Christ Mystical of the Blessed Union of Christ and His Members* (1893), from Gordon's own copy with an introduction on Gordon's theology, and Colonel Sir William Butler's *Charles George Gordon* (1889), the first volume in an 'English Men of Action' series published by Macmillan.

heroic attempt to save men, women and children from imminent and deadly peril (John xv.13).[97]

In Elizabeth Charles's trinity of martyrs there was a progression from the Christian towards the imperial; from Patteson the missionary bishop, through Livingstone, the missionary turned explorer, to Gordon, the devout layman and soldier. This trend may be seen as representative of a degree of secularization during the 1870s and 1880s of the motif of Christ-like, sacrificial death and of growing acceptance of imperial as opposed to specifically missionary motivations for overseas expansion. Even in relation to Gordon, however, that trend was by no means complete. In the meantime, however, the impact of the heroic myths of martyrdom associated with Gordon and Livingstone can be seen in influencing responses to later prominent deaths. When Edward VII died in 1910 Rudyard Kipling wrote of him, implausibly but emotively, 'Simply as any die in his service he died for us'.[98] In 1912 the deaths of Robert Falcon Scott and his men in the Antarctic replicated the sense of heroic failure associated with both Livingstone and Gordon, while Lawrence Oates's solitary last walk into the snow added the dimension of sacrificial death.[99] Above all, during the First World War, the image of the dead soldier as martyr remained influential.[100] In 1918, however, the publication of Lytton Strachey's compelling demolition of the Gordon myth was to have an enormous impact.[101] By contrast the image of Livingstone, for all the ambivalences of his 'martyrdom', was to prove much more adaptable to the mood of the twentieth-century world.[102]

[97] The Empire alluded to in the inscription was presumably that of China not of Britain, but the ambiguity appears intentional. Published memorial sermons include those by James Fleming (1890), T. Teignmouth Shore (1891) William Boyd Carpenter (1899) and John Phillips Alcot Bowers (1904).

[98] R. Kipling, *The Dead King* (1910).

[99] Cf. M. Girouard, *The Return to Camelot: Chivalry and the English Gentleman* (1981), 3–4; M. Jones, 'Heavy Mettle Fan Club', *Times Higher Education Supplement*, 3 April 1998.

[100] Wolffe, *God and Greater Britain*, 239–40.

[101] L. Strachey, *Eminent Victorians* (1986 edn), pp. ix, 189–267.

[102] MacKenzie, 'Livingstone: The Construction of the Myth', 37–40.

# 6

# *The Shades of Westminster:*
# Death and Politicians

The year 1865 saw the deaths in office of both the President of the United States, Abraham Lincoln, the victim of an assassin's bullet at Ford's Theatre on 14 April, and the British Prime Minister, Lord Palmerston, who succumbed to natural causes on 18 October. Both Lincoln and Palmerston died at the peaks of their fame and prestige, having recently enjoyed electoral triumphs that confirmed their tenure of office. In some respects the contexts were very different. The abrupt and violent death of a man of fifty-six had strong dimensions of shock and tragedy that were lacking in the peaceful end of a man of eighty who had lived life to the full. The United States was still in the final phases of a bitter civil war whereas Britain was enjoying a period of notable prosperity and stability. Nevertheless this striking and unique coincidence provides an instructive starting point for discussion in this chapter, especially as Palmerston has been the only British Prime Minister to die in harness since the assassination of Spencer Perceval in 1812.[1] Moreover his death had direct and important political implications in removing a substantial bastion of constitutional conservatism and beginning the chain of events that led to the second Reform Act of 1867 and the first Gladstone ministry of 1868–74. Arguably Lincoln's death and orderly succession by Andrew Johnson was more limited in its consequences.

In the United States the weeks after Lincoln's death saw a mood of intense mourning focused on the protracted progress of the murdered man's remains from Washington to Baltimore, Harrisburg, Philadelphia and New York and then west to his home at Springfield, Illinois.[2] In subsequent years the cult of Lincoln was to become a central strand in American civil

---

[1] In 1908 Sir Henry Campbell-Bannerman was terminally ill at the time of his resignation, but handed over to Asquith a few weeks before his death.

[2] M. D. Peterson, *Lincoln in American Memory* (New York, 1994), 3–24; T. R. Turner, *Beware the People Weeping: Public Opinion and the Assassination of Abraham Lincoln* (Baton Rouge, 1982).

religion.[3] There were some initial indications that reactions to Palmerston's death might follow a similar course. *The Times* leader surveyed his long career and felt that the death of 'one of the truest Englishmen that ever filled the office of Premier' would be felt by all 'with a feeling like that of personal bereavement'.[4] Indeed, Dean Stanley, who was in Scotland at the time, recalled telling a waiter who was bringing in his breakfast, and 'he almost fell down from the shock it gave him'.[5] *The Times* developed the idea that Palmerston was 'the Englishman of our ideal love and homage' and warmly commended the decision of the Queen and the new Prime Minister, Earl Russell, to hold a public funeral and interment at Westminster Abbey.[6] Although this arrangement overruled Palmerston's own expectation that he would be laid to rest at Romsey near his home at Broadlands, the newspaper felt that burial at Westminster was consistent with 'the deep national instinct'.[7] The funeral on 27 October, was the largest to take place in London since Wellington's thirteen years before, and the route from Piccadilly to the Abbey was densely crowded. The mourners—all male, as was still customary—were joined by the Prince of Wales.[8] The service itself was an impressive and solemn occasion.[9]

Nevertheless the mood lacked the intensity apparent in the aftermath of Lincoln's death, or indeed in the days after Prince Albert's death in December 1861. Although the funeral was described as a 'public' one, the arrangements were left to the undertakers and the Abbey authorities, without any involvement from those other agencies of government that had been active in the preparations for Wellington's obsequies.[10] The pro-

[3] Pierard and Linder, *Civil Religion and the Presidency*, 87–113.
[4] *The Times*, 20 Oct. 1865.
[5] WA, Stanley's Recollections, fo. 2.
[6] *The Times*, 24, 25 Oct. 1865. The decision was publicly attributed to the Queen, but Stanley's recollections make it clear that the initiative was Russell's. Generally Stanley jealously guarded his own prerogative of deciding on proposals for burial in the Abbey, but he noted that 'on occasions when the Prime Minister takes upon himself the responsibility of such an interment, the responsibility of consenting is removed from the hands of the Dean'. Stanley further insisted that the government take responsibility for the decision to grant Lady Palmerston's request to be allowed to be buried with her husband in due course (Recollections, fos. 3–5). This case was subsequently to be used as a precedent for also allowing Mrs Gladstone's burial in the Abbey with her husband.
[7] *The Times*, 24, 28 Oct. 1865.
[8] Ibid., 28 Oct. 1865.
[9] WA, Stanley's Recollections, fos. 5–6.
[10] Russell's correspondence on the funeral (PRO, PRO 30/22/15F, fos. 2–261 *passim*) suggests that there was considerable confusion over the arrangements. On 21 October the family was still envisaging that it would be at Romsey (fos. 91–2, William Cowper to Russell).

cession was accordingly a relatively modest one: it appeared 'shabby' and did not capture the public imagination to anything like the same extent as the Duke's had done.[11] The American minister in London did not notice anyone in tears outside the Abbey,[12] a notable contrast with the scene outside the White House and the Capitol six months earlier. Meanwhile obituarists might widely portray Palmerston as an archetypal Englishman, but he was also seen, even more perhaps than Wellington, as a survivor from a past era, whose prominence in the public mind was to wane rapidly after his death. At a period when many statues were still being erected to Prince Albert, there were but few for 'Old Pam'.

It was indeed generally observable that the British were relatively muted in their grief for politicians in contrast not only to the Americans but also to the French, as illustrated for example in reaction to the death of Léon Gambetta in 1882.[13] Irish feelings, as we have seen in relation to O'Connell and Parnell, could also be more intense. Reactions to prominent deaths had much more to do with the perceived symbolic status of the deceased than with any rational appraisal of the consequences of his or her death. In the American and French republics and in the Irish struggle for Home Rule, exceptional political leaders were more likely to acquire such an iconic national significance than they were in Britain, where such emotions were more usually centred upon royalty or on 'heroes' such as Nelson, Wellington or Gordon. Significantly *The Times* judged that Palmerston, although a 'great man', fell short of the 'heroic type of character, which we associate with a few—very few—historical names'.[14] Moreover, Palmerston had died in the midst of active political life with a dispatch box open beside his bed. The limits to public feeling were even more apparent in the cases of statesmen such as the fourteenth Earl of Derby or Earl Russell who died after retirement from the public eye, in 1869 and 1878 respectively. Both had private funerals. In the case of Russell, who had been out of the public eye

---

There was also ambiguity over its formal status: insofar as it took place in Westminster Abbey at the instigation and expense of the government it appeared to be a public funeral. The expenses of £2,079 were met from civil contingencies and repaid by a vote (BL, AddMS 44189, fo. 84). On the other hand, the new Parliament had not yet been sworn in, so could not pass a formal resolution, nor was the Earl Marshal or the Lord Chamberlain involved in any way. The precedent cited was that of George Canning in 1827 who had been buried 'privately' in Westminster Abbey in front of a 'large concourse of persons' (PRO 30/22/ 15F, fo. 66, Brand to Russell, 19 Oct. 1865; cf. note in PRO, WORKS 21/44).

[11] Gower, *Reminiscences* (1883), i. 219.

[12] J. Ridley, *Lord Palmerston* (1970), 584.

[13] A. Ben-Amos, 'Molding the National Memory: The State Funerals of the French Third Republic', University of California PhD thesis, 1988.

[14] *The Times*, 19 Oct. 1865.

for more than a decade, *The Times* observed that his death merely removed 'the shadow of a great name'.[15]

Politics, however, does merit consideration in this book mainly because of the two later Victorian cases that provided an exception to this pattern, those of Benjamin Disraeli, Earl of Beaconsfield, in 1881, and of William Ewart Gladstone in 1898. In death as in life these two great adversaries broke important new ground in British political culture, arguably achieving the 'heroic' status denied to Palmerston. Moreover in Gladstone's case the survival of numerous letters of condolence from the general public provides a valuable insight into popular feeling at a time of national bereavement.

The case in the previous generation that came closest to foreshadowing these instances was that of Sir Robert Peel, who died on 2 July 1850 from injuries sustained in a fall from his horse four days earlier. At the time of his death Peel was seemingly in the political wilderness following the split in the Conservative Party arising from his repeal of the Corn Laws in 1846. Nevertheless he was a figure of immense personal prestige, and at sixty-two was still young enough to offer the possibility of a comeback. Within days of his death, moreover, he had demonstrated his continuing political and personal vigour in his speech in the 'Don Pacifico' debate. His death therefore combined elements of shock and tragedy with a genuine and legitimate sense that a powerful force in British politics had been abruptly extinguished. Immediate public feeling was intense and widespread, numerous momentoes were manufactured, and fourteen towns and cities erected statues.[16]

Both Disraeli and Gladstone, at seventy-six and eighty-eight respectively, were substantially older than Peel when they died and, unlike him, suffered protracted final illnesses, which to some extent prepared public opinion for the worst. Gladstone had been in retirement for four years and although Disraeli died still leader of the Opposition, the prospects of a return to Downing Street were more theoretical than realistic. Nevertheless reactions to their deaths followed a similar pattern.

## Disraeli

Benjamin Disraeli died at his London home in Curzon Street early in the morning of Tuesday 19 April 1881. Almost exactly a year earlier his party had suffered a crushing defeat in a bitterly fought general election. Despite

[15] *The Times*, 25, 29 Oct. 1869; 29 May, 5 June 1878.
[16] D. Read, *Peel and the Victorians* (Oxford, 1987), 266–86, 294–301. Professor Read has here provided an extensive and suggestive account of responses to Peel's death that it would be superfluous to rework in detail in the present book.

his age, however, he had retained the leadership, saying that 'in the hour of failure he would not withdraw', although subsequent awareness of his own declining health led him to hope that 'my successor will soon appear'.[17] In the event, however, he was still in harness in late March 1881 when he developed the bronchitis that was to mark the onset of his final illness. After a few days his condition became serious, but he lingered for another three weeks. His death bed was attended by a small private circle, but was a focus of sustained public interest, the two spheres connected by regular bulletins on the one hand, and numerous telegrams and letters of sympathy on the other.[18] The Queen herself set the pattern, with repeated enquiries about Disraeli's condition, in response to which she received up to four telegrams or letters every day.[19] The bulletins clutched at straws of hope: the patient himself considered them too optimistic, while the Marquess of Donegall complained that they were 'incomprehensible compositions', and sought authentic information.[20] Meanwhile large crowds gathered in the street outside the house, including, in a striking indication of widespread consensus, both erstwhile political opponents of the dying man and a substantial proportion from the working classes.[21]

The end when it came was hardly a surprise, but only a limited circle had recognized its inevitability, and there was a sense of culminating drama. Dean Stanley wrote to the Queen, 'It is a close worthy of the wonderful life, . . . the intense interest of the people, the tragical fitness of the moment of the termination of that long political career.'[22] Lord Redesdale had been a boy at the time of Wellington's death and was to live to observe the response to Edward VII's, but he recalled that in April 1881, 'The mourning was universal all over the country; never, except in the case of King Edward's death, have I seen so much feeling shown.'[23] In the days after the death Disraeli's publishers could not satisfy the demand for copies of his novels, in spite of keeping the printers at work day and night.[24]

The aftermath of Disraeli's death saw an intriguing working out of two tensions inherent in mourning for a major and still active political figure. First, there was the endeavour to find a balance between private preference and public image. Second, to what extent, in death, could Disraeli transcend

---

[17] W. F. Monypenny and G. E. Buckle, *The Life of Benjamin Disraeli Earl of Beaconsfield*, 6 vols. (1910–20), vi. 577, 594–5.

[18] Monypenny and Buckle, *Disraeli*, vi. 612; Blake, *Disraeli*, 748.

[19] RA, VIC/Z 155, *passim*.

[20] Monypenny and Buckle, *Disraeli*, vi. 611; BodL, DisP, Dep. Hughenden 24/1, fos. 71–2, 18 April 1881.

[21] *Daily News*, 27 April 1881; *Lloyds Weekly Newspaper*, 24 April 1881.

[22] RA, VIC/Z 155/141.

[23] Redesdale, *Memories*, ii. 676.

[24] Laughton, *Henry Reeve*, ii. 292–3.

the strong political and religious partisanship that had been focused on him in life, and be presented as a truly 'national' figure? Both issues were complicated by the direct interest of the Queen, who grieved for Disraeli both as personal friend and as servant of the Crown.

When it became evident that Disraeli's illness was almost certainly terminal, Gladstone, now Prime Minister, consulted Earl Granville, the government leader in the Lords, about the funeral arrangements. They agreed that a public funeral should be offered and were concerned to be seen to act of their own volition rather than in response to royal or public pressure.[25] Meanwhile Gladstone asked his private secretary, Edward Hamilton, to investigate the precedents.[26] Accordingly, as soon as news of the death reached Gladstone at Hawarden in North Wales, at eight o'clock in the morning of 19 April, he telegraphed his offer of a public funeral to the executors.[27] He immediately followed his telegram with a letter to Lord Rowton (Disraeli's recently ennobled private secretary, Monty Corry) noting the event would be regarded with much 'mournful interest thoughout this country and beyond its limits'. Accordingly, he continued, 'I desire at once to inform you his Executors that, if it should be agreable to their wishes, I shall be prepared to give the necessary directions for a public funeral. In tendering this honour on the part of the Government I feel assured that I am acting in conformity with the general expectation and desire.'[28] Dean Stanley lost no time in himself calling at Curzon Street and endorsing the premier's implicit offer of a Westminster Abbey funeral.[29] By the time Gladstone had received a letter from the Queen giving her view that 'Tho' I think it will be declined a public funeral ought at once to be offered',[30] he had already had a negative response from the executors. Her letter also crossed with one from him giving the reasons for his magnanimity:

> Occasions like this, of deep and touching national interest are, in Mr Gladstone's view, governed by general rules entirely beyond the reach of the controversies which belong to differences between political parties.
>
> Mr Gladstone would not seek, nor would he earn, Your Majesty's regard by dissembling the amount or character of the separation between Lord Beaconsfield and himself. But it does not in any degree blind him to the extraordinary powers of the deceased Statesman, or to many remarkable

---

[25] E. Fitzmaurice, *The Life of Granville George Leveson Gower, Second Earl Granville*, 2 vols. (1905), ii. 196.

[26] BL, AddMS 48607B, fo. 30, Gladstone to Hamilton, 10 April 1881. For discussion of Hamilton's memorandum in response (AddMS 44189, fo. 84) see below, Appendix.

[27] RA, VIC/Z 155/145, Gladstone to the Queen, 20 April 1881.

[28] DisP, Dep.Hughenden 24/2, fo. 1, Gladstone to Rowton, 19 April 1881.

[29] Blake, *Disraeli*, 751.

[30] RA, VIC/Z 155/144, The Queen to Gladstone, 20 April 1881.

qualities, in regard to which Mr Gladstone, well aware of his own marked inferiority, can only desire to profit by a great example.[31]

The Queen, in forwarding a copy of what she considered a 'remarkable' letter to Rowton, chose to construe Gladstone's no doubt carefully worded final sentence as an unqualified admission of his own 'inferiority' to Disraeli and of his readiness to 'follow a great example'.[32] Nevertheless, the document is a significant one in clearly enunciating the position that for a statesman of Disraeli's stature, it was indeed appropriate to foster national mourning of a kind that transcended political partisanship. Disraeli moreover could hardly be perceived as a figure personally above party in the way that Peel, Wellington and Palmerston had all more or less become by the time of their respective deaths.

Rowton felt obliged to refuse Gladstone's offer of a public funeral because of Disraeli's clear instructions in his will that he should be buried beside his late wife, Mary Anne, in Hughenden churchyard on his Buckinghamshire estate, and that his funeral should be 'conducted with the same simplicity as hers was'.[33] The legal force of this document was reinforced both by Disraeli's 'verbally expressed desire' and by the discovery among his private papers of a letter from Mary Anne urging him to leave instructions that they should be buried in the same grave.[34] The final decision was in effect taken by the Queen. She summoned Rowton to Osborne on 20 April, and after a conversation with him concluded that Disraeli's 'wishes to be laid by the side of his devoted wife should be considered as sacred, and that he should rest at Hughenden, which he was so fond of'.[35]

The decision not to hold the funeral in Westminster Abbey attracted some criticism. Some felt that Disraeli was being denied the formal public tribute that was his due, and there was resentment from individuals and institutions who would have liked to be able to have paid their own respects

---

[31] RA, VIC/Z 155/7, Gladstone to the Queen, 20 April 1881.

[32] RA, VIC/ADD V 30/32, The Queen to Rowton, 21 April 1881.

[33] Blake, *Disraeli*, 751.

[34] DisP, Dep.Hughenden 24/2, fos. 4–5, copy by Rowton of letter from Mrs Disraeli (subsequently Viscountess Beaconsfield) of 6 June 1856, with note dated 26 May 1881. Hamilton judged that 'it is clear that the executors could have come to no other conclusion than they did' (Bahlman, *Hamilton*, i. 131). As Lady Beaconsfield had predeceased her husband (in 1872) the solution adopted in the cases of Palmerston and Gladstone, namely an undertaking that when the widow died she could also be buried in the Abbey, was impossible. Hamilton though wondered if the Queen might propose that her remains be disinterred from Hughenden and be moved to Westminster (BL, AddMS 44189, fos. 93–4, Hamilton to Gladstone, 20 April 1881).

[35] RA, VIC/Z 156/15, The Queen to Granville, 21 April 1881.

at the Abbey or on the streets of London.[36] The terms of the will were strictly applied: no consideration appears to have been given to the idea, voiced by some, notably the Duke of Cambridge, that a public funeral in the Abbey should have been followed by a private interment at Hughenden.[37] The Queen herself asked whether it might 'not be possible as the people seem so anxious to allow some public demonstration to be shown on the remains leaving London as it goes by road'.[38] The executors felt obliged to consider this suggestion carefully, but decided against it. They did not want to mar the 'simplicity' of the occasion, and were advised, presumably by the police, that if the remains were to pass publicly through the streets of London, control of the enormous crowds expected to gather would be a 'difficult matter' requiring extensive preparation.[39] Accordingly the coffin was moved secretly from London to Hughenden in the small hours of the morning of Sunday 24 April, although some newspaper reporters were alerted, and the Monday papers therefore carried eloquent accounts of the scene.[40] Nevertheless the predominant considered reaction was that the decision had been the right one. Lord Bradford's initial reaction even before Disraeli's wishes had been known had been to hope that 'there will be no "Westminster Abbey", but a romantic grave in a Buckinghamshire Churchyard'.[41] *The Times* felt that the place where a great man was buried was not of as much consequence as his place in the minds of the living. In any case, Buckinghamshire, 'the classic ground of English statesmen' and the locale in which Disraeli himself had 'loved to assume the ways of an English country gentleman' provided wholly appropriate surroundings for his burial.[42] The Queen appeared fully reconciled to the choice, writing to Lord Salisbury on the day of the funeral that 'the respect and true love and sorrow of the nation at large will be far more in unison with His feelings than the gloomy pomp of a so-called public funeral and the dismal dreariness of a grave in the great Metropolitan Abbey'.[43]

---

[36] DisP, Dep.Hughenden 24/2, fos. 57, 61–3, 64, E. Ashmead Bartlett, Blackburn Orangemen, Revd E. Fowler to Rowton, 21 April 1881.

[37] RA, VIC/Z 156/21, Duke of Cambridge to the Queen, 22 April 1881; see also letter from 'A. H. B.' in *The Times* of 22 April. Such a solution appeared relatively novel in 1881, but was to be adopted a mere four years later for Lord Shaftesbury in 1885, while for Lord Iddesleigh in 1887 a service at Westminster Abbey was held simultaneously with the actual funeral at Upton Pyne in Devon.

[38] RA, VIC/ADD V 30/34, Lady Ely to Rowton, 22 April 1881.

[39] RA, VICZ 156/26, Rowton to the Queen, 23 April 1881; DisP, Dep.Hughenden 24/2, fo. 9, Rowton to Lady Ely, 22 April 1881.

[40] *The Times*, 25 April 1881.

[41] DisP, Dep.Hughenden 24/2, fos. 33–4, Bradford to Rowton, 19 April 1881.

[42] *The Times*, 22 April 1881.

[43] RA, VIC/Z 156/51, The Queen to Lord Salisbury, 26 April 1881.

Moreover the ceremony on Tuesday 26 April, which Rowton somewhat disingenuously described as 'just a village funeral, no more!',[44] was actually attended by the Prince of Wales and two of his brothers, numerous present and former cabinet ministers, a large contingent of the diplomatic corps, many members of both Houses of Parliament, and by large crowds, both of local people and of Londoners brought down from the capital by special trains.[45] Gladstone's absence on grounds of pressure of work gave rise to adverse comment, even though he could hardly be regarded as a personal friend, and appears to have judged that his presence would have been regarded as intrusive.[46] Moreover in spite of the 'private' nature of the funeral, demand for tickets was considerable and the pressure to accept some representation from Conservative Associations was irresistible.[47] At a different social level, the future Lord Curzon, then an undergraduate at Balliol College, Oxford, wrote to solicit a ticket for the churchyard on the grounds of being the eldest son of a Conservative peer who was disinclined to 'become involved in the general crowd'. He was duly obliged.[48] Paradoxically the actual 'private' interment in the churchyard was visible, in virtue of the lie of land, to many thousands of people crowding the hillside, whereas only relatively small numbers would have been able to witness a 'public' burial in the transept of Westminster Abbey.

Although the ceremony was therefore hardly private, except in a technical sense, it was undeniably simple. The coffin, covered with white flowers, was wheeled by hand from the house to the church, followed by the mourners and dignitaries on foot. The Vicar, Henry Blagden, read the service in the church and the only music was the voluntaries played on the organ by his wife. The burial took place in the open air amidst a carpet of flowers, including the Queen's wreath of primroses with its famously

---

[44] RA, VIC/Z 156/53, Rowton to the Queen, 26 April 1881.

[45] *The Times*, 27 April 1881.

[46] Bahlman, *Hamilton*, i. 137 (8 May 1881). Philip Magnus (*Gladstone: A Biography* (1963), 280–81), who has been followed by other secondary authorities, misquotes a remark in Hamilton's diary (Bahlman, *Hamilton*, i. 187) 'As he (Disraeli) lived, so he died—all display, with an absence of reality and genuineness.' This observation was, however, made not in the immediate aftermath of Disraeli's death, but on 23 November 1881. It is, moreover, unclear whether Hamilton was recording Gladstone's exact words, paraphrasing them, or expressing sentiments that were more his own than Gladstone's. Certainly they appear at odds both with Gladstone's immediate response to Disraeli's death, and with his view that 'there is something very touching in his determination to be buried by the side of his wife' (*Gladstone Diaries*, x. 54).

[47] DisP, Dep.Hughenden 24/2, *passim*, 24/5, fos. 99–100. *The Times* (27 April) reported that five clerks had been employed throughout the day before the funeral acknowledging flowers and answering applications for tickets.

[48] DisP, Dep.Hughenden 24/2, fos. 104–5, Curzon to the executors, 23 April 1881.

ambiguous inscription 'His favourite flowers from Osborne', and daisies sent by children.[49] Participants were evidently moved: Prince Leopold found himself fighting back the tears, while Lord Salisbury, not a man given to hyperbole, told his wife that it was 'the most striking scene he ever witnessed'.[50] The large crowd was observed to be respectful and orderly, and according to Sir Henry Ponsonby's account for the Queen, there were 'many women crying' and 'much feeling shown by all present'.[51] The Prince of Wales, who was himself to play an important role in the development of such ceremonial during the next three decades, told his mother that 'It was a most striking and impressive sight and the simplicity and dignity with which everything was carried out pleased and touched everybody.'[52]

The immediate response to Disraeli's death transcended party lines. In the Prime Minister's absence, Lord Hartington and Sir William Harcourt were senior representatives of the government at the funeral.[53] The preceding week had seen numerous tributes to Disraeli from Liberal as well as Conservative speakers, even if the former, acknowledging their differences from him on matters of politics, tended to focus their comments more on his personal qualities. Admiration for the deceased as someone who had proved that the highest office was open to a man of talent and courage from comparatively humble origins was a widespread feature of such speeches.[54] Even an Independent minister, J. Baldwin Brown, who believed Disraeli's 'policy and political conduct' to have been 'disastrous' for the country, still acknowledged the virtue of his private character, expressed above all by his choice of his last resting place 'by the side of the wife whom he loved so well'.[55] *Lloyds Weekly Newspaper* acknowledged that 'all classes of his countrymen' had admired his political gallantry, magnanimity and self-command even as they opposed his principles and were angry at many of his actions.[56] In its leader on the funeral *The Times* perceptively, if complacently, contrasted the cross-party character of attendance and sym-

---

[49] *The Times*, 27 April 1881. The ambiguity in the inscription was whether 'His' referred to Disraeli himself or to the Prince Consort: it is conceivable that both were in the Queen's mind. See Redesdale, *Memories*, ii. 677; Blake, *Disraeli*, 752.

[50] RA, VIC/Z 156/58, Prince Leopold to the Queen, 27 April 1881; 156/55, Lady Salisbury to Lady Ely, 27 April 1881.

[51] RA, VIC/Z 156/43, Ponsonby to the Queen, 26 April 1881. Ponsonby's own notes on the funeral (RA, VIC/ADD A 12/622) suggest, however, that his personal feelings were of a less emotional kind.

[52] RA, VIC/Z 156/61, Prince of Wales to the Queen, 28 April 1881.

[53] *The Times*, 27 April 1881; Blake, *Disraeli*, 751.

[54] See for example the speeches by Sir Charles Forster, J. G. Talbot, and others reported in *The Times* of 22 April 1881.

[55] *The Times*, 25 April 1881.

[56] 24 April 1881.

pathy with the situation in 'the neighbouring country' where 'there would
be no considerable muster which would not exclude right and left, and
which would not utterly disown the character of a fair representation of
France as it is to-day'.[57]

Still there were dissentient voices. It was perhaps harder for Liberals
to be generous in places such as Exeter where local Tory domination
remained.[58] At a national level, Gladstone, still upset by criticism of his
absence from the funeral, was further distressed to find that his proposal
to erect a monument to Disraeli in Westminster Abbey was to be opposed
by the Radicals on his own back benches.[59] He carefully prepared the
ground for the subsequent debate, squaring the matter with his Cabinet,
and reporting with satisfaction that opposition seemed to be diminishing.[60]
When on 9 May he rose in the Commons to propose the vote he made no
attempt to gloss over his political differences from Disraeli, but paid tribute
to his personal qualities. He suggested that two non-partisan questions
should determine whether he was worthy of the honour. The first test was
whether he 'has sustained a great historic part and done great deeds written
on the page of Parliamentary and national history'; and, second, whether
his actions had been carried out on a constitutional basis with the full
authority of the nation. Both questions, Gladstone concluded, could be
answered strongly in the affirmative. Responding for the Conservatives,
Northcote warmly welcomed the Prime Minister's appeal to sentiments and
principles that transcended party, and felt that his stance was honourable
not only to himself but to the Commons as a whole. Henry Labouchere
led opposition to the vote, arguing that there was 'no precedent for a public
memorial being voted to one who has filled the office of Prime Minister,
unless there was in the House either a majority of his supporters or a
majority of those who considered that he had performed great and signal
services'. He therefore opposed the proposal on the grounds that it would
be construed as a retrospective endorsement of Disraeli's policies. However,
Labouchere evidently recognized that the sense of the house was against
him and wound up his speech rapidly. Following a brief and somewhat
scurrilous intervention from Arthur O'Connor, a vote was taken and,
swayed by Gladstone's magnanimous speech, the house endorsed the proposal by a majority of 380 to 54. The abstention of two Cabinet ministers,
Bright and Chamberlain, did not, however, escape notice.[61] Nevertheless

---

[57] *The Times*, 27 April 1881.
[58] See above, 99.
[59] RA, VIC/A 53/46, Gladstone to the Queen, 4 May 1881.
[60] Ibid.; RA, VIC/N 39/80, Gladstone to the Queen, 5–6 May 1881.
[61] *The Times*, 10 May 1881; RA, VIC/Z 157/24, Rowton to the Queen, 10 May 1881; 157/
28, Gladstone to Ponsonby, 12 May 1881.

the predominant mood was one of consensus and the parallel debate in the Lords was wholly uncontentious. The outcome gave significant endorsement to the principle that it was possible for Parliament and the nation to pay posthumous tributes to a distinguished statesman on the basis of a suspension of normal party divisions.

On the other hand the Conservative Party lost little time in exploiting the political potentialities of the Disraeli cult, which were all the more considerable precisely because of the extent to which in the aftermath of his death he had been portrayed as a genuinely national figure. Their cause was assisted by the strong public sympathy not only of the Queen but also of the royal family as a whole, who had perceived Disraeli as a keystone of the throne.[62] On 19 April the Queen had announced in the Court Circular that she 'received this morning with feelings of the deepest sorrow the sad intelligence of the death of the Earl of Beaconsfield in whom Her Majesty loses a most valued and devoted friend and counsellor, and the nation one of their most distinguished statesmen'.[63] Following the princely solidarity apparent at the funeral, Victoria herself travelled from Windsor to Hughenden on Saturday 30 April, inspected the grave, and laid a wreath. Although the Queen's visit had been shrouded in secrecy beforehand, it was widely reported afterwards, and, according to Rowton, it 'touched and pleased her people'.[64] Subsequently, a Conservative-led group promoting an additional memorial to Disraeli even ventured to approach the Prince of Wales to ask him to take the chair of their committee, but the latter declined, shrewdly detecting the precise point at which national consensus merged back into a more partisan agenda.[65] In November 1883 Lord Randolph Churchill, Sir Henry Drummond Wolff, John Gorst, and others were to launch the Primrose League designed to give institutional focus to their romantic vision of quasi-medieval social cohesion. Their task was no doubt considerably assisted by the parting image generated by the funeral and the burial at Hughenden, and by the powerful associations of the primrose motif itself. Whatever the realities of Disraeli's horticultural preferences in life, it linked him powerfully in death simultaneously both to the Crown and to a romantic ideal of rustic simplicity. On the third anniversary of his death in 1884 the

[62] The Duchess of Teck saw Disraeli's death as a 'national disaster' (RA, VIC/Z 156/8, 20 April 1881), while the Queen's own mood was evident in a letter to the Dean of Windsor in which she wrote of her expectation that 'dear Ld. Beaconsfield's followers will rally round the Throne inspired by his spirit and that God will not forsake her' (RA, VIC/B 63/51, 22 April 1881).

[63] RA, VIC/Z 155/131, telegram from Osborne with the text.

[64] *The Times*, 2 May 1881; RA, VIC/Z 157/8, Rowton to Lady Ely, 3 May 1881.

[65] RA, VIC/Z 157/40, 47, Northcote to the Queen, 18 May, 2 June 1881.

popularity of primroses and of other memorabilia continued unabated.[66] In April 1885 Disraeli's statue was draped with flowers and 'vast quantities' were strewn at the base.[67] Herein lay a powerful stimulus to a movement which, as Martin Pugh has shown, contributed very substantially to the recovery and maintenance of Conservative political fortunes in subsequent decades.[68]

The lingering image of that 'village funeral' was also apparent in other ways. Disraeli's obsequies both reflected and encouraged the general trend in later Victorian Britain towards simpler funerals, represented by the foundation of the National Funeral and Mourning Reform Association in 1875.[69] Floral tributes, which were so conspicuous at Disraeli's funeral, were still a relative novelty in 1881.[70] On the other hand the 'simplicity' he had requested led his executors to eschew the sombre display of mourning coaches, mutes and ostrich plumes, which had earlier been seen as normative for a high-status funeral. Individual tastes varied, and just as simple funerals even among the wealthy can be documented from the first half of the nineteenth century, there is evidence that more elaborate mourning trappings persisted into the 1890s beyond.[71] Nevertheless there is justification for seeing Disraeli's funeral as a pivotal and influential occasion in setting the trend of fashion. More specifically, for statesmen the rejection of Westminster Abbey and the metropolis in favour of interment in a romanticized provincial, preferably rural, graveyard also confirmed a pattern followed by most leading statesmen of all parties in the late nineteenth and twentieth centuries.

A final paradox in the response to Disraeli's death lay in its religious significance. In his lifetime since his formal teenage conversion to Christianity, Disraeli had been a conventional Anglican, venerating the Church of England as a great national institution, but displaying few indications of existential assent to its dogmatic teaching. His deathbed had been an essentially secular one, without the attentions of a clergyman, despite the occurrence on 17 April of Easter Sunday when Disraeli had normally received communion at Hughenden.[72] Nevertheless on the Sunday following

[66] Laughton, *Henry Reeve*, ii. 322.

[67] N. E. Johnson (ed.), *The Diary of Gathorne Hardy, later Lord Cranbrook, 1866–1912: Political Selections* (Oxford, 1981), 552 (19 April 1885).

[68] M. Pugh, *The Tories and the People 1880–1935* (Oxford, 1985), 12–13, 19–20 and *passim*.

[69] D. Cannadine, 'War and Death, Grief and Mourning in Modern Britain' in Whaley, *Mirrors of Mortality*, 192.

[70] Litten, *English Way of Death*, 170.

[71] Ibid., 170–71; Jalland, *Death in the Victorian Family*, 194–203.

[72] Monypenny and Buckle, *Disraeli*, vi. 616; DisP, Dep.Hughenden 24/3, fo. 179. Dr Quain, attending Disraeli, forbade the proposal that he be offered the sacrament on the grounds

his death numerous clergy, responding to an evident expectation among their congregations, referred to it in their sermons. For those uncertain of the deceased's spiritual condition the solution, as for his political opponents, was to dwell on his personal qualities. For example, J. A. Atkinson, preaching at Longsight near Manchester, found himself an apt text in Esther 9:4 and expounded the parallel between Disraeli and Mordecai, also a naturalized Jew who rose to high office. Disraeli, Atkinson acknowledged, had had his faults, but he was nevertheless an exemplar of qualities such as perseverance, imperturbable good temper, capacity to influence others, domesticity and conjugal devotion. His funeral would thus be representative of the feelings of the entire nation.[73] Similarly J. C. Ryle, the Evangelical Bishop of Liverpool, who owed his see to Disraeli, limited his eulogy at the University Church in Oxford to praising his qualities of persistence and courage, rather than drawing any spiritual lessons from his decease.[74] Other clergy, however, were more theologically ambitious: addressing a crowded congregation at St Paul's Cathedral, Canon Liddon used allusion to Disraeli as a powerful rhetorical support for his affirmation in an Eastertide sermon on the Emmaus Road (Luke 24) that 'No man, we know full well, ceases to exist at death'.[75] At Sandringham, preaching in front of the Prince of Wales, T. Teignmouth Shore wove together threads of political, patriotic and biblical imagery to conclude that 'His name, his fame, his deeds remain here in England's midst like the bones of some political Elisha, so that if ever the corpse of a dead patriotism were to touch them it must start forth to vigour and to life.'[76]

Meanwhile poetic tributes to Disraeli further imbued him with an aura of sanctity and merged the language of Christianity and patriotism. Striking in this respect was an anonymous poet who wrote of 'Ichabod . . . glory departed' and linked the imagery of Zion and England. The deceased himself was portrayed as the saviour of the nation:

> He was an Englishman! he of all others
> Worked for his country with heart, will and brain;

---

that it would lead him to give up the fight for life. In 1883 a curious rumour to the effect that Disraeli had made a deathbed conversion to Roman Catholicism was published in a Liverpool paper, causing some consternation among staunchly Protestant Tories (DisP, Dep.Hughenden 24/3, fos. 76–7, 79, 85–6). It appears however to have been wholly without foundation.

[73] Atkinson, *Earl of Beaconsfield.*

[74] *The Times,* 25 April 1881.

[75] Ibid.

[76] Ibid.

> Christian himself, he loved all men as brothers:
> Oh! would we call back DISRAELI again.[77]

The malleability of the boundaries of orthodox religious teaching and motifs was also apparent in the extent to which the expectation of a poet was fulfilled:

> That little church a Shrine for aye shall be,
> To Pilgrims coming over land or sea.[78]

In early May 1881 *The Times* reported that since Disraeli's funeral many people had travelled long distances 'to make a pilgrimage to his tomb'.[79] Sir Philip Rose, one of Disraeli's executors, wrote of 'the Holy Purpose of Her Majesty's recent visit to Hughenden Churchyard'.[80] Charles Dalrymple, MP, also explicitly used the language of pilgrimage.[81] Henry Blagden immediately sought to capitalize on the fashion by launching an appeal to 'complete and beautify the church he [Disraeli] loved so well'.[82] The executors were initially annoyed at what they regarded as self-interested opportunism,[83] but within a year sufficient funds were raised from general donations to redecorate the chancel, replace the organ and put stained glass in the west window. Meanwhile the Queen paid for an elaborate memorial tablet, and Oxford undergraduates and the executors themselves also donated stained glass windows.[84] On the first anniversary of Disraeli's death in April 1882 a dedication service overflowed into the churchyard, and it was observed both that almost all those attending were wearing bouquets of primroses, and that many young men were present, notably Oxford undergraduates. Mrs Blagden wrote of her satisfaction that the commemoration had been 'religiously observed': a political cult had acquired ecclesiastical sanction.[85]

In responses to the two most prominent political deaths of the later 1880s the themes of cross-party consensus and romanticized provincialism were self-consciously recapitulated. The circumstances of the death of the Earl of Iddesleigh (Stafford Northcote) in January 1887 were dramatic. Having just resigned as Foreign Secretary, he suffered a heart attack at 10

---

[77] Copy in RA, VIC/R 42/20.

[78] A. B. Cuming, *In Memoriam: The Earl of Beaconsfield* (1881).

[79] *The Times*, 2 May 1881.

[80] RA, VIC/Z 157/31, Rose to Lady Ely, 12 May 1881.

[81] DisP, Dep.Hughenden 24/3, fo. 191, Dalrymple to Rowton, 12 May 1881.

[82] DisP, Dep.Hughenden 24/3, fo. 32, reprographed announcement.

[83] DisP, Dep.Hughenden 24/3, fo. 33–41, Rose to Rowton and Rose to Blagden, both 8 May 1881.

[84] *The Times*, 20 April 1882.

[85] RA, VIC/R 42/2a, Mrs Blagden to Lady Ely, 20 April 1882.

Downing Street when about to see Lord Salisbury, and expired in the Prime Minister's presence. The shocking nature of the event combined with recollection of the dead man's personal amiability to produce expressions of grief that transcended party lines.[86] His funeral at Upton Pyne near Exeter[87] gave inspiration to a patriotic versifier who wrote of his being laid 'midst the hills of dear old Devon' in the 'England we are proud of' and the 'land of Drake and Raleigh'. The poem continued:

> And old England knows the lesson that is taught us by his life,
> And awhile suspends the bitter strokes and taunts of petty strife,
> For his mourners have no party—and are one—the good and brave,
> 'Tis the Englishman they honour by the wreaths upon his grave.[88]

A complementary image of latter-day patriotic political chivalry was stirred by the death of John Bright in March 1889. Just as Northcote was portrayed as the representative southern, Anglican, Tory country gentleman, Bright could be seen as the archetypal northern, Nonconformist, Liberal industrialist, but he too was a witness 'to the kind of thing that England honours and that England will not let die'.[89] His burial at the Quaker graveyard among the mills of Rochdale was at one level a striking contrast with the rural Anglican settings in which Disraeli and Northcote were laid to rest. *The Times* though still pointed up the similarities rather than the differences in evoking 'the green churchyards of their native land' in which many great Englishmen lay buried.[90] Bright's funeral also manifested a similar paradox of a technically 'private' event that was in practice more accessible (except from a metropolitan perspective) than a 'public' funeral in Westminster Abbey would have been.[91]

## Gladstone

At the time of Disraeli's death a sense of parallelism with his living Liberal counterpart was already apparent. When Dean Stanley proudly chose a location for Disraeli's statue in Westminster Abbey, he indicated that in due course he expected to place Gladstone opposite him.[92] The 'Grand Old

---

[86] *The Times*, 14–19 Jan. 1887.
[87] See above, Chapter 4.
[88] *Moonshine*, 22 Jan. 1887 (cutting in RA, VIC/R 42/55).
[89] C. J. Vaughan, *I Dwell Among Mine Own People* (1889), 14.
[90] *The Times*, 29 March 1889.
[91] *The Times*, 1 April 1889.
[92] Redesdale, *Memories*, ii. 677. In fact their statues stand side by side in the north transept of the Abbey.

Man', however, lived on for another seventeen years, long surviving Stanley himself, and forming two more governments, before he eventually died on 19 May 1898. His death and apotheosis had many similarities to those of Disraeli, but also manifested some striking and significant differences.

Gladstone's last illness, like that of his former rival, was the focus of intense attention from the press and public. Although he had retired from government in 1894 and from Parliament in 1895, he remained a very prominent public figure. While spending the winter of 1897–8 at Cannes he developed a painful facial cancer, which was diagnosed as terminal after his return to England in March 1898. The nature of Gladstone's illness was made public, and he returned to his home, Hawarden Castle in North Wales, to die. During subsequent weeks, as in Disraeli's last illness, the increasingly confined and private world of the sickroom was in counterpoint to detailed press reporting of every development in the dying man's condition.[93] His situation, however, contrasted with that of the widowed and childless Disraeli, in that public attention and sentiment also focused on the wife and family circle. Also, whereas Disraeli had had a metropolitan deathbed followed by a provincial funeral, in Gladstone's case the sequence was reversed, with Hawarden perceived like Hughenden as an idyll of romanticized rural peace. Thus John Morley was to conclude his narrative of the deathbed: 'Nature outside—wood and wide lawn and cloudless far-off sky—shone at her finest.'[94]

The letters of sympathy that poured into Hawarden amply support the impression that with Gladstone's death came 'a strange sense of incompleteness, as of something missing in the national life'.[95] The survival of over a thousand of these letters provides a unique opportunity for analysis of a cross-section of public reaction to a major death.[96] Individuals who chose to write were of course a self-selecting group, but they were drawn from a broad range of localities, social classes, and political and religious opinions.

---

[93] H. C. G. Matthew, 'Gladstone's Death and Funeral', *Historian*, 57 (Spring 1998), 20. For the final phase see *The Times*, 18, 19, 20 May 1898. At the family's urging, John Morley in his biography subsequently presented a truncated and idealized version of Gladstone's death, but newspaper reports at the time withheld little of the distressing nature of his illness (Jalland, *Death in the Victorian Family*, 184–6; J. Morley, *The Life of William Ewart Gladstone*, 3 vols. (1903), iii. 525–8).

[94] Morley, *Gladstone*, iii. 528.

[95] *Tablet*, 21 May 1898, p. 797.

[96] St Deiniol's Library, Hawarden, Glynne-Gladstone MSS [GG] 1037–1056 *passim*. Individual letters are not further classified, so are identified below by the file number, writer and date, which are all 1898 unless otherwise stated. It seems probable that the letters that survive are only a proportion of those originally received, but there is no indication of any systematic process of selection that would invalidate the presumption that they are a representative sample.

Many of them who had never met Gladstone were apparently responding as if to a personal bereavement. Seven broad themes can be categorized in the comment and reaction.

First, there were general tributes to Gladstone's personal qualities and stature as a statesman and public figure. To a young woman in Staffordshire he was 'the greatest and best on earth' and 'a synonym of all that is good and all that is true noble'.[97] An inmate of the Middlesbrough Workhouse felt him to be 'the one of England most purest and Generous and noblest Characters'.[98] For a writer in 'the lonely Kerry mountains', one of many from Ireland, he was quite simply 'the greatest man the proud land of England ever saw'.[99] Another sympathizer dwelt on the simplicity of his life, crowned by the glory of dying plain 'Mr Gladstone'.[100] His political career was perceived as that of a noble patriot and a great reformer, who had 'held aloft for so many years the banner of Freedom, Progress, Liberty and Humanity'.[101] In the opinion of Andrew Fairbairn, the Congregationalist Principal of Mansfield College, Oxford, 'that a man of his moral qualities and intellectual endowments shd have been an English Statesman, the most commanding & distinguished Statesman of our century, will in the eyes of posterity redeem English Statesmanship in our century from insignificance and commonplace'.[102] Furthermore, he was also felt to have rendered great service to humanity as a whole, being 'the true champion of oppressed races in every quarter of the globe' and an advocate for every 'suffering nation'.[103] Writers were stirred not merely by a wish to eulogize the deceased, but also by a sense that his inspiration and example had had, and would have, a much wider influence.[104] His memory would live on in the minds of his countrymen, and indeed 'the whole civilised world', while he would 'still speak to unborn generations'. He was portrayed as a role model for others in respect of qualities such as 'justice, righteousness and manliness', his ability 'to withstand the temptations of political life, and preserve his integrity', and his personal moral rectitude and 'domestic

---

[97] GG 1037, Cissy Rawlins, 20 May.

[98] GG 1038, Edward Wilkinson, 2 June.

[99] GG 1039, Maurice Humphrey, 18 May.

[100] GG 1037, Robert Johnstone, 21 May.

[101] GG 1037, Francis Drury, 20 May; 1038, 'A Hull Workman', 19 May; 1055, Hyde Division Liberal Association, 25 May.

[102] GG 1039, A. M. Fairbairn, 19 May.

[103] GG 1037, Henry A. H. Rott, 21 May; 1038, New Road Synagogue, Whitechapel, 27 June; 1055, United Methodist Free Church, Lincoln District, 24/25 May; 1039, Anon., Croft St., Roscommon, 21 May.

[104] GG 1037, F. Henderson, 20 May; 1038, 'A Hull Workman', 19 May; 1042, Robert Lethbridge, n.d.

virtues'.[105] Some were prompted to bemoan current moral decline or to seek reform: one writer despaired at the capacity of the 'present selfish age' to produce such a man,[106] while another proposed that his 'sterling principles' should be upheld for future generations by the formation of a 'Gladstone League'.[107]

Second, there was praise for Gladstone's distinctively Christian contribution to public life. Even primarily secular tributes frequently showed an implicit moral fervour, and when apparently non-religious sentiments are read in the context of a letter as a whole, spiritual perceptions become clear.[108] Many, however, perceived Gladstone's religion as the central feature of his life. Thus the Tottenham Pleasant Sunday Afternoon gathering felt his example of 'deep attachment to Christian principles will do much to raise the standard of public life by encouraging statesmen to aspire to loftier ideals and higher conceptions of duty'.[109] His political crusades were linked to his religion. In the eyes of a young man in Weymouth he had been a 'true and faithful worker for God and the working man'; a woman in North Wales saw him as modelling himself on his 'Divine Master especially in his loving sympathy with the oppressed'.[110] He was hailed as making it seem natural to believe that 'when we are face to face with political problems we are face to face with GOD'.[111] In the opinion of the Wimborne and District Liberal Association, he was the 'brightest example of a Christian statesman the nineteenth century has produced'.[112] Even such praise was, however, dim in comparison with that offered by a writer who judged him to have been the greatest man who had lived since Christ himself.[113]

Furthermore, Gladstone was recognized not only as an outstanding role model for Christian politicians, but also as 'the glorious defender'[114] of Christianity in general. As he lay dying, one Anglican clergyman wrote:

> For half a century the greatest orator of his age has by word and deed supported the principle that *Righteousness* exalteth a nation—and today the Churches would welcome a message from his matured Spirit in which he

---

[105] GG 1037, J. H. Standring, 5 Dec.; Wilmot L. Bryan, 22 May; Jessie Weir, 23 May; 1055, Sheffield Congregational Association, 19 May.

[106] GG 1038, Mary Foster, n.d.

[107] GG 1041, John Gill, 11 June.

[108] For examples see GG 1038, Edward Wilkinson, 2 June; 1037, Henry A. H. Rott, 21 May; 1039, John Dodgeon, 18 May.

[109] GG 1055, 22 May.

[110] GG 1037, W. L. Quick, 22 May; Mary Bradley, 30 May.

[111] GG 1041, Wilfrid Richmond, 19 May.

[112] GG 1053, 26 May.

[113] GG 1041, W. Croucher, 2 June.

[114] GG 1037, Mary Tyrel, 20 May.

should come again in this supreme moment, declare his unchangeable faith in a Personal God and an incarnate Saviour as the only source of Peace and joy.[115]

In Norwich he was remembered as a lover of the 'Holy Book of God', in Orkney as someone who refused to countenance 'modern theories of unbelief'.[116] A Baptist minister recalled hearing him speak in 1877 and recognizing in him 'a devoted lover of our Lord'. From that moment his admiration for Gladstone had 'passed into love'.[117] A Liverpool writer thought that his example had been instrumental in 'winning many souls to Christ', while it was reported that memorial services at Salvation Army halls were leading to further conversions.[118]

Third, many writers related Gladstone and his death in some way to their own needs and aspirations. At the crudest level there were requests for souvenirs, money, or assistance. One correspondent asked even before Gladstone had died for the hat he had been wearing in a recent photograph taken at Cannes, another for 'two or three of the late deceased's collars', considerately adding that Mrs Gladstone need not be in a hurry to send them.[119] One woman, with 'six little children' said that she would 'thankfully accept a Mourning garment'.[120] Another writer, in an evident attempt to emulate the Primrose League, asked what Gladstone's favourite flower had been, so that he could wear it on the day of the funeral.[121] A County Fermanagh man under threat of eviction paid effusive tribute to Gladstone's kindness and generosity, as a prelude to asking his widow to give him some assistance at her 'earliest convenience'.[122] A mother sought employment for her daughter as a lady's maid, while a Manchester woman asked for a loan to cover travelling expenses to go to Brighton for an interview.[123] Such importunate requests addressed to an aged and recently bereaved woman might appear the height of self-interested insensitivity, but also imply a perception of the Gladstones as possessed of superhuman qualities of compassion and sympathy.

More subtle and widespread, however, was a sense of a strong emotional tie to Gladstone that had given meaning and comfort to obscure and

---

[115] GG 1037, J. R. Baldwin, 18 May.

[116] GG 1055, St Peter's Wesleyan Men's Bible Class, Norwich, 24 May; 1039, David Johnston, 23 May.

[117] GG 1039, Geo. J. Knight, 24 May.

[118] GG 1037, T. E. Penn, 20 May; 1038, Hugh Shulver, 1 June.

[119] GG 1037, Joseph Barker, 15 May; Hy. Harrison, n.d.

[120] GG 1037, Lilly Nelson, n.d.

[121] GG 1037, William Martin, 22 May.

[122] GG 1038, Denis Leonard, 5 June.

[123] GG 1038, S. J. Frewin, 10 June; 1039, Emily Linfield, 30 May.

lonely lives, and now meant that his death was experienced as a personal bereavement. For some this was hero worship at an implicitly acknowledged distance; for others founded in the memory of some fleeting actual encounter.[124] Many though professed to regard Gladstone as a personal friend or father figure despite the fact that they had apparently never met him. One Salvation Army member felt that 'though I never had the honour to take hold of his hand in life, in spirit I have done so'. He had wept many times during the week following Gladstone's death.[125] A young woman's torrent of words conveyed similarly intense feelings:

> I feel we have lost someone from our side ... I thought about you on Saturday morning [the time of the funeral] when my mother was talking about it I do feel for you as with eyes blinded by tears I write to you I cant express in words what I feel for you but you have lived together a long time and loved one another long but by and by there will be a happy reunion with you and there will be no sorrow nor no tears for there God shall wipe all tears from our eyes and from yours.[126]

A Bristol woman who had never spoken to Gladstone, still felt him a 'dear and valued friend'; for one Londoner he had been a 'second father' since the death of the writer's own father sixteen years before.[127] Another writer perceptively attributed the intensity of his feelings for Gladstone to his own lack of close family.[128] Also suggestive in this connection were letters from children, for example from a six-year-old girl at Tain in the north of Scotland:

> Dear Mrs Gladstone I am only a little girl at school but I am very very sorry for you for my father and everybody is saying that the Great and Good Mr Gladstone is dead and we are all very sorry and I am sure you will be sorry too.
>     With deepest sympathy
>     yours truly
>     Reeta Macduff-Ross.[129]

In many cases Gladstone's death was related to personal bereavements

---

[124] GG 1037, Muriel Cambie, n.d.; Matthew Francis, 22 May; 1039, Geo. Watson, 24 May.
[125] GG 1038, Hugh Shulver, 1 June.
[126] GG 1038, Phoebe Ladley, 1 June.
[127] GG 1039, Sarah Ashley, 17 May; 'J.L.C.', 19 May.
[128] GG 1042, Ben Warhurst, 31 May.
[129] GG 1038, n.d. For other examples see 1037, Leonard Stern (aged 6½); 1039, William Ewart Lebrun, 19 May. A father reported that his seven-year-old son had of his own accord added to his prayers, 'Please God, take care of Mrs Gladstone' (1040, E. P. Alexander, 1 June).

and suffering. On the night he died his form was reported to have been standing at the bedside of a dying woman near Oxford.[130] Others might not claim such supernatural visitations, but among those also afflicted through cancer and terminal illness there were some who felt moved to write to express a sense of affinity.[131] One old man who died at almost the same time as Gladstone had been continually asking after the dying statesman.[132] The husband of a woman who had also died the same morning expressed his sympathy for Mrs Gladstone, although at least she had had time to prepare: his own wife's illness had been sudden, but in her last hours 'she did talk of Mr Gladstone'.[133] Some struggling to come to terms with the death of a father or spouse, found an outlet in using a letter of condolence as a trigger to write at length about their own departed loved one.[134] A doctor wrote from Chicago to draw an extended parallel between Gladstone and his own late wife, sharing elevated characters, strong personalities, brilliant minds, and deep religious convictions. One though was 'great and known and loved of all the world', while the other's talents were 'born to blush unseen' but still part of the epoch's common store of 'beauty and strength'.[135] A twelve-year old recalled that his own grandfather 'was buried a year ago today and he was God-fearing and patient like Mr Gladstone'.[136] Letters also conveyed accounts of more generalized loneliness and deprivation: from Bury in Suffolk came sympathy from 'a poor old woman who [has] seen great trouble in losing all i [*sic*] have not one left to cheer me up'.[137] A Lambeth woman sought to console Mrs Gladstone with the thought that at least she had been able to look up to her husband, whereas 'mine as [*sic*] deserted me and my 4 children'.[138] Both writers went on to testify to the strength they derived from God in the face of their troubles.

A fourth theme was to stress the universality of grief for Gladstone and sympathy for his family as a force that bridged the normal divisions and distinctions of humanity. A 'toiler in one room' in Willesden wrote of the throbbing of the 'National heart' made up of 'individual griefs for him <u>so</u>

---

[130] GG 1037, Louisa Castle, n.d.
[131] GG 1039, Mr and Mrs Miles, 19 May; 'C.B.', 20 May.
[132] GG 1038, Flora Holden, 2 June.
[133] GG 1037, Robert William Neal, n.d.
[134] GG 1037, Alfred Grose, 19 May, Isabella Gunn , 20 May.
[135] GG 1039, James Tucker, 19 May. The allusion is to the fourteenth stanza of Thomas Gray's Elegy, 'Full many a flower is born to blush unseen,/And waste its sweetness on the desert air.' (Starr and Hendrickson, *Gray*, 39).
[136] GG 1040, Mostyn Chich, 19 May.
[137] GG 1039, Henrietta Nunn, 23 May.
[138] GG 1038, Edith Smith, 31 May.

loved'.[139] Another writer visualized how the 'whole world's heart beats in unison'.[140] A old soldier from Bethnal Green was moved to verse:

> He sleeps, He sleeps, to wake no more,
> That brilliant Statesman's gone
> The pride of Dear Old England's shore
> His Death we sadly mourn
> But not alone, all Ireland, yes
> With Wales and Scotland too
> And every British Colony—ah!
> Respects that statesman true.[141]

An analysis of the locations from which letters were sent provides some objective corroboration of the wide extent of response to Gladstone's death, which did not merely reflect patterns of Liberal political allegiance. From a sample of 209 letters from individuals, 133 came from England. There was a perceptible predominance from London and the south, but nearly all parts of the country were represented. There were eight from Ireland, thirteen from Scotland, seven from Wales, and one from Jersey. Beyond the British Isles, the United States contributed twenty-three letters, continental Europe eight, southern Africa five, Australia four, India three, Canada two, with one apiece from China and New Zealand.[142] A striking feature of the letters from outside England was the manner in which Gladstone was perceived as an inclusive figure focusing the aspirations of all nationalities while also bridging divisions between them. Thus he was described as 'an honoured, and trusted friend of the people of Wales', while the Glasgow Branch of the Scottish Home Rule Association linked his name to its own aspiration for a measure 'which shall combine with Imperial Unity and supremacy Home Rule all round'.[143] Irish tributes were particularly effusive. A Dublin Roman Catholic priest expressed profound sorrow 'in common with millions of my countrymen throughout the world'.[144] An Irishman living in Essex felt that 'Ireland has lost her hero who sacrificed so much for her.'[145] From Ireland itself came strong feelings of regret for her 'best

---

[139] GG 1037, A. A. Hopper, n.d.

[140] GG 1040, Mary Burnett, 20 May.

[141] GG 1041, E. A. Pickett, 5 June.

[142] GG bundle 1039. Given the lack of any apparent organizing principle in the division of letters from individuals into bundles, this may be taken as constituting a random sample. The regional distribution within England was as follows: London 43; South and East Anglia 43; Midlands 17; North 30.

[143] GG 1039, Michael A. Ralli, 19 May; 1053, Glasgow Branch Scottish Home Rule Association, 26 May.

[144] GG 1037, John O'Hanlon, 20 May.

[145] GG 1037, Charles Shaw, 21 May.

and most noble friend', while one Dubliner noted the strong feelings of personal attachment felt by many of his compatriots. He declared his intention of travelling overnight to London in order to stand outside Westminster Abbey during the funeral.[146] Writers from the United States tended to use their letters to articulate their sense of continuing ties with Britain. A woman in Philadelphia recalled that she had in the past been a resident of Hawarden; a boy in St Louis told Mrs Gladstone that, although he had been born in America he felt himself to be 'heart and soul and every inch an English boy'.[147]

The inclusiveness of grief for Gladstone bridged political, religious, class and gender distinctions as well as geographical and national ones. Some writers acknowledged that they were Conservatives or Unionists, but still expressed great regard for Gladstone as having qualities that transcended party politics. The secretary of the Shirley Conservative Association in Southampton wrote:

> Remembering we are Englishman first and partisans after, although differing in politics, we cannot but admire with profound respect the statesmanlike qualities of the late Mr Gladstone and his earnest endeavours to promote the welfare of the country at large, and for the good of his fellow men. As a scholar there were few his equals. And his high moral character, his fervent Christian belief, his patience under great suffering; shows us one and all, by his example that we should endeavour to follow his steps.[148]

Religious minorities recalled his sympathy for their cause. Not only was there widespread acknowledgement of his general affinity with Nonconformists, but Unitarians still remembered with gratitude his advocacy of the Dissenters' Chapels Bill of 1844.[149] Meanwhile from 'poor Jews' in the East End of London came a tribute to his 'large heart which beat warmly for the oppressed in any country and especially towards the Jews'.[150] Numerous letters from the working classes expressed a sense that Gladstone had been a friend to the 'downtrodden' and had done much to improve their condition.[151] One such writer felt that he had 'lived for such as myself'

[146] GG 1039, Maurice Humphrey, 18 May; Anon. (Roscommon), 21 May; 1056, James O'Hara, 23 May.

[147] GG 1039, Mrs Peter Davis, 25 May; 1040, Mostyn Chich, 19 May.

[148] GG 1056, E. J. Clarke, 1 June.

[149] GG 1038, Wealdstone Baptist Church, 27 June; 1056, United Methodist Free Church Lincoln District Meeting, 24/25 May; Provincial Assembly of Presbyterian and Unitarian Ministers and Congregations of Lancashire and Cheshire, n.d.

[150] GG 1039, Simon Cohen, 19 May; cf. 1037, Michael Adler, 20 May; 1038, New Road Synagogue, Whitechapel, 27 June.

[151] For example GG 1038, J. Townsend, 22 June; 1055, St Peter's Wesleyan Men's Bible Class, Norwich, 24 May.

and testified to 'the bitter anguish that arises from thousands of hearts in this town of Leicester'.[152] Moreover such awareness could stir a sense that social distinctions among the living could be bridged. A 'humble Yorkshire Catholic' expressed sympathy, believing 'Heart speaks to heart; notwithstanding the disparity of social position'; a 'Christian Lad' in Swansea offered Mrs Gladstone extended spiritual counsel while trying to forget the difference in their respective stations in life.[153] Women, for their part, sometimes expressed a particular sense of affinity with Mrs Gladstone, hailed as a 'model for thousands', and a focus for the feelings of others experiencing the mixed sufferings and consolations of widowhood.[154]

A further three categories all relate to specifically religious sentiments, which were very widespread in the correspondence. In a substantial sample of 385 letters, 236, or 61.3%, were found to contain some kind of explicit religious reference.[155] These included tributes to Gladstone's Christian character in life as already described, while the remainder can be related to themes associated with death and bereavement.

First, Gladstone's deathbed was hailed as showing 'how a Christian should die'.[156] He had demonstrated how 'a great and good Christian man can be supported in the hour of suffering'.[157] One writer even saw the painful and prolonged character of his last illness as providential, in giving compelling evidence of his character and showing how he could bear his cross like Christ himself. This revelation, it was suggested, had 'done more for Christianity than all the sermons preached in England during his life'.[158] George Otto Trevelyan was struck how 'whatever one's creed, the more the body failed the greater impression he gave of the victory of the spiritual over the material'.[159] The sentiments of the letters were echoed in the view of *Reynolds Newspaper* that Gladstone's death had 'done more to strengthen

---

[152] GG 1039, Arthur Swift, 24 May.

[153] GG 1037, 'A Christian Lad', 20 May; 1040, 'A poor child of the Sacred Heart', 26 May. The fact that both writers chose to remain anonymous betrays an underlying insecurity about the possible reaction to their presumption.

[154] GG 1037, Jenine Sweatmann, 19 May; 1038, Louisa Barton Brown, 12 June.

[155] GG bundles 1037 and 1038 (see note 132 above).

[156] GG 1037, Alane G. Baggaley, 21 May.

[157] GG 1037, M. F. Macphee, 20 May.

[158] GG 1039, Malcolm MacColl, 29 May.

[159] GG 1041, 19 May. Such evidence of wider perceptions of Gladstone's deathbed serves substantially to modify the suggestion (Jalland, *Death in the Victorian Family*, 186) that a sanitized version was promulgated in conformity with public taste. *Pace* Jalland, many of Gladstone's younger contemporaries seemed quite as ready as their parents and grandparents to ascribe a spiritual significance to physical suffering.

the faith of the people as to the hereafter than any single act of this century'.[160]

Second, writers were prompted to reflect on the afterlife, and in doing so indicated the wide range of emphases current in the late Victorian period. The traditional Christian teaching that the dead were 'sleeping' until the Second Coming of Christ was only rarely stated.[161] More widespread was belief that the dead Gladstone was now consciously experiencing the immediate presence of God, finding himself to be made complete in Christ, and enjoying a new and richer life in heaven. Clergy such as Andrew Fairbairn offered the most eloquent statements of this broadly orthodox view, but it was also to be found in letters from the less theologically sophisticated.[162] Some went further, wondering about Gladstone's location in the geography of heaven, or speculating on the work he would be undertaking in his new sphere of existence.[163] Others visualized him as still looking down on the doings of human beings, and giving comfort to those who mourned his loss.[164] Much the most common line of reflection, however, was to dwell on the prospects for heavenly reunion with those still living. Some, apparently envisaging that life in heaven would be centred on reconstituted earthly families, offered such hopes primarily as comfort for the bereaved relatives, but others looked forward to themselves again encountering Gladstone on the other side of the grave.[165]

Finally there were assurances of intent to pray for the bereaved. A Glasgow woman felt she could not help writing to Mrs Gladstone: 'I can pray to our heavenly father to stranthen you and loved ones you have my prayers that the dear God may hold you up by his strenth may he bless you I know he dose.'[166] A 'working man' in Bradford prayed 'simpiely in the dear name of Jesus' that God would come very near to the family.[167] A Roman Catholic in Bristol linked her hope that God would give Mrs Gladstone strength to bear her sorrow to her prayers for the repose of her

[160] 29 May 1898.
[161] For an example see GG 1037, Henry A. H. Rott, 21 May.
[162] GG 1039, A. M. Fairbairn, 19 May; Arthur Swift, 24 May; Alice Pryor Pumphrey, 28 May; 1040, Mostyn Chich, 19 May.
[163] GG 1038, Mary Dexter, 8 June; 1055, New Church Missionary Society, 26 May (the perspective was characteristic of this group's Swedenborgian beliefs, but was also shared by others); 1040, Mary Burnett, 20 May.
[164] GG 1037, Edwin Drew, n.d.; 1038, Anon. (Cheltenham), 6 June; 1055, Spiritual Evidence Society, Newcastle-upon-Tyne, 23 May.
[165] GG 1037, Will Sharp Knight, 30 May; Phoebe Ladley, 1 June; 1039, Henry F. Hill, 17 May.
[166] GG 1039, Mary Craig, 23 May. Spelling and syntax as quoted.
[167] GG 1037, D. Haulasworth, 20 May.

husband's soul.[168] Other writers dwelt not so much on their own inter-
cessions, as on their hope that the united sympathy and prayers of the
nation as a whole would be a source of comfort and strength.[169]

The consensus of adulation and sympathy apparent in the letters was
also evident in public and official tributes. The Commons met formally on
the afternoon of Gladstone's death, but immediately adjourned as a mark
of respect.[170] The protracted and evidently hopeless nature of his illness
had made it possible for the Conservative government, prompted by a hint
from Gladstone's former private secretary Sir Edward Hamilton, to have
initial plans already in place.[171] During the closing days of Gladstone's life
the precedents were investigated, and the dying man's son, Henry, had
discreet meetings with Hamilton and Dean Bradley.[172] On Friday 20 May
Lord Salisbury and Arthur Balfour moved parallel resolutions in both
houses, which had been previously agreed with the Liberals. Balfour was
proud that their wording exactly followed precedent. They combined language used in 1778 with reference to Lord Chatham, with formulations
drafted by Gladstone himself in 1865 with reference to Palmerston, and in
1881 with reference to Disraeli:

> That an humble Address be presented to her Majesty that her Majesty will
> be graciously pleased to give directions that the remains of the Right Hon
> William Ewart Gladstone be interred at the public charge, and that a
> monument be erected in the Collegiate Church of St Peter, Westminster,
> with an inscription expressive of the high sense entertained of his rare and
> splendid gifts and his devoted labours in Parliament and in great offices of
> State . . .

The scrupulous endeavour to proceed on the basis of constitutional precedent and cross-party agreement was followed in the speeches, in which
divisive recollections were studiously avoided. Speaking in the Lords, Salisbury saw the basis of Gladstone's greatness as lying in 'the greatest and
purest of moral aspirations' and in the example of a 'great Christian man'.
The Liberal speakers, Kimberley and Rosebery, took their cue from the
Prime Minister and dwelt not on Gladstone's political achievements, but on
the 'moral qualities of the man'. In the Commons Balfour praised the
manner in which he had raised the whole tone of public life. Sir William
Harcourt, the Liberal leader, was similarly careful to emphasize Gladstone's

---

[168] GG 1039, Anon., 23 May.
[169] GG 1037, Evelyn Spilsbury, n.d.; Edwin J. Heys, 19 May.
[170] *The Times*, 20 May 1898.
[171] D. W. R. Bahlmann (ed.), *The Diary of Sir Edward Walter Hamilton 1885–1906* (Hull, 1993),
352–3 (11 May); *The Times*, 18 May 1898.
[172] Bahlmann, *Hamilton 1885–1906*, 353 (11, 16 May).

personal qualities and not to say anything that would jar on the ears of his Conservative opponents. The result was a series of tributes in which few of the most memorable events of the deceased's long career were even mentioned, but which served, according to *The Times*, as testimony to 'a generosity in English public life which Continental politicians do not find it easy to understand'. Balfour himself had acknowledged that such agreement was possible for Gladstone because he had been retired for several years, to a greater extent than for Disraeli who had died while still politically active.[173] Moreover in Salisbury's judgement the very fact that his government had been opposed to Gladstone made it impossible for it to appear grudging in giving him posthumous honour.[174]

The Queen, in notable contrast to her active involvement and interest in 1852 and 1881, stood aloof from the whole process. Although she acknowledged Gladstone to have been a 'good & very religious man' she genuinely believed that his political influence had been harmful. She sent a telegram to the family expressing her grief and sympathy, but refrained from any comment on the deceased.[175] It might have seemed unreasonable to expect more, had it not been for recollection of her expansive acknowledgement of Disraeli's death in the Court Circular in 1881. No such notice appeared for Gladstone, whereas, according to the *Daily Chronicle*, it was 'the unanimous verdict of all shades of opinion, political and social in this Empire' that 'every word applied by the Queen to Lord Beaconsfield applies with at least equal force to Mr Gladstone'.[176] On 24 May the Prince of Wales observed that 'the feeling of sentiment about him is so very strong among all classes in the country' and suggested that the Queen rectify the omission on the day of the funeral.[177] Salisbury also indicated his disquiet, while Hamilton reported that there had been 'a good deal of unfavourable comment'.[178] The Queen had initially planned to follow the Prince of Wales's suggestion, and a draft Court Circular announcement survives in the Royal Archives.[179] When, however, the *Daily*

---

[173] *The Times*, 20, 21 May 1898.
[174] RA, VIC/A 74/84, Salisbury to the Queen, 24 May 1898.
[175] RA, VIC/ADD U 32, The Queen to the Empress Frederick, 31 May 1898 (transcript); *The Times*, 21 May 1898.
[176] RA, VIC/L 17/81, cutting.
[177] RA, VIC/L 17/61, Francis Knollys to Arthur Bigge, 24 May 1898.
[178] RA, VIC/L 17/69, The Queen to Salisbury, n.d.; 17/73, Hamilton to Bigge, 28 May 1898. Hamilton was careful to dissociate the Gladstone family from the complaints.
[179] BL, AddMS 48599, Bigge to Hamilton, 31 May 1898. The draft Court Circular announcement (RA, VIC/L 17/64) is in the handwriting of Arthur Bigge, the Queen's private secretary. It reads 'The Queen heartily sympathises with today's national tribute to the memory of Mr Gladstone whose life, character and intellectual abilities have marked him as one of the most prominent statesmen of her reign.' A pencilled revision changes 'heartily' to 'sincerely'.

*Chronicle* printed its criticism on 26 May, on the government's advice she refused 'to seem to act on its dictation'.[180] Accordingly she compromised by merely publishing a further sympathetic telegram to Mrs Gladstone.[181] The Prince of Wales, by contrast, saw clearly that it was important for the royal family to associate itself with the public mood. He was actively consulted on the funeral preparations, and he and the Duke of York were pallbearers, an unprecedented role for senior members of the royal family at a non-royal funeral.[182] The Queen was annoyed, not so much because of her personal dislike of Gladstone, but because she feared that her son and grandson would be perceived as acting in a partisan fashion. She thought that the family had made a 'great mistake' in not holding the funeral at Hawarden.[183] The reality was that, with her judgement skewed by her own dislike for Gladstone, she had failed to grasp the unanimity of public grief. On the other hand, Hamilton wrote, the Prince of Wales's action was 'closely in accord with national feelings' and commanded 'universal respect'.[184]

The wider challenge for the Gladstone family and the government was to devise a funeral that would serve as a genuinely inclusive focus for the public mood. Gladstone's will allowed them considerable room for manoeuvre, provided that he could be buried where his wife might also lie, and that no 'laudatory inscription' was placed over him. It did however specify that the funeral should be 'private and very simple, unless they [his executors] shall consider there are conclusive reasons to the contrary'.[185] This formulation might be taken as implying a preference for Hawarden churchyard, and the family went through the motions of anticipating that

[180] RA, VIC/R 44/32, Salisbury to Akers-Douglas, 27 May 1898; VIC/L 17/69, The Queen to Salisbury, n.d.

[181] RA, VIC/L 17/74, Hamilton to Bigge, 31 May 1898. Hamilton judged this outcome satisfactory as the 'ordinary public will not discriminate between it and a notice in the Court Circular.'

[182] RA, VIC/R 44/31, Prince of Wales to the Queen, 27 May 1898; Bahlmann, *Hamilton 1885–1906*, 354–6 (21, 25, 27 May).

[183] Such appears to be the burden of a barely legible draft telegram to the Prince of Wales (RA, VIC/L 17/72, 28 May) in which the Queen complained that by being pall bearers the princes looked 'as if you were supporters of his policy'. For them merely to have attended would have been 'quite different'. Her fears however were groundless: as Salisbury and Balfour were also pall-bearers the non-partisan nature of the role was clear; also, as there had been no pall-bearers at Disraeli's funeral, the Prince of Wales could not be accused of favouring one great deceased statesman over the other.

[184] RA, VIC/L 17/73, Hamilton to Bigge, 28 May 1898.

[185] GG 1735. The prohibition of a 'laudatory inscription' meant that the parliamentary resolutions of 20 May could not be literally implemented, although a statue was duly erected in the north transept of the Abbey.

the interment would take place there.[186] Certainly, some public sentiment would have supported such an arrangement, seeing it as fitting for a man who had shrunk from honours in life, and had loved his home, family, and village church.[187] Nevertheless the weight of opinion quickly swung in favour of Westminster Abbey. There was a sense that 'he belonged ... to the nation'; that 'a great national act' was necessary 'to fix in peoples minds and hearts the great vision which one fears will fade'; and that 'the country cannot spare him even to Hawarden'.[188] Hamilton's personal feelings were in favour of Hawarden, but he was 'sure the public will be grievously disappointed if there is not a national funeral' and felt 'the most conspicuous Englishman of the 19th Century' should lie among the nation's worthies. Moreover there would be practical difficulties in managing the crowds that would flock to Hawarden.[189] In reality the family was already close to deciding in favour of Westminster,[190] although the 'one doubtful point' had been the condition regarding Mrs Gladstone. This matter was resolved in an exchange of telegrams with the Dean of Westminster on 20 May, and so that evening, after the parliamentary resolutions had been passed, Henry Gladstone announced their readiness to sacrifice their 'personal wishes' to 'the will of the nation'.[191] They did, however, make their agreement conditional on the funeral taking place within a week, and being conducted with all possible simplicity. The ostensible grounds for this decision were Gladstone's own wishes, and concern that a protracted delay before the funeral would add to the stress experienced by his frail widow. The effect, and very probably the intent, however, was to ensure that the ceremony would take a very different form from the martial excesses of Wellington's funeral, otherwise widely seen as the most recent relevant precedent.[192]

Without waiting for the Queen's formal approval of the Address, Lord Salisbury immediately referred the arrangements to the Earl Marshal, the first time either that dignitary or the College of Arms had been involved in a major funeral since 1852. Norfolk, at Salisbury's suggestion, sought assistance from Hamilton and from Reginald Brett (later second Viscount

---

[186] *The Times*, 20 May 1898.

[187] GG 1037, F. B. Rogers, 21 May; John Harding Giles, 20 May.

[188] GG 1037, T. E. Penn, 20 May; 1041, Wilfrid Richmond, 19 May; H. W. Primrose, 19 May.

[189] Bahlmann, *Hamilton 1885–1906*, 353 (16 May).

[190] Ibid. Matthew ('Gladstone's Death', 20) strains the evidence in suggesting that the family had already taken a firm decision before Gladstone died. As Hamilton had noted, whatever exploratory soundings the children might make, Mrs Gladstone's 'wishes must be consulted, when the end actually comes'.

[191] GG 1735. Correspondence in this bundle also makes clear that the decision regarding Mrs Gladstone was entirely a matter for the 'Abbey authorities' not the government.

[192] PRO, WORKS 21/44; Bahlmann, *Hamilton 1885–1906*, 354 (21 May).

Esher) at the Board of Works.[193] He convened an initial meeting at noon on Saturday 21 May, also attended by Aretas Akers-Douglas (First Commissioner of Works), Sir Matthew White Ridley (Home Secretary), and John Thynne (Westminster Abbey).[194] The Lord Chamberlain's department was not actively involved, and, with the Earl Marshal having no significant staff to support him, Brett felt that the 'whole strain' of the arrangements was carried by his own office.[195] Hamilton too felt that 'We are working at very high pressure.'[196] On the other hand the entrusting of the arrangements to a small group of people ensured a coherence and briskness of decision-making that had been notably absent at the time of Wellington's funeral. This was essential, because in conformity with the family's wishes, the date of the funeral was fixed for Saturday 28 May. That left barely a week to make all the arrangements, whereas Garter King of Arms had thought, presumably with the Wellington case in mind, that three or four weeks would be necessary for preparations.[197]

There was a tension between the requirement for simplicity and the pressure to make the funeral as public a spectacle as possible, in that it was felt that a lengthy procession through London was precluded. Hamilton, however, proposed squaring the circle by holding a public lying-in-state in Westminster Hall for the two days before the funeral. The family readily agreed.[198] Various other suggestions for facilitating wider public participation were put forward. For example, a writer to *The Times* suggested that the body should be conveyed to London by road rather than rail at a pace of four miles an hour, thus allowing a 'great concourse of mourners' to line the 180-mile route. The newspaper printed the letter, but in its leader dismissed the idea as 'an affected revival of medievalism' whereas Gladstone, it maintained, was 'a man of the nineteenth century' who 'exulted' over the improved communication brought by the railways.[199] Symbolism, practicality, and the requirement for speed all imposed constraints. A more realistic

---

[193] PRO, HO 45/9935/B26985; WORKS 21/44; BL, AddMS 46673, fo. 51, 19 May 1898 (a passage from Hamilton's diary not printed by Bahlmann). Not only had there been no obvious occasion for involvement from the Earl Marshal, but the 15th Duke of Norfolk had been a minor for some years following his father's early death in 1860. On Esher and Norfolk see Kuhn, *Democratic Royalism*, 58–81, 112–39.

[194] *The Times*, 23 May 1898.

[195] PRO, WORKS 21/44; Brett, *Esher*, i. 215; CA [128–9], [Mr] Gladstone's Funeral [Correspondence], Memorandum by Sir Spencer Ponsonby-Fane, 13 June 1898 (see below, 293). The Lord Chamberlain's Office file on the funeral (LC 2/147) contains only newspaper cuttings and a printed ceremonial.

[196] Bahlmann, *Hamilton 1885–1906*, 356 (26 May).

[197] BL, AddMS 48673, fo. 51, 19 May 1898.

[198] Ibid.

[199] *The Times*, 23 May 1898.

approach was to ensure that even if participation in the funeral could not be comprehensive it could at least be representative. Thus it was decided that all municipalities and county councils throughout the United Kingdom should be entitled to send their mayor, provost, or chairman to attend the funeral service. The intent was to ensure that the service would be expressive of national consensus rather than party feeling, and it was initially envisaged that political organizations would therefore not be represented.[200] The detailed lists of invitations that survive in the College of Arms indicate that great care was taken to ensure a representative attendance in relation to other aspects of national life, notably religious bodies and universities. On the other hand, requests for tickets from individual members of the public were relentlessly rejected.[201]

As Brett, Hamilton, and others worked hard through the weekend to draw up the plans that were made public on Monday 23 May, the intervening Sunday provided an opportunity for religious leaders to focus expression of the public mood. Introducing eight columns of reports of sermons, *The Times* leader writer was struck by the intensity of the emotions expressed, and by the manner in which tributes came from all strands of the Church of England and Nonconformity, as well as from Jews and Roman Catholics. Preaching in Canterbury Cathedral, the Dean, F. W. Farrar, said that the nation was more deeply stirred than it had been at Wellington's death, being 'united in spontaneous mourning'. He attributed the reaction to gratitude for Gladstone's integrity and simplicity, his sympathy with the oppressed and his 'sincere religion'. Rabbis acclaimed him as a devotee of Scripture and as a 'staunch friend of their race'. Above all, Nonconformist preachers acknowledged his responsiveness to their concerns, recalled their sense of affinity with him despite ecclesiastical difference, and praised his stainless Christian character.[202]

The Roman Catholic Church remained relatively aloof. No sermon comment was reported, and Cardinal Vaughan declined an invitation to the funeral, despite the hope of at least one of his co-religionists that he would attend.[203] Nevertheless a funeral march was played at the pro-cathedral in Kensington[204] and a sense of participation was stimulated by the key role

---

[200] *The Times*, 24 May 1898; GG 1727, Hamilton to Herbert Gladstone, 25 May. The organizers subsequently relented to the extent of permitting representatives of the National Liberal Federation to attend (EM 2996, Ross Spence Watson to Norfolk, 14 June 1898).

[201] CA, Gladstone's Funeral.

[202] *The Times*, 23 May 1898. For other sermon comment and religious observance from outside London see Chapter 4 above.

[203] CA, Gladstone's Funeral, Francis A. Moore, 24 May 1898; Norfolk to Garter King of Arms, 19 June 1898.

[204] *The Times*, 23 May 1898.

of the Duke of Norfolk in the arrangements. Vaughan wrote to Norfolk: 'You seem to be going on and on until the Catholic Premier Duke will become the darling of the English people. You are accomplishing a noble and signal work.'[205]

Although the Gladstone family professed to wish to keep the funeral 'simple', they were themselves responsible for two days of observances before the body even left Hawarden. The subsequent lying-in-state at Westminster Hall and the funeral itself meant that the great statesman's public apotheosis extended over five days in all. The proceedings began on Tuesday 24 May when the body was attired in evening dress and the brilliant scarlet robes of an Oxford Doctor of Civil Law, and laid on a couch in Gladstone's study. The setting thus symbolized the deceased's status as a man of letters. During the course of the day numerous visitors, apparently primarily local people, were allowed into the room in small groups.[206] Early the next morning the body, now closed in its coffin, was wheeled on a hand bier to the nearby village church, accompanied by members of the family. A private communion service was held, and later in the morning the church was opened to the public, who passed through in 'huge numbers' for the next six hours. The church was then closed, and further private devotions were held for the family, after which a procession formed to accompany the body to the railway station at Broughton Hall. At the front, preceded by a golden cross, were a choir and clergy. Following the bier were members of the family, the men on foot and the women in carriages. Watched by large crowds the procession passed through the park and in front of Hawarden Castle. It stopped several times to sing hymns, including Gladstone's favourite 'Rock of ages' and 'Praise to the holiest in the height'. Thus the Wednesday's events both recalled Gladstone as the great Christian and churchman, and also, in a form reminiscent of Disraeli's funeral, as the country gentleman, passing on his last journey before his mourning neighbours and dependants amidst the springtime glories of a peaceful pastoral landscape. In this way the family, while accepting the Westminster Abbey funeral, demonstrated their recognition of the power of such rustic romantic associations.[207] A significant contrast with Disraeli's funeral lay, however, in the absence of floral tributes, which was in accordance with Gladstone's own wishes.[208] His tastes in this respect appeared old-fashioned by 1898, and can be interpreted as reflecting his conservative understanding of Christian tradition, in which flowers could seem a distraction from the starker spiritual realities of death.

[205] EM 2992, Cardinal Vaughan to Norfolk, 31 May 1898.
[206] *The Times*, 25 May 1898.
[207] *The Times*, 26 May 1898.
[208] *The Times*, 20 May 1898.

The special train left for London shortly before 8 p.m. Many spectators waited by the railway line to pay their respects, and the train slowed as it passed through the major stations on its route, at Chester, Crewe, Stafford and Rugby, where large crowds stood silently on the platforms. At Rugby a band played the 'Dead March'. Rather than continue to the normal London and North Western Railway terminus at Euston, the train was switched to the underground system and travelled through to Westminster station, from where the body was carried directly by way of a subway into the precincts of Parliament itself. Thus a street procession was wholly avoided.[209] By 6 a.m. on the Thursday morning the simple polished oak coffin had been placed in Westminster Hall on a raised bier draped with black hangings and a white pall. The only other furniture was a brass cross and four silver candlesticks (see Plate 6).[210] This was the first public lying-in-state since 1852, and its character contrasted radically with the elaboration used for Wellington. Hamilton had advocated 'the grandeur of complete simplicity', while the family agreed that 'simplicity and dignity [would] determine the whole arrangement'.[211] Disagreement had arisen, however, over the family's initial wish to have the body exposed as it had been in the study at Hawarden, an arrangement that many felt would be distasteful and 'un-English'. A 'certain amount of peremptoriness' on the part of Hamilton and the Duke of Norfolk led to the idea being abandoned.[212]

Distant though recollection of the Duke of Wellington's lying-in-state might be, lessons had been learned. There was a heavy police presence, and careful thought had evidently been given to effective control of the crowds and to their smooth passage through the hall. The building was in any case much more suitable than Chelsea Hospital. Also—in notable contrast both to 1852 and to twentieth-century lyings-in-state—lengthy queues were avoided. Nevertheless during the two days nearly 300,000 people passed by the catafalque, and generally appeared deeply moved despite the lack of spectacle. Considerable social diversity was apparent. On the Friday evening, a concession was made to party loyalty insofar as representatives of the National Liberal Federation and of Liberal associations 'from Caithness to Cornwall' were allowed to file past the coffin and pay their last respects.[213]

---

[209] *The Times*, 26 May 1898.

[210] *The Times*, 27 May 1898. For the second day of the lying-in-state the four silver candlesticks were replaced with six brass ones (*The Times*, 28 May 1898).

[211] GG 1727, Hamilton to Herbert Gladstone, 22 May; Memorandum by Herbert(?) Gladstone. For Wellington's lying-in-state see above, Chapter 2.

[212] Bahlmann, *Hamilton 1885–1906*, 355 (23, 25 May); *The Times*, 25 May, letter from Lewis Morris.

[213] *The Times*, 27, 28 May 1898.

The hallmarks of the funeral itself were inclusiveness and an avoidance of unnecessary pageantry. The parliamentary consensus was represented by a large attendance of members of both houses and all parties, who walked in sombre procession to the Abbey. The pallbearers included Salisbury and Balfour, alongside Harcourt, Rosebery and Kimberley. Also striking was the presence of women and children among the family mourners, older boys even joining the procession, in notable contrast to the exclusively adult male attendance recorded at Palmerston's funeral. Mrs Gladstone took a prominent part in her husband's funeral while, in a moving scene, their young grandchildren knelt around his grave. Moreover, the ordinary people who had identified so much with Gladstone could feel themselves represented to some extent through a deputation of a hundred tenants, workmen and domestics from Hawarden.

Although this was also a state occasion at which royalty, headed by the Prince and Princess of Wales, turned out in strength, and foreign sovereigns and governments were duly represented, outward manifestations of status were severely limited. Only the Speaker and the Lord Chancellor appeared in ceremonial dress, and the chief mourner, the Revd Stephen Gladstone, wore his clerical robes, thus giving prominence to the dead man's parliamentary and ecclesiastical associations. Heralds marshalled the ceremony, but they wore morning dress rather than their traditional tabards. The only uniforms in sight were those of the police and the Eton College Rifle Volunteers, members of Gladstone's old school who had been invited at Brett's instigation[214] to form a guard of honour. The procession on foot traversed only the short distance between Westminster Hall and the west door of the Abbey. The funeral car, drawn by two horses, was 'simply a broad black platform' mounted on carriage wheels. Heraldic trappings, such as the ceremonial breaking of staves of office over the grave, were omitted. The service itself included impressive organ, brass, and choral music, but also three hymns that suggested an endeavour to connect with popular religiosity. Toplady's 'Rock of ages' and Newman's 'Praise to the holiest' again summed up the diverse springs of the dead man's spirituality, while the closing congregational singing of 'O God our help in ages past' was explicitly intended as 'a great national prayer'.[215]

Most participants and observers felt that the funeral had succeeded both as an appropriate tribute to Gladstone and as an authentic expression of the national mood. A member of the Handel Society who watched from the triforium of the Abbey found it 'extraordinarily impressive' and thought

[214] Brett, *Esher*, i. 215.

[215] *The Times*, 25, 30 May 1898; British Film Archive 4769 A(c)—a short but revealing sequence showing the hearse and the mourners processing to the Abbey; EM 2111, 2112, Report to the Queen by Norfolk. See above, 76.

that no 'display of pomp or ceremony would have added really to the effect'.[216] For those outside, the most powerful impression was of the 'intense and unexampled stillness' of the crowd in Broad Sanctuary and Parliament Square. Moreover, although only a small fraction of the population could be present at Westminster, the provision of memorial services throughout the country and beyond stimulated powerful echoes of the atmosphere in and around the Abbey.[217]

Some though felt the event fell between two stools, insofar as it lacked both pageantry and spontaneous popular resonance. Norfolk himself quietly amended the report in the London *Gazette* to make it clear that 'customs and regulations' had been modified in order to accommodate the 'expressed wishes of the deceased'. He was concerned that it should not be used 'as a precedent to deprive <u>future</u> public funerals of their grandeur'.[218] Meanwhile *Reynolds Newspaper* complained that it had been 'a cold, formal, official affair' marked by the hypocritical attendance of those who had been Gladstone's bitter enemies, and the exclusion of his real friends. It agreed that the avoidance of 'partisan celebration' had been right, but felt that it would have been far better if the actual funeral had been held at Hawarden and a simultaneous memorial service at Westminster. Then the 'great multitudes of Mr Gladstone's devoted followers' would have had more opportunity to pay their respects.[219] Ironically, the unspoken thought of the leader writer for this bastion of journalistic radicalism seemed to be that matters had been better handled for Disraeli.

In conclusion, Gladstone's obsequies can be set against the wider context suggested by the aftermath of Disraeli's death. Both funerals, through in particular their emphasis on simplicity, reflected and stimulated a significant evolution in both public and private funerals. Granted that the 'simplicity' was in neither case free from elements of disingenuousness or contrivance, it still carried sufficient conviction to strike a strong chord in the national consciousness. Disraeli's 'village' funeral indicated that a great statesman was in no way diminished by choosing to return at the last to his perceived rural roots; while Gladstone's showed that acceptance into the 'Valhalla' at Westminster was not incompatible with enduring populist appeal. Taken together their legacy was a complex one of subtle and somewhat ironic interplay between metropolitan and provincial associations. When Herbert Henry Asquith, the leading Liberal statesman of the next generation, died in 1928, Archbishop Randall Davidson hoped he too would be buried in Westminster Abbey on the grounds that 'great men belonged

---

[216] GG 1041, Philip G. L. Webb, 5 June.
[217] *The Times*, 30 May 1898.
[218] CA, Gladstone's Funeral, Norfolk to Garter King of Arms, 19 June 1898.
[219] *Reynolds Newspaper*, 29 May 1898.

to the nation'.[220] Asquith, however, was buried in the village churchyard at Sutton Courtenay near Oxford, a choice that his biographer, himself a leading politician, judged 'appropriate'.[221] Moreover Gladstone's funeral also showed how the panoply of state and heraldic tradition could be adjusted in line with personal preference and public opinion. This lesson was not lost on the two future kings among the pallbearers. The Prince of Wales was much impressed with the 'solemn simplicity' of the ceremony.[222] The Duke of York, when he succeeded as George V in 1910, decided to have a lying-in-state for his own father that took a form modelled much more closely on Gladstone's than on the distant royal precedents.[223]

The endeavours to build and sustain cross-party consensus on both occasions were striking in view of the controversial policies of both men in life. The achievement was a more fragile and limited one in 1881 than it was to be in 1898. Nevertheless, Gladstone's own magnanimity towards his dead rival had established an important precedent that Balfour and Salisbury were scrupulous in developing. In both cases the support of the royal family was helpful, with the impact of the Queen's personal affinities moderated by the Prince of Wales's shrewd appreciation of the dynamics of public opinion. In the short term at least the Conservatives were the main beneficiaries of both events. The Primrose League as it developed in the mid-1880s could present itself as being a national rather than merely partisan organization. In 1898, by generalized honouring of the dead and avoidance of allusion to past quarrels, the government could present itself as in some measure an inheritor of Gladstonian political values, in the face of the all too obvious limitations of Gladstone's successors in the Liberal leadership. In terms of wider national consciousness the aftermath of Gladstone's death provided a consensual expression of attitudes that were a significant counterbalance to the more militaristic and imperialist mood usually seen as characteristic of the period.[224]

Finally, the strongly religious tone of reactions to Gladstone's death sits in intriguing and revealing tension with the evidence that at this period the tide of Victorian religiosity was already ebbing.[225] Some indeed noted the contrast at the time, and hailed Gladstone's example and the spiritual aspirations stirred by his passing as a basis for successful Christian reassertion. For example a Calvinistic Methodist pastor in North Wales believed that 'His calmness, his Christian fortitude, his unshaken faith have

---

[220] Bell, *Davidson*, ii. 1178.
[221] R. Jenkins, *Asquith* (1978), 519.
[222] EM 2985, Francis Knollys to Norfolk, 28 May 1898.
[223] See below, Chapter 8.
[224] Cf. Matthew, 'Gladstone's Death', 24.
[225] H. McLeod, *Religion and Society in England, 1850–1914* (Basingstoke, 1996), 170–72.

doubtlessly done much to arrest the growing tendency in the present day to indifference and scepticism and to awaken the conscience of our Country to the stern realities of a life beyond.'[226] Such hopes rested to a considerable extent on the legacy of Gladstone's own distinctive personal qualities and his recent apologetic writings, but it was noteworthy that even the death of the much less pious Disraeli had stirred a significant measure of religious response. The events of both April 1881 and May 1898 demonstrated in different ways the inadequacy of straightforward analytical separations between the religious and the secular. On the one hand the churches, and the Church of England in particular, showed themselves to have a central and arguably growing role in giving expression to impulses of national mourning. On the other it still seemed to many in 1898 that the greatest compliment that could be paid to the memory of a leading secular politician was to acclaim him as a paradigm of Christian faith and conduct.

[226] GG 1055, Tabernacle Calvinistic Methodist Chapel, Ruthin, 30 May.

# 7

# *'It was too soon to die':*
# Death and the Royal Family
# 1861–1892

> It was too soon to die.
> Yet, might we count his years by triumphs won,
> By wise, and bold, and Christian duties done,
> It were no brief eventless history.

In such terms *Punch* mused on the death of Prince Albert at the age of only forty-two in December 1861.[1] For many older people the untimeliness of this national bereavement recalled the intensity of feeling that had followed the death in childbirth of Princess Charlotte in 1817.[2] Moreover, as in 1817, the royal family's tragedy was distressingly reminiscent of personal losses suffered by many of their subjects: just as Charlotte's fate was shared by many other young women, Albert, by dying in early middle age and leaving a numerous young family, epitomized another recurrent fear that clouded the horizon of the lives of ordinary people.

In later decades the Queen was also by no means a stranger to that most distressing of bereavements, the death of adult children, and thus could become further associated with the sufferings of many of her subjects.[3] This spectre was first raised by the dangerous illness of the Prince of Wales in 1871. He was to recover, but several of his siblings were not so fortunate: Princess Alice died in 1878, Prince Leopold in 1884, and Prince Alfred in 1900. Two of Victoria's sons-in-laws were also to predecease her, the Emperor Frederick in 1888, and Prince Henry of Battenberg in 1896. Most poignant of all was the death in January 1892, aged only twenty eight, of Prince Albert Victor, Duke of Clarence and Avondale, eldest son of the Prince of Wales and second in line to the throne. This long sequence of

---

[1] *Punch*, 41 (1861), 245.
[2] For example, Jeffreys, *Princes and Great Men*, 4–5.
[3] Jalland, *Death in the Victorian Family*, 277.

personal tragedies, spread across the last forty years of Victoria's reign, provided a significant recurrent focus for wider public attitudes both to death and to the royal family itself.

The period was a significant transitional one in the history of royal deaths. As we have seen, the eighteenth and early nineteenth centuries were characterized—with the significant exception of the short phase from 1817 to 1821—by limited and formalized responses that do not appear to have captured the public imagination. In the first half of the twentieth century, however, the deaths of successive sovereigns were to give rise to much more intense and widespread interest. Although the attempt to discern trends is limited by the obvious fact that no monarch died between 1837 and 1901, consideration of reactions to the deaths of other members of the royal family will serve to illuminate the reasons for the contrast. Analysis will be concentrated primarily on the two most prominent untimely cases, those of Prince Albert in 1861 and of Prince Albert Victor in 1892. Separated as they were by the space of almost exactly thirty years, they provide appropriate vantage points from which to assess the developments and trends of the second half of the nineteenth century.

## Prince Albert

Prince Albert had been in failing health for some years before his death, suffering from exhaustion and a chronic abdominal condition, conceivably a peptic ulcer, Crohn's disease or possibly stomach cancer. Even if his underlying problems were not terminal in themselves they would have undermined his capacity to fight infection. Certainly by early December 1861 he was seriously ill.[4] However, no public announcement of his condition was made until 8 December, when the Court Circular reported merely that he was suffering from a 'feverish cold'.[5] In reality the doctors already suspected typhoid, although that diagnosis itself appears dubious.[6] On 11 December it was publicly admitted that he had a 'fever' but 'unattended by any unfavourable symptoms'.[7] The Prime Minister, Lord Palmerston, feared the nation had to be prepared for worse news to come.[8] Only at 5 p.m. on 13 December did a bulletin suggest that the illness might

---

[4] S. Weintraub, *Victoria: Biography of a Queen* (1987), 295, 300n. Palmerston's correspondence with the royal household in early December shows that the Prince's condition was already giving grounds for concern (RA, VIC/R 1/2, 4, 5).

[5] *The Times*, 9 Dec. 1861.

[6] Weintraub, *Victoria*, 297.

[7] *The Times*, 12 Dec. 1861.

[8] RA, VIC/R 1/19, Palmerston to Phipps, 11 Dec. 1861.

be dangerous, although by that time the Prince and those around him had already recognized that he was almost certainly dying.[9] Hence when the end came little more than twenty-four hours later, at Windsor Castle at 10.50 p.m. on Saturday 14 December, the public at large had had very little time to adjust to the possibility. The Prince's death came 'without warning sufficient to prepare . . . for a blow so abrupt and so terrible'.[10] There was thus a notable contrast with the last illnesses of early nineteenth-century royalty, which had been conducted very much in the public eye insofar as frequent bulletins were issued and published in the newspapers.

The tension between the private and the public spheres inherent in all prominent deaths was particularly acute in Albert's case. Just as news of his illness had been largely kept from the public, the instincts of both the Queen herself and of the court seem to have been to find solace in strictly private mourning. Albert's death was indeed by any standards a profound personal tragedy, which left Victoria a widow in her early forties with numerous young children and the onerous state responsibilities from which Albert had done much to shield her over the twenty-one years of their married life. Nevertheless the event also had an important and inescapable public dimension. Despite the constitutional ambiguities of his position, Albert had played an important role in public affairs, and the Queen's capacity effectively to sustain her role without him was in 1861 an uncertain quality. Palmerston had thus observed during the Prince's last illness that his fate was 'a matter of the most momentous national importance'.[11] When the worst happened, the premier's letter of sympathy to Victoria well conveyed his sense that the recipient was in a very different position from any other bereaved widow:

> Your Majesty has sustained one of the greatest of human misfortunes and there is not one among the many millions who have the Happiness of being your Majesty's subjects, whose heart will not bleed in sympathy with your Majesty's sorrow. But that Almighty Creator who has placed your Majesty in a Position in which you so greatly sway the Destiny of so many millions of Fellow Creatures, has been pleased to endow your Majesty with a strength of mind and a sense of Duties commensurate with the Position which you hold.[12]

Albert's death indeed appears to have stirred a very extensive and intense public reaction. Adam Sedgwick, the geologist and Albert's secretary in his capacity as Chancellor of Cambridge University, was struck by a letter

[9] Weintraub, *Victoria*, 299.
[10] *The Times*, 16 Dec. 1861.
[11] RA, VIC/R 1/12, 10 Dec. 1861.
[12] RA, VIC/R 1/51, Palmerston to the Queen, 15 Dec. 1861.

he had received from his niece, wife of the clergyman at Fylingdales on the North Yorkshire Moors. The sad news arrived just as she had assembled her weekly Sunday class of farmers' daughters. 'We could not read', she wrote, 'but we all knelt down to pray for the Queen and wept bitterly.' She noted that in many parts of the moors the 'poor people' were all wearing marks of mourning, and that even in remote places churches and school buildings had been 'put in regular mourning' at the expense of the inhabitants. Sedgwick thought that a 'feather will show the direction of the wind better than a forest tree' and felt such incidents were more revealing of the 'deep penetration of the national feeling than the more formal ceremonials'.[13] Another revealing 'feather' in the wind was provided by an account of Bethnal Green on the day of the Prince's funeral. All the large shops were closed and the small ones were showing signs of mourning. People appeared unusually quiet and subdued and were gathering around ballad singers, whose utterances visibly moved their audiences.[14] The London City Mission witnessed a 'very general expression of deep concern and feeling' among the 200,000 poor families in the metropolis its agents visited, extending even to the 'very poorest'.[15] A hospital visitor reported that 'not one patient spoke to him of his own wounds or ailments while every one to whom he went up, was full of expressions of sorrow for the loss which the Country had sustained, and of tender enquiries about the Queen, in her cruel bereavement.'[16] Richard Monckton Milnes wrote: 'The peasants in their cottages talk as if the Queen was one of themselves. It is the realest public sorrow I have ever seen—quite different from anything else.'[17]

Even the radical Sunday press acknowledged the depth of public feeling. *Reynolds Newspaper* was backhanded in its tribute to Albert as 'the most respectable and meritorious German who ever lived upon the bounty of the British people', and regarded him as a pinnacle rather than as a pillar of the state. Nevertheless it acknowledged that he was an irreparable loss to his family and to the Queen, a 'truly noble lady' who had 'a just claim to the respect and affection of her subjects'.[18] *Lloyds Weekly Newspaper* reported that many were greatly affected by the news and thought there would not be 'a fireside in England that, in the midst of Christmas revelry, will not be, now and then, overshadowed' by awareness of his death.[19]

[13] RA, VIC/R 2/112, Sedgwick to Phipps, 10 Feb. 1862.
[14] RA, VIC/R 2/22, W. H. Wills to Miss Burdett-Coutts, 26 Dec. 1861.
[15] RA, VIC/R 2/41, Revd John Garwood to Revd G. Prothero, 31 Dec. 1861.
[16] RA, VIC/R 2/15, G. H. Seymour to Phipps, 25 Dec. 1861.
[17] T. W. Reid, *The Life, Letters and Friendships of Richard Monckton Milnes*, 2 vols. (1890), ii. 74.
[18] *Reynolds Newspaper*, 22 Dec. 1861.
[19] *Lloyds Weekly Newspaper*, 22 Dec. 1861.

The overall impression that emerges from newspapers and other sources is of a universal and palpably sombre public mood. In the first instance it spread out from the churches where many first learnt what had happened at service on the day after Albert's death, on to the streets where groups of people sought further news and mutual support. Anxiety was heightened by understandable concern for the Queen's own health.[20] John Rashdall, an Anglican clergyman, heard that many other people had been made dangerously ill by the shock.[21] On Monday 16 December the circulation of *The Times* broke all previous records and London shops found themselves faced with 'incalculable demand for mourning', from the poor as well as the wealthy.[22] In the middle of the week *The Times* judged that 'Never in our remembrance has there been such universal sorrow at the death of an individual.'[23] A similar feeling reportedly prevailed in Ireland.[24] This mood continued at least until the day of the funeral on Monday 23 December, when most places of business were closed even though no official instructions to that effect had been given.[25] When in early January the Home Secretary, Sir George Grey, felt able to present to the Queen some of the many hundreds of addresses of condolence that had been flooding in, he too emphasized the depth and universality of public grief.[26] If others did not share in the sentiments their feelings must have been perceived as so indecent that they were not recorded.

Such intense and extensive public reaction to a prominent death was certainly without parallel since 1817. At one level it lacks rationality. Why should so many be moved to tears and to a forgetfulness of their own problems by the death of someone whom they had never met, and whose passing had no perceptible practical impact on the fabric of their daily lives? Contemporaries were themselves intrigued by the phenomenon. Some

[20] *The Times*, 16, 17 Dec. 1861; *Leeds Intelligencer*, 21 Dec. 1861; *The Life of His Late Royal Highness the Prince Consort with an Account of his Last Moments* (1862), 12.
[21] BodL, Rashdall Diary, MS.Eng.misc.e.359, 22 Dec. 1861.
[22] Dasent, *John Thadeus Delane*, ii. 39; *ILN*, 28 Dec. 1861, p. 665. In a sermon on 22 December, John Cumming, minister of Crown Court Presbyterian church reported that the head of one of the largest drapery establishments had observed the poor coming 'in crowds' to buy mourning (*The Times*, 23 Dec. 1861).
[23] *The Times*, 18 Dec. 1861.
[24] RA, VIC/R 1/176, S. Ponsonby to Phipps, 21 Dec. 1861.
[25] *The Times*, 24 Dec. 1861; *ILN*, 28 Dec. 1861, p. 654. The town clerk of Hastings had enquired on 17 December whether any orders would be issued for the closing of shops, the inhabitants being anxious to express their 'deep grief' in every possible manner. In response the Lord Chamberlain's Office informed him that such demonstrations were a matter for the judgement and good feeling of individuals (PRO, LC 1/90, LC 1/92).
[26] RA, VIC/R 2/69, Grey to the Queen, 11 Jan. 1862. The Home Office log of addresses received survives in PRO HO 57/8.

remarked on the role the telegraph now played in providing for rapid communication of the news of the death, and thus giving a sense of immediate affinity with events even for those many hundreds of miles away from Windsor.[27] A clergyman in Penzance perceived the telegraph as a metaphor for the wider interplay of individual and collective emotion:

> The sensations which we individually experience, on the first tidings of some great sorrow, are doubled and redoubled as we find that every one we meet is occupied by the same sad story,—every member of a vast community in contact with the same electric chain, along which the tumultuous excitement is flashing from one end to the other.[28]

In Australia, which did not receive the sad news for two months, there was on the other hand a sense of dislocation in awareness that mourning was taking place 'at an advanced season'.[29] In the response to Albert's death one can thus detect a significant expression of a growing sense of the simultaneity of remote events, which, Benedict Anderson has argued, is both a key feature of the 'modern' concept of time, and an essential precondition for the development of nationalism. It also appears to have given heightened immediacy and intensity to public feeling.[30]

The texture of public sentiment was appreciably different from that which had prevailed in the aftermath of Wellington's death nine years before. The Duke's decease was a big event, but still one tacitly accepted as inevitable in the course of nature, and hence hardly a matter for profound concern or grief.[31] Albert's death on the other hand was doubly untimely, both in the light of his relative youth, and also because it removed a major public figure whose work was felt to be still very much incomplete. A sense that Albert's death was precipitating a sudden national crisis was accentuated by fears regarding the Queen's ability to carry on alone, an awareness of the inexperience of the young Prince of Wales, and knowledge of a possible confrontation with the United States looming over the Trent incident.[32] Such insecurities found further expression in suggestions by some

[27] Fletcher, *For the Prince Consort*, section V; Flower, *Prince Consort* (1862), 3.

[28] P. Hedgeland, *National Grief and Some of its Uses* (Penzance, 1861), 9.

[29] J. Carter, *Reflections on the Death of HRH Prince Albert* (Sydney, 1862), 11.

[30] B. Anderson, *Imagined Communities: Reflections on the Origin and Spread of Nationalism* (1983), 30–1. Anderson contrasts the modern concept of simultaneity as 'transverse, cross-time' and focused on the coincidence of events in different places, with the 'medieval' one of 'simultaneity-along-time' marked by 'prefiguring and fulfilment'.

[31] See above, Chapter 2.

[32] *The Times*, 16, 17 Dec. 1861; Sermon by the Dean of Westminster on 22 Dec. reported in *The Times* of 23 Dec. 1861.

churchmen that Albert's death should be seen as a divine judgement on the nation.[33]

In life, however, Albert had not been a particularly popular figure. Earlier suspicions of his German sympathies and unconstitutional influence had eased somewhat by 1861, but they had not disappeared.[34] Earl Russell acknowledged the important part he had played in the development of constitutional monarchy,[35] but only a limited circle appreciated the nature of his contribution. Obituarists were therefore liable to feel that their task was a delicate one.[36] For some indeed the intensity of their grief may well have been tinged with guilt at an earlier failure to appreciate the Prince properly while he was alive.[37]

In the immediate aftermath of Albert's death the mainspring of public sentiment was thus not so much regret for the Prince as an individual but rather a sense of affinity with the grief of the royal family as a whole.[38] Their personal loss was that which was in private life 'the deepest of all calamities'.[39] Within living memory the tragedies of royal women, notably Princess Charlotte and her mother Queen Caroline, had captured the public imagination and contributed to the shaping of domestic ideology.[40] Albert though, for the first time since the prime of George III three quarters of a century before, had presented the public with a perceived ideal of male conjugal and familial devotion. The point was made in both a secular and in a religious context. Gathorne Hardy saw the death as 'a sad break up to that happy family which has given so touching an interest to Royalty in this country'.[41] Lord Russell felt Albert had raised and sanctified the Crown as a supreme social as well as secular authority.[42] In the eyes of the Vicar of Doncaster the royal couple had achieved a 'moral revolution' by making their family a pattern for the nation as a whole.[43] The Bishop of London, A. C. Tait, grieved that 'now there is an end of all that happy married life which for 22 yrs has brought such blessings to England by exhibiting the

[33] Brooks, *The Rod of the Almighty*, 5–9; P. Hood, *Words from the Pall of the Prince* (1862), 23. Hood acknowledged, however, that some found the suggestion offensive: see above, 66–7.
[34] Redesdale, *Memories*, i. 165; Laughton, *Henry Reeve* ii. 77. Florence Nightingale pithily remarked 'He neither liked, nor was liked. But what he has done for our country no one knows.' (E. Cook, *The Life of Florence Nightingale*, 2 vols. (1913), ii. 10).
[35] RA, VIC/R 1/68, Russell to Phipps, 16 Dec. 1861.
[36] Laughton, *Henry Reeve*, ii. 77.
[37] C. Kingsley, *A Sermon on the Death of HRH the Prince Consort* (1862), 6–9.
[38] R. G. L. Blenkinsopp, *Britain's Loss and Britain's Duty* (1862), 3; Laughton, *Henry Reeve*.
[39] *The Times*, 23 Dec. 1861.
[40] Colley, *Britons*, 265–73; Davidoff and Hall, *Family Fortunes*, 150–55.
[41] *Gathorne Hardy A Memoir*, i. 153.
[42] RA, VIC/R 1/68, Russell to Phipps, 16 Dec. 1861.
[43] Vaughan, *Mourning of the Land*, 12.

best picture of what husband and wife shd be in the highest position in the nation'.[44] Tait pursued the link between the royal and the personal in his Christmas Day sermon at Fulham Parish Church. Christmas, he said, brought a sense of sadness to all families in that it recalled the faces missing among the joyful gatherings. Similarly the current sorrow touched everyone, and was national in a literal as well as conventional sense. Everyone felt as if they had lost a relative, and even the youngest children would have cause to remember the feelings experienced by their elders. Tait concluded that the Prince had greatly deepened attachment to the royal house by creating a model of Christian family life. In his opinion, the extent of current grief at the rupture of the royal circle was an indication of how much the ideal was valued by the people as a whole.[45] Some preachers went further, seeing the nation itself as one large family. A Liverpool clergyman maintained that the sorrow was both 'widely, yea universally, national' and at one and the same time 'deeply and tenderly domestic'.[46] Charles Kingsley suggested that the bereaved Queen should be taken to her people's hearts as 'the mother of her country', while the nation itself should see itself as a father to the orphaned Prince of Wales.[47]

Albert's death thus reinforced the status of the royal family and the Queen as points of focus for national consciousness and community. Indeed it would seem that bereavement strengthened this identification insofar as it reminded the Queen's subjects that, with all its privileges, royalty brought no exemption from the sufferings and losses experienced by ordinary people. As one preacher put it, 'Their own home-hearts know what Her affliction is, and enter into it.'[48] A popular ballad also expressed a strong sense of identification with the grieving royal family:

> In sorrow all classes are mingling,
> Grief in every quarter is seen,
> You mothers and daughters of England,
> Sympathise with your widowed Queen;
> Her loss now does sadly distress her
> With her children in pain do deplore,
> Let every Christian heart say, God bless her,
> Her dear consort alas is no more.[49]

The suddenness of Albert's death was also a major factor in contributing

---

[44] LPL, Tait Papers 75, fo. 75, Memorandum by Tait, 15 Dec. 1861.
[45] LPL, Tait Papers 384/6, MS notes.
[46] Falloon, *A Prince Fallen*, 4–5.
[47] Kingsley, *Prince Consort*, 14–15.
[48] RA, VIC/R 2/85, MS extract from sermon by Revd J. S. B. Monsell.
[49] RA, VIC/R 2/22, printed *Elegy on the Death of HRH Prince Albert*.

to the extent of its impact. The deaths of young women in childbirth or of young men in battle might appear equally untimely, but the circumstances themselves induced an awareness that risks were present. From the point of view of the general public, however, Albert's unexpected death was wholly a bolt from the blue. It also was a disconcerting reminder to his own still relatively youthful generation both of their own mortality and of the passage of time: as *The Times* put it, 'Prince Albert of the Queen's youth and our own ... is gone.'[50] Lord Overstone, the financier, who was more than two decades older than the Prince, found his thoughts wholly occupied by the event, which he contemplated in a 'religious light' as 'a startling admonition to us all of the short and precarious nature of life'.[51] If such sentiments were not already present in the minds of the unusually large congregations drawn to church in the aftermath of Albert's death, they were very likely to be prompted by exhortations from the clergy to be spiritually prepared for the possibility of a similar fate.[52] Charles Haddon Spurgeon, preaching on 22 December to a packed congregation at the recently-opened Metropolitan Tabernacle, concluded 'with a searching and impassioned appeal to his hearers to remember the uncertainty of life and to be ready to meet the Great Judge of all'.[53] On the same day John Rashdall preached in the morning on the text 'The grass withereth, and the flower thereof falleth away; but the word of the Lord endureth for ever' (1 Peter 1:24–5) , and in the evening on 'And the world passeth away, ... but he who doeth the will of God abideth for ever.' (1 John 2:17). He thought that many had been 'impressed' by sermons on the event.[54] The circumstances served to give credibility to the argument of an Episcopalian clergyman in Edinburgh that even when human beings excluded religion from other aspects of their experience, it would still always find a place in their response to death.[55]

The funeral service at St George's Windsor on 23 December was conducted away from the public eye and with a minimum of pageantry. Reaction against the empty heraldic spectacle last seen at the funeral of William IV was still strong, and a recent precedent had been set by the funeral of the Queen's mother, the Duchess of Kent, conducted in a private

---

[50] *The Times*, 23 Dec. 1861.

[51] D. P. O'Brien (ed.), *The Correspondence of Lord Overstone*, 3 vols. (Cambridge, 1971), ii. 980.

[52] For example see T. W. Aveling, *Princely Greatness Yielding Unto Death* (1861), 26–8; E. Mellor, *Be Still and Know that I Am God* (Liverpool, 1861), 7.

[53] *The Times*, 23 Dec. 1861.

[54] BodL, Rashdall Diary, 22 Dec. 1861. Rashdall seemed to be using the word 'impressed' in the strong and specialist sense of being stirred to repentance: he noted that there had been '2 or 3' such cases in his own congregation.

[55] J. H. Carr, *If He Sleep, He Shall Do Well* (Edinburgh, 1861), 3–7.

manner with limited ceremonial earlier in 1861.[56] Moreover Albert himself had apparently requested a 'private' funeral with limited ceremonial. No reference was made to the Queen and after a meeting with the Prince of Wales, Viscount Sydney, the Lord Chamberlain, considered himself commanded to carry out the funeral at his discretion. It was noted that 'It is not desired that references on matters of detail should be made to Windsor.' Sydney therefore decided to follow the model of the Duchess of Kent's funeral closely, on the assumption that it would best reflect the royal family's wishes.[57] There were significant continuities with the past, notably in the overpowering draping of the chapel with black, the erection of a platform in the nave, the use of a heavy embroidered pall, and the exclusively male attendance (see Plate 7). On the other hand, the funeral, like Queen Adelaide's and the Duchess of Kent's, was held in daylight hours, the heraldic content was limited, and there were musical innovations.[58] A further practical constraint limiting the extent of ceremonial was the need to hold the service before Christmas so as to avoid an incongruous prolongation of the initial phase of mourning over the festive season.[59] Even as it was, Sydney and his staff had to work under enormous pressure to make all the arrangements in the space of little more than a week.[60]

There was some pressure for the funeral to acquire a more public face so as to express both the sentiment of the nation as a whole and Albert's international standing. Despite a general limitation of invitations to individuals having some personal connection with the Prince, Cabinet ministers and the Archbishop of Canterbury were also included. Bishop Tait had made discrete representations on the latter's behalf, fearing lest 'the absence of the Heads of the Church might not be misconstrued'.[61] Foreign representation though was strictly limited to royal personages having a family connection with Albert. This rule provided a convenient pretext for

[56] *Ceremonial . . . Monday, December 23rd 1861* (copy in BL).

[57] PRO, LC 1/92, 16 Dec. 1861. A scrawled note from the Lord Chamberlain's Office, dated 5 p.m. on December 15, stated that the funeral would be on 23 December, 'on the Basis of the late Ds. of Kent' except that a hearse and some mourning coaches would be used. (PRO, WORKS 21/5/16/1).

[58] *The Times*, 17, 18, 24 Dec. 1861. The arrangements were made entirely by the Lord Chamberlain's Office, without any reference to the Earl Marshal or the College of Arms, except for the formal order for general mourning issued by the deputy Earl Marshal on 16 December (*The Times*, 17 Dec. 1861), and the presence of two heralds whom Sydney invited to assist him (LC 1/92, Sydney to Sir Charles Young, 18 Dec. 1861).

[59] Weintraub, *Victoria*, 304. Weintraub's authority for his assertion that the date was fixed by the Prince of Wales in consultation with the Duke of Cambridge is unclear, but it appears plausible.

[60] PRO, LC 1/90 and LC 1/92 contain much frenzied correspondence.

[61] LPL, Tait Papers, 79, fo. 263.

excluding both Marshal Vaillant who had been put forward to represent Napoleon III and any formal representation of King Louis-Philippe's widow, Queen Amélie. On the other hand the Orleanist Duc de Nemours was present by virtue of his marriage to Albert's cousin.[62] The only major foreign states to be represented were Prussia, through the attendance of the Crown Prince (Albert's son-in-law), Belgium, by the Duke of Brabant and the Count of Flanders (cousins of both Albert and Victoria), and Portugal (whose royal family was linked to Albert's by marriage), by the presence of its envoy in London. Indian connections though were symbolized by the participation in the procession of Maharaja Duleep Singh, a convert from Sikhism to Christianity and a favourite of the Queen's.[63]

The Mayor of Windsor pressed the case for members of the English public, as represented at least by his fellow citizens, to be allowed to see something of the ceremony. On 18 December he wrote to the Lord Chamberlain's Office to ask if tickets would be issued for the castle yard or the chapel, but received a negative response.[64] General Grey, one of Albert's private secretaries, however, took up the issue, and persuaded the Prince of Wales to approve an amended, more public, route for the procession. Instead of proceeding directly from the private apartments to the chapel through the Norman Gate, it would be taken down Castle Hill, and briefly out of the precincts altogether, before proceeding to the chapel by the Henry VIII Gate. Sydney was furious at this interference, feeling that it would compromise the 'private' character of the funeral. He refused to agree to the plan without authority from the Queen herself.[65] The matter was referred to Osborne, where the Queen had retired, and from where it was reported by Sir Charles Phipps that Princess Alice, the Queen's second daughter, was 'entirely of opinion' that her mother would prefer the more private arrangement. Moreover, Phipps pointed out, the 'invariable rule' for previous royal funerals had been to proceed by the Norman Gate.[66] Meanwhile, however, the Mayor of Windsor still persisted with strong representations to the royal household 'expressing the intense disappointment with which the determination to exclude everybody had been received, and his conviction that the anxiety to be allowed to see, at least the

---

[62] RA, VIC/R 1/130 Sydney to Phipps, 18 Dec. 1861; VIC/R 1/133, Phipps to the Duc de Nemours, 18 Dec, 1861.

[63] For lists of those present see printed *Ceremonial* and *The Times*, 24 Dec. 1861. On Duleep Singh see G. Beckerlegge, 'The Presence of Islam and South Asian Religions in Victorian Britain', in J. Wolffe (ed.), *Religion in Victorian Britain V: Culture and Empire* (Manchester, 1997), 232–3.

[64] PRO, LC 1/90, LC 1/92.

[65] RA, VIC/R 1/177, Sydney to Phipps, 21 Dec. 1861.

[66] PRO, LC 1/92, Note on draft of Sydney to Phipps, 21 Dec. 1861; RA, VIC/R 1/181, Phipps to Sydney, 22 Dec. 1861.

procession, were from the best motives'.[67] The matter was still unresolved on the evening before the funeral, when a harassed Sydney reiterated his determination to honour what he believed to be the wishes of both the Queen and the late Prince, and to keep the procession away from the public view, 'however much it may affront the Mayor of Windsor'.[68] In the event, although a few members of the public, including the Mayor and his family, were able to inveigle their way into the Castle, the numbers admitted were small and the crowd gathered at the bottom of Castle Hill saw nothing but empty carriages.[69] The confusion was entirely understandable given the circumstances, and Sydney's anxiety to protect the royal family from any unnecessary additional distress. The incident, however, was a revealing one in showing the strength of the preference for private funerals in royal circles and the extent of the distaste for the public pageantry associated with such occasions at both earlier and later periods. It is though interesting to note that the future Edward VII was already receptive to an alternative approach.

For the great majority of the British population, however, the question of whether or not a few thousand local people could see the procession was irrelevant to their own perception of the funeral, which inevitably had to be mediated by newspapers and magazines. The Lord Chamberlain's Office was content to give facilities to reporters and illustrators,[70] and hence accounts and images of the funeral became widely available during the ensuing days.[71] They provided a poignant description of what was, as Gladstone put it, 'a very solemn scene'.[72] The gloom and silence was broken only by tolling bells, minute guns, the slow movement of the procession, and the sombre chanting of the choir. The Prince of Wales struggled valiantly to control his emotions, but eleven-year-old Prince Arthur was in floods of tears and the Duke of Saxe-Coburg 'wept incessantly'. Dean Wellesley's voice repeatedly faltered as he struggled to read the service, and Garter King of Arms became inaudible as he proclaimed Albert's titles over the vault. The emotion was reportedly shared by all in the chapel, with the all-male assembly apparently feeling unconstrained in giving vent to their tears. Lord Torrington was inclined to think 'that more real sorrow was evinced at this funeral than at any that has taken place *there* [in St George's Chapel] for a vast number of years'.[73] Even today, accounts of Albert's

---

[67] RA, VIC/R 1/182, General Grey to Phipps, 22 Dec. 1861.

[68] RA, VIC/R 1/183, Note by Sydney, 22 Dec. 1861, 9.15 p.m.

[69] PRO, LC 1/90, Note by W. Scarbrook, 27 Dec. 1861; *The Times*, 24 Dec. 1861.

[70] PRO, LC1/90, Note by W. Scarbrook, 20 Dec. 1861.

[71] See in particular *The Times*, 24 Dec. 1861, *Daily Telegraph*, 24 Dec. 1861, as quoted by O. Bland *The Royal Way of Death* (1986), 170–73; *ILN*, 28 Dec. 1861.

[72] *Gladstone Diaries*, vi. 84.

[73] Quoted Dasent, *John Thadeus Delane*, ii. 40.

funeral make harrowing reading, and their impact on contemporaries must have been substantial. Such descriptions and images are likely to have deepened sympathy for the Queen and her family, highlighted the association between sincerity and relative simplicity in funeral observance, and reinforced the intangible but powerful links between patriotism, royalty, and religious responses to death.

In the meantime, despite the lack of organization or even encouragement from the government or royal household itself, the day of the funeral was marked by processions and church services in numerous towns and cities. Unlike the funeral itself these were very public occasions and appear to have attracted participation or at least interested observation from a much larger proportion of the population than those who normally attended church. These events were therefore expressions of national solidarity centred on the royal family as well as occasions for more orthodox Christian reflection on the impermanence of life and universality of death.[74] On a more private level Lord Overstone invited his whole household to attend prayers. He read the burial service to them, made 'a few remarks of my own on the character of the Prince and the solemnity of the event', and perceived all those present to be 'deeply affected'.[75] A Leeds newspaper asserted that 'Never before was the unity of feeling in subjects and their rulers so strongly evident, so feelingly displayed', and went on to contrast Britain favourably with the United States, which, it asserted, lacked a similar centre of devotion.[76]

A detailed account of the continuing 'cult of the Prince Consort' is outside the scope of this book, and is in any case already available elsewhere.[77] Three general points about Albert's prolonged apotheosis are, however, germane to our analysis. First, while it is difficult to unscramble cause and effect, it is noteworthy that the 1860s and 1870s saw a particular vogue for theological and popular literature on the afterlife. In particular there was William Branks's *Heaven our Home*, published in 1861 and reputedly read together by Victoria and Albert during the course of that year.[78] When Samuel Wilberforce, Bishop of Oxford, sought to console the Queen with a theologically nuanced account of the doctrine of the Communion of Saints, she responded with a confident assertion of her belief in future reunion. 'The thought,' she wrote, 'the <u>certain</u> feeling and belief that her adored Angel is <u>near</u> her, <u>loving</u> her, watching over her, praying for her and guiding her—is—next the blessed Hope of that Eternal reunion—her

[74] See above, Chapters 3 and 4.
[75] O'Brien, *Overstone*, ii. 980.
[76] *Leeds Intelligencer*, 28 Dec. 1861.
[77] Darby and Smith, *Cult of the Prince Consort*.
[78] Ibid., 4.

only comfort in her overwhelming affliction.'[79] In these convictions Victoria was reflecting widely-held beliefs. Certainly Branks quickly followed up his bestseller with two further publications on similar themes.[80] Subsequently, Edward Henry Bickersteth's epic poem on the afterlife, *Yesterday, Today and Forever*, first published in 1866, had run to eight editions by 1873.[81] It is at least plausible that the collective shock of Albert's death and the consequent desire to find religious comfort in the face of mortality gave an impetus to sentiments of this kind.

Second, the tone of the subsequent veneration of Albert in statues and other memorials showed a marked change of emphasis from the predominant sentiments in the immediate aftermath of his death. The images that developed during the 1860s were sometimes of Albert as a great individualist, a Carlylean hero, or latter-day knight errant. Alternatively—as in the Albert Memorial in Kensington Gardens—they expressed national or civic pride through tributes to the Prince as the patron of industry, science and the arts. Stained glass windows in churches paid tribute to his Christian virtues as a manifestation of the wider working out of God's grace in human lives.[82] Usually absent however was much evocation of Albert as a family man, the aspect of his life that had been a mainspring of popular sentiment in December 1861. The transition was especially suggestive in view of the reservations about Albert's influence still current at the time of his death, and the consequent tendency at that time to mourn him as the husband of the Queen rather than in his own right. It therefore seems probable that the later public urge to commemorate Albert was not closely connected to the immediate grief at his death, but arose rather because he was a convenient symbol for the expression of other things. The 1860s were a period when municipalities across the country were becoming wealthier and more conscious of their dignity. The erection of a memorial to Albert was an ideal way in which a town or city could simultaneously both demonstrate its loyalty and sympathy for the Queen and thus its solidarity with the centre of national life, and at the same time assert its own status and distinctiveness. Meanwhile he could serve as a model of practical and enlightened Christianity.[83]

[79] RA, VIC/R 2/136, The Queen to Wilberforce, 4 April 1862.

[80] *Meet for Heaven* (Edinburgh, 1862), *Life in Heaven* (Edinburgh, 1863). In the Preface to *Life in Heaven* (p. iv) the author noted that combined sales of the first two volumes already amounted to 75,000 in Britain alone.

[81] Wheeler, *Death and the Future Life*, 127–9, 426.

[82] For details see Darby and Smith, *Cult of the Prince Consort*; *The Memorial Window in St George's Chapel, Windsor Castle, by one of the Chapter* (Eton, 1863).

[83] For an early statement of this perspective on Albert see BL, 1878 d.12, a newspaper cutting reporting a eulogy in Birmingham Town Hall by George Dawson.

Finally, the public mood in December 1861 helps to give additional perspective to Victoria's subsequent reclusiveness and prolonged mourning. Granted that there was something pathological in her behaviour, the widespread and intense sympathy for her in the immediate aftermath of Albert's death may well have led her to feel that such conduct on her part would be acceptable indefinitely. What she failed to appreciate was that while her own grief indeed endured for the rest of her life, strong public sentiment disconnected from the reality of personal loss was a much more transient phenomenon. On the other hand, even as some criticized her reluctance to make public appearances, her very image as a devoted widow and a woman who suffered under the burden of immense sorrow was to enhance her role as a national symbol. This self-image was encouraged by those close to her, such as Bishop Boyd Carpenter, who wrote to her in 1892 that 'those who are crowned with sorrow are crowned with power to feel for and help the world'.[84] This was also the motif that could still be recalled at the time of her own death.[85]

In the shorter term, however, Victoria's perceived inactivity in the decade following Albert's death contributed to a significant growth in criticism of the monarchy, and even to an upsurge in overt republicanism. During the summer of 1871 the situation was becoming a matter of significant concern both to the government and to the Queen's children.[86] Then in the autumn of that year Victoria herself was seriously ill, and in December the Prince of Wales nearly died of typhoid. By an extraordinary and emotive coincidence, not only was he suffering from the very disease that had supposedly killed his father, but also his illness reached its most critical point on the tenth anniversary of Albert's death on 14 December.[87] The consequence was a striking resurgence in sympathy for the royal family, which was crystallized on 27 February 1872 by a thanksgiving service at St Paul's Cathedral for the Prince's recovery, a significant occasion in setting a precedent for the revival of public royal ceremonial.[88]

In 1878 the fateful associations of 14 December were again renewed when Princess Alice died on the seventeenth anniversary of her father's death, from diphtheria caught while nursing her own children through the disease. Lord Ronald Gower noted the 'profound national feeling of sorrow

---

[84] BL, AddMS 46720 (Boyd Carpenter Papers), fos. 9–12, Carpenter to the Queen 25 March 1892.
[85] For an example see C. F. Forshaw (ed.), *Poetical Tributes to the Memory of Her Most Gracious Majesty Queen Victoria* (1901), 90.
[86] W. M. Kuhn, 'Ceremony and Politics: The British Monarchy, 1871–1872', *Journal of British Studies* 26 (1987), 133–62; Weintraub, *Victoria*, 363.
[87] Ibid., 364–71.
[88] Kuhn, 'Ceremony and Politics'.

for and sympathy with our Queen and her family', which brought back memories of the 'black Sunday' of 1861.[89] A single-sheet poetical tribute to the Princess recalled her devoted care of her dying father, and visualized her, like him, now receiving a 'heavenly crown'.[90] As in 1861 the 14 December fell on a Saturday and so clergy again had an early opportunity to set the tone of national mourning in their sermons on the following day. The effect was further to reinforce the links between Christianity, female domestic virtue and royal bereavement.[91]

In March 1884 Prince Leopold, Duke of Albany, also died prematurely. Verses on his death encapsulate the manner in which such events could serve to bridge the gap between the Queen and her people:

> I don't know much about dukes
> And such high folks like, I confess;
> But the Queen's a mother, you'll grant,
> And a duke's son none the less.
>
> She's nothing to you, you say;
> Well, I'll not ask how that may be;
> But I'd like to tell you, my mates,
> Why she'll always be something to me.
>
> You see when we heard that the Queen
> Was mourning her youngest son,
> 'Twas natural like we should think
> Of the time when we lost our John.[92]

There was widespread public grief and sympathy, albeit with rather less intensity than in 1861, but driven in part by an awareness of the 'deep scars of her [the Queen's] past sorrows'.[93] In a sermon at St Paul's H. P. Liddon stated that a 'sound human interest' had drawn genuine sympathy 'from the poorest homes of the working classes'.[94] As in December 1878, the Queen made a public acknowledgement of her gratitude for the 'affectionate sympathy of my loyal people', while reminding them of her 'many sorrows

---

[89] Gower, *Reminiscences*, ii. 254.

[90] *A Tribute to the Memory of HRH the Late Princess Alice* (BL, 1871.e.2 (13)).

[91] *The Times*, 16 Dec.1878.

[92] Quoted in C. Bullock, *Ich Dien: I Serve: Prince Edward: A Memory* (n.d.), 71. The Queen had sent messages of sympathy and enquiry when the writer's son had been fatally injured in a mining accident.

[93] *The Times*, 29 March 1884.

[94] *The Times*, 7 April 1884.

and trials'. Such communications evoked fresh professions of renewed loyalty.[95]

## The Duke of Clarence

A further high point of sympathetic identification with the royal family came early in 1892. On 14 January after a week's illness, Prince Albert Victor, Duke of Clarence and Avondale, died at Sandringham in Norfolk from influenza. The circumstances were particularly poignant insofar as the Duke's engagement to Princess Mary of Teck had been recently announced and the royal wedding was being eagerly anticipated. Contemporaries immediately anticipated a strong public reaction. Edward Hamilton wrote: 'It really is too sad. Indeed if all the fates had been set to devise the saddest of occurrences, they could scarcely have selected an event more tragic or more calculated to arouse universal gloom.'[96] Similarly, Randall Davidson felt that 'there is something so tragic in all the circumstances of this sorrow, that it must, in a quite unusual degree, stir the very <u>heart</u> of everyone throughout the empire'.[97] Such predictions were to be amply fulfilled during the following week.

In contrast to Prince Albert, or even Princess Alice and Prince Leopold, Prince Albert Victor was an insubstantial figure. The public knew little of him except that he was second in line to the throne, and possessed of languid good looks and a pleasing amiability of manner. The reality was that he was a feckless young man of apparently limited intelligence, whose suitability for the throne was very questionable. Rumours regarding his private life would certainly have shocked the nun who wrote of him as dying with his 'baptism robes scarce sullied' and having 'no burden of grievous sin'.[98] It was, however, the very shortage of hard information—whether good or bad—about Clarence that made it possible for the public to project on to him in death an image of idealized British manhood (see Plate 9), while perceiving his recent engagement as a romantic love match.[99] Nevertheless, as Hamilton observed, public feeling was focused more on sympathy for

---

[95] *The Times*, 28 Dec. 1878, 17 April 1884.
[96] BL, AddMS 48657 (Hamilton Diary), fo. 29, 14 Jan. 1892.
[97] RA, VICZ 93/19, Davidson to the Queen, 14 Jan. 1892.
[98] RA, VIC/Z 97/22, Lines by an English nun. M. Harrison, *Clarence: The Life of HRH the Duke of Clarence and Avondale (1864–1892)* (1972) finds no evidence that Clarence had contracted syphilis, and rejects the charge that he was implicated in the Jack the Ripper murders, but suggests that he was associated with homosexual circles. See also Weintraub, *Victoria*, 520.
[99] For example see Emilia, Marchesa del Bufalo della Valle, *In Memory of Prince Albert Victor Edward* (Rome, 1892).

the surviving royal family than on grief for Clarence himself.[100] Such sentiment was all the more powerful because of its various points of focus.
There was the Queen herself, for whom her grandson's death was felt to
continue the sequence of previous grievous and untimely bereavements.[101]
Meanwhile, the aura of suffering was also assumed by the Prince and
Princess of Wales, whose royal status gave them no exemption from angu-
ished parental feelings.[102] Finally there was Clarence's fiancée, for whom his
death seemingly removed not only her future husband, but her eventual
hopes of becoming Queen. She acquired the stature of a tragic heroine:

> Since fond Heaven stooped through the ages hoary
> And illumined thy brow with love's tragic glory,
> Thy fair name's writ in unending story . . .[103]

This therefore was a bereavement with which all age groups of the population could identify, whether as aged and careworn grandparent, despairing
middle-aged parent, or distraught young lover. Moreover many others were
currently succumbing to the severe epidemic that had killed Clarence.
Accordingly his death and funeral provided a royal and national focus for
the personal fears and griefs of others.[104]

Clarence's death stirred an outpouring of public interest and feeling
comparable to that of December 1861. When it was announced on the
morning of 14 January large crowds gathered outside the Prince of Wales's
London home at Marlborough House.[105] In Edinburgh the *Scotsman* newspaper was deluged with requests for confirmation of the news and, during
the following week, expressions of 'sincere sorrow' were apparent among
all social groups.[106] Bishop Boyd Carpenter reported to the Queen that
'deep and widespread sympathy' met him everywhere. He had been particularly touched by the 'simple, rugged' words of a railway porter, which he
believed to be representative of more general working-class sentiment.[107] A
clergyman in Shoreditch shared this perception and, describing his parish
as one of the roughest in the East End, wrote that 'wherever I have gone

---

[100] BL, AddMS 48657, fo. 32, 19 Jan. 1892.
[101] For example see stanza ix of the poem by Alfred Austin, soon to become Poet Laureate,
published in *The Times* of 15 Jan. 1892.
[102] 'He that Comforteth', 12–13.
[103] Bullock, *Ich Dien*, 23.
[104] *The Times* of 15 Jan. 1892 reported the wider ravages of the influenza epidemic alongside
its accounts of Clarence's death.
[105] *The Times*, 15 Jan. 1892.
[106] *Scotsman*, 15 Jan. 1892; RA, VIC/Z 94/77, Miss F. Collins, 28 Jan. 1892.
[107] RA, VIC/Z 93/89, Boyd Carpenter to the Queen, 19 Jan. 1892.

among the poor people, I have found but one sentiment—predominating above all other feelings—that of grief and sympathy'.[108]

The occasional dissenting voices were liable to be drowned out. A meeting of representatives of the Miners' Federation refused, by a majority of nineteen to twelve, to pass a resolution of condolence with the royal family, but their conduct was subsequently repudiated by their own Lancashire and Cheshire branch.[109] Among Yorkshire miners the sentiment was voiced that the leader of the majority should go back to work down the pit, as he would do more good there.[110] When a resolution of sympathy was proposed at the Limehouse Board of Works in East London there were objections that it was extraneous to the business of the meeting, but it was still eventually passed unanimously.[111] Reynolds Newspaper argued that the sentiment was a mere following of a fashion sustained by the 'amazing trash' of other newspapers and the 'cant' of the clergy, but could not deny its pervasiveness.[112] Hamilton's impression that the public were 'giving vent to their hysterical feelings', and a newspaper allusion to 'cynics' who had 'deemed it an extravagance of emotion', also served to point up the strength of the dominant mood.[113]

There were, however, subtle but noteworthy differences from the tone of feeling apparent in December 1861. Although Clarence's death gave rise to some long-term fears for the succession to the throne,[114] it did not call into question the immediate functioning and image of the monarchy in the way that Albert's had done. Nor in 1892 was there an impending threat of war. If though the sense of crisis was less, preoccupation with the human and personal tragedy was, if anything, more intense. Sermons were widely reported in the secular press, and hence were a similarly prominent feature of public discourse as a whole, but they normally lacked reference to divine judgement, or direct exhortations to personal repentance in the face of the possibility of unexpected death.[115] Preachers tended rather to seek to encourage their hearers, for instance by speaking of Christ's comfort to the bereaved, or the positive impact of the wave of public feeling in drawing the nation together in loyalty to the throne, or in dwelling on the glories

---

[108] RA, VIC/Z 94/41, Revd J. F. Corbett-Williams, 18 Jan. 1892.

[109] The Times, 16, 19 Jan. 1892.

[110] Yorkshire Post, 19 Jan. 1892.

[111] East London Observer, 23 Jan. 1892.

[112] Reynolds Newspaper, 24 Jan. 1892.

[113] BL, AddMS 48657, fo. 33, 19 Jan. 1892; Western Times, 22 Jan. 1892.

[114] With hindsight such fears appear hard to understand. However in 1892 Clarence's only surviving brother, the future George V, was unmarried and had only recently recovered from a serious illness. His eldest sister, Princess Louise (or at least her husband, the Duke of Fife), was felt to be unsuitable (BL, AddMS 48657, fo. 33).

[115] For an exception see Anon., Christus Consolator (1892). See above, Chapter 3.

of resurrected life and reunion beyond the grave.[116] Some discerned a providential hand in the way that the nation was currently being stirred and united, but others evidently felt that God's mysterious purposes in the event would only become clear in the future.[117] Such gentler interpretation of Christian beliefs made it easier for other forms of tribute to adopt a broadly religious tone. The predominant tone of a collection of verses preserved in the Royal Archives expressed a diffused belief in the inscrutable purposes of God, and in the reality of the life beyond. Few of them were wholly secular.[118]

The sense of simultaneity was also noticeably stronger than it had been in 1861, and extended far beyond the shores of Britain. One preacher mused on the 'strange facilities for conveying news that mark our day, make the whole world kin, and quicken, as can never have been before, the widespread sympathies of men.'[119] Certainly reaction acquired a much stronger imperial and international dimension than it had done in 1861. Foreign expressions of grief and solidarity were received with gratification, as 'showing that whatever past differences or present difficulties or apprehensions for the future, the human heart is one, and that God has made of one blood all nations of the earth.'[120] In Rome the Italian government and people showed deep marks of sympathy and a writer penned memorial lines, while in distant Guatemala the flag on the presidential palace was lowered to half mast.[121] Within the Empire, in Canada there was reportedly deep feeling among all classes on account of 'the loss which has fallen on our beloved sovereign, and on those near and dear to her'.[122] Meanwhile the Anglican Cathedral in Adelaide was packed for a memorial service amidst numerous visible signs of grief and sympathy.[123] Even in territories whose loyalty might seem more questionable similar sentiments were manifested. From Cape Town it was reported that both English and Dutch inhabitants shared in feelings of genuine sympathy, and a Hindu speaker in the Bombay Legislative Council claimed that 'this sacred affection moves the nation, and fills the country with one universal sorrow'.[124] At Sandringham

---

[116] For examples see C. J. Vaughan, *The Sympathy of Jesus Christ with Sickness and Sorrow* (1892), 3–6, 13–15; A. W. Milroy, *In Memoriam* (Cowes, 1892), 4, 8–9.

[117] Macewan, *Distress of Nations*; Purey-Cust, *God's Ordering, Our Sufficiency*.

[118] RA, VIC/Z 97.

[119] F. F. Carmichael, *Honour the King* (Dublin, 1892), 11.

[120] Bullock, *Ich Dien*, 63, quoting sermon by Revd Newman Hall.

[121] RA, VIC/Z 93/107, Marquess of Dufferin and Ava, 21 Jan. 1892; Bufalo della Valle, *Prince Albert Victor Edward*; RA, VIC/Z 94/90, Audley Gosling, 17 Jan. 1892.

[122] RA, VIC/Z 93/135, Lord Stanley, 18 Jan 1892.

[123] RA, VIC/Z 98/30, Lord Kintore to Sir Henry Ponsonby, 26 Jan. 1892.

[124] RA, VIC/Z 94/88, Sir Henry B. Lock, 1 Feb. 1892; VIC/Z 93/144–5, Lord Harris, 5 Feb. 1892.

the Prince of Wales's staff struggled to deal with an avalanche of many thousand telegrams, with messages coming from 'all the small places in New Zealand, Australia and India'.[125]

The royal family showed a much greater awareness of the public as well as private importance of their bereavement than they had done in 1861. Both the Prince and Princess of Wales and the Queen issued messages to the nation expressing their gratitude for the sympathy that had been expressed. The Queen's message, greeted with adulation in the press, confirmed the image that had been increasingly self-consciously cultivated during the preceding years:

> My bereavements during the last thirty years of my reign have indeed been heavy. Though the labours, anxieties and responsibilities inseparable from my position have been great, yet it is my earnest prayer that God may continue to give me health and strength to work for the good and happiness of my dear Country and Empire while life lasts.[126]

The funeral arrangements gave some scope for public participation. There was a development of the precedents set by Prince Leopold's funeral in 1884, when there had been a procession through Windsor, a select number of onlookers had been admitted to the castle precincts, and the public had been allowed to view the floral tributes.[127] In 1892 the Prince of Wales had initially wanted to bring the body back to Windsor for interment by way of London, in response to public expectation of a procession through the streets from one railway terminal to another. He was dissuaded only because of the risks to the health of the soldiers who would have had to stand for hours to line the streets in the January cold in the midst of the continuing influenza epidemic. Accordingly the body was brought by train directly from Wolferton near Sandringham to Windsor.[128] Nevertheless opportunities were still provided for public participation. The body lay in state for two days in Sandringham Church amidst the overpowering scent of countless floral tributes,[129] and on the morning of the funeral on 20 January it was taken in procession from Sandringham to Wolferton station in front of numerous spectators. Although spectators were kept away from the special train while it was in transit, it arrived at Windsor at the London

---

[125] A. Ponsonby, *Sir Henry Ponsonby* (1942), 359–60. In the days following Clarence's death the columns of *The Times* carried numerous reports of tributes and expressions of condolence from around Europe and the Empire.

[126] *The Times*, 28 Jan. 1892. For the message from the Prince and Princess of Wales see *The Times*, 21 Jan. 1892.

[127] *The Times*, 6, 7, 9 April 1884.

[128] *The Times*, 18 Jan. 1892.

[129] *The Times*, 19, 20 Jan. 1892.

and South Western Railway station (now Windsor and Eton Riverside) which was a quarter of a mile further from the castle than the Great Western Railway station (Windsor and Eton Central). This arrangement suggests a positive attitude to a procession through the streets of Windsor, which duly took place in front of dense crowds. Meanwhile in further contrast to 1861, the Mayor and corporation of Windsor were observed making their way in state to St George's Chapel, this time as invited guests. Although foreign representation was limited by the same principle of family relationship as in 1861, the burgeoning of the royal family's connections during the intervening three decades gave rise to a substantially more international gathering.[130] Despite the practical constraints, the funeral thus assumed the appearance of a much more public and open event than the ceremonial following the Prince Consort's death had done.

Clarence's funeral also confirmed a trend already apparent in Prince Leopold's for gradual change in the setting and style of ceremonial as well as in liturgical content. In 1884, the Queen had taken an active role in settling the arrangements for her son's funeral,[131] and it indeed seems inherently unlikely that innovations would have been made without her explicit sanction. The Prince of Wales, although absent from Windsor until the eve of the funeral in order to escort his brother's body home from the south of France, took an active role in managing the details.[132] Whereas Albert's funeral had been very much a civilian occasion, with barely a uniform in sight apart from those of the guard of honour, Prince Leopold's had a noticeably military flavour. This was a significant change, for which the Queen herself was responsible. She had been influenced both by knowledge of her dead son's own wishes and by the funeral of the exiled Prince Imperial (heir of Napoleon III), which she had attended at Chislehurst in 1879.[133] A late decision was taken to convey Prince Leopold's coffin on a gun-carriage rather than a hearse from the station to the castle, thus setting an important precedent for the future.[134]

For Clarence a gun-carriage was again used and there was an extensive

---

[130] *The Times*, 21 Jan. 1892.

[131] PRO, LC 1/97, *passim*, particularly Davidson to Ponsonby-Fane, 31 March 1884, in which he reported that he had received 'definite commands' from the Queen on various points.

[132] LPL, DavP 4, fo. 33, Davidson to his father, 11 April 1884.

[133] RA, VIC/ADD 1/15/4215, The Queen to the Duke of Connaught, 4 April 1884. Victoria also confided to Connaught her satisfaction that the use of soldiers meant that no undertaker would touch the coffin. On her controversial attendance at the Prince Imperial's funeral see Weintraub, *Victoria*, 437–8.

[134] A rather cryptic telegram from Henry Ponsonby to Ponsonby-Fane on 2 April that 'Car must be abandoned impossibility of horse leaders and gun carriage to be substituted' (PRO, LC97) suggests that the immediate reason for the decision was practical rather than symbolic, but it was very much in accordance with the military tone of the funeral.

presence from both armed services. The Prince of Wales changed from civilian dress into uniform on the train from Sandringham to Windsor, so as to appear in attire consistent with the style of the successive phases of the funeral. A group of royal ladies, led by the Queen herself, was present in the chancel at Prince Leopold's funeral. In 1892 ladies watched from the window above the sanctuary. The use of heavy black drapings in the chapel was still continued in 1884, but these were eliminated altogether in 1892 in accordance with the wishes of the Prince and Princess of Wales. The heavy heraldic pall used for Albert gave way to a Union flag to cover the coffins of his son and grandson. Numerous floral tributes were received and displayed (see Plate 8). The overall effect of these developments was to cause royal funerals to assume a character that was more national and less dynastic, with the military providing colour and pageantry in lieu of the now marginalized heralds.[135]

Meanwhile the atmosphere in the rest of the country on the day of the funeral confirmed that Clarence's death had struck a very strong chord in public sentiment. According to Hamilton, 'London is, as it were, enveloped in a pall of gloom; and the manifestations of mourning are very marked and universal: theatres closed, shops shut, blinds drawn down, bells tolling, memorial services in churches and chapels of all creeds, flags flying half mast high, and even cabmen wearing little badges of black.'[136] At Horse Guards Parade a large crowd assembled while the minute guns were being fired. At St Paul's people were already arriving before 11 a.m. for the 3 p.m. memorial service, and by 1 p.m the cathedral was already almost full, while the crowd outside continued to grow. Westminster Abbey was similarly crammed to its absolute capacity, with several thousand people having to be turned away. At Bristol Cathedral an unpleasant crush occurred as the capacity of the building also proved entirely unequal to the demand.[137]

*The Times* leader writer considered that 'Never has mourning been more truly national than in the present case' and asserted: 'Loyalty—that compound of personal affection for the Head of State and her family, and of a sincere belief in monarchy as an institution—has never been stronger in Great Britain than now.' The revelation that there was such strong 'kinship in sorrow' was 'the reverse of mournful', because 'it is a feeling of this kind that is the basis of nationality'.[138] After the funeral *The Times*

---

[135] *The Times*, 2, 3, 4, 6, 7 April 1884, 21 Jan. 1892; St George's Chapel Archives, MS 148/1/16, Dean Eliot to his mother, 17 Jan. 1892. One observer found the military style incongruous at Prince Leopold's funeral in view of his 'health and occupations' (A. West, *Recollections 1832 to 1886* (1899), ii. 183–434), but Clarence had been a serving officer.

[136] BL, AddMS 48657, fos. 34–5, 20 Jan. 1892 (entry wrongly dated by Hamilton as 19 Jan.).

[137] *The Times*, 21 Jan.1892. See also above, Chapter 4.

[138] *The Times*, 20 Jan. 1892.

PLATE 1

Princess Charlotte's cortège here crosses the Lower Ward of Windsor Castle on its way to the south door of St George's Chapel, in an image representative of pre-Victorian nocturnal royal funerals. Artistic licence exaggerates the visibility of the scene.

PLATE 2

A dramatic representation of the breakdown of order in the crowd at the Duke of Wellington's lying-in-state on Saturday 13 November 1852. The problems arose from poor policing, and the convergence of two lines of access in a confined space.

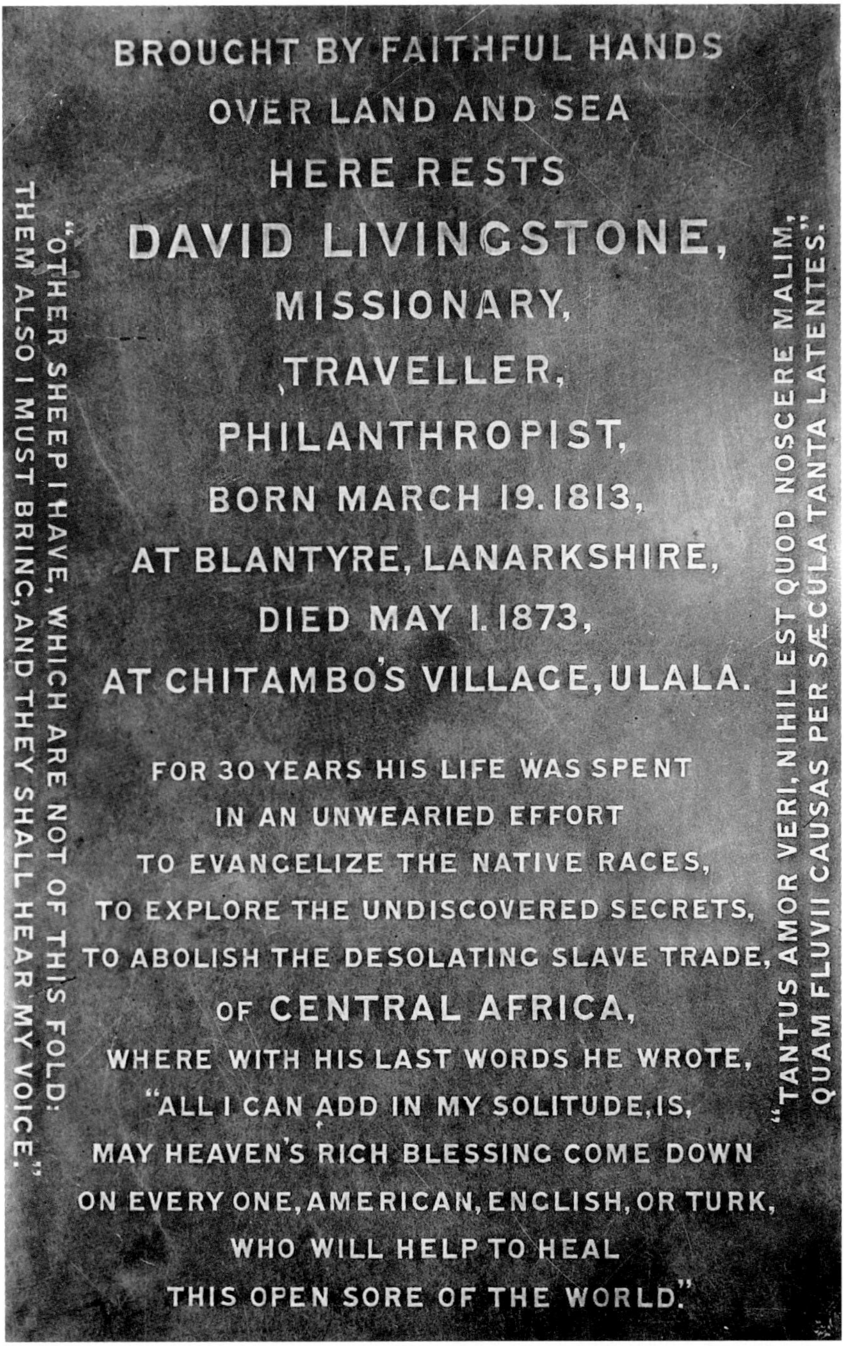

PLATE 3

BROUGHT BY FAITHFUL HANDS
OVER LAND AND SEA
HERE RESTS
DAVID LIVINGSTONE,
MISSIONARY,
TRAVELLER,
PHILANTHROPIST,
BORN MARCH 19. 1813,
AT BLANTYRE, LANARKSHIRE,
DIED MAY 1. 1873,
AT CHITAMBO'S VILLAGE, ULALA.

FOR 30 YEARS HIS LIFE WAS SPENT
IN AN UNWEARIED EFFORT
TO EVANGELIZE THE NATIVE RACES,
TO EXPLORE THE UNDISCOVERED SECRETS,
TO ABOLISH THE DESOLATING SLAVE TRADE,
OF CENTRAL AFRICA,
WHERE WITH HIS LAST WORDS HE WROTE,
"ALL I CAN ADD IN MY SOLITUDE, IS,
MAY HEAVEN'S RICH BLESSING COME DOWN
ON EVERY ONE, AMERICAN, ENGLISH, OR TURK,
WHO WILL HELP TO HEAL
THIS OPEN SORE OF THE WORLD."

"OTHER SHEEP I HAVE, WHICH ARE NOT OF THIS FOLD: THEM ALSO I MUST BRING, AND THEY SHALL HEAR MY VOICE."

"TANTUS AMOR VERI, NIHIL EST QUOD NOSCERE MALIM, QUAM FLUVII CAUSAS PER SÆCULA TANTA LATENTES."

The eloquent inscription on David Livingstone's gravestone, set into the centre of the nave of Westminster Abbey, well encapsulates the mythic qualities attributed to his life, death and apotheosis.

PLATE 4

The statue of David Livingstone in Princes Street Edinburgh was erected as an immediate response to news of his death, to a design by Mrs D. O. Hill.

PLATE 5

The location of Lord Iddesleigh's grave in the churchyard at Upton Pyne near Exeter was a notable parallel to Disraeli's at Hughenden in the selection of a rural setting, which was then romanticized in the press.

PLATE 6

The stark simplicity and quasi-ecclesiastical ambience of Gladstone's lying-in-state in Westminster Hall in May 1898 were in striking contrast to the elaborate heraldic fittings used on earlier such occasions. It set a precedent that was followed for Edward VII, subsequent sovereigns, and Sir Winston Churchill.

PLATE 7

The layout of St George's Chapel for royal funerals prior to the 1880s left little space for a congregation in the nave. Note also the all-male attendance, the heavy heraldic pall, and the poignant image of the young princes immediately behind their father's coffin.

PLATE 8

Floral tributes to the Duke of Clarence in January 1892 are laid out in the Albert Memorial Chapel at Windsor surrounding the monuments to the Prince Consort and the Duke of Albany. On Queen Victoria's death in 1901 the quantity sent to Windsor was even more overwhelming.

PLATE 9

The unfortunate Duke of Clarence might seem an unlikely St George, but this stained glass window at Sand Hutton Church near York illustrates the extent to which perceptions of idealized chivalric manhood were projected on to the dead Prince.

PLATE 10

In the dim light of a dank early February day, Queen Victoria's funeral procession passes along Piccadilly in front of enormous still crowds.

PLATE 11

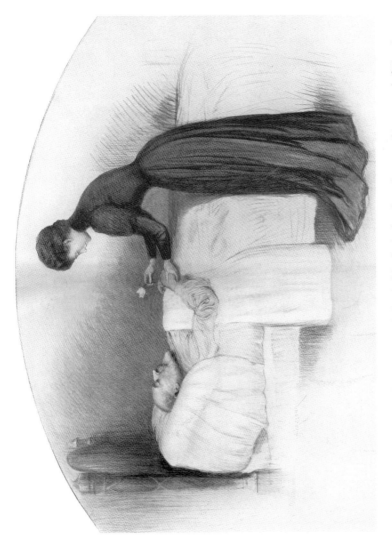

This image of Queen Alexandra placing a rose in the hand of the dead Edward VII shows a striking removal of Victoria constraints of privacy surrounding royal deathbeds and corpses. The caption refers to 'The sad, last token of undying love – an English rose', a romantic motif of royal death that had been associated with Prince Charlotte in 1817 and was to recur for Diana, Princess of Wales in 1997.

PLATE 12

Spectators find every possible vantage point in Windsor High Street for Edward VII's funeral. The disciplined ranks of the blue jackets hauling the gun-carriage contrast with the more casual disposition of the following royalty. The solitary carriage conveying Queen Alexandra is visible in the middle distance.

reiterated its perception that the monarchy was 'the embodiment of national life', a sentiment having 'its roots in the elementary notions of home and kindred as well as in the half-conscious traditions of national independence, unity, progress and renown'.[139] Lord Rosebery judged that 'it has been made more than ever manifest that the true bond of our Empire, which comprises every climate, race and perhaps as many constitutions as all the rest of the world put together, is our Sovereign'.[140] The Liberal *Daily News* acknowledged the presence of 'theoretical republicanism' especially among the working classes, but judged that in practice the monarchy focused in the person of the Queen was based on an 'impregnable rock of popular allegiance'.[141] Churchmen readily suggested a moral and spiritual dimension. Randall Davidson thought that 'It cannot but do good to the land to have this outburst of deeply sympathetic loyalty. It is absolutely everywhere.'[142] The anonymous writer of a Monthly Tract Society publication suggested that the Queen's great sorrows of 1861, 1871, and 1892 should be seen 'in the light of a threefold cord prepared by a loving and Divine hand' binding the Empire together, and calling the nation to hear the voice of God.[143] The Dean of Gloucester was struck that people had been drawn to church rather than to secular places of meeting, and saw this as an indication 'that England is still a religious country.'[144]

In this connection it is noteworthy that two of the Victorian age's most significant religious leaders chanced to die in the same month as the Duke of Clarence, Cardinal Manning on the identical morning, 14 January, and Charles Haddon Spurgeon, the great Baptist preacher, on 31 January. The passing of both men gave rise to widespread mourning and impressive spectacles. Manning's lying-in-state in his house at Westminster drew many thousands of people, and following his funeral at the London Oratory on 21 January (the day after Clarence's) there was an elaborate procession to Kensal Green cemetery with dense crowds thronging the four-mile route.[145] For some Roman Catholics indeed, Manning's death overshadowed Clarence's,[146] but feeling for him also appears to have extended to non-Catholics. In large measure this sentiment was attributable to the Cardinal's own record of sympathy for the underprivileged, leading members of the non-

[139] *The Times*, 21 Jan. 1892.
[140] RA, VIC/Z 93/115, Lord Rosebery, 21 Jan. 1892.
[141] *Daily News*, 21 Jan. 1892.
[142] DavP 18, fo. 84, Davidson to Archbishop Benson, 26 Jan. 1892.
[143] *Christus Consolator*, 13, 18.
[144] Spence, *England's Demonstration*.
[145] E. S. Purcell, *Life of Cardinal Manning Archbishop of Westminster*, 2 vols. (1895), ii. 813–16; *The Times*, 18, 22 Jan. 1892.
[146] See above, 90.

Catholic working classes to mourn his death as a personal loss.[147] *The Times*
though suggested that the 'national heart had been softened by the death
of the Duke of Clarence', and that among non-Catholics sentiment stirred
by the Prince was being extended to the Cardinal.[148] Manning's biographer
thought that the Cardinal himself would have been gratified by the subtle
linking of 'the sorrow and reverence manifested towards himself by the
people of England with the universal sorry and sympathy felt by the nation
at the death of the Prince'.[149] A similar inclusiveness was apparent on 11
February when the streets of south London were crowded with spectators
for Spurgeon's funeral procession from his Tabernacle at the Elephant and
Castle to Norwood cemetery five miles away. Randall Davidson attended
Spurgeon's funeral and as Anglican bishop of the diocese pronounced a
blessing at the graveside amidst a 'huge multitude' of people.[150]

Nevertheless it was apparent that reaction to Clarence's death overshadowed the responses to those of Manning and Spurgeon. Davidson
thought that Manning's death 'made far less stir than it would have done
had he died at any other moment'.[151] The fact that the loss of an untried
young prince could inspire more widespread public sentiment than the
deaths of two major religious figures might be interpreted as an indication
of secularity. That would, however, be a superficial reading. The contrast
was a relative one, and it was evident that by any other standards Manning's
and Spurgeon's deaths and funerals stirred extensive interest. Moreover, the
widespread religiosity of responses to Clarence's death has already been
noted. A more satisfactory interpretation is founded on an appreciation of
the multi–faceted character of late Victorian religion. The grand apotheoses
of their respective leaders were important demonstrations of the substantial
strength of the Roman Catholic and Nonconformist communities within
the increasingly pluralist fabric of national life. At the same time Clarence's
death stirred the expression of a collective moral and spiritual basis for
nationality, focused on the throne as a symbol of sympathetic devotion.
Preachers readily imbued such attitudes with an explicitly Christian
character.[152] In the response to untimely royal death national and religious
feelings found a fertile point of convergence.

---

[147] Purcell, *Manning*, ii. 811–12.

[148] *The Times*, 22 Jan. 1892.

[149] Purcell, *Manning*, ii. 807.

[150] S. Spurgeon and J. Harrald (eds.), *C. H. Spurgeon Autobiography Vol 2: The Full Harvest
1860–1892* (1973), 505–6; Bell, *Davidson*, i. 218–19.

[151] DavP 18, fo. 84, Davidson to Archbishop Benson, 26 Jan. 1892.

[152] Such sentiments were apparent in Nonconformist, Scottish Presbyterian and Jewish
sermons as well as Anglican ones (*The Times*, 18, 21 Jan. 1892).

## Changes and Continuities 1861–1898

It remains to set the royal cases analysed in the present chapter against the case studies examined in the two preceding chapters, and in so doing to suggest some overall characteristics and trends relating to the later nineteenth century as a whole. Three issues merit particular consideration: the nature of responses to death itself; the supposed 'invention of tradition' during this period; and the implications for a wider understanding of later Victorian religious life.

During the later nineteenth century general social and cultural preoccupation with death appears to have declined, probably primarily as a result of increasing longevity, which made the young and middle-aged less likely to see death as a potentially impending reality.[153] The deaths of prominent people, however, appear to have stirred stronger reactions than in earlier periods, probably precisely because they now seemed a greater and more shocking aberration than they had been in the past. It is indeed noteworthy that untimely deaths were particularly liable to evoke powerful public sentiment, as in 1861 and 1892. Meanwhile the growing perception that death should normally be avoidable until old age gave an enhanced dignity to perceived premature heroic and sacrificial death, as in the cases of Livingstone and Gordon.[154] Disraeli too, despite his more advanced years, seemed to fit something of the same pattern because he died still very much in political harness. Only in the case of Gladstone was it undeniable that the death was timely, and for him, as for Wellington, mourning could accordingly assume rather more of the quality of celebrating the values and achievements represented by his life. A further recurrent and distinctive feature of the period was a sense of sympathy for the family mourners as much as grief for the deceased. This phenomenon was especially evident in relation to royal deaths, but was also apparent in the aftermath of Gladstone's decease. It contrasted with earlier decades: sympathy for the surviving royal family had been conspicuous by its absence in 1817; in 1837 relatively few tears were shed for Queen Adelaide, who like Queen Victoria in 1861 lost her husband in her forties; little attention was paid to Wellington's family in 1852. All this implied a shift in subconscious sensibility from death being regarded as routine if regrettable, to becoming exceptional and for that very reason all the more traumatic and significant, except when it came inevitably in advanced old age.

The highpoint of elaborate funerals in private life came in the middle years of the century, and from the 1860s onwards there was a tendency

---

[153] Cannadine, 'War and Death', 193.
[154] Cf. ibid., 195.

towards more limited and restrained funerals and mourning practices.[155] The high-profile cases examined here were not inconsistent with this trend, but they do show significant dynamics of their own. In an earlier phase there was a reaction against eighteenth and early nineteenth century forms that had come to appear hollow. Thus Prince Albert's sombre funeral followed recent royal precedents in severely limiting heraldic display. Moreover the greatest possible degree of privacy and limitation of outward show of grief then appeared necessary if authenticity were to be achieved. From the 1880s, however, it began to be perceived that authenticity and simplicity did not necessarily require reclusive privacy and unrelieved gloom, and it is from that decade that a trend towards dignified but simple forms for high-profile funerals became apparent. Disraeli's village funeral set one kind of influential precedent, while the introduction by the royal family in 1884 and 1892 of a more colourful, military, and participatory approach also established a new direction. Then in 1898 Gladstone's funeral demonstrated that simplicity could be made compatible even with the grand and traditional surroundings of Westminster Abbey.

This sequence of development thus corresponds in some ways with the pattern discerned by David Cannadine in his seminal article on the 'invention of tradition'.[156] In particular the royal deaths and funerals of 1884 and 1892 were a significant complement to the jubilees of 1887 and 1897 in enhancing the ceremonial and public face of the monarchy. Nevertheless, in relation to funerals at least, the language of 'invention' would imply too radical a discontinuity: reverence for precedent was genuine, and intentional changes were not made lightly. Still, the very need to respond at short notice to unexpected contingencies, such as the Duke of Clarence's death, was itself a stimulus to sometimes unintended innovation. Moreover, whereas the Queen had only reluctantly accepted the thanksgiving service of 1872, by the 1880s the private preferences of the royal family were changing. In 1884 and 1892 there was, unlike 1872, no calculated intent to use ritual to strengthen popular royalism: in any case the funerals of Albany and Clarence were not witnessed by more than a few thousand people. Despite such limitations, however, extensive reporting of the funerals, and parallel provincial observance of them facilitated widespread identification with royal bereavements.

The recovery of popular affection for the monarchy in the late nineteenth century was an important historical phenomenon, which it is easier

---

[155] Jalland, *Death in the Victorian Family*, 194–203.

[156] D. Cannadine, 'The Context, Performance and Meaning of Ritual: The British Monarchy and the "Invention of Tradition", c. 1820–1977', in E. Hobsbawm and T. Ranger (eds.), *The Invention of Tradition* (1983), 115–35. For a critique of Cannadine's argument see Kuhn, *Democratic Royalism*, 1–10.

to demonstrate than to explain.[157] Certainly it was built on wider foundations than the 'invention of tradition'. The events analysed in this chapter add an important dimension to understanding the process. In particular by balancing celebration with sadness, they confirmed an image of an institution that reflected the darker as well as the lighter shades of human experience. The positive image of the later Victorian and Edwardian royal family was thus attributable not only to the increasingly elaborate pageantry but also to a feeling that it shared in the trials of ordinary humanity. The paradox of individuals perceived as elevated but yet accessible was central to the public appeal of royal ceremonial. Meanwhile the readiness of the monarchy to associate itself prominently with national mourning for Disraeli, Gordon and Gladstone (through the Prince of Wales) further contributed to its appeal.

Finally, the extensive religious dimension of responses to prominent deaths, even in the 1890s, is worthy of note. Pat Jalland is right to suggest that the Evangelical model of a 'good death', always more an ideal than a reality, was in decline in the later part of the century.[158] Its presence was still apparent however, in the appeal of Horace Waller's construction of Livingstone's death and in the widespread admiration accorded to Gladstone for his patient faith during his terminal illness. The Duke of Clarence had died in painful delirium, but his mother was still reported to have taken comfort from a sense that his passing had been a Christian one.[159] Moreover, the cases discussed above indicate that during the same period, other religious perspectives on death, above all that of self-sacrifice in the cause of Christ and humanity, tended to grow stronger. The expectation that the dead would be subject to divine judgment declined, but the very marginalization of hell made it possible to seize with greater enthusiasm on the prospect of heaven as a place of renewed personal fulfilment and of reunion with loved ones. Responses to prominent deaths in the later nineteenth century also reflected and stimulated a form of civil religion with a cultural resonance blending almost seamlessly into that of orthodox Christianity. Focal points of this framework of belief were veneration for the monarchy as an expression of suffering service and as the sacred focus for the providentially ordained empire; reverence for domestic and family life; and the hero worship of individuals such as Livingstone and Gordon, or even Disraeli, who seemed to represent an inspiring fusion of national and

---

[157] Cf. R. McKibbin, 'Why was there no Marxism in Great Britain?', *English Historical Review*, 99 (1984), 310–13.

[158] Jalland, *Death in the Victorian Family*, 39–58.

[159] Bullock, *Ich Dien*, 28.

spiritual values. The emphasis of beliefs was certainly changing, but these changes are not best understood by imposing a simple antithesis of the religious and the secular.

# 8

# *The Ending of Eras:*
# Victoria and Edward VII

She is our Mother still
Always in good or ill
    Faithful, serene:
So, we will sing it yet—
We, though our eyes are wet
We who can ne'er forget
    God save the Queen![1]

Such sentiment could not obscure the strong sense that an era ended at
Osborne House at 6.30 p.m. on 22 January 1901. The very fabric of national
life appeared abruptly to shift. Now with a male sovereign, even the words
of the National Anthem itself would change. The death of the monarch
had intrinsic dimensions that made it an event with a different quality
from the deaths of other individuals, however prominent. Although in
constitutional theory there was no hiatus, in that the Crown passed auto-
matically to the heir at the moment of the predecessor's death, in practice
there was a strong sense of dislocation and discontinuity.[2] In early modern
times the genuine political problem thus generated had led to the development of the doctrine of the king's two bodies, the body natural of the
mortal incumbent, and the body politic, which was transferred to his or
her succcessor. The ceremonial continuity between the two was symbolized
by the use of an effigy at the funeral.[3] Until the 1867 Reform Act, the
'demise of the Crown' led to the dissolution of Parliament and the holding
of a general election. By 1901 the decline in the practical political significance of the monarchy meant that such consequences no longer followed,
but the abrupt transfer of ultimate constitutional authority from experienced
to relatively untried hands could still induce a degree of anxiety. In both

---

[1] *The Queen's Best Monument: A Memorial Report from the Spectator* (1901), 59–60.
[2] For an example of a sense of cataclysmic change in 1901 see Fitzroy, *Memoirs*, i. 39.
[3] Woodward, *Theatre of Death*, 93–7.

1901 and 1910 such feelings were liable to be accentuated by a wider sense
of national crisis, over the Boer War and the Asquith government's clash
with the House of Lords respectively. Much more significant, however,
were the implications for the symbolic role of the monarchy, which had
greatly increased, even as its political role had receded.[4] Accordingly,
whereas the deaths of George IV in 1830 and William IV in 1837 passed
without strong public emotion,[5] the similarly close-spaced deaths of Victoria
in 1901 and Edward VII in 1910 stirred powerful and widespread feelings.
Further contributory factors were in 1901 the distinctive sentiment stirred
by Victoria's gender and the way in which the sheer length of her reign
reinforced a sense of disorientation at its end, and in 1910 the apparent
suddenness of the King's death.

In the aftermath of both deaths the sense of a need to sustain the
continuity of national life led to significant assertions of its essential underlying characteristics. On the ceremonial front, the liminal periods following
the deaths of sovereigns were particularly complex in that the formal
proclamation of the successor, in itself a celebratory occasion, had to
interrupt the process of mourning for the dead monarch. Nor did the
period of transition seem fully complete until the new sovereign had been
crowned many months later. For both Edward VII and George V therefore
the process of mourning for their predecessors was inextricably linked with
their respective needs to establish themselves as replacement focal points
for national and imperial unity. The same cause was served by elaborate
funeral pageantry, which, even as it provided a focus of public mourning
for the individual, served to demonstrate the continuity and prestige of the
institution. In the first decade of the twentieth century the British monarchy
was to rediscover the 'theatre of death'[6] to an extent not seen since the
Civil War, on a stage that had now acquired greatly expanded imperial and
international dimensions.

## Queen Victoria

At the time of the Duke of Clarence's fatal illness in 1892, Edward Hamilton
had remarked that 'They always make light of illness in court circulars.'[7]
Never was this tendency more apparent than in Queen Victoria's final
illness. She had been noticeably failing for some months before she became
seriously ill on Tuesday 15 January with 'head symptoms' including drowsi-

---

[4] Cannadine, 'British Monarchy', 120–1.
[5] See above, Chapter 1.
[6] Cf. Woodward, *Theatre of Death*.
[7] BL, AddMS 48657, fo. 28 (12 Jan. 1892).

ness, apathy, confusion and difficulty in speaking.[8] The Prince of Wales, however, allowed no bulletin to be issued until Friday 18 January, and even then the statement that she had 'not lately been in her usual health', and was being kept 'perfectly quiet', scarcely corresponded with the gravity of the situation.[9] Only at noon on Saturday 19 January did the issue of a more realistic bulletin admitting that she was 'suffering from great physical prostration accompanied by symptoms that cause anxiety', begin seriously to prepare the public mind for the worst.[10] Thus from the point of view of the world as a whole her death a mere three days later appeared to be a sudden one, and one for which, despite Victoria's eighty-one years, it was psychologically unprepared.

The flow of information continued to be carefully controlled in the final days and hours of the Queen's life, and despite the presence of a growing crowd of pressmen outside the gates of Osborne, public knowledge was largely limited to the official bulletins. Until the Queen's final hours, these tended to clutch at straws of hope, thus prolonging a feeling of suspense rather than promoting acceptance of the inevitable. There was also no allusion to aspects of the situation that might have marred the image of a serene deathbed, the worry that the Queen might live on for some time in a 'vegetable' state, or the distressing breathing difficulties that afflicted her at the end.[11] Perceptions of idealized family life and of Christian piety were also cultivated. The reality of the deathbed on which the attention of the world was focused was a very private one, with the Queen nursed only by her doctors and personal servants, and even her children only making short visits to the sickroom.[12] Nor, despite the presence at Osborne from the evening of Saturday 19 January of Randall Davidson, now Bishop of Winchester, who was closer to the Queen than any other clergyman, did she receive any pastoral visit until the very morning of her death.[13] In the meantime, however, the royal family assembled in the house and its vicinity, including, most dramatically and prominently of all, Kaiser Wilhelm II, who

[8] DavP 506, fos. 1–2, Sir James Reid to Davidson, 19 Jan. 1901. For a detailed, if somewhat unreliable, narrative account of the events surrounding Queen Victoria's death see Packard, *Farewell in Splendor*. The contemporary diagnosis of her medical condition was 'cerebral exhaustion' arising from impaired circulation to the brain (*Lancet*, 26 Jan. 1901, p. 276).

[9] *The Times*, 19 Jan. 1901.

[10] *The Times*, 21 Jan. 1901.

[11] DavP 19, no. 101, fos. 8–9. In 1935 George V still felt such 'intimate details' inappropriate for publication in Bishop Bell's life of Davidson, although his private secretary suggested that 'perhaps in another half-century the whole of the material may be able to be published' (LPL, Bell Papers 227, fos. 194–200, Sir Clive Wigram to Bell, 8 April 1935; 237, fos. 15–6).

[12] Packard, *Farewell in Splendor, passim.*

[13] Bell, *Davidson*, i. 352–3. Davidson did, however, spend time with other members of the royal family.

had travelled from Berlin to be present. *The Times* portrayed his journey as having 'sacred inner significance' and demonstrating 'that filial piety and that reverence for domestic ties which are ornaments of the German character'.[14] Privately, however, the Queen's children were much less enthusiastic about his presence.[15] Nevertheless, as the end drew near on the afternoon of Tuesday 22 January, they all assembled in the sickroom, as the Kaiser supported the dying Queen, the Prince of Wales knelt beside the bed, and Davidson said prayers.[16] Thus when the end came, the new King could truthfully inform the Lord Mayor that, 'My beloved mother, the Queen, has just passed away, surrounded by her children and grandchildren.'[17] Similarly, preaching on the following Sunday, Davidson portrayed the 'closing days' as characterized by 'family love, . . . deep and wide domestic happiness and motherliness and guiding care'.[18]

As the news of the Queen's death spread quickly around the country and the world during the early evening of 22 January, public reactions were immediate and tangible. Church bells shortly began to toll. Theatres and other places of entertainment abandoned their performances, without any indication of dissent from audiences, who quietly left. The streets were unusually crowded by people seeking and sharing news and impressions. In Dublin traffic in the city centre spontaneously stopped for several minutes. On the following day financial markets were closed and emblems of mourning were almost universally worn. In East London 'Wednesday was a day which will never be forgotten by those living. A feeling akin to despair came upon the people.' A similarly sombre mood and suspension of normal activity prevailed in all parts of the Empire. Foreign countries joined in the wave of sympathy and tributes, notably in the United States, where press and public interest was very strong, to a degree that even *The Times* New York correspondent evidently felt rather excessive. Although foreshadowed to some extent in January 1892 and May 1898, the strength and extent of the global response to Queen Victoria's death was on an unprecedented scale.[19]

---

[14] *The Times*, 21 Jan. 1901.
[15] M. Reed, *Ask Sir James* (1987), 205–6. The Queen's doctor, Sir James Reid, had, without consulting her children, telegraphed the Kaiser on 18 January informing him of the gravity of his grandmother's condition (Ibid., 203).
[16] Packard, *Farewell in Splendor*, 154–60.
[17] *The Times*, 23 Jan. 1901.
[18] Newspaper cutting in DavP 19, no. 101, fo. 20b.
[19] *The Times*, 22–24 Feb. 1901, *passim*; *East London Observer*, 26 Jan. 1901. There is no space here to discuss such international and world-wide reactions in any detail, but they are worthy of note in indicating the extent to which Victoria had acquired a global media image, of a kind unique in the nineteenth century that pointed forward to twentieth century developments. The implications of her death for international relations also merit consideration.

At a rational level the Queen's death could hardly be regarded as untimely or unexpected, but it still came as profound shock to many. In some measure this response was attributable to the apparent brevity of her final illness, but it also revealed the extent to which strong ingrained subconscious images of the Queen had imbued her with perceived super-human qualities. Alfred Austin, the Poet Laureate, wrote of the 'mellow, gracious Autumn of her days', that had led people to forget 'mortality's decree'.[20] The popular novelist, Marie Corelli, noted that her presence was so much 'a part of ourselves' and 'so deeply entwined in the very heart and life and soul of the nation' that the possibility of her death had been literally unthinkable.[21] A preacher in Chicago recalled that in his boyhood her name had become blended with his love of nature, and that loyalty to her had been 'almost a religion'.[22] Similarly Edward Hamilton judged that 'she had become a sort of fetish and was surrounded with a sort of sacred halo'. A week later, he noted that 5,000 telegrams had been delivered at Osborne in a single day and observed that there had 'never been such universal condoling and mourning before'.[23] Gradually, however, the initial sense of disorientation appears to have given way to sentiment reminiscent of that at Wellington's funeral half a century before, a sense of occasion and history as well as of sadness, and of acknowledgement of the inevitable passage of time. This more positive mood was stimulated in part by the ceremonies for the proclamation of the new King, on 24 January, which interrupted mourning and implied a sense of celebration and new begin-nings. Running through the whole period of mourning were powerful constructions of the image of the dead Queen as a continuing national symbol and inspiration, and a frantic endeavour to devise forms of cere-monial that could effectively serve both private feeling and public sentiment.

Tributes to Victoria on her death were dominated by the interlinked themes of Christian piety, idealized womanhood, domesticity, and sympath-etic suffering, that had already gained such currency during her lifetime. The specifically ecclesiastical strand constituted a significant proportion of published responses: of the 102 publications listed in the British Library catalogue that appeared in 1901 in tribute to the Queen or in direct response to her death, 32 were sermons or orders of service. Among other publications a more diffused religiosity was very much apparent. In a sample of 132 poems on Victoria's death, the proportion of poems founded on a sustained application of explicitly Christian theology was small, at 22 (16.6%),

---

[20] *The Times*, 24 Jan. 1901.

[21] M. Corelli, *The Passing of the Great Queen* (1901), 5.

[22] *Victoria the Queen: An Account of the Service at St James's Church, Chicago Saturday February 2 1901* (Chicago, 1901).

[23] BL, AddMS 48677, fo. 93 (22 Jan. 1901), fo. 102 (29 Jan. 1901).

but was only slightly exceeded by the 26 (19.7%) that were solely or very predominantly secular in sentiment. The remainder, 84 or 63.8% of the total, contained varying degrees of religious allusion, from passing references to the divinity or the afterlife, to more extended evocations of both.[24]

Most preachers and religious magazines dwelt at some point on the perceived strength of Victoria's personal religion. She was seen as consecrating herself to God at her accession, as maintaining constant prayerful and faithful observance throughout her life, and as being sustained by divine grace in carrying the great burden of royal duty, and, after 1861, in bearing the sorrows of her family life.[25] Marie Corelli extolled the Queen's simple, fervent piety and her unfaltering faith in God.[26] In the language of a poem read at a memorial meeting of the Society of American Women in London she had been a 'Righteous Ruler' who had planted her throne 'beneath the Cross'.[27] In the opinion of the *Morning Post*, 'One great distinctive feature marked the Queen's life—Religion.'[28] Such perceptions were further pointed up by the nervous drawing of contrasts between Victoria and her successor who was thought to be 'not a godly man'.[29]

Victoria's gender was also important in understanding reactions to her death.[30] She was imbued with an image of spotless purity, felt to be symbolized by the white pall chosen for her coffin. A newspaper suggested that a committee of representative ladies should subscribe towards a pure white marble statue of the Queen to be located 'in some low part of the East End of London, as a memorial and symbol of her pure, white life'.[31] She was regarded as having been an active force for moral rectitude at court and an influence that ultimately permeated the whole country.[32] Prominent women writers readily acclaimed her as a role model for their sex. To Charlotte M. Yonge she had been 'The Mother of the Homes of

---

[24] Forshaw, *Poetical Tributes*, 1–151.

[25] H. H. Henson, *A Sermon Preached in Westminster Abbey on the Occasion of the Death of Queen Victoria* (1901), 9–10; S. A. Brooke, *A Memorial Sermon on the Funeral of the Queen* (1901), 4–5; *Go Forward: YWCA Monthly Journal for Secretaries and Workers*, 15 (1901), 58–60.

[26] Corelli, *Great Queen*, 14, 16.

[27] *At Rest*, in BL collection of elegies, 10804 f. 19. For the more complex reality of Victoria's personal religious life see J. Wolffe, 'The End of Victorian Values? Women, Religion and the Death of Queen Victoria', in W. J. Sheils and D. Wood (eds.), *Studies in Church History 27: Women in the Church* (Oxford, 1990), 482–3.

[28] *Morning Post*, 23 Jan. 1901.

[29] LPL, Frederick Temple Papers, 48, fo. 191, George N. Herbert to Temple, 27 Jan. 1901.

[30] Cf. D. Thompson, *Queen Victoria: The Woman, the Monarchy and the People* (1990).

[31] T. R. H. Sturges, *Queen Victoria the Good* (1901), 13.

[32] H. J. Wilmot-Buxton, *Full of Days and Honour* (1901), 14; A. F. Winnington-Ingram, *The After-Glow of a Great Reign* (1901).

the Nation', a true woman and devoted wife, who had never stepped out of her place and had given religious instruction to her children and servants.[33] To Marie Corelli she was the incarnation of womanhood at its best, an inspiration to others to be 'content with their husbands and their homes' and the 'supreme example of what mothers should be'.[34] The anonymous author of a publication entitled 'The Reign of Women under Queen Victoria' argued that during her reign women had gained greatly in self-respect and influence. The supreme example of 'the Great Woman who has just passed "into the silences" ' should point them to the duties and pleasures of home and family as the essential foundations of national purity and stability.[35] Such themes were taken up with notable enthusiasm in Jewish sermons, in which Victoria's 'Judaic virtues' were dwelt upon.[36] An East End rabbi noted the readiness with which the poorest costermongers brought their small tributes to the memory of a woman whom he described as 'the ideal mother of her people'.[37]

Some felt a need to address a perceived tension between the essential qualities of a woman and the duties of a ruler. One approach was to make an explicit separation between her different functions. As woman, Victoria was felt to conform to a pattern of subordination and humility, but when acting as Queen she was held to have left her womanhood behind, assuming for the occasion certain masculine qualities with which providence had considerably endowed her.[38] The alternative approach was to link together the roles of Queen and of woman in presenting her as the mother of her people, ruling the nation as the matriarch of a large family. To Charlotte M. Yonge it was precisely through the consistent maintenance of her essentially feminine virtues that she became 'the greatest and most respected sovereign of our time'.[39] One preacher saw her success as a constitutional monarch as founded in her sense of being a 'national mother' who made 'her country a home' by patiently reconciling the childish squabbles of her subjects.[40]

Victoria's gender also informed the more radical comment of *Reynolds Newspaper*, where she was described as a 'bourgeoise Queen', the 'ideal

---

[33] *Mothers' Union Journal*, 54 (April 1901), 40–1.

[34] Corelli, *Great Queen*, 8, 11.

[35] *The Reign of Women Under Queen Victoria: The Argosy Memorial Number* (1901), 145–7.

[36] J. A. Goldstein, *A Sermon on the Occasion of a Memorial Service Held in Memory of Her Late Most Gracious Majesty Queen Victoria* (1901), 7.

[37] J. F. Stern, *The Queen* (1901), 7–10.

[38] Harrison, *A Queen Indeed*, 12–14; A. T. Wirgman, *Queen Victoria of Blessed Memory: A Voice from Her People Over the Seas* (1901), 5–6; *Mothers in Council*, April 1901, p. 70.

[39] *Mothers' Union Journal*, 54 (April 1901), 40–41.

[40] Sturges, *Queen Victoria*, 11.

British matron', with 'simple virtues' that appealed to the common people. Their gratitude to her was exaggerated, but nevertheless:

> Her life has had one great use. It has taught us the power we are wilfully allowing to go to waste in the womanhood of the nation. If Victoria has been all her flatterers say, then there are many thousands of possible Victorias in the kingdom. No longer can it be argued, without casting stones at the memory of the dead monarch, that women are unfitted for public duties. The feature of the twentieth century probably will be the utilization of this rich reserve of force. If it be so, that will be the greatest result of the reign of the Queen.[41]

The writer could not resist a dig at the Tory government, alleging that it had hastened her death by parading her about in order to popularize the Boer War. Although the article derided those who exaggerated Victoria's virtues by writing 'revolting nonsense', its own overall drift tended to affirm the consensus rather than subvert it.

A further quality widely attributed to the Queen was a capacity for profound sympathy and identification with suffering. To a significant extent this image was one she had cultivated for herself over the past decades through the spectacle of her indefinite mourning for Albert and the continued recollection of her other bereavements. It was also supported by her spontaneous gestures of kindness and concern.[42] According to the Revd H. J. Wilmot-Buxton: 'She was no secluded and unapproachable mysterious potentate, but a woman with a tender, loving heart—a woman who felt ready sympathy for the cares and sorrows of her people; a widow who could mingle her tears with other widows, a mother in whom all worthy mothers found a friend.'[43] The Vicar of St Austell saw her name as an inspiration to the humblest peasant and the poorest seamstress, who felt that their 'kind-hearted Queen' would assist them if she could.[44] The circumstances of the closing months of her life gave increased depth and patriotic resonance to such perceptions, in that Victoria had been known to be deeply concerned for the suffering of the soldiers fighting in South Africa:

> Sorrows and cares had filled life's closing chapters,
>     War's bitterest sorrows pierced that aged heart;
> Yet through it all her people's grief was her grief,
>     And nobly, bravely did she do her part.[45]

---

[41] *Reynolds Newspaper*, 27 Jan. 1901.

[42] Anon., *The Light of Life Eternal* (1901); Winnington-Ingram, *After-Glow.*

[43] Wilmot-Buxton, *Full of Days*, 5.

[44] Harrison, *A Queen Indeed*, 4.

[45] *Women*, 30 Jan. 1901.

On the day after her death, there was widespread press comment to the effect that anxiety about the war had shortened her life, and hence that, as the *Star* put it, 'She died as she lived—for England.'[46]

The power of such constructions of Victoria lay in their capacity to bridge the gulf between the personal, the imperial, and the universal. The very same woman who was felt to have had a capacity for sympathy in the sorrows of everyone had also been the symbolic centre of a worldwide Empire. Just as some had adopted Gladstone as a father figure,[47] the Queen had come to assume a comparable psychological role as ideal surrogate mother for a substantial number of people. Her perceived role as a super-human sympathizer with suffering also invites comparison with the functions of the Virgin Mary in contemporary French Roman Catholicism.[48] Viewed in such perspective it becomes easy to see why her death could be experienced as an almost personal bereavement and spiritual impoverish-ment by many who had never met her.

At the same time the Queen was judged to have been 'the symbol of Empire, the golden link of the race, the magnetic idea that drew the passionate affection and allegiance of her subjects to the centre'.[49] It is striking how universal and inclusive her role in this respect was felt to have been. In Grahamstown, South Africa, a preacher portrayed her as a 'mother in Israel', holding together the Empire as it now existed.[50] Memorial sermons and services in Australia shared the public appeal and immediacy of their counterparts in Britain, with only a passing acknowledgement that the death they were mourning had occurred 'far off across the sea'.[51] Nor was her appeal limited to white Christians. In London as she lay dying, Muslims in the city who had assembled to celebrate Eid, the festival marking the end of Ramadan, also offered prayers for her, as 'the Sovereign of the greatest number of The True Believers in the world'.[52] Similarly in India the mood was intensified by the coincidence with Eid and 'great congre-gations' were led in fervent prayers. Hindus and 'other sects' also offered special worship and prayers.[53] After she died, the Viceroy, Lord Curzon, told Edward VII that Indians had invested her 'with almost saintly attibutes'.

[46] *Star*, 23 Jan. 1901; cf. *Leeds Mercury*, 23 Jan. 1901; *Sheffield Telegraph*, 23 Jan. 1901; *South Wales Daily News*, 23 Jan. 1901.

[47] See above, Chapter 6.

[48] Cf. R. Gibson, *A Social History of French Catholicism* (1989), 145–51; P. Butry, 'Marie, la Grande Consolatrice de la France au XIXe Siècle', *L'Histoire*, 50 (1982), 31–9.

[49] *Daily Telegraph*, 23 Jan. 1901.

[50] Wirgman, *Queen Victoria*, 8–9.

[51] A. Harper, *In Memoriam Her Gracious Majesty Queen Victoria* (Sydney, 1901), 3; National Library of Australia, Canberra, Queen Victoria In Memoriam folder.

[52] *The Times*, 21 Jan. 1901.

[53] *The Times*, 24 Jan. 1901.

'To all of them', he wrote, 'she was at one and the same time the Great Queen and the loving mother.' Throughout the subcontinent memorial meetings 'of all races and religions' were being held and telegrams of sympathy poured in.[54] Maharaja Bahadur Sir Jotindra Mohun Tagore, a leader of the Bengal aristocracy, suggested that the Queen had strikingly shared in the attributes of 'the Great Universal Mother, who is worshipped as the *Adya-Sakti* of our [Hindu] mythology'. Similarly Surendranath Bannerjea, a leading moderate in the Indian National Congress, paid fulsome tribute to her 'fascinating influence' which made her seem to be a living representative of 'our own Seeta and Sabriti of legendic fame'. Indian Jewish and Parsi leaders joined in the chorus of adulation.[55] On the day of the funeral a vast crowd gathered on the Maidan in Calcutta and sat mourning throughout the day.[56]

Indeed any rare signs of tension in the apparent imperial consensus were attributable rather to division among professing Christians. In Ireland, sectarian and political divisions brought controversy to the normally formal procedure of passing a resolution of condolence.[57] In Canada, in the face of extensive public mourning for the Queen,[58] a sharp private dispute between the Governor-General, the Earl of Minto, and the Prime Minister, Sir Wilfrid Laurier, revealed some of the practical difficulties that arose in finding appropriate forms of commemoration in a religiously divided dominion. When Minto declared his intention of holding a 'state memorial service' in the Anglican cathedral in Ottawa, Laurier expressed 'very strong objection' on the grounds that there was no state church in Canada.[59] Minto argued that such a ceremony would have been fully in accord with public sentiment, but accepted the premier's advice, albeit with obvious bad grace.[60] Laurier was concerned at the Governor-General's 'manifestly disappointed' tone and reiterated that an official Anglican service would not have had 'harmonious' results.[61] Minto was anxious to maintain an appearance of unanimity,[62] but in a subsequent letter to Joseph Chamberlain, as Colonial Secretary, he attributed the problem to 'bigotted [sic] Roman Catholic' and 'small parochial' views in the Canadian Cabinet. Laurier, he thought, was

---

[54] RA, VIC/W 1/1a, Curzon to the King, 24 Jan. 1901.
[55] R. J. Mitter, *Bengal's Tribute to Her Late Majesty the Queen-Empress* (Calcutta, 1901), 17, 39, 48, 52. On Bannerjea see J. M. Brown, *Modern India: The Origins of an Asian Democracy* (Delhi, 1985), 149 and *passim*.
[56] D. Gilmour, *Curzon* (1994), 234.
[57] See above, Chapter 4.
[58] *The Times*, 23 Jan. 1901.
[59] NLS, MS 12557 (Minto Papers (4th Earl)), Minto to Sir Charles Tupper, 27 Jan. 1901.
[60] Ibid., MS 12563, fos. 58–9, Laurier to Minto, 28 Jan. 1901.
[61] Ibid., MS 12557, Minto to Laurier, 29 Jan. 1901.
[62] Ibid., MS 12563, fos. 60–63, Laurier to Minto, 29 Jan. 1901.

out of touch 'with the strong Imperial feeling here.'[63] In Britain too the Roman Catholic Church, despite expressions of grief and sympathy by its adherents, was subject to some verbal attacks because of its perceived antagonism to the Empire and its lamented Protestant Queen.[64]

Awareness of the vast weight of symbolism and sentiment focused on Queen Victoria had its corollary in a sense that her death was an historic moment, the end of an era. For some it implied dark thoughts over the future of the Empire itself, a feeling that its very survival was in danger without the 'beloved Monarch' under whose rule it had largely been created.[65] Marie Corelli feared that Victoria's death coincided with a national turning away from those values of Christian faith and 'pure and modest' womanhood that the Queen had so powerfully represented.[66] From Persia Cecil Spring Rice wrote that local people believed that the Queen had been 'the good angel who saved us from destruction and that our glory is gone with her'. He half agreed with them himself.[67] Arthur Balfour, moving the Commons address of sympathy and congratulation to the King, attributed the deep-seated and universal nature of public grief not only to the loss of the individual, but also to a feeling 'that the end of a great epoch has come'.[68] The *Spectator* felt that the Queen's passing had induced 'a distinct and unexpected diminution in . . . [people's] faith in the stability of things'.[69]

Edward VII had a shrewd appreciation of the nature of the public mood following his mother's death and of the high expectations thereby transferred to him. His immediate action, as expressed in his well-received speech at his Accession Council, was to stress continuity, both with the immediate past, by declaring his 'constant endeavour' to walk in his mother's footsteps, and with a more remote history, by his decision to take the name Edward, 'which has been borne by six of my ancestors'. This decision prompted others to set the event in an historic perspective. *The Times* thought the King wise to spurn the 'foreign' name of Albert, agreed that Edward 'is a good old English name', and thought that those 'who value the historical continuity of a nation' would rejoice at its associations. It offered its readers a quick survey of the previous kings of that name, despite embarrassment about Edward II and Edward V.[70] A clergyman in Australia

[63] Ibid., MS 12557, Minto to Chamberlain, 15 Feb. 1901.
[64] Corelli, *Great Queen*, 47–8; *The Queen's Best Monument*, 8–9.
[65] Sturges, *Queen Victoria*, 4.
[66] Corelli, *Great Queen*, 11–12, 19.
[67] S. Gwynn (ed.), *The Letters and Friendships of Sir Cecil Spring Rice*, 2 vols. (1929), i. 331.
[68] *The Times*, 26 Jan. 1901.
[69] *The Queen's Best Monument*, 12.
[70] *The Times*, 24 Jan. 1901. Lord Acton thought the King had perpetrated a 'howler' as Edward V and Edward VI were not his lineal ancestors, but few others appear to have worried about such historical precision (Fitzroy, *Memoirs*, i. 44).

drew inspiration from the coincidence that King Alfred had died exactly a thousand years before Victoria, and had had a worthy successor in his son Edward the Elder. He developed an extended comparison between Alfred and Victoria as shown in 'the Bible of our national history' and then in his evening sermon drew similarly sustained parallels between the two Edwards.[71]

Queen Victoria's was the first full-scale state funeral since the Duke of Wellington's half a century before and constituted a decisive departure from the limited Windsor obsequies of early nineteenth-century monarchs. The essential starting point was the Queen's own written instructions, dictated in a memorandum dated 25 October 1897 addressed to the Prince of Wales and Princess Beatrice with a supplement dated 25 January 1898.[72] In a significant irony, Victoria decisively rejected many of the trappings of a supposedly 'Victorian' funeral. There was to be no lying-in-state and the funeral itself was to be 'simple and with as little pomp as possible'. Her coffin was to be carried by non-commissioned officers and her Highland attendants, and was to be borne on a gun-carriage, modified so as to 'go smoothly and noiselessly'. She specifically noted that this decision was inspired by the 'two most striking and touching Military Funerals' of Prince Leopold and of Prince Henry of Battenberg (in 1896). As head of the army she considered that she too had a right to a military funeral.[73] The horses were not to be black, and the pall was to be satin and gold with the royal arms embroidered on the corners. The 'Dead March' was not to be played,[74] nor were there to be any black drapings. She initially asked that her remains should be taken directly to Frogmore and not first to St George's, but in her supplementary instructions indicated that she would not object if for practical reasons the first part of the service were after all to be held in St George's. Should she die abroad or away from Windsor she wished 'all my directions to be carried out as much as possible'.

There were two major challenges facing the King and others responsible for the funeral. The first was the practical one of organizing such an elaborate event within the space of ten days: Victoria died on the evening of Tuesday 22 January; her funeral cortège left Osborne on Friday 1 February. By contrast, preparations for the Duke of Wellington's funeral had been spread over two months. Despite the Queen's age, no plans had been made in advance, apart from her own instructions. Although com-

---

[71] H. L. Jackson, *Two Pages in a Nation's History: AD 901–AD1901* (Huntingdon, NSW, 1901).
[72] RA, VIC/F 23/1, VIC/F 23/2.
[73] It should be noted that this decision pre-dated the Boer War.
[74] Her tastes had changed since 1852, when she had approved of its use at Wellington's funeral (see above, 40). Her dislike of the piece dated back at least to the mid-1880s (RA, VIC/ADD A 15/4215).

munications had greatly improved since 1852, at least in the month before
Wellington's funeral all the major players in the arrangements had been in
London or Windsor. In 1901 on the other hand continual liaison with the
King and his staff at Osborne was required. Moreover, the funeral was to
begin at Osborne and end at Frogmore, after a journey of well over a
hundred miles, spread over several days and involving numerous different
forms of transport and ceremony. Secondly, there was the conceptual
problem of devising ritual that as a whole would reflect the diverse perceptions and emotions centred on the dead Queen. On the one hand there
were the quiet, private images of personal Christian devotion and ideal
family life; on the other awareness of the military and imperial aspirations
of which she had been such a potent symbol. At the same time she was
both a national icon and an international figure. The sense that a whole
era was being interred with her had to be recognized, but it was equally
important to affirm continuities. The most recent funeral of a sovereign
had been in 1837, and this precedent was very little use to anyone.

In the actual form of the arrangements Edward VII, while not doing
anything manifestly inconsistent with his mother's wishes, indulged his own
taste for ceremony and stimulated the creation of a unique pageant—or
rather a series of pageants—that provided a successful focal point for
public mourning.[75] He summoned the Lord Chamberlain (the Earl of
Clarendon) and Lord Esher, as secretary of the Office of Works, for a
meeting in the evening of 23 January, the day after Victoria's death. The
resulting 'rough memorandum of the King's commands given to me [Clar-
endon] verbally by His Majesty' established the broad outlines of the
ceremonial. The coffin was to be removed from Osborne to Cowes on
the afternoon of 1 February on a gun-carriage with Indian rubber tyres,
and then carried across the Solent on a royal yacht in a procession through
the Channel Fleet. There were to be salutes and guards of honour. The body
would remain on board the yacht at Portsmouth overnight. The following
morning a special train would convey the coffin, royal family and suites to
Victoria Station in London where NCOs would transfer it to a gun-carriage
drawn by eight cream-coloured horses. Followed by the King and royalty
on horseback, it would proceed through the centre of the capital to Paddington Station with a military escort and guard of honour. Troops would
line the route. Nevertheless, the King stipulated that 'all needless pomp
was to be avoided'. From Paddington a second special train would take the
coffin to Windsor where it would be placed on a further gun-carriage for
the procession to St George's Chapel. At the conclusion of the service, it

[75] Lord Esher commented after the funeral: 'Ceremonial he [the King] loves. Not so much
as a setting after the Napoleonic manner, but as an end in itself.' (Churchill College,
Cambridge, Esher Papers, 2/10, 6 Feb. 1901). See Cannadine, 'The British Monarchy', 135–6.

would be taken to Frogmore Mausoleum for the final sentences and interment, with the King and the royal family following on foot.[76]

As in 1852, a bewildering range of agencies and individuals were
involved in the funeral arrangements, including the Earl Marshal, the Lord
Chamberlain's Office, the Office of Works, various members of the
immediate royal staff, the army, the navy, the police, the Dean and Chapter
of Windsor, the undertakers (Bantings), and the railway authorities. Bishop
Davidson was an influential force in relation to the religious aspects of the
proceedings. In 1901, unlike 1852 or 1898, senior members of the government did not take an active role, an indication that the funeral of the
sovereign, unlike that of the former Prime Ministers, Wellington and Gladstone, was perceived as a non-political matter.[77] At the outset the overall
direction of the event was a matter of contention. It was initially assumed
that the Lord Chamberlain would be in charge, but the Duke of Norfolk,
as hereditary Earl Marshal, claimed responsibility on the basis of historic
precedent, and persuaded the King to accept his claim. According to
Esher, Clarendon was 'much chagrined', and despite his own professions
of willingness to co-operate with Norfolk, it seems that the officials of the
Lord Chamberlain's Office were less than wholly supportive.[78] On Friday
25 January, Norfolk convened a meeting attended by Esher, Clarendon,
Earl Roberts (Commander-in-Chief), the Duke of Portland (Master of the
Horse), Sir Edward Bradford (Metropolitan Police Commissioner) and Sir
Spencer Ponsonby-Fane (Comptroller of the Lord Chamberlain's Office),
whose experience of royal funerals stretched back to 1861. It discussed 'the
London part of the arrangements'.[79] In relation to the earlier and later
phases in the ceremonial, however, members of the immediate royal staff
took a leading role. Notable among them was Queen Victoria's assistant
private secretary Frederick ('Fritz') Ponsonby, to whom the King directly

---

[76] CA [132], Queen Victoria's Funeral, fo. 17; RA, LC Funeral Queen Victoria, Letters
Received, fos. 50–53, Norfolk to Clarendon, 24 Jan. 1901. The King initially envisaged that
the St George's service would be immediately followed by interment at Frogmore, whereas
in the event this final phase of the ceremonial was delayed until Monday 4 February, with
the Queen's body lying in the Albert Memorial Chapel in the meantime.

[77] The Duke of Norfolk was a staunch Tory, but in his capacity as Earl Marshal he was not
a government appointee.

[78] Brett, *Esher*, i. 277; Fitzroy, *Memoirs*, i. 43. Packard (*Farewell in Splendor*, 210–11) describes
a meeting at Osborne on Saturday 26 January, at which, he asserts, Clarendon and Norfolk
again 'locked horns' over the matter of overall direction and the King had to arbitrate. I
have not, however, found this meeting recorded in any contemporary source, and Clarendon's
letter to Norfolk pledging his 'hearty cooperation', dated 24 January, indicates that the matter
had already been resolved by the Thursday (CA, Queen Victoria's Funeral, fo. 74).

[79] Esher Papers, 2/10, 25 Jan. 1901. For Ponsonby-Fane's involvement in the arrangements
for Albert's funeral see RA, VIC/R 1/176, VIC/R 2/13.

delegated responsibility for the processions at Windsor.[80] The King himself decided all difficult or important points. He was careful to avoid clashes of responsibility, and thus he was the only person with an overview of the whole sequence of events, and his own views and sensibilities were very much apparent in the general shape of the ceremonial.[81]

According to Ponsonby-Fane, the days before the funeral were characterized by the most 'extraordinary hurly burly of confusion'.[82] Norfolk, whose organization of Gladstone's funeral had been such a triumphant success, perhaps underestimated the demands of the task he was now taking on at short notice. Certainly he was hampered by the lack of any secretariat attached to his office, other than the heralds of the College of Arms. According to Fritz Ponsonby, these worthies 'being accustomed to work out coats of arms and genealogical tables at their leisure, were swept off their feet with the urgent arrangements for the funeral'.[83] Ponsonby-Fane and Esher were also scathing about the ineffectiveness of the heralds.[84] Meanwhile Norfolk complained about Fritz Ponsonby's 'rudeness' to the heralds, and Esher thought that the Lord Chamberlain and his department were being 'unhelpful' to the Earl Marshal.[85]

Nevertheless, despite the haste, confusion, and personal tensions, the eventual result appeared successful and well organized, except to those on the inside. Norfolk was slow to announce arrangements, but this delay indicated thoroughness and the need for consultation with the King rather than inefficiency.[86] There were also some careful rehearsals of potentially problematic aspects of the proceedings.[87] Despite his criticism of the heralds, Ponsonby acknowledged that the Earl Marshal himself was 'a

---

[80] RA, LC Private Memoranda, Queen's Funeral (by Ponsonby-Fane); F. Ponsonby, *Recollections of Three Reigns* (1951), 84, 87; Packard, *Farewell in Splendor*, 210–1.

[81] *The Times*, 28 Jan. 1901; Ponsonby, *Recollections*, 84. The King's comment at a particular juncture that 'we shall never get on if there are two people giving contradictory orders' (Ponsonby, ibid., 89) appears symptomatic of his general attitude to the management of the funeral.

[82] RA, LC Private Memoranda, Queen's Funeral.

[83] Ponsonby, *Recollections*, 85.

[84] RA, LC Private Memoranda, Queen's Funeral; Brett, *Esher*, i. 281.

[85] Ponsonby, *Recollections*, 86; Esher Papers, 2/10, 31 Jan. 1901. Esher originally wrote and scored through 'and disloyal to the King'. Kuhn (*Democratic Royalism*, 122ff.) characterizes the controversy stirred by Norfolk's assertion of the prerogatives of his office as a clash between hereditary privilege and modern bureaucracy. Bureaucracy, however, is no safeguard against small-mindedness and sectional interest, and Norfolk's achievement in establishing a degree of overall co-ordination should not be underestimated.

[86] *The Times*, 29, 30, 31 Jan. 1901.

[87] *The Times*, 30 Jan. 1901; Ponsonby, *Recollections*, 91–2.

thoroughly businesslike and capable man' who worked 'like a cart-horse'.[88] Although Ponsonby-Fane complained that the meetings 'of a kind of committee' convened by Norfolk never settled anything, in all probability these gatherings were an important channel of communication between representatives of the key agencies involved.[89] The only problems on the day were minor ones. At Windsor station the horses who were to pull the gun-carriage broke their traces, but this was an unforeseeable mishap, which was handled successfully by inspired improvisation when the naval guard of honour picked up the broken harnessing and pulled the gun-carriage themselves.[90] The printed order of service merely mechanically reproduced the Prayer Book, including the reference to 'our dear *brother* [*sic*] here departed'.[91] Arrangements for the allocation of seats for St George's Chapel were confused, meaning that although many applicants for tickets had been turned away, in the event the building was no means full.[92] Over-stressed officials, such as Ponsonby-Fane, might magnify the significance of such faults, but as far as the general public was concerned the proceedings went without a visible hitch.

The challenge of responding to the range of perceptions of the Queen was met through the numerous separate phases of the ceremonial, each of which had a distinctive character. The sequence of events is summarized schematically in Table 1.[93] Some aspects were foreshadowed in the funerals of Clarence and Gladstone. Queen Victoria's funeral, however, had an unprecedented degree of complexity. To a considerable extent its character was shaped by the contingent circumstance of the Queen's death at Osborne, which provided the opportunity for the magnificent waterborne phase in the crossing of the Solent. On the other hand, the body could have been brought across to the mainland with much less ceremony, and at an earlier date almost certainly would have been. Similarly, there was no practical necessity for taking the procession through London, as a train could easily have been run directly from Portsmouth to Windsor. The inclusion of phases 4 and 5 therefore built on the success of the Diamond

---

[88] Ibid., 86.

[89] RA, LC Private Memoranda, Queen's Funeral. Attendance at the meeting on 28 January included Norfolk, Esher, Clarendon, Ponsonby-Fane, Roberts, Portland, Bradford, Weldon (Norroy King of Arms), Sir Henry Ewart (Crown Equerry), William Forbes (general manager of the London, Brighton and South Coast Railway), and the Earl of Pembroke (Lord Steward) (*The Times*, 29 Jan. 1901).

[90] Ponsonby, *Recollections*, 89.

[91] *Burial of the Dead: St George's Chapel, Windsor Castle, 2 February 1901* (1901).

[92] RA, LC Private Memoranda, Queen's Funeral.

[93] The sources for the following table are *The Times*, and the eye-witness accounts by Fritz Ponsonby (*Recollections*, 87–94) and Randall Davidson (DavP, 19, no. 101; substantial extracts in Bell, *Davidson*, i, 354–7). Cf. Packard, *Farewell in Splendor*, 237–68.

Jubilee of 1897 by using the funeral as a popular demonstration of royal prestige, military power and imperial might, which was all the more desirable in the face of the continuing war in South Africa. By keeping the London procession almost exclusively military in character such images were sustained, and not confused, as they had been at Wellington's funeral, by the presence of civilian representatives.

The funeral was also an occasion of hitherto unprecedented international significance. In addition to the four reigning monarchs who accompanied Edward VII in the procession, eight other nations were represented by members of their royal families, and twenty-one further countries by ambassadors or special envoys.[94] It is probable that the King wished to emulate the impressive funeral accorded to Alexander III of Russia, which he had attended in 1894.[95]

Grandiose militaristic ceremonial was, however, balanced by other images. Thus in phase 6 the historic setting of Windsor combined with the presence of the heralds to emphasize tradition and continuity, while the choice of an indirect route from the station to the chapel ensured visibility. Civilian institutions and dignitaries were recognized in the congregation at St George's Chapel. The walking processions of royalty in phases 3 and 9 gave prominence to an image of family coherence and devotion, especially through the unprecedented inclusion of women on foot. In phase 9, the procession even included royal children, notably the six-year-old future Edward VIII, now second in line to the throne.[96] Although crowds at these phases were more limited than in the grand ceremonies of phases 4, 5 and 6, their presence was still encouraged. In phases 2 and 10 the admission of the press ensured that accounts of supposedly private events would go into general circulation. Thus, except for the minority of the population who were able to witness one or more phases in person, impressions of all parts of the sequence were in practice no more or less accessible. Even in relation to phase 1, readers of *The Times* were able to learn, through a discreet 'leak' that the dead Queen lay on her bed 'with an expression of perfect peace' with her hands crossed so as to leave her wedding ring visible.[97] At the end of phase 10 they could read that she now rested 'beside the husband whose love was her solace and support during his lifetime, and whose memory was cherished with such touching fidelity

---

[94] This calculation ignores the numerous representatives of the smaller German states and dynasties.

[95] *The Times*, 26 Jan. 1901; Cannadine, 'British Monarchy', 129.

[96] Brett, *Esher*, i. 282; Duke of Windsor, *A King's Story* (1953), 23. The young Prince later observed that 'at seven [*sic*] one's sense of destiny is limited', but he was nevertheless conscious of the mood of his elders.

[97] *The Times*, 24 Jan. 1901.

**Table 1.** Rituals following the death of Queen Victoria

| Phase | Date/Time | Location | Description |
|---|---|---|---|
| 1 | Monday 22 January to Friday 25 January | Queen's Bedroom, Osborne House | The Queen's body was laid out on her bed, and was visited by members of the family, and servants and tenants on the Osborne estate. Davidson conducted services for the royal family in the room on 22 and 23 January, and Holy Communion on 24 January. |
| 2 | Friday 25 January to Friday 1 February | Dining Room, Osborne House | Having been closed in its coffin the body was moved downstairs to a *chapelle ardente.* Emblems of royalty were placed above and beneath the coffin, and sacred pictures and floral tributes surrounded it. A temporary altar was set up, and further services were held. Four Grenadiers stood guard. Selected friends, local people, artists and journalists were admitted to the room, and reports and images of the scene appeared in the press. |
| 3 | Friday 1 February 1.45 p.m. to 3.00 p.m. | East Cowes | The coffin was laid on a gun-carriage, covered with a white pall, and taken in procession from Osborne House to Trinity Pier. Both male and female members of the royal family walked behind. There was a military escort, troops lined the road, a band played the Chopin funeral march, and substantial crowds watched. |
| 4 | Friday 1 February 3.00 p.m. to 4.30 p.m. | Solent: Cowes to Portsmouth | The coffin was placed on the deck of the royal yacht 'Alberta', underneath a crimson canopy. Preceded by an escort of eight destroyers, and followed by the 'Victoria and Albert' with the King and Kaiser aboard, the Alberta sailed past an impressive line of warships moored all along the track of the procession. Salutes were fired as it passed. A number of foreign ships were also present. Large sombrely dressed crowds watched from the shore and from boats. |
| 5 | Saturday 2 February 11.00 a.m. to 1.00 p.m. | London: Buckingham Palace Road—The Mall—St James's Street—Piccadilly—Hyde Park—Edgware Road—Boundary Road—London Street—Praed Street | The cortège spent the night at Portsmouth and Gosport, and then proceeded from Clarence Yard to London by train. Accompanied by massed bands and numerous military and naval detachments, the coffin was conveyed on a second gun-carriage through the streets of the capital from Victoria to Paddington. The King followed on horseback, accompanied by the |

**Table 1.** *cont.*

| Phase | Date/Time | Location | Description |
|---|---|---|---|
| | | | Kaiser, the Kings of Greece and Portugal, and numerous other members of British and foreign royal families. The procession was essentially military in character. Royal ladies and elderly men (including the King of the Belgians) travelled in coaches. Troops lined the route and enormous crowds looked on. |
| 6 | Saturday 2 February early afternoon | Windsor: High Street—Park Street—Long Walk—Sovereign's Entrance—Norman Gate—Lower Ward | The coffin and royal mourners travelled from Paddington to Windsor by train. The procession at Windsor required a third gun-carriage, which following the mishap with the horses at the station, was drawn by sailors. The procession was almost entirely on foot, and included heralds and representatives of foreign countries, republics among them, who had not participated in the London procession. The royal ladies went directly to the castle, but the main procession took a circuitous route to accommodate the many thousand spectators. Bands played funeral marches. |
| 7 | Saturday 2 February late afternoon | St George's Chapel, Windsor Castle | The impressive choral service was attended by leading civilian representatives, such as members of the government, the judiciary, and municipal leaders, who had not taken part in the procession. It was the formal religious climax of the funeral. |
| 8 | Saturday 2 February to Monday 4 February | Albert Memorial Chapel, Windsor Castle | The coffin remained in the Albert Memorial Chapel for two days, while Sunday services were conducted in the nearby main chapel. A private evening service for the royal family was held in the Memorial Chapel, in which the professional singer, Mme Albani, participated. |
| 9 | Monday 4 February 2.50 p.m. to 3.30 p.m. | Windsor Great Park | A further walking procession of the King, members of the royal family, and foreign royalty followed the coffin and gun-carriage on the final stage of its journey from Windsor Castle to Frogmore. Troops lined the route, military bands played, guns fired, and spectators were allowed into the park to watch part of the route of the procession. |
| 10 | Monday 4 February 3.30 p.m. | Frogmore Mausoleum | The committal service in the mausoleum was quite elaborate and included a hymn and anthems. It was private, but detailed accounts were published. |

during the long years of her lonely widowhood'.[98] The sequence thus showed a circular movement from the privacy of the bedroom to the ultimate privacy of the tomb, by way both of the splendour of public military display, and the celebration of familial solidarity.

Running through this process were the important religious dimensions of the ceremonial. *The Times* correspondent on board HMS Majestic off Portsmouth on 1 February observed that in the scene in the Solent 'there was nothing of a show, but that dignity and solemn treatment which elevated everything and made of this pageant a deeply touching, if not a religious, function'. A kind of quasi-religious awe did indeed imbue much of proceedings, whether the object of veneration was the nation, family life, the living King or the dead Queen herself. At another level of interpretation though, there was a clear division and balance between phases 1, 2, 7, 8, and 10 that were marked by formal religious observance, and the essentially secular character of phases 3, 4, 5, 6 and 9. Although phases 6 and 9 had their destinations in religious buildings, at no time did robed clergy or choristers participate in the public outdoor processions:[99] they waited for the funeral at St George's Chapel and at the mausoleum. The exclusively secular and military tone of the procession through London apparently distressed some Christians,[100] but in that respect it differed little from Wellington's funeral procession in 1852.

Although Christian observance was limited largely to the private and semi–private phases of Victoria's obsequies, it is evident that the King himself set considerable store by it.[101] He shared Davidson's concern that the religious highpoint of the funeral at St George's Chapel should be carefully judged so as to ensure that it did not offend any strand of public opinion.[102] Nor were the religious preoccupations of the King and the royal family merely a matter of public image: private services were held on at least six occasions before the body left Osborne, and also at Portsmouth before departure for London and in the Albert Memorial Chapel at Windsor.[103] Indeed at one point the King's pious zeal appears to have disconcerted even Davidson, who on 24 January was surprised to find

---

[98] *The Times*, 5 Feb. 1901.

[99] Davidson and the Vicar of Whippingham, Clement Smith, walked with the Household in the procession from Osborne to Trinity Pier, but did not wear their robes (Bell, *Davidson* , i. 356). At Clarence Yard, Cosmo Lang, then Vicar of Southsea, conducted a short service before the coffin was landed from the 'Alberta', and then walked with the coffin to the train. This ceremony, however, was not a public one (*The Times*, 4 Feb. 1901).

[100] DavP 326, fo. 101, M. F. Macaulay to Davidson, 15 May 1910.

[101] DavP 19, no. 101, fo. 23.

[102] Ibid., fos. 25–7; see above, 79. Packard (*Farewell in Splendor*, 229–30) fails to understand the religious sensibilities that Edward VII himself evidently fully appreciated.

[103] DavP 19, no. 101, *passim*; J. G. Lockhart, *Cosmo Gordon Lang* (1949), 140.

himself 'imperatively' commanded to conduct a Holy Communion service for the royal family around the Queen's body.[104] At Portsmouth, Cosmo Lang, after conducting a short service on board the 'Alberta', was touched to see the King and Kaiser spontaneously kneel side by side at the foot of the coffin.[105] At Frogmore, the King and Queen made their young grandson Prince Edward kneel with them beside the grave.[106] Such private gestures suggest that, stirred by the emotions of personal bereavement and by the challenge of at last inheriting the Crown, Edward VII saw his mother's funeral as a moment for personal spiritual rededication and for affirmation of the sacramental and religious dimension of the monarchy.

Something of this sentiment transmitted itself to a wider public. The widespread reports of packed churches in the fortnight following the Queen's death suggest that many found their sense of national bereavement led them to turn to Christian ritual and language. Outside London and Windsor, religious services were generally the central focus of local observance on the day of the funeral itself. A Free Church mission to London that had chanced to coincide with the period between the death and the funeral proved to be unexpectedly successful.[107] In a sample of Yorkshire parishes Anglican confirmation figures for 1901 were noticeably higher than in immediately preceding and succeeding years, especially for females.[108]

The intense public mood reached its culmination on the day of the funeral. Even *Reynolds*, which had initially doubted whether the public really were deeply moved, referred on 3 February to 'the wave of emotion which has passed over the country on the death of the Queen—whose immense popularity there are too many evidences to doubt'. The mood on the streets of London on the day was not apparently one of unrelieved gloom[109] and a few spectators cheered Earl Roberts and the King as they passed in the procession. Nevertheless the great majority frowned upon such gestures and a sombre atmosphere predominated, finding visual expression in the universal wearing of black. As the gun-carriage passed there was a sepulchral

[104] DavP 19, no. 101, fo. 17.
[105] Lockhart, *Cosmo Gordon Lang*. Shortly after the outbreak of the First World War, Lang, by then Archbishop of York, made an ill-judged public allusion to this 'sacred memory' of the Kaiser and was subjected to torrents of abuse (Lockhart, *Lang*, 248–50).
[106] Bell, *Davidson*, i. 357. The Prince's father, the future George V, was absent because of illness.
[107] *The Times*, 2 Feb. 1901.
[108] Wolffe, 'Death of Queen Victoria', 496–7.
[109] Packard, *Farewell in Splendor*, 249; Corelli, *Great Queen*, 39.

hush and the densely packed spectators stood absolutely still.[110] Certainly the crowds in the capital and at Windsor were enormous (see Plate 10), with the authorities experiencing problems in controlling the flow in the Marble Arch and Edgware Road areas. Such a massive turnout was all the more significant in the face of the chilly early February weather. Elsewhere, notably in Birmingham, crowds gathered around statues of the Queen and left floral tributes. Meanwhile an overwhelming quantity of flowers was sent to Windsor Castle.[111] The Labour leader Keir Hardie might criticize the cost of the funeral and suspect that it was being used to rally support for the war, but even he implicitly accepted the reality of the popular grief.[112] Beatrice Webb wrote on 10 February:

> We are at last free of the funeral. It has been a true national 'wake', a real debauch of sentiment and loyalty—a most impressive demonstration of the whole people in favor of the monarchical principle. The streets are still black with the multitude in mourning from the great ladies in their carriages to the flower girls, who are furnished with rags of crepe. The King is hugely popular and evidently intends to play his part well.[113]

If feelings of grief and loss were beginning to be overlaid by a sense of occasion and of new beginnings, the former reaction remained widespread, while the latter one was testimony to the success of the funeral itself in providing a resolution and a conclusion to the public sorrow.[114]

---

[110] *Lloyds Weekly Newspaper,* 3 Feb. 1901. Verbal descriptions are corroborated by photographs and films of the procession that give a striking impression of very large crowds filling every available vantage point and standing absolutely still (for example, British Film Archive 827 A(d)).

[111] *The Times,* 4 Feb. 1901; St George's Chapel Archives, XVII.29.2, Dean and Chapter Memorandum Book, 1 Feb. 1901.

[112] K. O. Morgan, *Keir Hardie: Radical and Socialist* (1975), 120.

[113] N. MacKenzie (ed.), *The Letters of Sidney and Beatrice Webb II Partnership 1892–1912* (Cambridge, 1978), 134–5.

[114] In their anthropological analysis of royal funerals in Renaissance France, Huntington and Metcalf observe (*Celebrations of Death,* 166–7), 'The ritual becomes expressive of great dyadic tension: the triumph of death versus the triumph over death, church ritual versus state ritual, grief versus joy, all revolving around the body of the mortal king and the effigy of the immortal royal dignity.' Such an analysis appears readily applicable to Victoria's funeral, with the significant qualification that now, in the absence of an effigy, the symbol of 'immortal royal dignity' became her living successor.

## Edward VII

Edward VII outlived Queen Victoria by less than a decade, but his reign was still sufficient for him to establish a very strong public image as King. In view of the strong quasi-religious devotion inspired by his predecessor, the contrast with Victoria may helpfully be characterized in terms of a theological analogy. The secluded Victoria had acquired a transcendent quality, whereas Edward through his genial accessibility and substantial ceremonial presence became an incarnate focus for popular devotion. In both cases millions of people appear to have had a powerful sense of direct connection with the monarch, but for Victoria the public consciousness was of a sympathizing but distant presence; for Edward one of personal friendship. Such was the strength of Victoria's transcendent image, that when she died it was initially hard for many to come to terms with the reality of her mortality, and subsequently in death as in life she was perceived as an exceptional being. Edward's death, on the other hand, was felt as the abrupt and untimely termination of a human life that seemed much closer to the reality of his subjects' experience. She died at Osborne, removed from the centres of national power and social life; he at Buckingham Palace, in the heart of his capital.[115]

Two circumstances contributed substantially to the impact of Edward VII's death. The first was the constitutional crisis, which reached a critical point in the spring of 1910. The initial clash between the two houses over Lloyd George's radical 1909 Budget had been resolved by the narrow Liberal victory in the general election of January 1910. In mid-April, however, the Prime Minister, H. H. Asquith, announced that, if the Lords rejected resolutions curtailing their powers, his government would resign unless the King agreed to dissolve Parliament and to guarantee that, if the Liberals won the subsequent general election, he would create enough new peers to swamp the Lords.[116] This was how matters stood when the King died at 11.45 p.m. on 6 May, leaving polarized positions and an acute dilemma for his successor. Second, the death was startlingly sudden and unexpected. At sixty-eight, the King had not seemed an old man. On 27 April, he had returned from Biarritz in apparently good health and had gone to Sandringham for the weekend. On Monday 2 May he developed bronchitis, but his illness did not initially seem life-threatening. Moreover he insisted on continuing to get up and receive visitors. On Thursday 5 May he was unable to meet the Queen at the station on her return from the Continent and that evening a first bulletin was issued indicating that his condition caused 'some anxiety'. Within little more than twenty-four hours he was dead,

---

[115] Redesdale, *Memories*, i. 188.
[116] For a full account see Jenkins, *Asquith*, 194–211.

from heart failure triggered by the bronchitis. For a world that knew little
of his chronic chest complaints, and was unaware of the risks of smoking,
his death seemed like a bolt from the blue.[117]

Immediate reactions to Edward VII's death accordingly had a shocked
and hysterical edge. Asquith recalled that he 'felt bewildered and indeed
stunned'.[118] *The Times* wrote that his loss 'at a moment when we stand
committed to the gravest domestic crisis of our time, is indeed a public
calamity'.[119] According to Lord Redesdale, 'a deadly pall fell over the
country'.[120] Crowds gathered outside Buckingham Palace during the evening
of the King's death, and although many went home after being told the
sad news, others remained in a silent vigil into the small hours of
the morning. Throughout the following weekend enormous crowds stood
silently outside the Palace. Tokens of mourning were almost universally
worn. Unusually large congregations swamped the churches and extra
services were hastily arranged.[121] John Morley wrote: 'The feeling of grief
and sense of personal loss throughout the country, indeed throughout
Western Europe, is extraordinary, and without a single jarring note. It is in
one way deeper and keener than when the Queen died nine years ago, and
to use the same word over again, more personal.'[122]

Indeed the perception that everyone felt the King's death as a personal
bereavement was continually repeated during the ensuing days. As we have
seen, something of the kind was apparent in responses to the deaths of
both Gladstone and Victoria, but it was much more generally and emphatically attested in 1910. The phenomenon may therefore in part be seen as
a trend arising from the ever-increasing press coverage of prominent individuals and the royal family in particular, but was also attributable to
Edward's own human qualities. His gregariousness, tact, courtesy, and
evident zest for life all appealed to many. He was perceived as the model
English gentleman, who had a genuine interest and concern for the underprivileged. Hence the 'poor toiling masses' could hail him as 'Good old
Teddy' or 'our dear old Dad'.[123] From County Durham it was reported that
'One hears on all sides the expression "I feel as if my own Father had

[117] The medical reports reprinted in *The Times* of 7, 10, and 12 May 1910 give revealing
insights into the state of knowledge. They were also much franker and more detailed than
the corresponding accounts of Victoria's last illness.
[118] Quoted Jenkins, *Asquith*, 194.
[119] *The Times*, 7 May 1910.
[120] Redesdale, *Memories*, i. 187.
[121] *The Times*, 7, 9 May 1910; *Lloyds Weekly Newspaper*, 8 May 1910.
[122] NLS, MS 12740, p. 36, Morley to Minto, 12 May 1910.
[123] *The Times*, 7 May 1910; Cannadine, 'British Monarchy', 121; A. W. Gibbons, *A World in
Mourning!* (1910?).

gone." '[124] A large banner in a London street declared: 'Loved by his people, not as King alone but as friend.'[125] It may have been true that, as Beatrice Webb put it, the late King's virtues were 'somewhat commonplace',[126] but implicit recognition of his very limitations heightened the sense of popular affinity with him. One pamphleteer scathingly dismissed the general 'prostration of judgement', but by consigning Edward VII 'to a very ordinary position among what may be termed monarchs of a middle-class character', gave a suggestive hint as to the nature of his appeal to substantial portions of the population.[127] According to *Reynolds* 'he was a very average typical Briton in his tastes and habits, and the man in the street saw in him a glorified portrait of himself'.[128]

The extent and inclusiveness of feeling was striking. Enoch Edwards, the Labour spokesman in the Commons, assured the House when it passed its address of condolence that 'Nowhere will sorrow be truer, more sincere, or deeper than among the humblest of the poor.'[129] Keir Hardie and Ben Tillett had already paid tribute to the individual while affirming their continuing critique of the institution of the monarchy. George Lansbury attributed the sorrow of 'Socialists who did not believe in Royalty and that kind of thing' to their realization that King Edward 'was a man and that he loved his fellow-men and fellow-women'.[130] A driver in the Essex Territorials wrote that what he had heard about him 'was only good and [if] I could have saved His life by giving my own I would have done so willingly'.[131] Sympathy in Ireland was notably strong, with dissenting voices in a much smaller minority than they had been at the time of Queen Victoria's death.[132] According to Lord Minto, now Viceroy of India, the King's death 'sent a shock' through the subcontinent and there was 'a universal expression of deep grief'.[133] In Canada too the sense of personal loss was widespread, and 'deep and genuine ... distress' was felt even 'by thousands who had never been within 3000 miles of England'.[134] A ship' cook, who had served in the navy with the new King, wrote to him in familiar terms from Three

[124] RA GV/AA 55/252, Joseph Homer to Sir Charles Cust.
[125] British Film Archive, 203670A.
[126] N. and J. MacKenzie (eds.), *The Diary of Beatrice Webb*, 4 vols. (1982–5), iii. 139.
[127] A. Canmore, *The Late King Criticised* (Edinburgh, 1910), 6.
[128] *Reynolds Newspaper*, 8 May 1910. Cf. McKibbin, 'Why Was There No Marxism in Great Britain?', 312.
[129] *The Times*, 11 May 1910.
[130] *The Times*, 9 May 1910.
[131] RA, GV/AA 54/97, Reginald Odell, 9 May 1910.
[132] *The Times*, 9 May 1910; see above, 133–4.
[133] NLS, MS 12740, p. 72, Minto to Morley, 12 May 1910. For further testimony to grief in India, see NLS, MS 12740, *passim* and RA, GV/AA 54/51; GV/AA 55/23, 251.
[134] RA, GV/AA 54/99, Lord Gray to George V.

Rivers, Quebec, expressing his heartfelt sorrow and adding that 'sympathy is the <u>cord</u> which binds us Man to Man'.[135] The *Sydney Morning Herald* reported that, in Australia, 'a latent but overwhelmingly powerful sentiment' was touched: "It is our people's head, our friend who is dead." '[136]

The general tone of reactions was perceptibly more secular than it had been in 1901. Christian leaders and preachers were presented with an unspoken dilemma in that Edward VII, unlike Victoria, could not readily be presented as a role model for personal and domestic piety. On the other hand, in the light of the general public mood, any clerical criticism of the late King's spiritual and private life would almost certainly have given grave offence to many. Whereas in 1901 Archbishop Temple paid tribute in the House of Lords to Queen Victoria as a 'truly religious woman',[137] in 1910 Archbishop Davidson decided when the House passed its address of condolence that the discreet course of action was not to speak at all.[138] Some preachers alluded delicately to the tension between veracity and loyalty: for example H. Montagu Butler said that he 'would not willingly be guilty of a word less that truth on a day like this'.[139] W. R. Inge, then Lady Margaret Professor of Divinity at Cambridge, said that the House of God 'was not the place for any encomiums, even of the dead, that were not absolutely sincere'.[140]

Two approaches to the problem were generally adopted. The first was to give endorsement to the secular consensus regarding the King's qualities as the affectionate father of his people, a successful constitutional monarch, and a reconciler and peacemaker both at home and abroad. Such an approach could be given a more spiritual gloss by reference to Christian ideals of service and self-sacrifice or to the seventh Beatitude, 'Blessed are the peacemakers'.[141] It was also possible to acknowledge his outward and apparently sincere reverence for Christianity both in his public gestures and utterances as King, and in his private religious observance.[142] Indeed his very lack of dogmatic Anglicanism could encourage other religious groups to claim him as their own. Thus the leading Congregationalist C. Silvester Horne thought that he 'would gladly have given Godspeed to every body of Christian worshippers in his kingdom, being consistently on

---

[135] RA, GV/AA 55/278, William James Lewis to George V, 10 May 1910.
[136] Quoted in *The Times*, 12 May 1910.
[137] E. G. Sandford (ed.), *Memoirs of Archbishop Temple*, 2 vols. (1906), ii. 367.
[138] DavP 581, fo. 20.
[139] Butler, *For Kings*, 9.
[140] *The Times*, 9 May 1910.
[141] Ibid.
[142] J. B. McGovern, 'Death of Edward VII' (Extract from parish magazine of St Stephen's Charlton on Medlock in BodL); *The Times*, 9 May 1910 (address by Rector of Sandringham).

the side of peace, not only international, but ecclesiastical'. Similarly Cardinal Bourne acknowledged his 'courteous consideration' towards Roman Catholics, and the Chief Rabbi, Hermann Adler, praised his 'absolute freedom from racial and sectarian prejudice'.[143] The Maharaja of Bikaner sent a fulsome letter to the new King, describing the sentiment of 'loyal Hindus' who had prayed for Edward VII in his illness and had regarded him as a god.[144] At a meeting in London the Muslim League passed a resolution expressing the 'deep and heartfelt sorrow' of their co-religionists, and noting that half the Islamic world was under British rule.[145]

The second approach was to use the dramatic and unsettling circumstances of the King's death as a prompt for discussion of wider issues of national and divine purpose. Such was the stance adopted by both Anglican archbishops. Addressing an enormous hushed congregation at Westminster Abbey on Sunday 8 May, Archbishop Davidson expounded his sense of a divine hand and Christian purpose at work in British history through the life of the late King. He felt that he had 'said what was wanted'.[146] Preaching in York Minster, Archbishop Lang suggested that everyone had been looking to the late King to resolve their political differences for them, but by removing him at this juncture God was calling the nation to restrain party heat and vindictiveness and to face its problems 'with a mind and a will, humbled, chastened, deepened' by the divine act. Similarly at St Margaret's Westminster, Hensley Henson called for 'a new spirit of conciliation' in political life, as being an appropriate memorial to the King, while at the City Temple R. J. Campbell urged prayer that 'clamour and strife might be stilled'.[147]

The funeral was organized without the sense of frantic improvisation apparent in 1901. The task was more manageable for a variety of reasons. There was now recent precedent and experience to build upon; three more precious days were allowed for preparation; all the arrangements and key participants were in London or Windsor. Above all, the Earl Marshal could now assert his overall control at the outset, and appointed a wide-ranging *ad hoc* committee to assist him.[148] This group held its first meeting at

---

[143] *The Times*, 9 May 1910.

[144] RA, GV/AA 54/51, Sir Ganga Singh to George V, 8 May 1910.

[145] *The Times*, 12 May 1910. Such sentiments were echoed by the Imam of the Shahi Mosque in Lahore in front of a crammed congregation on the day of the King's funeral (*Punjab In Memoriam: Death of His Majesty King Edward VII, Emperor of India* (Simla, 1910), 193).

[146] Davidson, *From Strength to Strength*; *The Times*, 9 May 1910; DavP 581, fo. 15.

[147] *The Times*, 9 May 1910.

[148] The membership, as subsequently reported to the House of Commons (*Hansard* fifth series, 17, col. 1037, 13 June 1910), was as follows: Duke of Norfolk (Earl Marshal, Chairman); Randall Davidson (Archbishop of Canterbury); Earl Beauchamp (Lord Steward);

Norfolk House on Monday 9 May, and was able immediately to agree and announce the general outline of arrangements.[149] Subsequent arrangements were carried out 'under great pressure of time',[150] but appear to have been effectively managed and co-ordinated. Nevertheless some errors and tensions were inescapable: mistakes in the published version of the Windsor ceremonial had to be hastily corrected, and George V was less than impressed with the Duke of Norfolk's business capacities. Matters of protocol and precedence also proved troublesome.[151] From the public perspective, however, the ceremonial was well regulated and most effective.

The structure of the funeral as a whole, as summarized in Table 2,[152] was simpler than Queen Victoria's had been, but the proceedings were still protracted and designed to convey a variety of image and atmosphere. As at Queen Victoria's funeral there was an endeavour to find effective points of balance between continuity and innovation, public display and private grief, and secular and religious ritual. In the face of the constitutional crisis, George V himself and the court, military and civil service circles primarily responsible for the planning of the funeral were concerned to stress the continuity and dignity of the monarchy and its capacity to transcend the death of a single individual. Hence the new King, even in the midst of personal grief, was alert to the symbolic significance of the Royal Standard, and insisted that it be flown at full-mast on Marlborough House to signify his own presence, even while all other flags were at half-mast in mourning

---

Viscount Althorp (Lord Chamberlain); Earl of Granard (Master of the Horse); Viscount Esher (Deputy Constable of Windsor Castle); Sir Schomberg MacDonnell (Secretary, Office of Works); Sir William Carrington (Keeper of the Privy Purse); Sir Edward Ward (Secretary, War Office); Sir Douglas Dawson (Controller, Lord Chamberlain's Department); Sir Edward Henry (Commissioner of Metropolitan Police); Sir Alfred Scott-Gatty (Garter King of Arms); General Codrington (Commanding Home District); Commodore Trowbridge (Admiralty); Lewis Harcourt (First Commissioner of Works). Harcourt was thus the only representative of the government. The inclusion of Davidson was a significant recognition of the ecclesiastical and religious dimension of the ceremony. George V took a very active interest, discussing aspects of the proceedings in personal interviews with Davidson and presumably also with other members of the committee, and having his wishes formally reported through Dawson and Carrington (EM 2145, Minutes of meeting at Norfolk House, 9 May 1910; DavP, 581, fos. 15, 17, 29–30).
[149] BodL, MS.Harcourt.dep.adds.161 (Lewis Harcourt Papers), Notes of Meeting at Norfolk House, 9 May 1910; *The Times*, 10 May 1910.
[150] BodL, MS.Harcourt.dep.adds.161, Norfolk to Harcourt, 26 June 1910.
[151] K. Rose, *King George V* (1983), 77–8.
[152] Sources for table: *The Times, passim*; DavP, 581; Duke of Windsor, *King's Story* (1953), 73–5.

**Table 2.** Rituals following the death of Edward VII

| Phase | Date/Time | Location | Description |
|---|---|---|---|
| 1 | Saturday 7 May to Saturday 14 May | King's Bedroom, Buckingham Palace | For a whole week the King's body was left in the room where he had died, with the face exposed. Queen Alexandra allowed select family members, close friends, and political leaders to visit it. Religious services were held in the room on 9 and 11 May. |
| 2 | Saturday 14 May to Tuesday 17 May | Throne Room, Buckingham Palace | The body was closed in its coffin and ceremonially but privately moved to the Throne Room. A temporary altar was set up in place of the chair of state, and the coffin placed in front of it, covered with the white pall made for Queen Victoria. Symbols of kingship rested on the coffin and bier. Four Grenadiers kept a motionless vigil. Prayer stools were set up. Services were held in the Throne Room on the evenings of 15 and 16 May. |
| 3 | Tuesday 17 May 11.30 a.m. to 12 noon | The Mall—Horse Guards Parade—Whitehall | Following a final short service at the Palace, the coffin was placed on a horse-drawn gun-carriage and taken in procession to Westminster Hall. The participants included a military escort, senior officers, and members of the royal family and the royal household. All the men, led by George V and his two eldest sons, were on foot, while ladies (and the young Prince Henry) followed in carriages. |
| 4 | Tuesday 17 May to Friday 20 May | Westminster Hall | The two Houses of Parliament assembled to receive the body, and the Archbishop of Canterbury led a short service. The coffin was placed in the centre of the hall, and covered by the pall and the Royal Standard. Crown, orb and sceptre were laid on the top. A processional cross stood at the head of the coffin and soldiers kept guard. From 4.00 p.m. to 10 p.m. on 17 May and from 6.00 a.m. to 10.00 p.m. on 18 and 19 May the public were allowed to file past. |
| 5 | Friday 20 May 9.00 a.m. to 12 noon | Whitehall—Horse Guards—The Mall—St James's Street—Piccadilly—Hyde Park—Edgware Road— | A mounted 'procession of sovereigns and princes of Europe', including nine reigning monarchs (George V, the Kaiser, and the Kings of Norway, Greece, Spain, Bulgaria, Denmark, Portugal and Belgium), moved from Buckingham Palace to Westminster |

**Table 2.** *cont.*

| Phase | Date/Time | Location | Description |
|---|---|---|---|
| | | Oxford and Cambridge Terrace — London Street — Praed Street | Hall. Carriages followed, bringing royal ladies and children and other leading participants, including the former US President, Theodore Roosevelt, and the French Foreign Minister. At Westminster Hall the coffin was brought out and laid on the gun-carriage and the procession, now preceded by numerous military detachments, continued to Paddington Station. Troops lined the route and enormous crowds, some of whom had waited all night, packed the pavements and parks, and all available vantage points. |
| 6 | Friday 20 May 12.30 p.m. to 1.30 p.m. | Windsor: High Street — Park Street — Long Walk — Sovereign's Entrance — Norman Tower — Lower Ward | Naval ratings drew the gun-carriage — an arrangement that this time had been planned from the start. Military detachments and senior officers preceded it. Male royalty and representatives of foreign countries followed on foot with a single carriage carrying Queen Alexandra and her sister, the Dowager Russian Empress. Other royal ladies proceeded directly to the chapel. As in London, the crowds in Windsor were very substantial (see Plate 12). |
| 7 | Friday 20 May 1.30 p.m. | St George's Chapel, Windsor Castle | Among a congregation of leaders from many spheres of national and imperial life, clergy and heralds received the coffin and processed into the choir for the service. George V escorted Queen Alexandra up the aisle. The coffin was lowered into the royal vault while Garter King of Arms proclaimed the late King's titles. |

for his father.[153] In his speech at his accession council he spoke of his

---

[153] Duke of Windsor, *King's Story*, 73–4; DavP 581, fos. 17–18. During the late Victorian period the halfmasted Royal Standard was flown as a token of mourning for royalty independently of the presence of the living sovereign or of the remains of the deceased. Following the death of the Duke of Albany in 1884, the Tower of London was unsure whether to half-mast the Union flag or the Royal Standard (PRO, LC 2/97) and for the Duke of Clarence the Royal Standard was flown at half-mast from the Round Tower of Windsor Castle while the Queen herself was at Osborne and the Duke's remains were at Sandringham (*The Times*, 15 Jan. 1892). The Royal Standard was flown at half-mast at Windsor throughout the week after Queen Victoria's death (*The Times*, 4 Feb. 1901). In 1901 Edward VII, during Queen Victoria's funeral passage across the Solent, objected to a half-masted

endeavour to follow in his father's footsteps,[154] as he was to do symbolically by walking behind his coffin on the streets of London and Windsor. The procession at phase 5 also achieved an unprecedented degree of magnificence. Films of the occasion convey an impression of substantially greater precision in the ceremonial than at Queen Victoria's funeral.[155] With the luxury of hindsight the splendid display of military power and monarchical solidarity is too readily dismissed as ironic and fragile: at the time it seemed to be a powerful expression of the stability and international standing of the British Crown. At the same time, however, George V, having spoken of his endeavour 'to uphold the constitutional government of these Realms', was concerned to present a 'democratic' and accessible face. Thus, in contrast to Victoria's funeral, leading representatives of the two major republican nations, France and the United States, were given prominent positions in the procession.[156]

The most significant innovation was the public lying-in-state (phase 4) in Westminster Hall. The idea originated with George V himself.[157] It was a significant departure from precedent for the funeral of a sovereign to be preceded by a public lying-in-state in central London, in contrast to the arrangements at Windsor in 1820, 1830 and 1837, and at Osborne in 1901. The planners of Edward VII's funeral were almost certainly inspired by the success of Gladstone's lying-in-state in 1898, and accordingly decided that the late King's coffin should be placed in Westminster Hall for several days before the funeral. The decision attracted weighty private criticism from Lord Esher, who argued that the only royal association of Westminster Hall was a 'very unhappy one' and that as Gladstone had been 'a great subject and a great commoner' that precedent was inappropriate. He also thought that the lying-in-state of a sovereign should have 'some Ecclesiastical significance', which pointed to Westminster Abbey or St

---

Royal Standard on his own vessel (S. Lee, *Edward VII*, 2 vols. (1927), ii. 8), but did not countermand its use on the one carrying the dead Queen's body (*The Times*, 2 Feb. 1901). Similarly, George V had the Royal Standard flown at half-mast on the Victoria Tower of the Palace of Westminster during the lying-in-state of his predecessor (PRO, WORKS 21/6/1/14) as an acknowledgement of the actual presence of the dead sovereign's body.

[154] *The Times*, 9 May 1910.

[155] British Film Archive, A02P922, 203670A, 603956A, 604265A. One might speculate that a consciousness of the unforgiving record provided by the movie camera, as opposed to the more fleeting impressions of the human observer, was itself beginning to influence the organizers.

[156] Monsieur Pichon, the French Foreign Minister, felt, however that he had not been treated with due respect, especially when he observed Orleanist princes among the royalty ahead of him (Rose, *George V*, 77–8).

[157] DavP 581, fo. 15.

Paul's.[158] Esher, however, missed the point that Westminster Hall provided an ideal setting in which to give ritual expression to the mediating role of constitutional monarchy, in bridging divides between the aristocratic and the democratic, and the sacred and the secular. As the dead King's body was brought in on 17 May, it was received by both Houses of Parliament— so bitterly at odds with each other in recent months—and was literally placed between them. Meanwhile the historic parliamentary associations of Westminster Hall made it possible for a novel development in royal funerals to be perceived paradoxically as linking the monarchy even more firmly to ancient and honoured national tradition.[159] Esher's reservations indicate that the decision was accompanied with a degree of risk, but it was amply vindicated by the outcomes.

Admission was open to all and George V intended the ceremony to be 'as democratic as possible'.[160] The early opening at 6 a.m. was specifically intended to accommodate workmen on their way to work.[161] There was an explicit prohibition of messenger boys holding places for others,[162] and accordingly even the wealthy had little option but to stand in line themselves if they wished to view the lying-in-state. The queue itself thus became symbolic of a kind of social equality.[163] As the ceremony was held within the Palace of Westminster it was impossible to avoid giving some privileged rights of admission to MPs and peers, but at the prompting of the King even these were curtailed as far as possible.[164] The degree of resentment stirred among those who felt themselves entitled to privileged admission, but found that they had no option but to join the queue, was an indication of the rigour with which the policy was implemented.[165] The appeal of the spectacle was very considerable. Up to 350,000 people, showing considerable

---

[158] PRO, WORKS 21/35, fo. 84, Esher to Schomberg McDonnell, 9 May 1910. The 'very unhappy' association Esher had in mind was presumably the trial of Charles I.

[159] *The Times*, 18 May 1910. George V had, however, rejected a proposal that his father should be buried in Westminster Abbey rather than at Windsor. In putting forward this suggestion Davidson wrote of 'the growing sentiment in favour of some new development of the Abbey's historic status as the burial place of England's greatest' (DavP 326, fo. 4, Davidson to Bigge, 7 May 1910). The King did not 'make little of the suggestion' but felt his mother's strong personal preference for Windsor had to be honoured (ibid., fo. 21, Davidson to the Dean of Westminster, 9 May 1910).

[160] DavP 581, fos. 29–30.

[161] PRO, WORKS 21/35, letter to Arthur Bigge, 11 May 1910.

[162] *The Times*, 17 May 1910, 'Admission to Westminster Hall'.

[163] *The Times*, 18, 19, 20 May 1910.

[164] DavP 581, fos. 29–30. Cf. BodL, MS.Harcourt.dep.adds.160, *passim*, for the grumbling of MPs about the severe restrictions placed on their entitlement to bring guests.

[165] BodL, MS.Harcourt.dep.adds.161, R. Farquharson, Ian Malcolm to Harcourt, 18 May 1910.

social diversity, passed by the coffin, and at times the queue of those waiting to enter Westminster Hall was five miles long, reaching all the way to Chelsea before doubling back to Parliament Square. When the doors were closed at 10 p.m. on Thursday 18 May an estimated twenty to thirty thousand people were left disappointed in the queue, and it seems highly probable that, with a longer period of opening, many thousands more would have attended.[166] Moreover, every effort was made to convey the sense of the occasion to the wider audience not able to attend in person, through pictures and description in the press.[167] Thus the sense of popular pilgrimage was widely diffused.

Meanwhile George V had consulted Randall Davidson closely about the arrangements for the lying-in-state with a view to giving the ceremony 'some sacred character'. Initially monarch and primate jointly proposed that all visitors would be handed a card 'with two or three prayers or texts', but this idea was abandoned when the police pointed out that when people stopped to read it they would disrupt the flow of the queue. Nevertheless Davidson, with the King's sanction, obtained a large cross from St Paul's to stand over the coffin, and arranged a short service to be held in front of the royal family and both Houses of Parliament when the body was first brought to the hall.[168] The Archbishop's address on that occasion was widely disseminated and is worth quoting at some length:

> Brothers, the Sovereign whom his Empire and the World delighted to honour is suddenly taken from our head ... Here in the great Hall of English history we stand in the presence of Death. But Death is, to us Christians, swallowed up in a larger Life. ... We thank God for a Ruler devoted to the service of his people; we thank God for the peace and prosperity which have marked King Edward's reign; we thank God for teaching us still to see His hand in the story of our Nation's well-being. And we pray: we pray God that as we are united by this great sorrow we may be united for the tasks which lie before us, for the fight against all that is unworthy of our calling—as the Christian inheritors of a great Empire—the fight against selfishness and impurity and greed, the fight against the spirit that is callous or profane. Let us pledge ourselves afresh from this solemn hour to a deliberate and unswerving effort, as Christian folk, to set forward what is true and just, what is lovely and of good report,

---

[166] *The Times*, 18, 19, 20 May 1910. There was no exact count of attendance. Some estimates were as high as 400,000 (Anon., *In Memoriam Edward VII King and Emperor* (1910?)). The police estimated the flow past the catafalque at 8500 to 9000 an hour (PRO, WORKS 21/35, fo. 105), while *The Times* counted about 160 people a minute, equivalent to nearly 10,000 an hour. The hall was open for a total of 38 hours.

[167] PRO, WORKS 21/35; *ILN*, 21 May 1910.

[168] DavP 581, fos. 15–19, 29–32.

in the daily life, both public and private, of a people to whom much is
given and of whom much will be required.[169]

This passage provides a striking articulation of a form of civil religion
expressing the convergence of church and state at a moment of national
grief. Particularly noteworthy was Davidson's repeated assumption that his
entire audience identified themselves as Christians, his readiness to sacralize
generalized moral virtue, and his easy shift between the 'great Hall of
English [*sic*] history' and the Empire as a whole. The King and the archbishops endeavoured to encourage general religious observance, by urging
that bishops and clergy should officiate in their own cathedrals and parishes
on 20 May in order that 'the Funeral shall, as far as possible, be made a
universal rather than a local Service'. The King, according to Davidson,
was 'somewhat full' of this subject.[170] As in 1901, very numerous and well-
attended services throughout the country and Empire were indeed a primary
focus for public observance of the funeral.[171]

Other aspects of the arrangements confirmed a more populist approach
than that adopted in the aftermath of Queen Victoria's death. George V
decided that the government should not itself erect stands in the royal
parks for privileged viewing of the funeral procession and thereby take
space away from the public. This policy, like the arrangements for admission
to the lying-in-state backfired to the extent that it irritated some MPs and
was denounced as constituting shabby treatment of the people's elected
representatives. Lewis Harcourt was subsequently obliged to defend it in
the Commons, while being unable to reveal the King's direct responsibility.[172]
George V also endeavoured to limit excessive and disruptive mourning:
he indicated his wish that people should take advantage of the normal
'opportunities . . . for . . . amusement' on the Whitsun bank holiday, which
fell on 16 May. He asked that the theatres should be kept open, except on
the day of the funeral, so as to avoid putting their staff out of work.[173] He
initially proposed to keep the period of general mourning, which had
extended for three months after Queen Victoria's death, as short as possible,
'until the Saturday after the Funeral, but not longer'.[174] Davidson, however,
expressed a more conservative view. He appreciated 'the King's desire to

---

[169] Bell, *Davidson*, i. 610–11.
[170] DavP 326, fo. 84, Davidson to Canon Alexander, 14 May 1910.
[171] *The Times*, 21 May 1910; see above, Chapters 3 and 4.
[172] *Hansard* fifth series, 17, cols. 1036–7, 13 June 1910; BodL, MS.Harcourt.dep.adds.161, 15
June 1910, Harcourt to Lord Edmund Talbot; *Reynolds Newspaper*, 22 May 1910.
[173] *The Times*, 10 May 1910.
[174] EM 2145, Norfolk to FitzRoy, 9 May 1910.

prevent distress from unemployment in many trades', but observed that 'the King presumably does not wish to inaugurate a system of reducing to the barest minimum all public recognition of great national sorrows'.[175] The Archbishop's view prevailed in the initial announcement of six weeks full general mourning, followed by a further six weeks of half mourning.[176] Significant discontent followed among the textile trades who feared they would suffer severely from their consequent inability to sell coloured dresses.[177] Hence after the funeral, the King compromised by having the period of half mourning concluded at the end of June, thus leaving some weeks of the London Season when coloured dresses could be worn.[178]

The sequence of the funeral, when compared with 1901, showed a significant shift in the balance between the public and the private. Only phases 1 and 2 were conducted wholly away from the public eye, and even these were extensively reported. Thus the public were aware that phase 1 had been prolonged by Queen Alexandra's reluctance to agree to the removal of the King's body from his bedroom,[179] and a sentimental image of her with her dead husband was published in the illustrated magazines (see Plate 11). It was also reported that Queen Maud of Norway had been 'much affected as she looked at her dead father', while the liveliness of her young son Prince Olaf[180] provided an element of relief to 'a pathetic scene of family grief'.[181] In phases 3 and 5 the occupants of the carriages were more visible and responsive to the crowds than they had been in 1901. At Windsor, Queen Alexandra set a new precedent for the visible presence of women at royal funerals, both by taking part in the street procession, and by walking up the aisle of St George's behind the coffin. Women were present in the congregation, albeit generally as wives of the male personages invited. George V's children also participated in public as well as private phases of the ceremonial, thus reinforcing messages regarding the continuity of the monarchy, and its associations with domesticity and family life. A further poignant hint of the late King's private life was given by the inclusion

---

[175] DavP 326, fo. 26, Davidson to FitzRoy, 10 May 1910.

[176] EM 2145, Notice dated 11 May 1910. Davidson had discussed the matter with Lord Knollys (Edward VII's private secretary), Sir Arthur Bigge (George V's private secretary), and Lord Crewe (government leader in the Lords), an alliance the King would have found it hard to resist (DavP 326, fo. 47, Davidson to FitzRoy, 11 May 1910).

[177] *The Times*, 14, 17 May 1910.

[178] *The Times*, 25, 26 May 1910.

[179] *The Times*, 14 May 1910.

[180] The future King Olaf V.

[181] *The Times*, 10 May 1910.

in the procession of his fox terrier, Caesar, being led behind the gun-carriage.[182]

The lying-in-state had brought a religious dimension into the heart of the public phases of the ceremonial. Davidson evidently took great satisfaction from this, but accepted that overall a balance between the religious and the secular was needed. Thus he tried to quell the concerns of zealous correspondents who felt that there should be an ecclesiastical presence in the outdoor processions. Phases 5 and 6, he argued, were 'the Military transfer of the King's Remains from Westminster Hall, where religious services will have been held, to St George's Chapel, Windsor, where the great Funeral Service will be held'. He considered that it would be anomalous and inconvenient for clergy to participate in the street processions.[183] On the other hand the private phases 1 and 2 had been punctuated by religious observance with Davidson himself taking the service in the late King's bedroom on 11 May. 'Nothing', he wrote, 'could have been more simple, reverent, homely and yet dignified than the whole incident.'[184] Still, for Davidson, private piety, even that of a bereaved Queen, could not be allowed to determine the religious content of a state occasion, as was evident in his determination to remove from the St George's service material that he judged inappropriate.[185] By making the religious aspects of the proceedings unintrusive and uncontroversial they could then be general in their appeal.

As in 1901, the mood on the streets of London and Windsor suggests that in its later phases the funeral provided a kind of resolution for the public sentiment of the previous fortnight. The sombre expressions of personal sorrow in phases 3 and 4 were lightened somewhat by the pageantry of phases 5 and 6, a process assisted by the fine weather on 20 May. A sense of occasion began to supersede feelings of grief, even if the clothing and demeanour of the crowds continued to express consciousness of national mourning. Despite the disapproval of some, the occasion was aggressively commercialized by the sale of seats in stands and buildings along the route. If anything, sincere grief proved most enduring among the lower classes. Entrepreneurs found their expensive seats difficult to sell, but the free space on the pavements and in the parks was densely crowded. If class tensions were apparent, the late King himself was perceived as having been above them, an image reinforced by the lying-in-state. One

---

[182] Caesar was subsequently the purported author of a touching little book, *Where's Master?* (1910). From internal evidence, it would seem that the actual author was someone close to Queen Alexandra.

[183] DavP 326, fo. 84, Davidson to Canon Alexander, 15 May 1910.

[184] DavP 581, fo. 23.

[185] See above, 80–1.

man, though, was heard to grumble: 'When he was alive, he never wanted such a sight o' policeman an' sojers to keep the people off. Not he—he liked to see an' be seen an' be one of the crowd like.' [186]

The political aftermath of the King's death was significant but temporary. There were some mutterings that Asquith and his colleagues were responsible for it through exposing him to the strain of the constitutional crisis.[187] The Kaiser heard rumours that members of the government had been hissed in the streets. Such sentiments, however, do not appear to have been prevalent outside right-wing circles.[188] A more powerful current of reaction was that the suspension of political conflict was the only decent response to his death: Harcourt had warned Asquith that 'we should incur much public odium if we were thought to be unduly pressing the Crown at this time'.[189] The result was a constitutional conference between the two parties, which, although unsuccessful, provided a breathing space and postponed further open confrontation for six months. At the end of the year, however, George V found himself having to deal with exactly the same situation as that which had faced his father in April.[190]

Thus, as in 1901, the country adapted quickly to its new King and the period of intense grief for the departed sovereign was a short and transient one in the context of currently ongoing political and social developments. Nevertheless the brevity of the phase should not obscure its significance as an expression and affirmation of national consciousness. At a moment of constitutional crisis it served to portray the continuity and appeal of the monarchy as a force for national unity, a recollection that arguably was of importance in securing its survival during the subsequent turbulent years. Ongoing affection for the memory of late King was apparent in a report in 1913 that visitors to Windsor were 'constantly' asking where his monument was, and expressed 'surprise, disappointment and grief' when told that no monument had yet been erected.[191] Also at the very time when the fortunes of many of the churches at the grassroots were beginning to decline, it provided a reaffirmation, and even a strengthening, of the part of religious observance in national ceremonial and of popular belief in the afterlife. In one place on the streets of London, as the crowd waited for

---

[186] *The Times*, 18–21 May, *passim*. The remark quoted was overheard by *The Times* reporter on 17 May, but resentment was again voiced on 20 May against the obstruction of the view by the soldiers lining the route.

[187] Bod, MS.Harcourt.dep.adds.161, Geo. Hooper to Harcourt, 11 May 1910.

[188] J. A. Spender and C. Asquith, *Life of Herbert Henry Asquith, Lord Oxford and Asquith* (1932), i. 282–4.

[189] Bod, MS.Asquith.12, fo. 136, Harcourt to Asquith, 9 May 1910.

[190] For details see Jenkins, *Asquith*, 212–32.

[191] St George's Chapel Archives, XVII.5.3, anonymous memorandum.

the procession to pass, some started chants of 'I know that my Redeemer liveth' and 'I am the Resurrection and the Life'. *Lloyds* commented on the general religiosity of the occasion:

> While the doctrinaires have sometimes come near to robbing us of our trust and hope in the future by their controversies, the heart of the people has clung to the promise of the hereafter, with its hope of reunion with the loved ones gone before, and has refused to be robbed of the solace thus given to the otherwise unbearable sorrow of separation.[192]

Finally, the funeral was a ritual high point of a period in which it seemed possible to glorify death more than to fear it. It is a revealing irony that the second stanza of Laurence Binyon's 'For the Fallen', written little more than four years later, seems a much more apt reflection of sentiment at the time of Edward VII's funeral than of the brutal new reality of the First World War:

> Solemn the drums thrill: Death august and royal
> Sings sorrow up into immortal spheres.
> There is music in the midst of desolation
> And a glory that shines upon our tears.[193]

---

[192] *Lloyds Weekly Newspaper*, 22 May 1910.
[193] *Collected Poems of Laurence Binyon*, 2 vols (1931), i. 210. Cf. J. Hatcher, *Laurence Binyon: Poet, Scholar of East and West* (Oxford, 1995), 193.

# 9

# *'A vast dumb tenderness':*
# Prospect and Retrospect

> What is a Nation's love? No little thing:
> A vast dumb tenderness beyond all price ...[1]

These lines by John Masefield, inspired by the public response to the death of George VI in 1952, evoke a mood that was to recur on several occasions during the twentieth century. The intensity and universality of reactions to the deaths of Victoria and Edward VII were a culmination of trends in the preceding period, but they also, despite the dislocation brought by war and rapid social change, established a pattern that was to be replicated in successive generations. In this concluding chapter a survey of the twentieth century will be offered, concentrating particularly on the five most prominent cases, the interment of the 'Unknown Warrior' in 1920, and the deaths of George V in 1936, George VI in 1952, Sir Winston Churchill in 1965, and Diana, Princess of Wales in 1997. Particular attention will be given to pursuing the central focus of this book on the religious dimensions of public response and ceremonial and their wider implications for the role of religion in national life. In the light of this perspective, overall conclusions will then be drawn.

## From the Unknown Warrior to the People's Princess

As we have seen, in the decades before the First World War personal identification with national bereavement was widespread, in viewing the Duke of Clarence as son or lover, Victoria as an ideal grandmother, or Gladstone and Edward VII as surrogate father figures. Such prominent deaths could both stir and release painful memories of family bereave-

---

[1] J. Masefield, 'At the passing of ... King George VI', in *The Life of King George VI as Recorded in the Pages of 'The Times'* (1952), 15.

ments.[2] At the same time, however, the emotive power of such events also lay in a sense that the dead personage was on a pinnacle of eminence that, by association, lifted all the millions of mourners out of the mundane reality of their daily lives. Such a paradox of immediacy and remoteness, already very much apparent in the nineteenth century, was heightened during the course of twentieth century. The burial of the Unknown Warrior was a logical if unconscious ritual extension of the representative dimension of other great deaths. Here the deceased's claims to veneration entirely transcended his personal qualities and achievements, and it was possible for many to believe that the body just might be the actual remains of their own loved one. In the case of Diana, Princess of Wales at the other end of the period such literal identification was precluded, but in the media-saturated 1990s the dead woman's image, life story, joys, and tragedies loomed large in everyone's consciousness. Remote as she was from the reality of most lives, she still assumed the qualities of ideal role model, mother, daughter, even lover. In the intervening three-quarters of a century, the growing role of radio, film and eventually television had meant that general shared consciousness of national loss would become ever more vivid.

During the decade following 1910 the experience of untimely personal bereavement was to touch almost every family in the land. Such an accumulation of individual losses had, however, a different quality from the feelings stirred by the deaths of single prominent individuals. Some incidents prior to the outbreak of war are indicative of the dynamics of public sentiment. A few days after Edward VII's death in May 1910 a colliery disaster at Whitehaven in Cumberland resulted in the deaths of 136 miners. Nevertheless this large-scale human catastrophe was greatly overshadowed in most of the press coverage and in public feeling by the single death of the King.[3] Even when it was recognized that eighty families in Whitehaven were experiencing 'mourning of a deeper hue',[4] their loss was implicitly seen as merely a personal and local one, rather than a national bereavement. The harsh reality was that whereas millions had felt that they somehow knew the late King, only a limited circle was in any way acquainted with a bereaved Cumberland mining family. Nor was this merely a matter of class. In April 1912 the *Titanic*'s collision with an iceberg resulted in the drowning of well over a thousand people. Although the disaster made a powerful impact, expressed in a packed memorial service in St Paul's and extensive

[2] Such feelings were made explicit by a West London man who wrote to George V on the day of the late King's funeral, recalling all his own family bereavements (RA, GV/AA 55/306, Alfred Tapp to the King, 20 May 1910).

[3] *The Times*, 14 May 1910 and *passim*.

[4] *Reynolds Newspaper*, 15 May 1910.

contributions to the Lord Mayor's appeal, the intensity of reactions still appeared relatively muted when measured against those to the single death of Edward VII. Again the contrast is explained by the recognition that only a minority could feel a personal link to any of the *Titanic*'s passengers.[5] In the following February, the strong popular feeling stirred by news of the deaths in the Antarctic of Robert Falcon Scott and his four companions was a further illustration, reminiscent of Livingstone and Gordon, of the emotive power of perceived individual heroic sacrifice, despite the relatively small actual loss of life.[6]

From August 1914 onwards the First World War brought collective death on a qualitatively different scale, and struck heavily upon a generation for whom the untimely death of the young had otherwise become much less familiar than for their parents and grandparents.[7] Nevertheless an ordinary soldier was known only to his family and friends, and hence even as wartime bereavements were commonplace, they were often likely to be experienced in relative isolation. Despite the mutual support networks that readily developed, wider popular and institutional responses to numerous but obscure military deaths could be matter-of-fact and at times even callous.[8] Meanwhile, amidst all the other casualties of the summer of 1916, the single high-profile death of Lord Kitchener when his ship was sunk off the Orkneys had a powerful impact on public opinion.[9]

Against such a background it is easy to understand the instant widespread appeal of the 'Unknown Warrior', who could became a surrogate son or husband for those who had lost their own menfolk through the war. This association was greatly reinforced by the anonymity of the body. Any rational calculation of statistical probabilities in the face of the vast numbers of the unidentified war dead was liable to be outweighed by the psychological appeal of the belief that the 'unknown' might in reality be

[5] *The Times*, 16–23 April 1912, *passim*. Predominant in the reports is emphasis on enquiry as to what happened and the mistakes that had been made, rather than testimony to universal grief such as that apparent in May 1910. Cf. D. Davies, 'The Week of Mourning' in T. Walter (ed.), *The Mourning for Diana* (Oxford, 1999), 4–5. In the long term, however, a reversal occurred: whereas the loss of the *Titanic*, with its enormous dramatic and symbolic potential, has had an enduring place in the twentieth-century imagination, the impact of Edward VII's death was limited to those alive at the time.

[6] *The Times*, 12–15 Feb. 1913.

[7] Cannadine, 'War and Death', 193–8.

[8] J. Winter, *Sites of Memory, Sites of Mourning: The Great War in European Cultural History* (Cambridge, 1995), 31–53.

[9] *The Times*, 7–14 June 1916, *passim*. The juxtaposition of the numerous column inches devoted to Kitchener with the mere listing of other casualties elsewhere in the paper is striking.

their own loved one.[10] In any case for civilians at least, focus on a representative individual proved more emotionally manageable and satisfying than attempts to respond to the sheer tragic immensity of the overall slaughter. The collective national focus on a single funeral provided a sense of solidarity and mutual support in grief that had hitherto been lacking.[11]

The interment of the Unknown Warrior at Westminster Abbey on Armistice Day, 11 November 1920, was thus both a delayed ceremonial resolution of the collective grief at the carnage of the Great War, and a natural development of the tendency of the public to identify personal griefs with national ones. It was a late addition to Cabinet plans for the unveiling of the Cenotaph in Whitehall that initially had had little or no explicitly Christian content.[12] Archbishop Davidson had protested to the Prime Minister, Lloyd George, at the proposed omission of prayer.[13] The Cabinet, it seemed, was sensitive not only to the 'fear of Nonconformist criticism about the Church's taking the prominent place' but also to awareness that Muslims and Hindus were among the dead.[14] Davidson, however, stood his ground, and following negotiations between him and Lord Curzon, the chairman of the Cabinet committee planning the ceremonial, the unveiling was preceded by the singing of 'O God our help in ages past' led by massed choristers in surplices, and the saying of the Lord's Prayer.[15] According to Davidson, 'there was unanimous expression of thankfulness that we had thus marked our Christian fellowship'.[16] Curzon and his officials, for their part, having once abandoned the idea of a wholly secular ceremony, were considerably exercized by the desirability of securing representation from religions other than Christianity.[17] Offered a list of fifteen Christian denominations other than the Church of England that might be represented, Curzon slimmed it down to six, while still insisting on the inclusion of the Chief Rabbi, and Muslim and Sikh representatives.[18] In the event Hinduism

---

[10] A. Gregory, *The Silence of Memory: Armistice Day 1919–1946* (1994), 27. In fact the secret decision of the Cabinet committee responsible for the arrangements was to select the body of a man killed early in the war, who was thus almost certainly a regular British soldier rather than a volunteer, colonial or conscript (PRO, CAB 27/99, 5; cf. Gregory, *The Silence of Memory*, 46, n74).

[11] Gregory (ibid., 27–8) suggests that ex-soldiers, who had encountered the brutal and messy reality of death in the trenches, found the whole thing much less meaningful.

[12] PRO, CAB 23/22, 14 Oct. 1920, p. 270. For an evocative discussion of the cultural significant of war memorials see Winter, *Sites of Memory*, 78–116.

[13] PRO, CAB 27/99, p. 34.

[14] DavP 14, fo. 76.

[15] PRO, CAB 27/99, p. 16; WORKS 21/1/3/115; *The Times*, 12 Nov. 1920.

[16] DavP 14, fo. 76.

[17] PRO, CAB 27/99, p. 52.

[18] PRO, WORKS, 21/1/3/162, 21/1/3/186.

was represented by the attendance of several Indian princes. Sant Basant Singh, the family priest of the Maharaja of Patiala, represented the Sikhs, while the Imam of the Woking Mosque was invited to attend, but was unable to do so due to illness.[19] The occasion thus provided a significant precedent for future national ceremonies.

It was, however, Herbert Ryle, the Dean of Westminster, who gave the whole proceedings an unmistakable Christian cast through his proposal, which was readily adopted, that the body of an Unknown Warrior should be buried in a central position in the Abbey, a few feet inside the west door.[20] A military procession brought the body from Victoria Station in front of immense sombre crowds. After the King had unveiled the Cenotaph and the two minutes' silence had been observed, a procession of clergy, royalty, members of the government and the military moved on to the Abbey with the body of the Unknown Warrior. The King was chief mourner. As the dignitaries gathered round the grave the burial service was read, punctuated by two hymns, 'Lead kindly light' and 'Abide with me', which conveyed a tone more Christian than patriotic. The opening and closing hymns in the Abbey, Arkwright's 'O valiant hearts' and Kipling's 'Recessional' evoked reflections of a more national kind, but in an appropriately reflective vein. *The Times* leader writer perceived the ceremony as one whole, 'the most beautiful, the most touching and the most impressive that . . . this island has ever seen'.[21] It inextricably linked national and Christian associations. Preaching that evening on Hebrews 12:1, Davidson equated the war dead with the 'great cloud of witnesses' of the text. He stressed the representative nature of the Unknown Warrior, and that he had died 'that England might live'. He saw such sacrifice as an inspiration to Christian endeavour to make family life more 'sacred' and thus lift the quality of national life as a whole.[22]

The effect of Ryle's coup in 1920 was to secure the enduring position of his great church as a focus for national feeling and ceremonial. The location of the grave, on the boundary between secular and ecclesiastical space, was a particularly suggestive one, and contrasted significantly with the wholly secular location of the grave of the French Unknown Warrior, who was interred on the same day under the Arc de

[19] *The Times*, 12 Nov. 1920.
[20] PRO, CAB 23/22, 15 Oct. 1920, p. 282; CAB 27/99, p. 9; Gregory, *Silence of Memory*, 24–5.
[21] *The Times*, 12 Nov. 1920. Davidson also stressed the continuity between the Cenotaph and the Abbey phases, recalling that 'for the ending of our service we moved to West[minster] Abbey' (DavP 540, fo. 217).
[22] DavP 540, fos. 217–28.

Triomphe.[23] Immediately after 11 November it was the grave in the Abbey that became the primary focus for personal pilgrimage by the bereaved, even though, for practical reasons, it was the Cenotaph that formed the focus for public ceremonial.[24]

The elaborate inscription on the tombstone, unveiled in 1921, strongly asserted an Anglican sense of identification between church and nation. It was engraved with biblical texts and sonorous phrases and concluded: 'Thus are commemorated the many multitudes who . . . gave the most that man can give life itself for God for King and Country for loved ones home and empire for the sacred cause of justice and the freedom of the world.' There was a clear continuity with the sentiments voiced by Randall Davidson at Edward VII's lying-in-state. The wording had indeed been roughed out at a gathering at Lambeth Palace even before the interment had taken place.[25] It superseded earlier ideas for a much briefer and purely secular inscription.[26] The choice of the text, 'In Christ shall all be made alive', gave rise to a Jewish complaint on the grounds that there was no way of knowing that the unknown was a Christian. Ryle, however, argued that the choice was justified as 'nine-tenths of the mourners who visit the grave are Christian people' and 'the great majority of our brothers who fell in France were Christians either by conviction or profession'.[27] Despite all that had happened during the previous decade the centrality of Christianity in national mourning had been successfully reasserted.

Such associations were renewed in November 1925 when the death of Queen Alexandra was marked with widespread church services and a lying-in-state, as well as a funeral service, in Westminster Abbey. This was also the first major death that was communicated to the nation by the new medium of radio and the announcement was followed by a short broadcast memorial service.[28] By the time of George V's death in January 1936, radio had done much to facilitate a feeling of more immediate contact between the public and the monarchy. In the King's annual Christmas broadcasts,

[23] For continental comparisons see G. L. Mosse, *Fallen Soldiers: Reshaping the Memory of the World Wars* (1990), 94–8.
[24] Gregory, *Silence of Memory*, 27–8. In attributing a greater appeal to the Cenotaph (Mosse, *Fallen Soldiers*, 96) confuses public ceremonial and private devotion.
[25] WA 58673, Davidson to Ryle, 1 Nov. 1920. The inscription also comes close to echoing a sentence in Davidson's sermon on the evening of Armistice Day 1920: 'the British Nation will never forget the multitudes of men . . . who gave the most that men can give, life itself, for their country, for the cause of justice, and the freedom of the world'. (DavP, 540, fo. 219).
[26] WA 58671, Cabinet Memorandum, 15 Oct. 1920.
[27] M. H. FitzGerald, *A Memoir of Herbert Edward Ryle* (1928), 314–16.
[28] *The Times*, 21, 23, 28 Nov. 1925.

his actual personality and beliefs began to have an immediate impact. George V had a straightforward Christian faith, apparently more sincere than his father's and certainly less complex than his grandmother's, which *The Times* judged to be 'typically English'.[29] His broadcasts of the early 1930s expressed his sense of dependence on God, and presented a homely vision of Christmas as the festival of the family, not only in a literal sense, but also in the 'spirit of one great family' uniting 'this Realm and Empire'.[30] Thus a major Christian festival was imbued with patriotic significance. In his Silver Jubilee broadcast in May 1935 the King also struck a spiritual note, expressing his thankfulness to God and looking to overcome future anxieties 'with God's help'.[31]

Accordingly, public reaction to his death linked the intensity of mourning for a quasi-personal loss with a strongly Christian dimension. In a broadcast message to the nation on the day after the King died, the Prime Minister, Stanley Baldwin, spoke explicitly of God's calling to him. In his tribute in the House of Commons he asserted that 'the spiritual power of the Crown is ... far greater than it ever was'.[32] Such language was less specific than that employed by churchmen, but it still constituted a significant setting of the national tone. The Archbishop of Canterbury, Cosmo Gordon Lang, rose to the occasion with a speech in the Lords, a sermon at Westminster Abbey and an address at a service broadcast by the BBC on the Sunday before the funeral. In doing so he was able to give wide publicity to his own perception of the King's character and to apostrophize him as speaking from beyond the grave 'O my people, remember, remember the Lord God of your fathers.'[33] Among the complimentary letters Lang received was one from Lord Beaverbrook, who judged his speech 'the most effective and powerful' he had ever heard in the Lords.[34] Dame Beatrix Lyall felt the Archbishop had confirmed the 'wonderful feeling' people had that the late King really did live his life 'in the sight of God'. She continued:

> The good your words to-night did to the millions who heard you is incalculable and of the greatest value not only from the Christian point of view as an example to be followed, which many will follow, but also it will

---

[29] *The Times*, 23 Jan. 1936.

[30] *The Times*, 27 Dec. 1934, 27 Dec. 1935. Archbishop Lang, who was a close personal friend of the King, had a substantial hand in the drafting of these two last Christmas broadcasts and of the Silver Jubilee broadcast (LPL, Lang Papers 218, fo. 22).

[31] *The Times*, 7 May 1935.

[32] *The Times*, 22, 24 Jan. 1935.

[33] *The Times*, 24, 27 Jan. 1936.

[34] LPL, Lang Papers 191, fo. 189, Beaverbrook to Lang, 25 Jan. 1936.

have effect in binding the nation more and more in unity, with respect and love for the monarchy, and what it stands for.[35]

Certainly public observance in the days following the King's death gave some substance to such hopes. A lying-in-state in Westminster Hall closely followed the pattern set in 1910. There was again a religious service to receive the body and a prominent processional cross stood beside the coffin.[36] With longer opening hours than in 1910, attendance was at least double, with a count of 809,182 thought 'probably [to] underestimate the numbers very considerably'. At one time on Sunday 26 January the waiting time came close to eight hours.[37] After passing the catafalque thousands then went on into Westminster Abbey where 'repeated short memorial services had to be arranged'.[38] Church services continued to be a focus for national mourning, above all on the day of the funeral itself, Tuesday 28 January, when under the headline 'A Nation at Prayer', *The Times* reported huge congregations and concluded that 'at heart we are a deeply religious race'. In Scotland too there were very large church attendances.[39]

A further significant feature of the response to George V's death was an aspiration for joint action between the Church of England, the Church of Scotland, and the Free Churches, which was now felt appropriate on a 'National occasion'.[40] The time, however, proved too short to agree a common special form of service, although the Moderator-designate of the General Assembly of the Church of Scotland read prayers before the Archbishop's address at the broadcast memorial service on 26 January.[41] It was indeed apparent that the late King was sufficiently innocent of ecclesiastical subtleties for his piety to have as strong an appeal among Scottish Presbyterians as among English Anglicans.[42]

One measure of continuity in religious consciousness since 1901 is provided by a comparison of an anthology of poems written in response to the death of George V, with the similar volume compiled after the death of Victoria.[43] The proportion of orthodox Christian statements had declined

---

[35] Ibid., fo. 190, Lyall to Lang, 27 Jan. 1936.

[36] Lockhart, *Lang*, 393; photograph in *The Times* supplement of 28 Jan. 1936, p. iv.

[37] PRO, WORKS 21/100.

[38] LPL, Lang Papers 218, fo. 17.

[39] *Scotsman*, 29 Jan 1936.

[40] LPL, Lang Papers 36, fo. 222, memorandum by A. C. Don (chaplain), 22 Jan 1936; fos. 223, 231, 237, correspondence between Don and Oswald Milligan of the Church of Scotland Committee on Public Worship, 23, 24, 28 Jan. 1936.

[41] *The Times*, 27 Jan. 1935.

[42] See for example the address by Dr Archibald Fleming at St Columba's Church, reported in *The Times* of 27 Jan. 1936.

[43] *King George V Commemoration Book of Verse* (1936?), containing 132 poems. See above, 225–6.

slightly from 16.6% to 13% and predominantly secular poems had risen from 19.7% to 31%. Nevertheless the majority of the poems, 56%, were still broadly religious in content. Moreover the evidence of high church-going in response to the King's death suggests that organized Christianity remained a natural point of reference for many, and a culture of diffuse rather than dogmatic Christianity continued to provide particularly fertile soil for an easy equation of Christian and national values.

In many respects the public mood following George VI's sudden death in February 1952 resembled that in January 1936. It derived additional intensity from a sense that the death was untimely, and that the fifty-six-year-old monarch had sacrificed his own health through his commitment to his duties, above all during the war. It is thus arguable that mourning for him acquired a dimension of belated collective catharsis for the trauma of the Second World War, analogous to the role of the funeral of the Unknown Warrior in relation to the Great War. Like his father George V, the late King was also readily presented as epitomizing an idealized family life and domestic piety. Religious allusions were widespread. A significant example is provided by Winston Churchill's memorial broadcast, in which the Prime Minister spoke of the way the King had been sustained 'by the sincerity of his Christian faith'. He went on to speak of the 'mysterious link—indeed, I may say, the magic link' between the Crown and the Commonwealth.[44]

The ceremonial and observances leading up to the King's funeral closely followed the pattern of 1936 and retained the strong religious content. The BBC broadcast a memorial service on Sunday 10 February, prefaced by an address from the Archbishop of Canterbury, Geoffrey Fisher, in which the primate spoke of how the late King, when 'England [*sic*] was in peril, . . . embodied our heritage, our hope and faith'. George VI had made two perfect marriages, one to the Queen and the other to his people, both of them founded on vows 'made before God and to God' to whom he always looked 'with a simple, trustful, unswerving obedience'.[45] On the following day the lying-in-state was again opened with a short service, identical to that used for George V, except that, at Elizabeth II's request, the hymn was changed from 'Praise my soul the King of heaven' to 'Abide with me'. The choice appeared to reflect the new Queen's personal preference, but it was one that linked her father's lying-in-state to a hymn with particularly strong popular appeal.[46] Once again there were enormous queues, although

---

[44] *George VI in the Pages of the Times*, 13.
[45] LPL, Fisher Papers 103, fos. 38–41.
[46] Ibid., fos. 4, 20. On the place of 'Abide with me' in popular culture see H. J. Garland, *Henry Francis Lyte and the Story of Abide with Me* (Manchester, n.d.).

at 305,806[47] the recorded attendance was less than half that for George V. The discrepancy, however, can be largely attributed to the fact that in 1936 Westminster Hall had been open for four days including a Saturday and a Sunday, whereas in 1952 it was open for only three days, all of them weekdays. *The Times* readily applied the language of pilgrimage, suggesting that those who passed through Westminster Hall were brought into the presence of 'some transfigured reality'.[48] On the day of the funeral itself large church attendances were reported, despite the availability of the alternative option of watching or listening to broadcasts of the funeral itself at home. St Paul's Cathedral was crammed to capacity half an hour before the service was due to start, and in Birmingham 15,000 people crowded into Victoria Square for an interdenominational open-air service. In Edinburgh queues formed outside St Giles's long before the beginning of the memorial service there.[49]

The appeal of Christian observance and symbols as a focus for national mourning overlaid a more complex reality. In a leading article *The Times* reflected on the subtle connections between the throne and 'the faith of Englishmen'. In the writer's view, although many did not go to church, 'the sentiments evoked by the death and accession of monarchs have a quality which it is no impiety to call religious'. Monarchy was representative of the Christian view of leadership, while even mere temporal loyalty constituted 'one approach to the understanding of religious truth'.[50] Archbishop Fisher, preaching to a congregation of over 3,000 at St Paul's on the following Sunday, sought to turn sentiments of this kind towards religious revival. The King, he said, had been a symbol and sacrament of the nation's unity, an inspiration to hold firm to moral duty and religious faith. Moreover the new Queen's sincerity and devotion should be a spur to a 'united, a youthful reformation of manners and morals'. He called on the press and the clergy to lead such a reformation, which could not be achieved 'without a return to the Christian religion and the Christian Church'.[51] This sermon evoked some enthusiastic comment, and the Vice-Chairman of Lloyds Bank volunteered the services of his organization to circulate printed copies to thousands of influential people.[52] There was indeed a considerable distance between 'temporal loyalty' and fully committed Christianity, but that distance was perceived as one between points on a spectrum rather than between opposing sides of a gulf.

[47] PRO, MEPO 2/9682.
[48] *The Times*, 13 Feb. 1952.
[49] *The Times*, 16 Feb. 1952.
[50] *The Times*, 15 Feb. 1952.
[51] *The Times*, 18 Feb. 1952.
[52] LPL, Fisher Papers 103, fos. 67, 68, 75, 77, 81.

The aftermath of George VI's death also saw a consolidation of the moves towards greater recognition of the Church of Scotland and the Free Churches than had been apparent in 1936. The Moderator of the General Assembly of the Church of Scotland wrote to Fisher the day after the King's death. He recalled that the Kirk had been represented at George VI's Coronation and at the marriage of the then Princess Elizabeth, and continued: 'I need scarcely say that, in Scotland where sympathy for the Royal Family is deep, widespread and personal, great importance would be attached to the giving of a like place at the forthcoming service at Windsor to the official head of the national Church.'[53] The Archbishop agreed, and it was arranged that the Moderator, together with the Moderator of the Free Church Federal Council, would join the procession of clergy at Windsor and stand in the sanctuary during the service. Moreover their presence was formally noted in the order of service.[54] Both Moderators also took part in the broadcast memorial service on 10 February.[55] In addition, the Metropolitan of Thyateira, representing both the Oecumenical Patriarch and the Orthodox community in Britain, was given a stall in the choir of St George's.[56] On the other hand, there is no record in Fisher's papers of any approach to the Roman Catholic Church, although it was probably assumed that any invitation would be refused.[57] Nor, while Fisher responded warmly to news that prominent Muslims had attended a memorial service for the King in Baghdad,[58] does it appear to have occurred to him or to anyone else that representation from faiths other than Christianity might have been appropriate in London and Windsor.[59]

The response to Sir Winston Churchill's death in January 1965 had some affinities to that to the Duke of Wellington's in 1852 in that it recalled heroic defence of the nation in time of crisis, and evoked a sense of the passage of time. Similarly, given the great age of the deceased, it could hardly be a cause for particular grief. Church and state again combined to produce splendid ceremonial, which had been secretly planned for several

[53] Ibid., fo. 12, W. White Anderson to Fisher, 7 Feb. 1952.
[54] Ibid., fos. 19, 35, 127. The final decision on such matters lay with the Dean of Windsor, not the Archbishop, but Lambeth Palace applied a strong steer.
[55] Ibid., fo. 35.
[56] Ibid., fos. 45, 47.
[57] The Catholic community could, however, feel itself to be prominently represented in the person of the Duke of Norfolk, as Earl Marshal, even though the Church as an institution was not.
[58] LPL Fisher Papers 103, fos. 71–2, 86.
[59] The issue was explicitly raised in connection with Elizabeth II's Coronation in the following year, but in the face of Fisher's adamant opposition nothing was done (E. Carpenter, *Archbishop Fisher—His Life and Times* (Norwich, 1991), 251).

years.[60] In Westminster Hall, a golden cross once more stood by a coffin, this time draped with the Union flag, as hushed crowds filed past.[61] The state funeral at St Paul's, broadcast on television and on all three radio channels, stirred memories of the cathedral's role as a national symbol at the time of Churchill's 'finest hour'. Churchill's burial at Bladon, in an archetypal English country churchyard,[62] served to evoke the enduring emotional links between the church, a rural idyll, and the nation's history and identity. Nevertheless, the reality of 1965 was different from that of 1952. In part this was a contingent effect of personality: Churchill had been no more than a nominal Christian;[63] Michael Ramsey, who had succeeded Geoffrey Fisher as Archbishop of Canterbury in 1961, perceived state occasions as an embarrassment rather than an opportunity.[64] Accordingly the pre-conditions for linkages of the kind so readily made in 1936 and 1952 were lacking. More fundamentally, the underlying climate of opinion seemed to be best reflected in a secular national commemoration in which the Christian dimension was more decorative than central. The Archbishop's main practical task was to distribute an inadequate allocation of tickets for other church leaders.[65] He was given a five-minute television slot in Westminster Hall shortly before Sir Winston's body arrived, in which he called for thankfulness to God for the life of such a great man, but it was hard to escape the impression of a mere pious interlude.[66]

By this period the advent of television was having a decisive impact on the forms of public participation. Even in 1952 the police had observed that the crowds on the streets of London were smaller than they had been in 1935,[67] and in 1965 there were widespread reports that the turnout was less than anticipated. The officer in command of the Whitehall and Charing Cross area suggested that on a future such occasion policing could be reduced by 25 per cent. He noted that 'a large section of the public' now preferred 'to view the spectacle from the comfort of their own homes where they can see through the eyes of the cameras coverage of the whole route from vantage points they could not otherwise hope to attain.'[68] This trend also greatly reduced the importance of simultaneous memorial services

---

[60] See for example PRO, MEPO 2/9922, 'Personal and Confidential' circular of 22 Nov. 1960.

[61] For a particularly evocative photograph see the *Observer* magazine of 7 Feb. 1965.

[62] Cf. Richard Dimbleby in *Supplement to Radio Times*, 28 Jan. 1965, p. 7.

[63] K. Robbins, 'Britain, 1940, and "Christian Civilization" ', in D. Beales and G. Best (eds.), *History Society and the Churches* (Cambridge, 1985), 280–81.

[64] O. Chadwick, *Michael Ramsey: A Life* (1990), 121–2.

[65] LPL, Ramsey Papers 74, fos. 205, 220, 229, 239–40.

[66] Ibid., fos. 226–7, 230; Chadwick, *Ramsey,* 123.

[67] PRO, MEPO 2/9682.

[68] PRO, MEPO 2/9930, Report by Chief Supt. J. A. Rennie.

as mechanisms for the public to express their sense of participation and identification: now that television gave them immediate visual access to the central ceremonial, attendance at the local church seemed unnecessary.

During the three decades following 1965, it would have seemed plausible to argue that Churchill's funeral also marked the end of an era in the public acknowledgement of prominent deaths. Late twentieth-century Britain seemed to be reverting to a pattern of more perfunctory public mourning, as in the eighteenth century. Even in the aftermath of the assassination of Earl Mountbatten in 1979, the most dramatic major death of these years, the popular mood showed only limited echoes of the 'vast dumb tenderness' Masefield had discerned in 1952. Then, as in 1861 and 1892, the wholly unexpected occurred.

The impact of the car accident in Paris on 31 August 1997 that killed Diana, Princess of Wales, showed that whatever else might be changing in the later twentieth century, the potentiality remained for the death of a major public figure to stir intense and widespread reaction. The complex dynamics of the role of the media in helping to stimulate the very emotions it was reporting need to be carefully evaluated. Nevertheless the palpable expressions of grief among the crowds in the streets and parks of London, and the sentiments that prompted an avalanche of flowers and of expressions of condolence and quasi-personal bereavement were real enough. Such feelings were not universal, but those who dissented from them, or even—like the royal family themselves—chose to mourn in a less outwardly demonstrative manner, felt themselves constrained and pressurized by the dominant mood.[69]

In some respects the religious dimension of reactions was noteworthy. As on earlier such occasions St Paul's Cathedral found itself so crowded that it had to turn away potential worshippers;[70] and local clergymen found themselves arranging extra services in response to public demand. For example the Vicar of Ottery St Mary in Devon told his local paper, 'It seems that the public do want a way to express their grief and feelings at this time, and that is why we are putting on this service.'[71] Churches were a focal point for expressions of grief and condolence, particularly in the leaving of flowers. Moreover, the public perception of Diana, in death if not in life, was that of a Christlike suffering 'saviour of the world'.[72] Such an understanding of her life might be a sign of theological inexactitude, but

[69] Davies, 'Week of Mourning', 3–18; W. Merrin, 'Crash, Bang, Wallop! What a Picture! The Death of Diana and the Media', *Mortality*, 4 (1999), 41–62.
[70] *Daily Telegraph*, 1 Sept. 1997.
[71] *Express and Echo*, 5 Sept. 1997.
[72] The phrase appeared on a poster outside Kensington Palace, quoted by R. McKibbin, 'Mass Observation in the Mall', *London Review of Books*, 2 Oct. 1997.

this was nothing new in British popular religion, and it also indicated the continuing cultural resonance of Christian motifs. The Poet Laureate, Ted Hughes, wrote a brief tribute replete with religious allusion, and concluding:

> Love is broken on the Cross.
> The Flower on the Gun.[73]

The analogy between the crucified Christ and the 'English rose' borne on a gun-carriage to her funeral was inescapable.

The central act of public mourning, the funeral in Westminster Abbey, drew the largest British television audience hitherto recorded, amounting to three-quarters of the adult population. It was an eclectic ritual reflecting the changing and diverse forms of religious and national life. There were important continuities. The location revived and enriched the Abbey's historic links with national mourning, while the singing of the Croft sentences showed that these were likely to outlast the twentieth century as well as the nineteenth. Three of the hymns, 'I vow to thee my country', 'The King of love my Shepherd is', and 'Guide me, O thou great Redeemer' evoked a range of traditional Christian associations. They were redolent respectively of the religious patriotism of the earlier twentieth century, of the gentler aspects of Victorian piety, and of Welsh revivalism and national self-expression. By contrast, 'Make me a channel of your peace' evoked a more contemporary religious idiom, despite the supposed derivation of its words from St Francis of Assisi. Further explicit Christian content was present, most notably in the prayers led by the Archbishop of Canterbury, and also in the reading by the Prime Minister, Tony Blair, from 1 Corinthians, a striking symbolic expression of his own neo-Gladstonian sense that political leadership had a Christian dimension. On the other hand, the address by Earl Spencer, brother of the deceased Princess, was remarkable for many reasons, but in the present context it was notable for adopting a secular tone, albeit softened by some passing allusions to God, within the framework of a church service. The poems read by Diana's sisters were also essentially secular in their perceptions of death and the passage of time. Other musical features of the service provided something of a bridge between the Christian and the secular. It is noteworthy, however, when Randall Davidson's objection to the inclusion of the Russian Kontakion in Queen Victoria's funeral is recalled,[74] that not only John Tavener's setting of words from this office, but a section of Verdi's Requiem had an uncontroversial place in the service. No one now needed to worry seriously about Protestant objections to prayers for the dead. Also absent from the service, indeed, were the carefully calculated ecumenical and inter-faith gestures that were becoming a feature

---

[73] *Express and Echo*, 6 Sept. 1997.
[74] See above, 79–80.

of more conventional and predictable national occasions. Meanwhile Elton John's 'Candle in the wind' linked a diffuse spirituality with a romantic patriotism. The song described the Princess as 'England's rose' and 'the grace that placed yourself/Where lives were torn apart' and asserted 'Now you belong to Heaven/And the stars spell out your name.' Such material arguably did much to make the ritual meaningful to the large constituency of those who had little or no connection with organized religion.[75]

The religious ambivalences of the funeral itself were symptomatic of the wider public response. Evaluated against the measure suggested by the Victorian and Edwardian cases examined in this book, as opposed to the predominant secularity of Britain in the 1990s, the formal religiosity of the aftermath of Diana's death should not be exaggerated. Extra church services were indeed held, but they were by no means as numerous as on such occasions a century earlier, and attendance at them was relatively a minority pursuit. Visits to churches to leave flowers or to sign condolence books a matter of individual pilgrimage rather than participation in collective worship. Tributes and words of consolation from religious leaders were given limited coverage by television and radio, and a few column inches in the newspapers, but this was still a long way short of the numerous columns of reports of memorial sermons and services in equivalent nine-teenth- and early twentieth-century newspapers. To the extent that the media felt the need for moral and spiritual reflection on the event, it commissioned its own, generally secular, pundits rather than sending reporters to listen to sermons. Nevertheless, if a more expansive under-standing of religion is adopted, then much in the behaviour of the mourners could be equated with it. In particular there was veneration of Diana as a quasi-saint or angel, and the creation of shrines and points of pilgrimage. Thousands of condolence messages made extensive use of broadly religious language.[76]

Further detailed analysis of the response to Diana's death would fall outside the scope of this book.[77] The material examined in earlier chapters does, however, suggest an important historical perspective that has been largely absent hitherto from both journalistic and academic interpretation of this event. Despite the evidence of change, the public mood of early

---

[75] For the order of service and a revealing eye-witness account see *Sunday Times*, 7 Sept. 1997.

[76] For a selection of messages sent to a tabloid newspaper see the *Sun*, 6 Sept. 1997. Theologically informed Christian responses to death were conspicuous by their rarity.

[77] For a range of comment and analysis see I. Ang and others (Re:Public) (eds.), *Planet Diana: Cultural Studies and Global Mourning* (Kingswood, NSW, 1997); M. Merck (ed.), *After Diana: Irreverent Elegies* (1998); B. Campbell, *Diana Princess of Wales: How Sexual Politics Shook the Monarchy* (1998); Walter, (ed.) *The Mourning for Diana*.

September 1997 can still be fitted into a recurrent long-term pattern. The immediacy of media coverage meant that events unfolded more rapidly and emotions were cultivated in a more hothouse atmosphere than in, say, 1910 or 1861. There were also the particular contingent circumstances of romantic interest, a wider sense of crisis in the royal family, and the advent of 'New Labour' in government. In many other respects, though, the continuities were striking. Once again, sudden high-profile death brought to the surface the existential uncertainties and obscured griefs of millions, focused on the image of a person whom they had never met. Once again, the various agencies involved found themselves engaged in frantic activity in order to identify and organize an appropriate ritual means of assuaging febrile popular sentiment. Once again, the 'vast dumb tenderness' of humanity brought into collective encounter with death became powerfully apparent.

## Conclusions

At the level of broad impressions the overall pattern that emerges is one of underlying continuity. In 1997 as in 1805 or 1817, the death of a conspicuous and popular individual had the power to shock and, super-ficially at least, to unite the nation. In this respect the nineteenth and twentieth centuries had more in common with each other than with the period that preceded them.[78] Accordingly in terms of the history of death, the material presented in this book should serve as a check to the drawing of simplistic contrasts between supposedly 'Victorian' and post-Victorian attitudes.

More specifically, the chronology of response to prominent deaths suggests that the highpoint of such collective commemoration occurred not so much in the middle of the century, as in the decades immediately before the First World War. It was at this later period that the nation showed itself to be most uninhibited in mourning its prominent dead. The Duke of Wellington's funeral, which is widely cited as epitomizing the Victorian 'celebration of death', appeared, by contrast with the funerals of Gladstone, Victoria and Edward VII, to be more of a show of pageantry, and less of an expression of genuine mourning. The Duke's obsequies were certainly a powerful national rite of passage, in marking a sense of final transition from the Napoleonic to the Victorian era, but they were only to a limited extent a reflection of common grief. Conversely, when Prince Albert died, feelings of public grief were much more intense, but they lacked a commensurate ceremonial and ritual focus. From the 1880s

[78] See Chapter 1 above.

onwards, however, there was greater official recognition of the dynamics of popular sentiment, scope for participation in observance was widened, and such opportunities enthusiastically taken. In suggesting that Queen Victoria's funeral was 'far less elaborate' than Wellington's, David Cannadine only conveys half the picture.[79] He is correct to the extent that in 1901 the procession through London lacked the baroque extravagances (such as the funeral car) of 1852, but his observation implies a disregard of the numerous other earlier and later phases of the ceremonial. He also fails to take into account the numerous parallel commemorations throughout the United Kingdom and beyond, both on the day of the funeral and during the ten days after Victoria's death. Viewed in this perspective, history can record few more elaborate and protracted celebrations of death than the stately progress of Queen Victoria's body from her bedroom at Osborne to her mausoleum at Frogmore.

There is no inconsistency here with the indications that in private life declining mortality was reducing preoccupation with death. There was a strong element of shock and surprise in the response to the deaths of both Victoria and Edward VII. Part of the power of public reactions lay precisely in the fact that the death of the monarch brought many people into a collective encounter with death that was disconcerting because now relatively unfamiliar. There were also wider forces at work, particularly a growth in a consciousness of coherent national community fostered by newspapers, railways and the telegraph and a corresponding awareness of major personages as common reference points for collective identity. There was the renaissance of the monarchy itself in popular esteem, a process assisted, as we have seen, by the sympathies inspired by earlier royal deaths, but also supported by other grand occasions such as Victoria's jubilees and Edward VII's coronation. Both among politicians and among potentially disruptive sectional and national forces the psychology of response to death triggered an anxiety to affirm underlying consensus and community rather than to subvert it. Herein lay the appeal of large-scale funerary ceremonial in which the mood of celebration in 1897 and 1902 was readily transformed into that of mourning in 1901 and 1910, in sustaining an aura of impressive stability.

At the same time significant innovations in funerary and commemorative observance established a greater sense of sincerity and affinity with popular taste. Gone, despite the personal assertiveness of the Duke of Norfolk, was all but the shadow of influence from the heralds. In their place the church and the armed services were somewhat incongruous collaborators in the construction of funerals that fully exploited their comp-

[79] Cannadine, 'War and Death', 193. The parallel contrast Cannadine draws between Palmerston's and Gladstone's deaths also needs to be refined.

lementary capacities for effective ceremonial and reinforced patriotic and nationalistic associations. Developments such as street processions and lyings-in-state permitted a wider sense of participation, while a relaxation of the gloom and rigour of earlier mourning regulations meant that national grief could become less contrived and burdensome to the participants. Meanwhile the use of flowers in the expression of grief, first conspicuous in 1881, and confirmed by the extravagance of the floral tributes to Clarence, Victoria and Edward VII, further mitigated earlier more sombre customs. It is important to note that these trends were under way long before the First World War was associated with a decisive break in earlier mourning conventions.[80]

Within the broad trends identified, something of the specific response to individual great deaths can be explained in terms of contingent circumstances of context and personality. There was a dominant note of untimely tragedy in 1861 and 1892, and of heroic dedication and sacrifice in 1874 and 1885. In 1852, 1898, and, above all, in 1901, the sense that a whole era had been wrapped up in the life of the deceased meant that mourning for the individual could readily transmute into wider reflection on the passage of time and the transience of human life. Such thoughts though could detach themselves from the specific context. As Almeric Fitzroy watched the procession carrying Edward VII's coffin to Westminster Hall he felt 'with a force there was no gainsaying, the profound grief that lies at the heart of things, do what we can to conceal or forget it'. Such occasions, he thought, could even bring healing to a people 'that knows not the significance of Sorrow'.[81]

Emile Durkheim's observations on the communal dimension of mourning are pertinent here:

> When someone dies, the family group to which he belongs feels itself lessened and, to react against this loss, it assembles. A common misfortune has the same effects as the approach of a happy event: collective sentiments are renewed which then lead men to seek one another and to assemble together.... Not only do the relatives, who are affected the most directly, bring their own personal sorrow to the assembly, but the society exercises a moral pressure over its members, to put their sentiments in harmony with the situation.

According to Durkheim, people then influence each other and 'a veritable panic of sorrow results'. Shared grief, however, strengthens the group and indicates that in the face of pain and loss 'the society is more alive and active then ever'. The point is readily extended from the family and small com-

---

[80] Cf L. Taylor, *Mourning Dress: A Costume and Social History* (1983), 120–63, 206.
[81] Fitzroy, *Memoirs*, ii. 407.

munity context of individual death to the much broader impact of the death of national figures. Here communal grieving is a paradoxical manifestation of Durkheim's general sense of the role of ritual in the affirmation of the underlying ideas and sentiments that give unity to society.[82]

In their interpretation of the Coronation of Elizabeth II in 1953, Edward Shils and Michael Young made a controversial application of Durkheim's analysis of communal ritual. They viewed the Coronation as a ceremonial collective expression of shared moral and spiritual values to an extent that led them to describe it as 'a great act of national communion'.[83] Shils and Young were subsequently criticized for confusing the language of the Coronation service with the reality of popular belief in a society where explicit Christianity was only a minority commitment.[84] In 1977 Steven Lukes offered a more wide-ranging critique of these and other 'neo-Durkheimian' approaches, arguing that they implied an 'excessively simple answer' to the 'exceedingly complicated problem' of what holds society together. Moreover, Lukes pointed out, underlying social coherence needed to be demonstrated rather than assumed. In Lukes's view it is banal merely to see ritual as 'expressing-producing-constituting value integration'. A more fruitful approach, he argued, is to acknowledge its cognitive dimension and to set it in the context of a 'class-structured, conflictual and pluralistic model of society'. According to Lukes, such rituals can therefore be seen 'as modes of exercising, or seeking to exercise, power along the cognitive dimension'.[85] In other words, he saw the organizers of state ceremonial as consciously manipulating—or attempting to manipulate—popular sentiment to their own ends, rather than as instruments for the expression of a genuine consensus.

A parallel approach arises from anthropological analysis of royal funerals in a wide range of geographical and historical contexts. Surviving rulers used mortuary ritual for their deceased predecessors as a means of establishing and legitimizing their own power and authority. Thus for example the protracted and elaborate rites that followed the deaths of the kings of Thailand—such as Rama VI in 1926—served both to reassert the prestige of the royal court and to demonstrate the continuity of kingship.[86] In nineteenth-century Bali, the funeral ceremonies of important men assumed qualities of high drama, and constituted aggressive assertions of

---

[82] E. Durkheim, trans. J. A. Swain, *The Elementary Forms of the Religious Life* (1915), 375, 399–402, 427–8.

[83] E. Shils and M. Young, 'The Meaning of the Coronation', *Sociological Review*, 1 (1953), 63–82.

[84] N. Birnbaum, 'Monarchs and Sociologists', *Sociological Review*, 3 (1955), 5–23.

[85] S. Lukes, *Essays in Social Theory* (1977), 52–73.

[86] Huntingdon and Metcalf, *Celebrations of Death*, 124–30.

status in a politically fragmented country.[87] Richard Huntingdon and Peter Metcalf conclude their survey of this phenomenon with the observation: 'It seems that the most powerful natural symbol for the continuity of any community, large or small, simple or complex, is, by a strange and dynamic paradox, to be found in the death of its leader, and in the representation of that striking event.'[88]

In their analysis of Queen Victoria's Diamond Jubilee in Cambridge, Elizabeth Hammerton and David Cannadine are very sensitive to the social tensions and political power struggles that came to the surface in the course of planning local observance. Nevertheless they note that conflicts were resolved in advance of the actual celebrations, and that points at issue had always been merely concerned with the forms celebration should take. In public at least, everyone was agreed that the Jubilee should be celebrated, and the events of the day itself were 'not ritualized *conflict* but ritualized *consensus*'.[89] Similarly, in her account of late Tudor and early Stuart royal funerals Jennifer Woodward emphasizes the propagandistic dimension of such occasions. Nevertheless she recognizes the extent to which the expectations of the mass of participants and observers limited the capacity of the organizers to manipulate ritual to their own ends. Moreover, it was not possible to use spectacle to manufacture a popular mood. When, as in the case of the funeral of Anne of Denmark in 1619, the intended message of ceremonial lacked affinity with public sentiment, the result was an expensive farce.[90]

Some aspects of the response to the great deaths examined in this book can indeed be interpreted as primarily propagandistic exercises on behalf of particular power élites. The royal circle was explicit about its motivation for using the Duke of Wellington's funeral as an expression of continuity with the glories of the national past. The aspirations for grand ceremonial and maximum public participation following the deaths of Victoria and Edward VII implied an anxiety to assert the status and importance of the monarchy in the face of the decline of its actual political influence. The search for consensual responses in the aftermaths of Disraeli's and Gladstone's deaths can be seen as an endeavour to express the underlying solidarity of traditional parliamentary groupings in the face of newer and potentially subversive forces. In Ireland the funerals of Daniel O'Connell

[87] Ibid., 130–2; C. Geertz, *Negara: The Theatre State in Nineteenth-Century Bali* (Princeton, 1980), 116–20.

[88] Huntingdon and Metcalf, *Celebrations of Death*, 182.

[89] E. Hammerton and D. Cannadine, 'Conflict and Consensus on a Ceremonial Occasion: the Diamond Jubilee in Cambridge in 1897', *Historical Journal*, 24 (1981), 111–46.

[90] Woodward, *Theatre of Death*, 12–13, 166–70.

and Charles Stewart Parnell provided rallying points for promoting regrouping among their now leaderless supporters.

Nevertheless the further development of such lines of argument would quickly become heavily dependent on circumstantial and somewhat tendentious interpretations. The balance of the evidence weights conclusions much more towards an impression of widespread genuine consensus on most of the occasions discussed. Such consensus, however, might reflect a diversity of inward views and attitudes, and sometimes, as in Cambridge at the time of the Diamond Jubilee, it was the outcome of prior resolution of conflict. Three considerations are of particular importance in supporting this interpretation.

First, the detail adduced of the organization of funerals and commemoration is redolent much more of improvisation than of any considered strategy.[91] With the sole exception of the Duke of Wellington's funeral, the time allowed for planning and the making of arrangements was very short in comparison with the funerals of the early seventeenth century. There was accordingly little or no leisure for the development of conscious political strategies. Moreover any monolithic view of the state as a force in the organization of funerals breaks down in face of an awareness of the wide range of agencies and individuals involved in the formulation and implementation of policy. Those directly responsible were more usually preoccupied with personal and sectional corporate status than with national institutions as a whole. In the face of such potential for confusion, if not chaos, the actual emergence of successful and well-supported ceremonial was indicative of substantial underlying consensus. It was true that in the latter part of the period more coherent forms of organization began to develop, under the leadership notably of Sir Edward Hamilton, Lord Esher and the Duke of Norfolk, but the ethos was an administrative rather than political one. Until Lord Curzon took charge of the arrangements for the interment of the Unknown Warrior in 1920, no senior statesman felt a need to invest detailed personal effort in the planning of a funeral, however eminent the deceased personage might be.

Second, the funerals themselves were part of a much wider range of responses to prominent deaths, most of which owed little to specific official

---

[91] The process was reminiscent of that described by Ralph Giesey in relation to Renaissance France: 'Time and again . . . I have emerged with the conviction that some crucial innovation in the ceremonial first occurred quite haphazardly, although a contemporary chronicler may have tried to give it some plausible explanation *ex post facto*, and later generations when reenacting it embellished it with clear-cut symbolism' (*The Royal Funeral Ceremony in Renaissance France* (Geneva, 1960), Preface). The process whereby naval ratings pulled the gun-carriage in an emergency in 1901, but by design in 1910, is a striking and by no means unique example.

action at the centre, and some of which reflected spontaneous movements of popular sentiment. Civic bodies held special meetings and processions, countless organizations passed resolutions of sympathy, congregations assembled to hear funeral sermons and express solidarity. Crowds gathered in public places, and the near universal adoption of mourning clothes or emblems was illustrative of a sense of general participation. Such sentiment extended to Scotland and Wales, and even, albeit in more limited measure, to Ireland. Motivations were undoubtedly mixed: statutory and voluntary bodies took the opportunity to assert their own status; social convention and a sense of 'respectability' influenced individuals. Nevertheless the breadth and depth of such manifestations defy any explanation other than the obvious and simple one, namely that very large numbers of people were deeply moved by a sense of loss, and felt the need to express that sentiment in visible and collective forms. Popular responses to Prince Albert's death owed little or nothing to the private funeral ceremonial. The case of Livingstone shows that, on this occasion at least, indications of popular feeling put the government under irresistible pressure to support a funeral from which it had initially attempted to distance itself. Although on other occasions official agents of the state were somewhat more pro-active, they seldom, if ever, manifested a degree of energy sufficient to suggest a capability of stimulating sentiment that did not already exist.

Finally, the rarity and marginalization of explicit dissent must be reiterated. Despite the relatively recent experience of the rather less than fully consensual funerals of the Duke of York in 1827, George IV in 1830 and William IV in 1837, critical sentiments were already unusual by 1852. In 1881 the parliamentary opponents of the Disraeli memorial were made to appear not merely factional, but indecent in their perceived lack of reverence for the dead. In 1892, the miners' leaders who refused to pass a resolution of condolence with the royal family were not only denounced by the conservative press but also disowned by some of their own supporters.[92] In 1910 even Irish nationalists were made to feel very uncomfortable in placing themselves outside the consensus. The universal sense of awe inspired by death pushed the boundaries of social and cultural cohesion to their limits: any differences over modes of commemoration that might be apparent on more joyful occasions were now liable to be suppressed, except in the most extreme circumstances. In this respect the British case differs significantly from the French one, in which the commemoration of promi-nent deaths was much more liable to reflect the sectional sense of community of particular political groupings rather than the coherence of the nation as a whole. Even the relatively broadly-based funeral of Victor Hugo in 1885 was designed to consolidate the republican centre against both the

---

[92] *Yorkshire Post*, 16, 19 Jan. 1892.

right and the extreme left.[93] It was true that the alternative potentialities of deaths and funerals as triggers for the expression of dissent and conflict in Britain were apparent in the aftermath of Queen Caroline's death in 1821. In Ireland too the impact of the deaths of both O'Connell and Parnell were important in the development of nationalism, a pattern that was to be repeated in more extreme form after the execution of the leaders of the Easter Rising of 1916. Nevertheless such sequences of events were exceptional and their very rarity serves to point up the strength and significance of the dominant state of mind.

Communal and ritual observance of prominent deaths had a demonstrably religious dimension, not only in a functionalist Durkheimian sense, but also in a more specifically institutional and cognitive fashion. Sermons and religious publications constituted a substantial proportion of the public discourse that appeared on such occasions. Although in the later part of the period the influence of sermons declined somewhat relative to the press and to biographies and other forms of memorial tributes, they were still by no means wholly eclipsed. Moreover newspapers themselves continued extensively to report sermons. Even superficially secular publications, notably poems, often showed a strong religious reference. Organized religious observance was a central feature both of the funerals themselves and of the local commemorations through which individuals could express their participation in the larger whole. Both in 1852 and again from the 1880s onwards, secular and military ceremonial was also prominent, but through the re-invention of the public lying-in-state in 1898 and 1910 a form of observance was established that effectively blended the Christian and the national. Under the leadership of men such as A. P. Stanley and Randall Davidson, the Church of England showed that declining constitutional and political privilege was no bar to ceremonial prominence at times of national mourning, while their example was emulated by numerous provincial clergy. Here, more than among secular politicians, one can detect an implicit and sometimes explicit agenda for the use of mourning rituals to sustain institutional prestige. Meanwhile, the Church of Scotland, Nonconformists, Jews, and eventually Roman Catholics came to favour participation rather than abstention. For its part, the state in general, and the monarchy in particular, positively welcomed and encouraged the involvement of organized religion, partly from genuine sympathy, partly from an awareness of the added legitimacy and dignity that ceremonial thereby obtained. The sacral associations of monarchy heightened the religious tone of mourning as did the personal piety of figures such as

---

[93] A. Ben-Amos, 'Les funérailles de Victor-Hugo' in Pierre Nora (ed.), *Les lieux de mémoire* (Paris?, 1997), 426. For wider discussion of French state funerals, which emphasizes their generally factional rather than consensual character, see id., 'Molding the National Memory'.

Livingstone, Gordon, Gladstone and Queen Victoria. Nevertheless in various ways the church showed itself able to sacralize such seemingly unpromising material as Dickens, Disraeli, Darwin, Edward VII, and the Unknown Warrior.

Such evidence of the religiosity of public grief needs to be assessed in the context of the evidence that, in Hugh McLeod's phrase, a 'religious crisis' occurred in the decades preceding the First World War. According to McLeod, the elements of this 'crisis' included declining attendances, the advance of agnosticism or at least unorthodoxy, the rise of alternative leisure activities, the decline of paternalist social structures, and the marginalization of the social and cultural contribution of the churches.[94] There was also a trend, explored particularly by Simon Green in his study of West Yorkshire,[95] towards associational rather than experiential models of religious commitment, which made the churches very vulnerable to institutional failings. In 1900 an incumbent in Middlesbrough listed among hindrances to his ministry the 'rapid spread of cheap easy going sentimental religion void of true repentance and full of P[leasant] S[unday] A[fternoon]s and entertainments'.[96] As this quotation suggests, however, the difficulty facing organized religion lay not in outright hostility but rather in lukewarm commitments that merged into indifference. Such popular attitudes were entirely consistent with a readiness to revert to religious participation on occasions of collective mourning as a response to the insecurity stirred by awareness of death and change, and an impulse to express solidarity on a national and communal occasion. Arguably, such occasional observance even became more widespread as core commitments declined and irregular churchgoers could become more confident that the sermons they would hear on such occasions would be sources of comfort rather than disconcerting calls to repentance. This book provides important confirmation and extension to other evidence of the very large penumbra of affinity and sympathy that surrounded the active minority of regular churchgoers.[97] It is evident, moreover, that the patriotic element in such associations worked particularly to the advantage of the Church of England and the Church of Scotland, which were best placed to serve as vehicles for national and imperial sentiment. In the early twentieth century, the Established Churches suffered less numerical decline than the Nonconformists did.

Accordingly approaches such as Pat Jalland's, which emphasize the

---

[94] McLeod, *Religion and Society*, 169–220.

[95] S. J. D. Green, *Religion in the Age of Decline: Organization and Experience in Industrial Yorkshire, 1870–1920* (Cambridge, 1996).

[96] Borthwick Institute of Historical Research, York, 1900 Archbishop's Visitation Returns, B.Bp.Vis. 1900/249.

[97] Cf. J. Cox, *The English Churches in a Secular Society: Lambeth, 1870–1930* (1982), 90–128.

implications for responses to death of declining Christian conviction in the late nineteenth and early twentieth centuries, need to be balanced by an awareness that the relationship between death and religion was dynamic and two-way.[98] As Alan Gilbert points out, 'the fact of death remains the great, inescapable reminder of human powerlessness and insecurity'. Accordingly, he argues, 'while all people continue to die, some people will continue to be religious'.[99] The assertion is open to some debate at a theoretical level, but as an empirical historical observation relating to the persistence of widespread residual religious belief in twentieth-century Britain it carries conviction. It is consistent with the view advanced by Douglas Davies, noted in the early pages of this book, that collective responses to death can inspire social and spiritual regeneration.[100] In earlier periods too, scholars have observed a dynamic of religious renewal associated with death, in tension with other cultural trends.[101] Even as death itself became more secular it paradoxically also served to check the process of secularization, and to stir modified forms of civil religiosity, such as the cult of the war dead, and the complex mix of sentiment, patriotism, and diffuse Christianity inspired by the passing of monarchs. Granted that in more self-consciously secular societies, such as the France of the Third Republic or in Soviet Russia,[102] such impulses were channelled into correspondingly secular civic rituals, the cultural climate in Britain was conducive to an eclectic blend of traditional and more novel religious motifs.

There are hence important implications for understanding the distinctive character of national consciousness in the United Kingdom. Linda Colley, in her analysis of the development of national identity, demonstrates the considerable extent to which between 1707 and 1837 Britishness was 'invented' and superimposed on an enduring structure of English, Scottish, Welsh, regional and local divides. A sense of common Protestantism, reinforced by successive wars with Roman Catholic states, lay at the core of this process. Further stimulus came from an awareness of common economic interests, a shared involvement in imperial expansion, and, during the reign of George III in particular, the appeal of the monarchy as a

---

[98] P. Jalland, 'Victorian death and its decline: 1850–1918', in Jupp and Gittings, *Death in England*, 248–53.

[99] A. D. Gilbert, *The Making of Post-Christian Britain: A History of the Secularization of Modern Society* (1980), 62, 137.

[100] Davies, *Death, Ritual and Belief*, 9–19, 184–98. See Chapter 1 above.

[101] J. McManners, *Death and the Enlightenment: Changing Attitudes to Death among Christians and Unbelievers in Eighteenth-Century France* (Oxford, 1981), 444–5; Rugg, 'From Reason to Regulation', 202, 215, 226–7.

[102] Davies, *Death, Ritual and Belief*, 185–6; Kselman, *Death and the Afterlife in Modern France*, 106–7.

symbol of collective identity.[103] Such factors remained very influential in the period between 1837 and 1945. Even Protestantism, albeit more problematic after the Union with Ireland in 1800 and the granting of Catholic Emancipation in 1829, was still a persistent point of focus.[104] Only in the later twentieth century, especially with the loss of Empire, was there a decisive weakening of the factors that had contributed, in Colley's phrase, to the 'forging of the nation' in the eighteenth century, and a consequent loosening of a sense of 'British' identity in favour of a resurgence of English, Scottish and Welsh consciousness.[105]

Responses to 'great deaths' were a significant part of this overall picture. The continuing importance of war in national consciousness was shown in the responses to Wellington's death, despite its occurrence in peacetime, and to Gordon's. Livingstone's apotheosis gave expression to a sense of common Protestantism. Imperial sentiment was apparent not only in reactions to Livingstone's and Gordon's deaths, but also in mourning for members of the royal family. The contention of this book is that these occurrences did not merely reflect wider trends but also contributed to their development. Above all, from 1861 onwards, the impact of royal deaths was a major factor in the resurgence of the monarchy as a pre-eminent focus for British national identity, through the cultivation of sympathy for the survivors and the expression of solidarity linked to idealized images of domesticity and public service. Queen Victoria's insistence on making mourning a way of life certainly irritated some, but increasingly its net effect was to provide many more with an enhanced sense of affinity with the monarchy. Similarly Gladstone by 1898 had acquired a quasi-royal symbolic status, and could readily be presented as the model paterfamilias, and as a statesman whose sympathies transcended distinctions of class, religion and nation. The inclusive nature of such events was very much apparent in provincial England, as in Scotland and Wales, and even in Ireland they were a perceptible counterweight to separatist nationalism. The widespread religiosity of public observance imbued it with additional legitimacy in the eyes of a population that was at least residually Christian, and reinforced the linkages of religion and national consciousness that were strongly apparent in the decades before the First World War.[106] The very decline in the cultural influence of traditional Christian dogmatic teaching

[103] Colley, Britons.
[104] J. Wolffe, The Protestant Crusade in Great Britain 1829–1860 (Oxford, 1991); J. Wolffe, 'Change and Continuity in British Anti-Catholicism', in F. Tallett and N. Atkin (eds.), Catholicism in Britain and France since 1789 (1996), 67–83.
[105] For my own survey of interactions between religion and national consciousness between the mid-nineteenth and mid-twentieth centuries see Wolffe, God and Greater Britain.
[106] Wolffe, God and Greater Britain, 225–36.

meant that civil religion of this kind could find easy and extensive acceptance.

Intense popular sentiment on such occasions only lasted for a few days or weeks, but its impact was more enduring. On the day after the Duke of Wellington's funeral *The Times* speculated that 'in the year 2000 AD, there will be a few score [elderly people] . . . who will relate what their . . . fathers told them about it'.[107] There is indeed anecdotal evidence of the long-term persistence of memories. For example, in the late 1930s a man in his nineties could still recall being taken at the age of five to see the Duke of Wellington's funeral, and told a twelve-year-old boy about the experience. By such means the oral tradition was transmitted to the very end of the twentieth century.[108] For some, such as Lord Redesdale, who described in his autobiography reactions to great deaths from the Duke of Wellington to Edward VII, they were landmarks against which to measure the passage of time.[109] Writing in the early 1960s, Geoffrey Gorer opened his study of responses to death in contemporary Britain, with the observation that 'some of the most vivid memories of my early childhood are concerned with the death of Edward the Seventh'. Gorer was just five in May 1910.[110] Memories from early childhood were likely to be shaped by adults, but such mediation in itself served to ensure that they have an enduring place in the child's consciousness. Indeed, parents often appeared concerned that their off-spring should participate actively in national mourning, precisely in order to imbue them with abiding memories.[111]

Historical analysis needs to give due weight to the impact of the exceptional as well as to that of the routine in collective human experience. The extent of the legacy of personal and shared memory in the conscious-ness of individuals and society at any given period is too readily neglected. In one sense the aftermath of the Duke of Wellington's death ended when his body was lowered into the crypt of St Paul's in the November twilight of 1852, but in another it lasted well into the twentieth century. It provided a means by which seemingly remote generations could feel a tenuous personal linkage to a heroic past. Similarly, while Queen Victoria's death seemed to break a link with the age to which she had given her name, the subsequent recollection of it could give individuals a sense of their own location in history. A feeling of shared grief and mourning could foster an

---

[107] *The Times*, 19 Nov. 1852.

[108] Letter from Mr Gordon Lavy to the author, 7 Dec. 1999.

[109] Redesdale, *Memories, passim.*

[110] G. Gorer, *Death, Grief and Mourning in Contemporary Britain* (1965), 1.

[111] See above, 45; *Yorkshire Post*, 21 May 1910. For analysis of the role of children in public mourning in the light of the response to Diana's death see J. Hockey and A. James, 'The Children's Princess' in Walter, *The Mourning for Diana*, 77–88.

illusion and even a reality of social and cultural cohesion. The mingled sentimental, martial, religious and patriotic resonances of the deaths examined in the late Victorian and Edwardian periods are very relevant to understanding the frame of mind in which the British people faced the First World War and the personal bereavements then experienced by so many. Even if such sentiments lacked the emotional and psychological depth of individual grief, they still drew great power from the extent to which they were being shared or at least acknowledged by the whole nation simultaneously. Just as biographers readily appreciate the effect of personal bereavements on their subjects, an awareness of the dynamics of collective loss should inform a rounded understanding of national histories.

# Appendix.
# The Organization of Funerals[1]

During the eighteenth century, the declining role of the College of Arms in the organization of funerals was associated with a distinction between 'private' funerals in which the heralds were no longer involved, and increasingly rare 'public' or 'state' funerals.[2] The latter were normally funded by the state, and the hereditary Earl Marshal (the Duke of Norfolk) and the College of Arms had a major share of responsibility. A 'public' funeral was automatic only for deceased sovereigns, although at the time of Queen Charlotte's death in 1818 a memorandum had stated that the Earl Marshal also had responsibility for the funeral of the 'Queen [consort] or Heir apparent'.[3] The position though was confused in 1821 by the ambiguities of Queen Caroline's status and in 1849 by Queen Adelaide's preference, honoured by Queen Victoria, for a 'private' funeral. In 1861 Albert was not covered by the precedents, such as they were, relating to the spouses of male sovereigns, and there was hence no technical impediment to the decision to hold a private funeral. Accordingly not until the death of Queen Alexandra in 1925 was there again to be a 'public' funeral for a consort. No heir apparent died during the period covered by this book. The Duke of Clarence came closest to that status, but, although his funeral was relatively elaborate, it was still technically 'private' and its organization did not involve the Earl Marshal or the College of Arms. There was moreover a general ambiguity about the 'private' funerals of royalty insofar as costs were usually met from public funds.[4]

For non-royal personages, 'public' funerals were normally held to

---

[1] The purpose of this Appendix is to introduce the documents printed below by drawing together information on the organization of funerals that is otherwise scattered through the book. Authority for statements not specifically referenced here will be found in the relevant chapters.

[2] Fritz, 'From "Public" to "Private" ', 61–79.

[3] PRO, LC 2/45, fo. 5.

[4] See the numerous bills and accounts in PRO, LC 2, *passim*.

require a prior parliamentary resolution, of which the only nineteenth-century instances after 1806 were those of Wellington and Gladstone. There were though some marginal cases. Palmerston's funeral was described as 'public', although it did not meet the procedural criteria and Parliament refunded the costs only after the event. On the other hand, Livingstone's funeral, although 'privately' organized by the Royal Geographical Society [RGS], was supported by a government grant. The confusions were very much apparent in memoranda drawn by Edward Hamilton for Gladstone's benefit in 1881 when possible arrangements for Disraeli's funeral were under consideration.[5] Hamilton could only find three non-royal cases in the previous half century in which public funds had met the full costs of funerals: Wellington, Palmerston and Livingstone. Small contributions had, however, been made to costs for Lord Clyde (Sir Colin Campbell, commander-in-chief in India during the Mutiny, died 1863), the Earl of Mayo (Viceroy of India, assassinated 1872), and Sir John Burgoyne (soldier, died 1872). Canning (1827), Wilberforce (1833) and Macaulay (1859) had been buried in Westminster Abbey, but without any public grant. Public funerals were offered to Peel (1850) and Russell (1878), but declined. Gladstone's own sense of the imprecision of past practice is evident in his comment on Hamilton's memorandum: 'The general upshot is I think affirmative shd the need arise.'[6]

Arrangements for 'private' funerals, however extensive the popular interest, were, as in Disraeli's case, the responsibility of relatives and executors, with decisions on matters such as policing being made on an *ad hoc* basis. For Livingstone the RGS assumed the responsibility on behalf of the relatives. It should be noted that even 'public' funerals had their 'private' phases, such as the Hawarden portion of Gladstone's obsequies or the Isle of Wight part of Queen Victoria's. The Lord Chamberlain's Office was in theory in overall control of the 'private' funerals of royalty. A memorandum of January 1875 apparently laid down its specific duties on these occasions, but this document has not been traced.[7] In practice the arrangements were liable also to involve unofficial action by immediate royal staff such as equerries and private secretaries, and direct interventions from bereaved royalty themselves. The scope for this involvement was extended in February 1875 when the Queen countermanded the 'custom of the Remains being taken possession of by the Lord Chamberlain'. She required that no

---

[5] BL, AddMS 44189 (Gladstone Papers), fos. 84–5, 87.

[6] Ibid., note on fo. 85.

[7] It was stated in 1875 to be 'bound up at the beginning of the Funeral Book' (PRO, LC 1/293), but no such volume has been identified in the Lord Chamberlain's Office papers deposited at the Public Record Office. It is conceivable that it remains among the working papers of the Lord Chamberlain's Office, to which researchers have no access.

'official person' should 'interfere or be present when the last sad duties are performed by the Personal attendants of the deceased, unless especially called upon to do so by any written instructions to that effect'.[8]

The organization of 'public' funerals was complicated in particular by the competing jurisdictions of the Lord Chamberlain and the Earl Marshal. The then Lord Chamberlain, the Duke of Devonshire, seemed to have scored a decisive victory in relation to George II's funeral in 1760 when he 'directed the whole ceremony by authority of Council'.[9] The ascendancy of the Lord Chamberlain was still apparent in 1852 in the first extract printed below. Nevertheless, even on this occasion, the reality was that the Earl Marshal took his instructions directly from the Prime Minister and Prince Albert. The latter's active involvement as the Queen's personal representative meant that the question of which officer had overall jurisdiction could be diplomatically left unresolved. In 1898 and 1901, however, the fifteenth Duke of Norfolk successfully reasserted the claim of the Earl Marshal to lead the organization of public funerals.

The two documents reproduced below provide snapshots of a fluid and complex situation at two points in the period. Both originated in the Lord Chamberlain's Office. The first was drawn up in 1852 to inform plans for Wellington's funeral. Even in relation to the other agencies involved, the pre-eminence of the Lord Chamberlain's position was less clear-cut than is implied. The document was also less than comprehensive in its identification of responsibilities. In particular the Home Secretary, not mentioned in the document, had an acknowledged responsibility in respect of military and police arrangements. The Foreign Office also had a role with regard to representation from other countries, which was to assume much greater importance for Victoria's and Edward VII's funerals. Nevertheless the memorandum is of considerable interest in providing a contemporary survey of some of the tasks involved in the organization of a major 'public' funeral. The wide-ranging responsibilities given to the undertaker are of particular note. It graphically conveys the complexity of such occasions, the more so when the reader is aware that its tendency is towards over-simplification.

The second document, a memorandum by Sir Spencer Ponsonby-Fane, Comptroller of the Lord Chamberlain's Office, relates specifically to Gladstone's lying-in-state. It gives useful insights both into acknowledged areas of responsibility, but also into the potential for confusion, conflict, and omission in the face of overlapping and contested jurisdictions. Although these issues were satisfactorily resolved in May 1898, the substan-

---

[8] LC 1/293, Memorandum signed by Lord Hertford (copy in LC 2/97).
[9] Quoted Fritz, 'From "Public" to "Private" ', 79.

tially greater complexity of arrangements for Queen Victoria's funeral three years later was to test the structures to the limit.

It should also be noted that the realities of each occasion were different in the face of the impact of specific contingent circumstances and personalities. For example, under Lord Esher the Office of Works assumed enhanced importance, while Randall Davidson became an influential representative of general Anglican interests as distinct from the particular responsibilities of the Deans of St Paul's, Westminster and St George's.

*Document 1: Precedents of Public Funerals which may be applicable to the Funeral of the Duke of Wellington*[10]

Different Departments concerned in the Arrangements of a Public Funeral are

The Lord Chamberlain
The Earl Marshal
The Commander in Chief
The Commissioners of Works
The Dean of the Cathedral
The Commissioners of the Metropolitan Police
The Lord Mayor of London

The Lord Chamberlain has, in all instances, received The Sovereign's Commands, either Personally, or through the Secretary of State, to take upon himself the Charge of Public Funerals. He communicates with the other Departments and requests their assistance, in making the various Arrangements. His Officers have usually superintended the Removal of the Body to the Place, where it has lain in State, and, though not formally delivered to him, he may be considered to have the custody of the Body from the Lying in State to the Day of Interment. The Ceremony of the Lying in State has been altogether under the Lord Chamberlain's management, and every Order involving Expenditure proceeds from him, excepting for the Work done by the Office of Works; a more particular description of the Orders to Tradesmen is given hereafter. The Lord Chamberlain's first step is to communicate with The Earl Marshal.

The Earl Marshal who has deputed Garter King of Arms to frame the Ceremonial of the Interment for the Approval of the Sovereign. From The Earl Marshal's Office notice is sent to those, who are to form part of the Procession, and of the Ceremony of Interment, and the Special Duties to

[10] PRO, LC 2/75. The punctuation of the original has been slightly adjusted.

be performed by each are assigned to them from thence, and the whole Solemnity of the Interment is marshalled by the Officers of Arms.

The Commander in Chief, or Adjutant General, is made acquainted by The Lord Chamberlain with the Day and hour when the different parts of the Ceremony are appointed to take place, and he makes the military arrangements accordingly, for the Removal of the Body to the Lying in State, for the Ceremony of the Lying in State, and for the Interment. The arrangements when made are communicated to The Lord Chamberlain. They are framed upon Precedents preserved at the Horse Guards and sometimes in concert with the Lord Chamberlain to meet particular exigencies. That part of them relating to the attendance of the Military in the Procession more particularly relates to the Earl Marshal.

The Commissioners of Works are requested by The Lord Chamberlain to give Orders for such temporary constructions, as may be necessary to adapt the Building, selected for the Lying in State, and the Erections of Platforms, Seats for the Procession and Spectators at the Place of Interment, and all other Scaffolding and Wood work rendered necessary for the accommodation of large concourse of People present at these Ceremonies. When these works are completed the Rooms and the Cathedral are hung with black, under the superintendence of The Lord Chamberlain's Office. The Office of Works, in connexion with the Dean of the Cathedral, would also have charge of the Vault and of the Machinery for lowering the Coffin into the Vault.

The Dean of the Cathedral is made acquainted by the Lord Chamberlain with the Day of the Funeral, and the hour when the Procession may be expected to arrive. He performs the Burial Service at the Choir and at the Grave. The Choirs of the Chapel Royal St. James and Westminster Abbey have been placed in communication with the Dean to render the singing more effective. Frequent communications take place between The Dean, The Lord Chamberlain, and Garter, as to the Position and Space required for the Procession during the different parts of the Service, and respecting the appropriation of the Seats.

The Commissioners of Metropolitan Police are acquainted by The Lord Chamberlain from time to time with the arrangements with reference to an effective supply of Police Constables.

The Lord Mayor of London gives Orders for the Attendance of the Police within the City of London and makes the regulations for the ordering of carriages and keeping the Streets free within the City.

*The Lord Chamberlain's Orders to Tradesmen*    The Lord Chamberlain gives every Order involving Expenditure except for work executed by the Office of Works, and the Account is made up at his office, and finally transmitted to the Treasury for Audit. The following comprise the greater part of the Orders given—

The Undertaker Provides the Coffins, Palls, and the 2 Canopies, one of which is suspended over the Coffin during the Lying in State, and the other attached to the Funeral Car during the Procession. He fits up the Rooms appointed for the Lying in State, hanging with Black Cloth and Flannel the Walls, Ceilings, Barriers and Passages, and covering the Floors with Baize. He provides the Sconces and Candlesticks for the Lying in State, and attends to the lighting up of the Rooms, and, under the superintendence of the College of Arms, fixes up the Eschucheons [*sic*] of Arms on the Pall and Canopy, and round the Rooms, and otherwise makes preparations for the viewing of the Lying in State by the Public.

He provides the Hearse, the Bearers, and Mourning Coaches for the Attendants employed in removing the Body from where it lies to the Rooms selected for the State, attends to the Fittings of the Attendants upon that occasion, and inspects the Route by which the Body is to be conveyed— if by Special Train he would place himself in communication with the Railway Authorities respecting the details of the conveyance. He fits up with Velvet Hangings the Funeral Car which conveys the Body to the Place of Interment and in the case of Lord Nelson's Funeral the Undertaker constructed the Car altogether, according to an artist's design, at an expense of nearly £700. He fits up the Place of Interment with Mourning Hangings to the Choir, and covers all the Seats, Barriers, Platforms, etc., erected by the Office of Works. He provides all the Mourning Coaches, Horses and Attendants for those forming part in the Procession who do not go in their own carriages, (at Lord Nelson's Funeral there were 31 Mourning Coaches so employed), and it is his business to make up either from his own or from the Office Materials, the whole of the Scarfs, Hatbands, and Gloves, provided to those forming the Procession, the Clergy, etc., and to deliver them according to Lists furnished from the Lord Chamberlain's Office in concert with Garter. He also fits with Crape the Uniforms, Sword Knots etc. of those in the Procession who wear Military or Navy Uniforms, on production of Tickets for attending the Procession signed by Garter.

Besides the above work he would be instructed to fit with Mourning Hangings any Churches or Chapels which it may be thought right to place in Mourning from having been attended by the Deceased.

[There then follow statements of the responsibilities of other tradesmen, the joiner, the wax chandler, the herald painter, the silk mercer, the woollen draper, the military accoutrement makers, the tailor, the king's printer, and the engraver.]

## Document 2: Memorandum by Sir Spencer Ponsonby-Fane, 13 June 1898[11]

The Duke of Norfolk called on me on the 22nd May and told me that Mr Gladstone's Family had accepted a Public Funeral, and that Lord Salisbury had desired him to carry it out, but that he had been informed at Heralds College that the Lord Chamberlain under such circumstances should take possession of the Body, and give the necessary instructions for 'lying in State, &c'. He was unable to give me any definite information as to what the 'lying in State' was to be, but said that the Office of Works had undertaken the full responsibility of carrying it out in Westminster Hall. I told the Duke that if the precedent to be followed was that of Mr. Pitt or the Duke of Wellington, the Lord Chamberlain was clearly responsible for the 'taking possession of the Body &c', and was perfectly ready to do so, but that if the more recent case of Lord Palmerston, in which there had been no lying-in-State, were to be followed, this would not be so. The Duke's instructions on these points were very vague, the only precise instructions being, that the Ceremony, whatever was finally decided about it, was to be carried out on the 28th Instant. After considering the matter it appeared to us that the only function of the Lord Chamberlain would be to instruct Banting [the undertaker] to bring up the Body from Hawarden, after placing it in the Coffin, and land it in Westminster Hall, and that under these circumstances His Lordship's intervention might perhaps rather hamper than help the speedy carrying out the work, and that it would be better to leave the whole matter in the hands of the Duke. It is clear that no precedent should be quoted from this incident.

[11] CA, Gladstone's Funeral.

# Bibliography

Arrangement
A. Manuscript and Archive Sources
B. Newspapers and Contemporary Periodicals
C. Sermons
D. Other Printed Primary Sources
E  Secondary Sources
The place of publication in sections C, D, and E is London unless otherwise stated. Anonymous publications are listed in chronological order at the beginning of the appropriate section.

## A. Manuscript and Archive Sources

Arundel Castle, Sussex
   Earl Marshal's Papers (15$^{th}$ Duke of Norfolk).

Bodleian Library, Oxford
   Asquith Papers.
   Disraeli (Hughenden) Papers.
   Lewis Harcourt Papers.
   John Rashdall Diary.

British Film Archive, London
   Films of the funerals of Gladstone, Queen Victoria and King Edward VII.

Borthwick Institute of Historical Research, York
   Archbishop's Visitation Returns, 1900.

British Library, London
   Balfour Papers.
   Boyd Carpenter Papers.
   Gladstone Papers.
   Address to Miss Gordon (1885).
   Hamilton Papers.
   Iddesleigh Papers.
   Liverpool Papers.

Facsimile of memorandum by Sir Herbert Taylor on the death of the Duke of York (1827).

College of Arms Archives, London
Correspondence and papers relating to the funerals of King William IV, the Duke of Wellington, Gladstone, Queen Victoria and King Edward VII. (These collections are cited in the text by their substantive volume titles, although the enumeration of a hand-written listing is also given in parenthesis at first citation.)

Devon Record Office, Exeter
Exeter Chamber/Council Minutes.

Dublin City Hall
Dublin Council Minutes.

Edinburgh District Council Archives
Edinburgh Council Minutes.

Glamorgan Archive Service/Cardiff Central Library
Cardiff Council Minutes.

Lambeth Palace Library, London
Bell Papers.
Davidson Papers.
Fisher Papers.
Lang Papers.
Ramsey Papers.
Tait Papers.
Frederick Temple Papers.

Leeds City Archives
Council Minutes.
File Case 32.
Town Hall Committee Minutes.

Liverpool Record Office
Derby Papers (14th and 15th Earls).

National Library of Australia, Canberra
Queen Victoria and King Edward VII In Memoriam folders.

National Library of Scotland, Edinburgh
Photocopies of material relating to David Livingstone.
Minto Papers (4th Earl).

New College, Edinburgh
Chalmers Papers.

Public Record Office, Kew
  Cabinet Office (CAB 23, CAB 27).
  Home Office (HO 45, HO 57, HO 129).
  Lord Chamberlain's Office up to 1901 (LC 1, LC 2).
  Metropolitan Police (MEPO 2, MEPO 5).
  Russell Papers (PRO 30).
  Office of Works (WORKS 21).

Royal Archives, Windsor Castle
  Papers of Queen Victoria, Prince Albert and King George V.
  Lord Chamberlain's Office from 1901.
  (Edward VII's papers do not survive).

St Deiniol's Library, Hawarden, Flintshire
  Glynne-Gladstone MSS.

St George's Chapel Archives, Windsor Castle
  Correspondence and papers relating to royal funerals and interments.

St Paul's Cathedral Library, London
  Chapter Minutes (including memoranda on the Duke of Wellington's funeral).
  Newbolt Scrapbooks.

Trinity College Library, Dublin
  Correspondence relating to the Grattan Statue.
  Irish Ballads Collection.

Westminster Abbey Muniments, London
  Certificate by Sir William Ferguson relating to Livingstone's body (1874).
  Dean Stanley's Recollections.
  Correspondence and papers relating to the interment of the Unknown Warrior
  (1920).
  Service sheets.

## B. Newspapers and Contemporary Periodicals

*Annual Register*
*Baptist Magazine*
*British Quarterly Review*
*Cardiff and Merthyr Guardian*
*Cardiff Times*
*Congregationalist*
*Daily News*
*Daily Telegraph*
*East London Observer*
*Exeter Flying Post*

*Exeter and Plymouth Gazette*
*Express and Echo*
*Free Church Magazine*
*Freeman's Journal*
*Go Forward: YWCA Monthly Journal for Secretaries and Workers*
*Glasgow Herald*
*Hansard*
*Illustrated London News*
*Inverness Courier*
*Irish Times*
*Lancet*
*Leeds Intelligencer*
*Leeds Mercury*
*Lloyds Weekly Newspaper*
*Morning Post*
*Mothers in Council*
*Mothers' Union Journal*
*New York Observer*
*North British Daily Mail*
*Observer*
*Proceedings of the Royal Geographical Society*
*Punch*
*Radio Times*
*Record*
*Reynolds Newspaper*
*Scotsman*
*Sheffield Telegraph*
*South Wales Daily News*
*Spectator*
*Star*
*Star of Freedom*
*Sun*
*Sunday Times*
*Tablet*
*The Times*
*Wesleyan Methodist Magazine*
*Western Mail*
*Western Times*
*Witness*
*Women*
*Yorkshire Post* (formerly *Leeds Intelligencer*)

## C. Sermons

*A Sermon Preached on the Sunday After the Funeral of the Rt Hon Lord Viscount Nelson* (1806).
*Christus Consolator* (1892).
*'He that Comforteth': A Plain Sermon on the Death of HRH the Duke of Clarence* (1892).
*The Light of Life Eternal* (1901).
*The Long Home* (1910).
Adler, H. N., *The Nation's Lament* (1892).
Allen, J. T., *A Sermon Preached in the Parochial Chapel of Clitheroe . . . On Occasion of the . . . Death of HRH Prince Frederick Duke of York and Albany* (1827).
Atkinson, J. A., *Lessons From the Life of the Earl of Beaconsfield, KG* (Manchester, 1881).
—— *In Memoriam Victoria and Albert* (1901).
Aveling, T. W., *Princely Greatness Yielding unto Death* (1861).
Baines, J., *Honorable Sepulture the Christian's Due* (1852).
Baker, F., *An Address Delivered to the Children of the Sunday School, Bank Street, Bolton, on the Death of a Sunday Scholar* (Bolton, 1826).
Barnett, H. N., *The Victor Vanquished* (1852).
Bedford, J., *Britain's Loss and Lesson* (Stockport, 1852).
Bentley, J., *A Sermon Preached on . . . Occasion of the Death of Lord Beaconsfield* (1881).
Berry, C., *A Sermon on the Death of Caroline, Queen of England* (1821).
Biddulph, T. T., *National Affliction Improved* (Bristol, 1820).
Bingham, R., *The Duty of Watchfulness Enjoined on the Church Collectively, and On Individuals Particularly . . .* (1836).
Blenkinsopp, R. G. L., *Britain's Loss and Britain's Duty* (1862).
Blomfield, C. J., *The Mourning of Israel* (1852).
Boutell, C., *The Hero and His Example* (1852).
Bowerbank, T. F., *A Sermon Preached in the Parish Church of Chiswick* (Chiswick, 1817).
Bowers, J. P. A., *The Secret of a Great Life* (1904).
Bowhay, J. H., *A Pulpit Tribute to the Memory of . . . the Duke of Wellington* (1852).
Brady, N., *A Sermon Upon Occasion of the Death of Our Late Sovereign King William; and Her Present Majesty's Happy Accession to the Crown* (1702).
Bradley, R., *Britain in Sorrow for the Loss of A Prince and a Great Man* (Manchester, 1827).
Brooke, S. A., *A Memorial Sermon on the Funeral of the Queen* (1901).
Brooks, J. W., *The Rod of the Almighty* (Nottingham? 1861).
Brownlow, W., *A Sermon Occasioned by the Death of . . . the Duke of Wellington* (Manchester, 1852).
Butler, H. M., *An Address Delivered in Great St Mary's Church, Cambridge . . . at the Hour of the Interment . . . of the Right Hon William Ewart Gladstone* (Cambridge, 1898).
—— *For Kings and All that are in High Places* (1910).
Carmichael, F. F., *Honour the King* (Dublin, 1892).

Carpenter, W. B., *The Hidden Life* (1899).

Carr, J. H., *If He Sleep He Shall Do Well* (Edinburgh, 1861).

Carter, J., *Reflections on the Death of HRH Prince Albert* (Sydney, 1862).

Cecil, R., *The Pageant is Over* (1852).

Chalmers, T., *A Sermon Delivered in the Tron Church, Glasgow, on Wednesday November 19 1817, the Day of the Funeral of HRH the Princess Charlotte of Wales* (Glasgow, 1817).

Clayton, J., *A Discourse on the Death of Her Late Majesty the Queen* (1821).

Close, F., *National Obsequies Sanctioned by Holy Writ* (1852).

Collyer, W. B., *The Royal Preacher* (1818).

Conway, W., *The Victory Over Death* (1865).

Croly, G., *A Sermon on the Death of the Duke of Wellington* (1852).

Crowther, S., *A Sermon Occasioned by the Lamented Death of His Majesty King George the Third* (1820).

Cumming, J. *The Lord Taketh Away* (1852).

—— *From Life to Life* (1861).

Cunningham, J. W., *A Sermon Preached . . . on the Death . . . of George the Third* (1820).

Dakeyne, J. E., *Virtutis Fortuna Comes* (Wolverhampton, 1852).

D'Arblay, A. C. L., *The Vanity of All Earthly Greatness* (1830).

—— *The Path of the Just* (1833).

Davidson, R. T., *From Strength to Strength* (1910).

Dibdin, R. W., *The Patriot Palmerston: Was He Saved?* (1865).

Dibdin, T. F., *The Patriot King* (1837).

Evans, J., *A Sermon Preached at the Independent Chapel, Malmesbury . . . Occasioned by the Death of . . . Queen Caroline* (1821).

Falloon, W. M., *A Prince and a Great Man Fallen* (Liverpool, 1861).

Fleming, J., *The Death of a Patriot* (1887).

—— *Napier and Gordon* (1890).

Fletcher, A., *A Sermon on the Death of Her Late Majesty Queen Caroline* (1821).

Flower, W. B., *An Extract from a Sermon on the Death of HRH the Late Prince Consort* (1862).

Fox, W. J., *A Funeral Sermon for Caroline Queen of England* (1821).

Gardiner, J., *A Tribute to the Memory of Lord Nelson* (Bath, 1805).

Garnett, C., *Mr Gladstone: Scholar, Statesman, Saint* (Manchester, 1898).

Gilbart, T., *Britain's Song* (Dublin, 1820).

Goldstein, J. A., *A Sermon on the Occasion of a Memorial Service Held in Memory of Her Late Most Gracious Majesty Queen Victoria* (1901).

Good, J. E., *Britannia's Tears at the Decease of Her Sovereign* (Gosport, 1837).

Gretton, F. E., *Barzillai: The Very Aged, the Very Great Man* (1852).

Hall, R., *A Sermon Occasioned by the Death of Her Late Royal Highness the Princess Charlotte of Wales* (Leicester, 1818).

Harper, A., *In Memoriam Her Gracious Majesty Queen Victoria* (Sydney, 1901).

Harrison, J., *A Queen Indeed* (1901).

Hatchard, J. A., *Romanism Overthrown by Wellington* (1852).

Hawtrey, C. S., *A Funeral Sermon on the Death of . . . the Princess Charlotte Augusta* (1817).

Heathcote, C. J., *A Sermon Preached on the Sunday After the Funeral of the Duke of Wellington* (Hackney, 1852).

Hedgeland, P., *National Grief and Some of its Uses* (Penzance, 1861).

Henson, H. H., *A Sermon Preached in Westminster Abbey on the Occasion of the Death of Queen Victoria* (1901).

Hitchens, H., *On the Death of General Gordon* (1885).

Holland, W. B., *A Sermon Preached in the Parish Church of Walmer of September 19th 1852* (1852).

Hood, P., *Words from the Pall of the Prince* (1862).

Howarth, H., *On Human Greatness* (1852).

Hugo, T., *The Voice of the Dead* (1852).

Jackson, H. L., *Two Pages in a Nation's History: AD901–AD1901* (Huntingdon, NSW, 1901).

James, W. B., *National Blessings a Ground for National Gratitude and Obedience* (1830).

Jeffreys, J., *Princes and Great Men* (1862).

Kingsley, C., *A Sermon on the Death of HRH the Prince Consort* (1862).

Lane, E., *Hope for Africa; or a Memorial to Dr Livingstone* (1874).

MacEwan, A. R., *The Distress of Nations* (Glasgow, 1892).

MacLean, A. M., *Queen Victoria and Her Time* (Edinburgh, 1901).

Mardon, B., *The Evanescence of Human Glory* (1837).

Maude, F. H., *The Mighty Man of Valour* (Ipswich, 1852).

Mellor, E., *Be Still and Know that I am God* (Liverpool, 1861).

Meyer, S., *A Funeral Sermon on the Death of His Late Majesty George IV* (1830).

Miller, E., *The Battle-Axe of God* (Chichester, 1852).

Milroy, A. W., *In Memoriam* (Cowes, 1892).

Morison, J., *Patriotic Regrets for the Loss of a Good King* (1820).

Oakley, J., *The Mid-Lent Gospel* (Manchester, 1889).

Pollock, B., *Fellowship with the Deceased* (1911).

Purey-Cust, A. P., *God's Ordering, our Sufficiency* (York, 1892).

Reade, R., *The Conqueror's Rest* (1852).

Rodgers, R. R., *Queen Victoria* (Birmingham, 1901).

St Leger, W. N., *The World Passeth Away* (1852).

Sandford, C. W., *The Queen and Mother of Her People* (Oxford, 1901).

Spence, H. D. M., *England's Demonstration of Sympathy and Loyalty* (1892, privately printed, RA, VIC/Z98/23).

Saunders, S., *A Sermon Occasioned by the Death of the Rt Hon William Huskisson* (Liverpool, 1830).

Sherlock, W., *A Sermon Preached at the Temple Church December 30 1694 upon the Sad Occasion of the Death of Our Gracious Queen* (1694).

Shore, T. T., *General Gordon* (1891).

Sinclair, W. M., *Gordon and England* (1885).

Sprague, W. B., *A Discourse Commemorative of the Rev Thomas Chalmers* (Edinburgh, 1847).

Stanley, A. P., *Sermon Preached . . . in Westminster Abbey, June 19 1870 . . . being the Sunday following the Funeral of Charles Dickens* (1870).

—— *Sermons on Special Occasions* (1882).

Stern, J. F., *The Queen* (1901).

Stinton, B., *A Discourse of Divine Providence: Occasion'd by the Demise of Her Late Majesty Queen Anne, and the Happy Accession of Our Present Sovereign King George* (1714).

Stovel, C., *National Bereavement Improved* (1837).

Sturges, T. R. H., *Queen Victoria the Good* (1901).

Styles, J., *A Tribute to the Memory of Nelson* (Newport, IOW, 1806).

Thornton, T., *Religion in Humble Life: A Sermon on the Death of Betty Adamson, a Weaver* (1863).

Tucker, H. F., *A Tribute to the Memory of General Gordon* (Melbourne, 1885).

Van Mildert, W., *A Sermon Preached . . . on the Assassination of the Rt Hon Spencer Perceval* (1812).

Vaughan, C. J., *The Mourning of the Land, and the Mourning of the Families* (Cambridge, 1861).

—— *I Dwell Among Mine Own People* (1889).

—— *The Sympathy of Jesus Christ with Sickness and Sorrow* (1892).

Watts, I., *The Religious Improvement of Publick Events* (1727).

Wilmot-Buxton, H. J., *Full of Days and Honour* (1901).

Wilson, D., *Death the Last Enemy of Man* (1827).

Winnington-Ingram, A. F., *The After-Glow of a Great Reign* (1901).

Wirgman, A. T., *Queen Victoria of Blessed Memory: A Voice from Her People Over the Seas* (1901).

## D. Other Printed Primary Sources

*Britannia's Tears: A Satyrical Dirge by Way of Lamentation on the Deplorable Death of Her Late Gracious Majesty Queen Anne . . . and as a Chastisement to all Her Merry Mourners* (Dublin, 1714).

*The Order of the Procession at the Funeral of His Grace John Duke of Marlborough* (1722).

*Verses on the Death of Her Late Most Excellent Majesty Queen Caroline* (1738).

*Neil's Pocket Melodist, or, Vocal Repository*, No. XXII (c. 1806).

*An Official and Circumstantial Detail of the Grand National Obsequies at the Public Funeral of Britain's Darling Hero, the Immortal Nelson* (1806?).

*The Order to be Observed in the Publick Funeral Procession of the Late Vice-Admiral Horatio Lord Nelson* (1806).

*Services and Anthems to be Used upon Thursday the 9th Day of January 1806, Being the Day Appointed for the Public Funeral of the Late Lord Viscount Nelson* (1806).

*Order to be Observed in the Publick Funeral Procession of the Late Right Honourable William Pitt* (1806).

*The Virtuous Life and Lamented Death of HRH the Princess Charlotte, Including Every Interesting Particular Relative to Her Accouchement and Death!* (1817?).

*Authentic Memoirs of Our Late Venerable and Beloved Monarch, George the Third*, by 'Robert Southy' (1820).

*Radicals and True Patriots Compared; or Living Evidences from New York of Paine's Character and Last Hours Contrasted with those of the Patriotic Duke of Kent and the Late Great and Good King George III* (1820).

*An Authentic and Impartial Account of the Funeral Procession of Her Late Most Gracious Majesty Queen Caroline* (1821?).

*Ceremonial for the Interment of His Late Most Sacred Majesty King George the Fourth* (1830).

*The Last Moments of Our Late Beloved Sovereign George IV* (1830?).

*Funeral of Dr Chalmers, in a Letter to a Friend by an Englishman* (1847).

*Programme of Arrangements for the Funeral of the Rev Dr Chalmers* (Edinburgh, 1847).

*Funeral of the Late Field Marshal Arthur Duke of Wellington* (Directions by Metropolitan Police Office, 1852, BL, Tab.597.a.1(1)).

*The Wellington News* (1852).

*Ceremonial . . . Monday, December 23rd, 1861* (BL).

*Services Held in Windsor Castle on the Anniversary of the Lamented Death of the Prince Consort, December 14 1862*.

*Service in the Royal Mausoleum at Frogmore on 18th December 1862*.

*The Memorial Window in St George's Chapel, Windsor Castle*, by one of the Chapter (Eton, 1863).

*David Livingstone: A Missionary Poem: In Memoriam* by W. J. H. Y. (1874).

*The Last Years of Livingstone* (Toronto, 1874).

*O'Connell Centenary Record* (Dublin, 1878).

*A Tribute to the Memory of HRH the Late Princess Alice* (BL, 1871.e.2 (13)).

*Gordon: A Life of Faith and Duty*, by W. J. G. (1885).

*The Hero Sacrificed: Stray Cuttings from the Portfolio of an Old Soldier*, by O. S. (1885).

*In Memoriam: Epitaphs on C. G. Gordon* (1885).

*Who is the White Pasha? A Story of Coming Victory* (1889).

*At Rest* (1901, BL, 10804 f. 19).

*Burial of the Dead: St George's Chapel, Windsor Castle, 2 February 1901*.

*The Proclamation of King Edward VII: An Account of the Ceremony at Ipswich on the XXV January MDCCCCI*.

*The Queen's Best Monument: A Memorial Report from the Spectator* (1901).

*The Reign of Women Under Queen Victoria: The Argosy Memorial Number* (1901).

*Special Forms of Service in Commemoration of Her Late Majesty Queen Victoria* (1901).

*Victoria the Queen: An Account of the Service at St James's Church, Chicago Saturday February 2 1901* (Chicago, 1901).

*Official Programme and Illustrated Souvenir of the Unveiling of the Queen Victoria Memorial Statue* (Leeds, 1905).

*In Memoriam Edward VII King and Emperor* (1910?).

*The Order of Service for the Burial of His Majesty King Edward VII* (1910).

*Punjab In Memoriam: Death of His Majesty King Edward VII, Emperor of India* (Simla, 1910).

*St Bartholomew's Church, Brighton: On the Occasion of the Funeral of His Late Most Gracious Majesty Edward VII, May 20th 1910, Solemn Requiem at 11.*

*Special Forms of Service in Commemoration of His Late Majesty King Edward VII* (1910).

*Sunday School Union: Form of Memorial Service, May 22nd 1910.*

*Souvenir of the Unveiling of the Parnell Monument* (Dublin, 1911).

*George V Commemoration Book of Verse* (1936?).

*The Life of King George VI as Recorded in the Pages of 'The Times'* (1952).

Archer, T., *'The Duke' A Sketch* (1852).

Argyll, 8th Duke of, *Autobiography and Memoirs*, 2 vols. (1906).

Bahlman, D. W. R. (ed.), *The Diary of Sir Edward Walter Hamilton 1880–1885*, 2 vols. (Oxford, 1972).

—— (ed.), *The Diary of Sir Edward Walter Hamilton 1885–1906* (Hull, 1993).

Bell, G. K. A., *Randall Davidson Archbishop of Canterbury*, 2 vols. (1935).

Benson, A. C. and Esher, Viscount (eds.), *The Letters of Queen Victoria 1837–1861*, 3 vols. (1907).

Besant, A., *Gordon Judged Out of His Own Mouth* (1885).

Binyon, L., *Collected Poems*, 2 vols. (1931).

Brett, M. V. (ed.), *Journals and Letters of Reginald Viscount Esher* 4 vols. (1934).

Branks, W., *Heaven Our Home* (Edinburgh, 1861).

—— *Meet for Heaven* (Edinburgh, 1862).

—— *Life in Heaven* (Edinburgh, 1863).

Brewster, P., *Wellington 'Weighed in the Balance' or War a Crime, Self-Defence a Duty* (Paisley, 1853).

Bufalo della Valle, Emilia Marchesa del, *In Memory of Prince Albert Victor Edward* (Rome, 1892).

Bullock, C., *Ich Dien: I Serve: Prince Edward: A Memory* (1892?).

Butler, W., *Charles George Gordon* (1889).

Campbell, A. E., *Livingstone* (1875).

Charles, E., *Three Martyrs of the Nineteenth Century: Studies from the Lives of Livingstone, Gordon and Patteson* (1885).

Coe, C. C., *General Gordon in a New Light: The Cause of War, and the Advocate of Peace* (Bolton, 1885).

Cook, E., *The Life of Florence Nightingale*, 2 vols. (1913).

Cooper, T., *The Life of Thomas Cooper Written by Himself* (1872).

Corelli, M., *The Passing of the Great Queen* (1901).

Coxe, W., *Memoirs of the Duke of Marlborough*, 3 vols. (1896).

Cuming, A. B., *In Memoriam the Earl of Beaconsfield* (1881).

Cumming, J., *Wellington: A Lecture* (1853).

Dasent, A. I., *John Thadeus Delane Editor of 'The Times'*, 2 vols. (1908).

Donisthorpe, G. T., *An Account of the Origin and Progress of the Devon and Exeter Albert Memorial Museum* (Exeter, 1868).

Edgecumbe, R. (ed.), *The Diary of Lady Frances Shelley 1818–1873*, 2 vols. (1913).

Farningham, M., *A Working Woman's Life: An Autobiography* (n.d.).

Eliot, P., Letters to his mother relating to the funeral of the Duke of Clarence, in *Report of the Society of the Friends of St George's and the Descendants of the Knights of the Garter*, 1968, pp. 382–4.

Evans, S., *Sonnets on the Death of the Duke of Wellington* (Cambridge, 1852).

FitzGerald, M. H., *A Memoir of Herbert Edward Ryle* (1928).

Fitzmaurice, E., *The Life of Granville George Leveson Gower, Second Earl Granville*, 2 vols. (1905).

Fletcher, J., *For the Prince Consort: A Lay* (1861?).

Foot, M. R. D. and Matthew, H. C. G. (eds.), *The Gladstone Diaries*, 14 vols. (Oxford, 1968–94).

Forshaw, C. F. (ed.), *Poetical Tributes to the Memory of Her Most Gracious Majesty Queen Victoria* (1901).

Frith. W., *General Gordon or the Man of Faith* (1884).

Fry, A. A., *A Dissertation Upon Funeral Orations* (1839).

Gathorne-Hardy, A. E. (ed.), *Gathorne Hardy, First Earl of Cranbrook: A Memoir*, 2 vols. (1898).

Gibbons, A. W., *A World in Mourning!* (1910?).

Gower, R., *My Reminiscences*, 2 vols. (1883).

Gregory, Mrs J. H., *Lines on the Interment of HRH the Late Lamented Duke of Sussex in Kensall Green Cemetery* (1843?).

Gwynn, S. (ed.), *The Letters and Friendships of Sir Cecil Spring Rice*, 2 vols. (1929).

Harpur, C., 'Wellington' in G. Dutton (ed.), *The Heritage of Australian Poetry* (South Yarra, 1976), 31–2.

Henson, H. H., *Gordon: A Lecture* (Oxford, 1886).

Hodder, E., *The Life and Work of the Seventh Earl of Shaftesbury, KG*, 3 vols. (1887).

Hughes, T., *David Livingstone* (1889).

Hurwitz, H., *The Tears of a Grateful People: A Hebrew Dirge and Hymn Chaunted in the Great Synagogue, St James's Place, Aldgate, on the Day of the Funeral of His Late Most Sacred Majesty King George III* (1820).

Johnson, N. E. (ed.), *The Diary of Gathorne Hardy, later Lord Cranbrook, 1866–1912: Political Selections* (Oxford, 1981).

Jones, I. G. and Williams, D. (eds.), *The Religious Census of 1851: A Calendar of the Returns Relating to Wales* 2 vols. (Cardiff, 1976).

Kingdon, A., *Gordon the Christian Hero: A Book for the Young* (1885).

Kipling, R., *The Dead King* (1910).

Laughton, J. K. (ed.), *Memoirs of the Life and Correspondence of Henry Reeve*, 2 vols. (1898).

Lee, S., *Edward VII*, 2 vols. (1925–7).

Lockhart, J. G., *Cosmo Gordon Lang* (1949).

Long, C. C., *The Three Prophets: Chinese Gordon, Mohammed-Ahmed (Ed Maadhi), Arabi Pasha* (New York, 1884).

Macaulay, J., *Gordon Anecdotes: A Sketch of the Career, with Illustrations of the Character of Charles George Gordon, RE* (1885).

MacCabe, W. B., *The Last Days of O'Connell* (Dublin, 1847).

McCrie, T. ('Scoto-Britannicus'), *Free Thoughts on the Late Religious Celebration of the Funeral of HRH the Princess Charlotte of Wales* (Edinburgh, 1817).

MacKenzie, N. (ed.), *The Letters of Sidney and Beatrice Webb: II Partnership 1892–1912* (Cambridge, 1978).

MacKenzie, N. and J. (eds.), *The Diary of Beatrice Webb*, 4 vols. (1982–5).

MacLean, N., *The Life of James Cameron Lees* (Glasgow, 1922).

Malmesbury, 3rd Earl of, *Memoirs of an Ex-Minister*, 2 vols. (1884).

Mann, A. Y., The *Last Moments and Principal Events Relative to the Ever to be Lamented Death of Lord Viscount Nelson* (1806).

Milman, H. H., *Annals of St Paul's Cathedral* (1869).

Mitter, R. J., *Bengal's Tribute to Her Late Majesty the Queen-Empress* (Calcutta, 1901).

Monypenny, W. F. and Buckle, G. E., *The Life of Benjamin Disraeli Earl of Beaconsfield*, 6 vols. (1910–20).

Morley, J., *The Life of William Ewart Gladstone*, 3 vols. (1903).

Murray, J., *Wellington: The Place and Day of His Birth Ascertained and Demonstrated* (Dublin, 1852).

O'Brien, D. P. (ed.), *The Correspondence of Lord Overstone*, 3 vols. (Cambridge, 1971).

O'Hanlon, J., *Report of the O'Connell Monument Committee* (Dublin, 1888).

Perceval, A. P., *Thoughts on the Delayed Interment of the Remains of the Late Duke of Wellington* (1852).

Plomer, W. (ed.), *Kilvert's Diary 1870–1879* (1986).

Ponsonby, A., *Sir Henry Ponsonby* (1942).

Ponsonby, F., *Recollections of Three Reigns* (1951).

Prothero, R. E., *The Life and Correspondence of Arthur Penrhyn Stanley, DD*, 2 vols. (1894).

Redesdale, Lord, *Memories*, 2 vols. (1916).

Reid, T. W., *The Life, Letters and Friendships of Richard Monckton Milnes First Lord Houghton*, 2 vols. (1890).

Ricks, C. (ed.), *The Poems of Tennyson*, 3 vols. (2nd edn., Harlow, 1987).

Rutter, J., *Gordon Songs and Sonnets* (1887).

Sandford, F., *The Order and Ceremonies Used for, and at the Solemn Interment of the . . . Duke of Albemarle* (1670).

Sinclair, W. M., *Memorials of St Paul's Cathedral* (1909).

Stanley, A. P., *Historical Memorials of Westminster Abbey* (1882).

Starr, H. W. and Hendrickson, J. R. (eds.), *The Complete Poems of Thomas Gray* (Oxford, 1966).

Strachey, L. and Fulford, R. (eds.), *The Greville Memoirs 1814–1860*, 8 vols. (1938).

Sykes, J., *An Account of the Death and Funeral Procession of HRH Frederick Duke of York* (Newcastle-upon-Tyne, 1827).

――― *An Account of the Last Moments and Death of His Majesty King George the Fourth* (Newcastle-upon-Tyne, 1830).

Welch, G., *Life of General Gordon* (Melbourne, 1885).

Wemyss, Mrs R., *Memoirs and Letters of the Rt Hon Sir Robert Morier*, 2 vols. (1911).

West, A., *Recollections 1832 to 1886*, 2 vols. (1899).

Wilson, H. C., 'The Theology of General Gordon', Introduction to Joseph Hall's *Christ Mystical of the Blessed Union of Christ and His Members* (1893).

Windsor, Duke of, *A King's Story* (1953).

Yeats, W. B., *Collected Poems* (1950).


## E. Secondary Sources

Anderson, B., *Imagined Communities: Reflections on the Origins and Spread of Nationalism* (1983).

Anderson, O., 'The Growth of Christian Militarism in Mid-Victorian Britain', *English Historical Review*, 86 (1971), 46–72.

Ang, I. and others (Re:Public) (eds.), *Planet Diana: Cultural Studies and Global Mourning* (Kingswood, NSW, 1997).

Ariès, P., *The Hour of Our Death* (1981).

Barringer, T., 'Fabricating Africa: Livingstone and the Visual Image, 1850–1874' in MacKenzie and Skipwith, *David Livingstone*, 171–96.

Beckerlegge, G., 'The Presence of Islam and South Asian Religions in Victorian Britain' in J. Wolffe (ed.), *Religion in Victorian Britain: V Culture and Empire* (Manchester, 1997), 221–267.

Behrendt, S. C., *Royal Mourning and Regency Culture: Elegies and Memorials of Princess Charlotte* (Basingstoke, 1997).

Bell, P. M. H., *Disestablishment in Ireland and Wales* (1969).

Bellah, R. N., 'Civil Religion in America', in R. G. Jones and R. E. Richey (eds.), *American Civil Religion* (1974), 21–44 (originally published in *Daedalus*, Winter, 1967).

Ben-Amos, A., 'Molding the National Memory: The State Funerals of the French Third Republic', University of California PhD thesis, 1988.

――― 'Les Funérailles de Victor-Hugo' in P. Nora (ed.), *Les Lieux de Mémoire* (Paris?, 1997).

Binfield, C., *So Down to Prayers: Studies in English Nonconformity 1780–1920* (1977).

Birnbaum, N., 'Monarchs and Sociologists', *Sociological Review*, 3 (1955), 5–23.

Blake, R., *Disraeli* (1966).

Bland, O., *The Royal Way of Death* (1986).

Bocock, R., *Ritual in Industrial Society: A Sociological Analysis of Ritualism in Modern England* (1974).

Bond, M., 'The Burial Places of English Monarchs', *Report of the Society of the Friends of St George's and the Descendants of the Knights of the Garter*, 1969–70, pp. 30–40.

Briggs, A., *Victorian Cities* (1963).

Brown, C. G., *Religion and Society in Scotland since 1707* (Edinburgh, 1997).

Brown, J. M., *Modern India: The Origins of an Asian Democracy* (Delhi, 1985).

Brown, S. J., *Thomas Chalmers and the Godly Commonwealth in Scotland* (Oxford, 1982).

Butry, P., 'Marie, la Grande Consolatrice de la France au XIXe Siècle', *L'Histoire*, 50 (1982), 31–9.

Callanan, F., *The Parnell Split 1890–1891* (Cork, 1992).

Cameron, N. M. deS. (ed.), *Dictionary of Scottish Church History and Theology* (Edinburgh, 1993).

Campbell, B., *Diana Princess of Wales: How Sexual Politics Shook the Monarchy* (1998).

Cannadine, D., 'War and Death, Grief and Mourning in Modern Britain' in Whaley (ed.), *Mirrors of Mortality*, 187–242.

—— 'The Context, Performance and Meaning of Ritual: The British Monarchy and the "Invention of Tradition", c. 1820–1977', in E. Hobsbawm and T. Ranger (eds.), *The Invention of Tradition* (1983), 101–64.

Carpenter, E., *Archbishop Fisher: His Life and Times* (Norwich, 1991).

—— (ed.), *A House of Kings: The History of Westminster Abbey* (1966).

Chadwick, O. *Michael Ramsey: A Life* (1990).

Clark, D. (ed.), *The Sociology of Death: Theory, Culture, Practice* (Oxford, 1993).

Coleman, B. I., *The Church of England in the Mid-Nineteenth Century* (1980).

—— 'The Nineteenth Century: Nonconformity' in N. Orme, (ed.), *Unity and Variety: A History of the Church in Devon and Cornwall* (Exeter, 1991), 129–55.

Colley, L., 'The Apotheosis of George III: Loyalty, Royalty and the British Nation 1760–1820', *Past and Present*, 102 (1984), 94–129.

—— *Britons: Forging the Nation 1707–1837* (1992).

Cox, J., *The English Churches in a Secular Society: Lambeth 1870–1930* (New York, 1982).

Curl, J. S., *The Victorian Celebration of Death* (Newton Abbot, 1972).

—— *A Celebration of Death: An Introduction to Some of the Buildings, Monuments, and Settings of Funerary Architecture in the Western European Tradition* (1980).

Daly, M. E., *Dublin the Deposed Capital: A Social and Economic History 1860–1914* (Cork, 1984).

Darby, E. and Smith N., *The Cult of the Prince Consort* (New Haven, Conn., 1983).

Darke, J., *The Monument Guide to England and Wales* (1991).

Daunton, M. J., *Coal Metropolis: Cardiff 1870–1914* (Leicester, 1977).

Davidoff, L. and Hall, C., *Family Fortunes: Men and Women of the English Middle Class 1780–1850* (1987).

Davies, D. J., *Death, Ritual and Belief: The Rhetoric of Funerary Rites* (1997).

Davies, J., *Cardiff and the Marquesses of Bute* (Cardiff, 1981).

D'Avray, D. L., 'The Comparative Study of Memorial Preaching', *Transactions of the Royal Historical Society* fifth series, 40 (1990), 25–42.

—— *Death and the Prince: Memorial Preaching Before 1350* (Oxford, 1994).

Durkheim, E., *The Elementary Forms of the Religious Life*, translated J. A. Swain (1915).

Fraser, D. (ed.), *A History of Modern Leeds* (Manchester, 1980).

Fritz, P. S., 'From "Public" to "Private": The Royal Funerals in England, 1500–1830' in Whaley (ed.), *Mirrors of Mortality*, 61–79.

—— 'The Trade in Death: The Royal Funerals in England, 1685–1830', *Eighteenth-Century Studies*, 15 (1981–2), 291–316.

Garland, H. J., *Henry Francis Lyte and the Story of Abide with Me* (Manchester, n.d.).

Geertz, C., *Negara: The Theatre State in Nineteenth-Century Bali* (Princeton, NJ, 1980).

Gibson, R., *A Social History of French Catholicism* (1989).

Giesey, R., *The Royal Funeral Ceremony in Renaissance France* (Geneva, 1960).

Gilbert, A. D., *The Making of Post-Christian Britain: A History of the Secularization of Modern Society* (1980).

Gilley, S., 'Pearse's Sacrifice: Christ and Cuchulain Crucified and Risen in the Easter Rising, 1916', in J. Obelkevich, L. Roper and R. Samuel (eds.), *Disciplines of Faith* (1987), 479–97.

Gilmour, D., *Curzon* (1994).

Gittings, C., *Death, Burial and the Individual in Early Modern England* (1984).

Girouard, M., *The Return to Camelot: Chivalry and the English Gentleman* (1981).

Gorer, G., *Death, Grief and Mourning in Contemporary Britain* (1965).

Gray, R. Q., *The Labour Aristocracy in Victorian Edinburgh* (Edinburgh, 1976).

Green, S. J., *Religion in the Age of Decline: Organization and Experience in Industrial Yorkshire, 1870–1920* (Cambridge, 1996).

Gregory, J., *The Silence of Memory: Armistice Day 1919–1946* (Oxford, 1994).

Hammerton, E. and Cannadine, D., 'Conflict and Consensus on a Ceremonial Occasion: The Diamond Jubilee in Cambridge in 1897', *Historical Journal*, 24 (1981), 111–46.

Hamilton, C. I., 'Naval Hagiography and the Victorian Hero', *Historical Journal*, 23 (1980), 381–98.

Harrison, M., *Clarence: The Life of HRH the Duke of Clarence and Avondale (1864–1892)* (1972).

Hatcher, J., *Laurence Binyon: Poet, Scholar of East and West* (Oxford, 1995).

Helly, D. O., *Livingstone's Legacy: Horace Waller and Victorian Mythmaking* (Athens, Ohio, 1987).

Hendrickson, K. E., *Making Saints: Religion and the Public Image of the British Army 1809–1885* (1898).

Houlbrooke, R. (ed.), *Death Ritual and Bereavement* (1989).

—— *Death Religion and the Family in England, 1480–1750* (Oxford, 1998).

Huntington, R. and Metcalf, P., *Celebrations of Death: The Anthropology of Mortuary Ritual* (Cambridge, 1979).

Hyland, A. D. C., 'Imperial Valhalla', *Journal of the Society of Architectural Historians*, 21(3) (1962), 129–39.

Jalland, P., *Death in the Victorian Family* (Oxford, 1996).

—— 'Victorian Death and its Decline: 1850–1918', in Jupp and Gittings, *Death in England*, 230–55.

Jeal, T., *Livingstone* (1973).

Jenkins, R., *Asquith* (1978).

Johnson, D., 'The Death of Gordon: A Victorian Myth', *Journal of Imperial and Commonwealth History,* 10 (1982), 285–310.

Jones, M., 'Heavy Mettle Fan Club', *Times Higher Education Supplement,* 3 April 1998.

Jouffre, V.-N. (translated A. Moyon), *The Panthéon* (Rennes, 1996).

Jupp, P. C. and Gittings, C. (eds.), *Death in England: An Illustrated History* (Manchester, 1999).

Karl, F., *George Eliot: A Biography* (1995).

Kselman, T. A., *Death and the Afterlife in Modern France* (Princeton, NJ, 1993).

Kuhn, W. M., 'Ceremony and Politics: The British Monarchy, 1871–1872', *Journal of British Studies* 26 (1987), 133–62.

—— *Democratic Royalism: The Transformation of the British Monarchy, 1861–1914* (Basingstoke, 1996).

Laderman, G., *The Sacred Remains: American Attitudes to Death 1793–1883* (New Haven, Conn., 1996).

Lambert, R. S., *The Cobbett of the West: A Study of Thomas Latimer and the Life of Exeter* (1939).

Laqueur, T. W., 'The Queen Caroline Affair: Politics as Art in the Reign of George IV', *Journal of Modern History,* 54 (1982), 417–66.

Larkin, E., *The Roman Catholic Church in Ireland and the Fall of Parnell 1888–1891* (Liverpool, 1979).

Litten, J., *The English Way of Death: The Common Funeral Since 1450* (1991).

Longford, E., *Wellington Pillar of State* (1972).

Lukes, S., *Essays in Social Theory* (1977).

MacKenzie, J. M., 'David Livingstone: The Construction of the Myth', in G. Walker and T. Gallagher (eds.), *Sermons and Battle Hymns: Protestant Popular Culture in Modern Scotland* (Edinburgh, 1990), 24–42.

—— 'David Livingstone and the Worldly After-Life: Imperialism and Nationalism in Africa', in MacKenzie and Skipwith, *David Livingstone,* 201–16.

—— 'Heroic Myths of Empire', in J. M. MacKenzie (ed.), *Popular Imperialism and the Military 1850–1950* (Manchester, 1992), 109–38.

MacKenzie, J. M. and Skipwith, J. (eds.), *David Livingstone and the Victorian Encounter with Africa* (1996).

McKibbin, R., 'Why was there no Marxism in Great Britain?', *English Historical Review,* 99 (1984), 297–331.

—— 'Mass Observation in the Mall', *London Review of Books,* 2 Oct. 1997, 3–6.

MacLaren, A., *Dublin: The Shaping of a Capital* (1993).

McLeod, H., *Religion and Society in England, 1850–1914* (Basingstoke, 1996).

McManamon, J. M., *Funeral Oratory and the Cultural Ideals of Italian Humanism* (Chapel Hill, SC, 1989).

McManners, J., *Death and the Enlightenment: Changing Attitudes to Death among Christians and Unbelievers in Eighteenth-Century France* (Oxford, 1981).

Magnus, P., *Gladstone: A Biography* (1963).

Martin, R. B., *Tennyson: The Unquiet Heart* (1980).

Martineau, G., *Le Retour des Cendres* (Paris, 1990).

Marwick, W. H., 'Municipal Politics in Victorian Edinburgh', *The Book of the Old Edinburgh Club* 33(1) (1969), 31–41.

Matthew, H. C. G., 'Gladstone's Death and Funeral', *The Historian*, 57 (Spring 1998), 20–24.

Merck, M. (ed.), *After Diana: Irreverent Elegies* (1998).

Merrin, W., 'Crash, Bang, Wallop! What a Picture! The Death of Diana and the Media', *Mortality*, 4 (1999), 41–62.

Mitchell, B. R., *Abstract of British Historical Statistics* (Cambridge, 1962).

Moore, J. R., 'Charles Darwin Lies in Westminster Abbey', *Biological Journal of the Linnaean Society*, 17 (1982), 97–113.

Morley, J., *Death, Heaven and the Victorians* (1971).

Morgan, K. O., *Keir Hardie: Radical and Socialist* (1975).

—— *Rebirth of a Nation: Wales 1880–1980* (Oxford, 1981).

Morton, G., *Unionist Nationalism: Governing Urban Scotland 1830–1860* (East Linton, 1999).

Mosse, G. L., *Fallen Soldiers: Reshaping the Memory of the World Wars* (1990).

Newman, G., *The Rise of English Nationalism: A Cultural History 1740–1830* (1987).

Newton, R., *Victorian Exeter 1837–1914* (Leicester, 1968).

Packard, J. M., *Farewell in Splendor: The Passing of Queen Victoria and Her Age* (1995).

Peterson, M. D., *Lincoln in American Memory* (New York, 1994).

Pierard, R. V. and Linder, R. D., *Civil Religion and the Presidency* (Grand Rapids, MI, 1988).

Pugh, M., *The Tories and the People 1880–1935* (Oxford, 1985).

Read, J. C., *A History of St John's Cardiff and the Churches of the Parish* (Bridgend, 1995).

Reed, M., *Ask Sir James* (1987).

Ridley, J., *Lord Palmerston* (1970).

Robbins, K., *Nineteenth-Century Britain: Integration and Diversity* (Oxford, 1988).

—— 'Britain, 1940, and "Christian Civilization" ', in D. Beales and G. Best (eds.), *History, Society and the Churches* (Cambridge, 1985), 279–99.

Rowell, G., *Hell and the Victorians: A Study of the Nineteenth-Century Theological Controversies Concerning Eternal Punishment and the Future Life* (Oxford, 1974).

Rose, K., *King George V* (1983).

Rugg, J., 'From Reason to Regulation: 1760–1850', in Jupp and Gittings, *Death in England*, 202–29.

Schor, E., *Bearing the Dead: The British Culture of Mourning from the Enlightenment to Victoria* (Princeton, NJ, 1994).

Shannon, E. F., 'The History of A Poem: Tennyson's *Ode on the Death of the Duke of Wellington*', *Studies in Bibliography*, 13 (1960), 149–77.

—— and Ricks, C., 'A Further History of Tennyson's *Ode on the Death of the Duke of Wellington*', *Studies in Bibliography*, 32 (1979), 125–57.

Sheehy, J., *The Rediscovery of Ireland's Past: The Celtic Revival 1830–1930* (1980).

Shils, E. and Young M., 'The Meaning of the Coronation', *Sociological Review,* 1 (1953), 63–82.

Stanley, B., *The Bible and the Flag: Protestant Missions and British Imperialism in the Nineteenth and Twentieth Centuries* (Leicester, 1990).

Strachey, L., *Eminent Victorians* (1986 edn.).

Taylor, L., *Mourning Dress: A Costume and Social History* (1983).

Thompson, D., *Queen Victoria: The Woman, the Monarchy and the People* (1990).

Thurmer, J. A., 'The Nineteenth Century: The Church of England' in N. Orme (ed.), *Unity and Variety: A History of the Church in Devon and Cornwall* (Exeter, 1991), 109–28.

Turnbull, M. T. R. B., *Monuments and Statues of Edinburgh* (Edinburgh, 1989).

Turner, T. R., *Beware the People Weeping: Public Opinion and the Assassination of Abraham Lincoln* (Baton Rouge, 1982).

Van Gennep, A., *The Rites of Passage,* translated M. B. Vizedom and G. L. Caffee (1960).

Walter, T. (ed.), *The Mourning for Diana* (Oxford, 1999).

Weintraub, S., *Victoria: Biography of a Queen* (1987).

Whaley, J. (ed.), *Mirrors of Mortality: Studies in the Social History of Death* (1981).

Wheeler, M., *Death and the Future Life in Victorian Literature and Theology* (Cambridge, 1990).

Winter, J., *Sites of Memory, Sites of Mourning: The Great War in European Cultural History* (Cambridge, 1995).

Wolffe, J., 'The End of Victorian Values? Women, Religion and the Death of Queen Victoria', in W. J. Sheils and D. Wood (eds.), *Studies in Church History 27: Women in the Church* (Oxford, 1990), 481–503.

—— *The Protestant Crusade in Great Britain 1829–1860* (Oxford, 1991).

—— *God and Greater Britain: Religion and National Life in Britain and Ireland 1843–1945* (1994).

—— 'Change and Continuity in British Anti-Catholicism', in F. Tallett and N. Atkin (eds.), *Catholicism in Britain and France since 1789* (1996), 67–83.

Woodward, J., *The Theatre of Death: The Ritual Management of Royal Funerals in Renaissance England, 1570–1625* (Woodbridge, Suffolk, 1997).

# Index